STAR BODIES AND THE EROTICS OF SUFFERING

CONTEMPORARY APPROACHES TO FILM AND MEDIA SERIES

A complete listing of the books in this series can be found online at wsupress.wayne.edu

STAR BODIES AND THE EROTICS OF SUFFERING

Edited by Rebecca Bell-Metereau
and Colleen Glenn

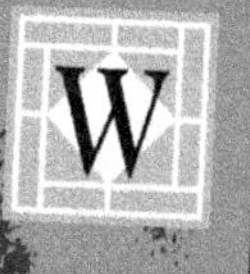

Wayne State University Press
DETROIT

Manufactured in the United States of America.

19 18 17 16 15 5 4 3 2 1

ISBN 978-0-8143-3939-8 (paperback)
ISBN 978-0-8143-3940-4 (ebook)

Library of Congress Control Number: 2015938561

Published with the assistance of a fund established by
Thelma Gray James of Wayne State University for the publication
of folklore and English studies.

Designed and typeset by Bryce Schimanski
Composed in Adobe Caslon Pro

We
dedicate this to
Jean-Pierre Metereau,
Marisa and Thea Bell-Metereau;
the Glenn family, especially Thomas and Blanche;
mentors, editors, colleagues and friends;
and to the stars who
inspire us
all.

CONTENTS

ACKNOWLEDGMENTS

WE WISH TO THANK OUR CONTRIBUTORS FOR THE INSIGHTFUL AND VARied pieces they contributed to this collection, for their willing and prompt revisions, and for their enthusiasm, energy, and patience. This book originated from a panel entitled "Star Bodies and the Erotics of Suffering" that we presented at the Society for Cinema and Media Studies conference, held in New Orleans in 2011. A year later, as we moved forward with the project, we explored the intersection of stars and suffering yet again at the SCMS conference (in Boston) in a panel called "Private Parts: Shame and Star Identities." These two panels formed the foundation of our anthology, and we are thankful to the panelists as well as attendees who offered feedback and useful questions at those sessions.

Our heartfelt thanks go to Barry Keith Grant and Annie Martin at Wayne State University Press for their interest and steadfast support of this project. Along the long road from proposal to finished manuscript, thoughtful readers suggested useful ideas for trimming, focusing, and improving the depth and parameters of our research for this volume. We owe our thanks to these unknown scholars. James Naremore and Alan Nadel provided early insightful suggestions and continued support for the project, as did Victoria Smith, Elizabeth Skerpan-Wheeler, and Dennis Bingham. Thanks to Sam Girgus, Peter C. Pugsley, Dhamu Pongiyannan, and Ben McCann for their generosity, patience, and intellectual contributions during development of the collection. We also offer thanks to Sally Angelica, Michel Elliott, Matthew Parrott, and Amanda David, who helped in early phases of the editing process. In addition to providing enormous assistance with manuscript preparation and copyediting, Eric Wright helped with images and other technical issues. Murray Pomerance and James Lighthouse also advised and assisted with illustrations and other technical aspects of PDFs and image capture. We owe deep gratitude to Jean-Pierre Metereau, who provided encouragement, ideas, and a keen eye for editing, detail, and accuracy. Special thanks go to Daniel Glenn, John Bruns, Catherine Thomas, and Franklin Ashley for their continued support of this project. Eric Schramm deserves thanks for painstaking copyediting and generous patience through the revision process. We are also grateful to Bryce Schimanski for his creativity and willingness to work through multiple iterations of the cover design until he found exactly the design to convey the collection's unifying central focus. Finally, we would like to thank everyone at Wayne State University Press, including Sarah Murphy, Emily Nowak, Kristina Stonehill, and Carrie Teefey, for helping to shepherd us through this process

Introduction

Rebecca Bell-Metereau and Colleen Glenn

> Once the film is over, the actor becomes an actor again, the character remains a character, but from both their union is born a composite creature who participates in both, envelops them both: the star.
>
> Edward Morin, *The Stars* (1972)

> The cult of love in the West is an aspect of the cult of suffering . . . [and] the sensibility we have inherited identifies spirituality and seriousness with turbulence, suffering, passion.
>
> Susan Sontag, *Against Interpretation*

WHAT HAPPENS WHEN MOVIE STARS SUFFER IN THEIR PRIVATE LIVES OR when personal dramas and bodily changes eclipse and alter their screen identities? What happens to the actor who wishes to break away from typecasting and take on a challenging role, as Marilyn Monroe did in her tortured portrayal of Roslyn in *The Misfits* (1961)? To what extent was Mickey Rourke's critically acclaimed performance in *The Wrestler* (2008) tied to his shocking metamorphosis from sexy bad boy to monstrous hulk? How has Halle Berry's star status been affected by painful struggles with gender and racial boundaries? What "star rules" did Joaquin Phoenix break with his bizarre behavior and disheveled appearance on *The Late Show with David Letterman* promoting the hoax movie *I'm Still Here* (2010)? These actors who suffer onscreen and in private—intentionally or unintentionally—disrupt the glamorous, idealized narratives of their star personae.

They challenge us to reconsider such issues as typecasting, audience expectations, and the tensions at play among a star's roles as private individual, public disaster site, artistic product, and cultural icon.

Stardom is typically associated with celebrity, wealth, beauty, and youth, and we often equate star status and box office success with an actor's ability to maintain a coherent and enduring image over the course of a career. Yet iconic performances often grow out of unglamorous suffering, brought on by such vicissitudes of life as physical abuse, accidents, personal failure, or simple aging. This collection examines the fissures and fractures in a representative range of fourteen stars' lives from the last seven decades in order to better understand how suffering—including emotional or physical pain and adverse bodily changes—shapes stars' onscreen and offscreen performances. Each chapter focuses on a star whose career has been marked by suffering, creating in viewers a sense of intimate relationship to the actor whose physical or psychological pain is incorporated into a distinctive star persona and repertoire, at times emerging as intentional display, at other times appearing as desperately hidden secrets or skillfully negotiated tactics. These essays demonstrate the powerful connection between the ethereal star image and the human experience of suffering, exploring how physical or emotional pain and transformation help define star personae. This process, and the intimacy that is established between the star and audience via the star's acts of suffering, we call "the erotics of suffering."

While considerations of filmic suffering often link sadomasochistic identification with feelings of disempowerment on the part of the spectator, suffering also provides a dramatic tension that invites audience identification or empathy, distinguishable from the position of victimhood.[1] By focusing attention on the personal dimensions of pain in stardom and its impact on the star image, this volume lays the groundwork for a thematic and affective consideration of the transformations inherent in suffering, aging, and reconfiguring star and personal identities. Although the essays that follow take a variety of approaches—including personal memoir, photo essay, and traditional scholarship—they seek a set of common denominators in the connections between private and public performance of stars in the midst of pain, both acted and experienced. We divide their discussion into four categories, corresponding to four parts in this volume. "Extreme Makeovers" considers physical transformations and dramatic reinventions of Method and non-Method actors; "Suffering in Silence" examines relationships between public fame and stars' attempts to conceal private suffering; "Growing Pains" deals with those who struggle to break out of a constrictive star persona or to maintain their identity as aging occurs; and "Damage

Control" reveals articulations among competing versions of star personae, as actors attempt to manage or manipulate publicity about difficulties in their personal and celebrity lives.

THEORIZING THE EROTICS OF SUFFERING

Untangling the complex phenomenon of stardom as a set of subtle interactions among the actor's image, the film text, and the audience's sense of knowing the actor calls for a new blend of approaches, along with reinterpretations of older models of analysis. In 1964, Susan Sontag suggested replacing hermeneutics, the search for textual understanding, with what she called "erotics of art," which would bring us closer to the direct experience of a work. Although she did not precisely define "erotics of art," this evocative phrase struck a chord in popular culture by pointing toward a more sensual, emotional, and personal avenue to understanding our responses to artistic production. Sontag's quest for an erotics of art was more than a catchy phrase, however. Indeed, her personal history as a public intellectual contained a special relationship to suffering, as she wooed and eventually won the heart of renowned *Vogue* photographer Annie Liebowitz, later inspiring her to turn her fashion camera lens toward real-world suffering in war-torn areas, and eventually toward Sontag's own painful death from ovarian cancer. The erotics of art became a way of understanding the world. For some, Sontag's concept appears simply as an extension of aestheticism or "art for art's sake," but for others it signals an attempt to locate the private and even physical sources for our appreciation of artistic expression. This type of emotional and sometimes idiosyncratic response to art constitutes an attempt to account for both private and public perception and reception of art.

Subsequent feminist approaches that captured film hermeneutics—allied to semiotics, psychoanalysis, and other methodologies—sidelined Sontag's critical stance for decades. As a possible corrective to this neglect of erotics and the visceral appeal of art, Erika Balsom argues that considering "not only what the form of a work *is,* but what it *does* and the desire it produces might open a new space in which to consider the generation of a textual pleasure that would be grounded in the sensory, affective experience of the work of art."[2] In focusing on emotive reception and the erotics of art, we seek to understand the dynamics of stars' suffering, aging, or disruptions of their images and to consider how these factors intersect with performance.

Suffering itself has not been isolated as a specific component of stardom, but it has figured as a key element in theorists' consideration of viewer interaction with film narratives. For example, in looking at melodrama, Mary Ann Doane argues that "in films addressed to women, spectatorial pleasure is often indissociable from pain."[3] Shifting the focus from genre and narrative, Jackie Stacey counters this notion of passivity or masochism in female audiences by exploring these dynamics through responses from particular spectators. She observes that instead of creating masochistic surrender, viewer identification with certain struggling characters may prompt neither identificatory anguish nor submission but "rebellious feelings and a desire to fight the dominant system."[4] Our study considers how the apparent pain and vulnerability of particular stars offer multiple points of identification and entry to the varied psychological appeals these stars consciously or unconsciously bring to their roles. It also considers how and why certain actors are immortalized, branded, and irrevocably altered by their association with pain. Even supposedly timeless star images change over time as scholars reread their performances, especially in light of previously unknown personal information. In a process similar to Patricia White's theory of "retrospectatorship," we can reinterpret a star image to identify responses of various spectators—including lesbian, gay, and other groups—over different eras.[5] Star identities expand beyond their historical context and moment of popularity, and, as Paul McDonald observes, "Star status is contingent on the commercial performance of films" and therefore is "never fixed."[6]

Stars may not have a fixed status, but they distinguish themselves from actors by virtue of the accumulated weight of meanings they carry with them from role to role. Emerging from what Adorno and Horkheimer called a "culture industry" that coincided with the rise of a mass consumer-capitalist society (epitomized during the classical Hollywood era of filmmaking), the designation of "star" refers to the highly mediated personalities and endlessly reproduced images in the entertainment industry that are generated and consumed by mass culture. Karen Alexander describes a star as "that combination of an immediately seductive image with the larger-than-life projection of a persona,"[7] while Richard Griffith, in an early treatise on movie stars, argues that stars emerge from society's collective unconscious and articulate societal desires.[8] John Ellis, drawing our attention to economic mechanisms, defines a star as a "performer in a particular medium whose figure enters into subsidiary forms of circulation" which then feed "back into future performances."[9] Star personae contain a multitude of meanings that include their film characters as well as the public personality or star image, generated by a variety of sources (press releases, photographs, television appearances, magazine stories).[10] Yet despite their larger-than-life personae and successively reproduced simulacra, stars also personify the masses of non-stars who consume their images. In his landmark work *Stars*, first published in 1979, Richard Dyer notes that many of the most powerful film stars embody social types, such as "The Good Joe," "The Rebel," or "The Pin-up," thus typifying the society that produces them, albeit on an exaggerated scale.[11] Stars function as reflections of an idealized society, then, even as their physical or emotional struggles capture our attention by representing the contradictions and tensions of the culture itself. On some level, we see ourselves in the stars, and just as we triumph with them, we also suffer with them.

Popular interest in stars' personal distress and occasionally shocking physical alterations can be understood as a desire to discover the illusory "real" person behind the veil of stardom. As Dyer has observed, "The whole media construction of stars encourages us to think in terms of 'really'—what is [the star] really like? Which biography, which word-of-mouth story, which moment in which film discloses [the star] as she really [is]?"[12] Stars of the stage and screen are caught in a continual tension concerning the relationship between their "real" selves and the characters they play. As Dyer observes, fan magazines and the news media invest in creating "a rhetoric of sincerity or authenticity" about stars.[13] Indeed, the potency of a star's image, which can often be attributed to a misguided perception of the star as "authentic" or "genuine," is inherently at odds with the very notion of stardom, which is predicated on public *performance*. Stars always, already, contain multiple identities, a truth that becomes particularly evident when scandal, misfortune, and physical alterations occur, whether through accident, indiscretion, or aging. It is at these moments that yet another identity surfaces, splintering the star persona into before-and-after dyads (Woody Allen pre- and post-scandal, for instance).

Beyond such image-altering revelations, star personae frequently encompass multiple sets of other dichotomies. When Dyer suggests that the most compelling stars represent a "magic reconciliation of . . . apparently incompatible terms," he is speaking of the capacity of the star persona to contain and manage mutually exclusive elements.[14] Indeed, the impossible contradictions that stars negotiate—Marilyn Monroe's ability to represent both innocence and sexuality, for instance—enhance their magnetism. Another important contrast that stars incorporate includes their simultaneous status as both extraordinary and ordinary beings.[15] This important tension that characterizes stardom and our relationship to it—the star is like us (emotional, imperfect, struggling, vulnerable), but unlike us (more beautiful, famous, wealthy, talented)—accounts for how interruptions to the idealized star persona often pique audience interest. When scandals hit or wrinkles set in, seemingly "perfect" stars are suddenly rendered more ordinary, more human, and yet they remain stars, that is, extraordinary. Like us, they suffer, makes mistakes, and grow old; unlike us, they suffer on the public stage.

We experience stars quite differently from the way we view ordinary actors because the star persona eclipses the character of any single role. The sense of sincerity that successful stars transmit, causing viewers to experience them as "real" or "genuine," derives from their ability to "collapse the distinction between the actor's authenticity and the authentication of the character s/he is playing."[16] Far from being a slight to their talent as performers, this phenomenon actually speaks to the capacity of the star image to generate a powerful sense of a real individual that we could know. Dyer comments on the contradictory nature of public response to stars: "People often say that they do not rate such and such a star because he or she is always the same. In this view, the trouble with say, Gary Cooper or Doris Day, is that they are always Gary Cooper and Doris Day. But if you like Cooper or Day, then precisely what you value about them is that they are always 'themselves'—no matter how different their roles, they bear witness to the continuousness of their own selves."[17]

James Naremore also considers the authenticity of the "self" and suggests that "by analyzing the paradoxes of performance in film, by showing how roles, star personae, and individual 'texts' can be broken down into various expressive attributes and ideological functions, we inevitably reflect upon the pervasive theatricality of society itself."[18] He implies here that it may be no easier to identify where personal identity ends and acting begins in private life than it is onscreen. Indeed, as the essays in this collection demonstrate, the blurred lines between the public and private lives of stars result in dramatic performances, whether planned or unplanned, filmed or not filmed, when scandal, tragedy, or misfortune intervene. These ruptures, in turn, increase rather than diminish many spectators' sense of identification with their favorite stars. Ultimately, the Möbius strip of the star's self creates a kind of amplified image of a human, one who offers an intriguing promise or fantasy of realness, despite the constructed and mediated nature of the image.

In addition to amplifying and managing suffering, and then suturing the emotional fissures inherent in contradictory social expectations, stars' disastrous escapades represent a market opportunity for publicists and managers. This extra-filmic material includes information about the erotic aspects of star bodies—their physical attractiveness or deterioration, love affairs, personal dramas, and sexual orientation. In distinguishing the appeals and differences between soft-core erotic films and hard-core pornography, Linda Ruth Williams offers "reference to the 'reality' of the filmmaking situation: were they really doing it or not?"[19] as a key factor in viewer response. In a sense, this audience hunger for "reality," the desire to pin down and witness lived experience, bleeds over into viewers' perception of a character's pain; the viewer desires certainty that the actor feels pain in the same way that the character—and by extension, the viewer—does. Marxist theorist Paul McDonald views this kind of dynamic as a marketable phenomenon and emphasizes the star's "dual status as both capital and labour," arguing that "the tensions witnessed over the control of star images do not represent stars attempting to challenge or oppose the capitalist logic of the film industry but rather to become something more than just labour by recognising and consolidating their status as capital."[20] Thus, "studying the star system demands understanding both the industry's *power over the star* and those actions that demonstrate the *power of the star*."[21] In this sense, suffering constitutes another product, as stars' labor and capital include on- and offscreen lives, bodies, faces, and every other element of their images. Because the star persona belongs to the public audience, personal tragedies belong to the public market as well.

A careful look at the efforts of individual stars to maintain, transform, or exploit their iconic identities and to manage or mine the suffering experienced both onscreen and in their personal lives reveals patterns, but also a surprising unpredictability. Such variety prompts a reconsideration of how to frame the star persona and physical embodiment of roles. Richard Maltby talks about an actor's "two bodies,"[22] as does Bertolt Brecht, but it may be more fruitful to speak of multiple and mutable bodies—performed, refashioned, accessorized, surgically improved, aged, deconstructed, rejuvenated and re-presented to the public in multiple iterations—all interacting with audiences that receive and interpret these images in myriad ways. For example, Mickey Rourke and Joaquin Phoenix, both discussed in this work, underwent drastic and unsightly bodily changes, one permanently and the other temporarily, providing examples of just how confounding and compelling the mutability of a star's body can be. Christian Bale's stunning series of transformations—from strong and muscular in *American Psycho* (2000) and the *Batman* trilogy (2005, 2008, 2012) to dangerously emaciated in *The Machinist* (2004) and *The Fighter* (2010) to overweight with a bulging gut in *American Hustle* (2013)—all reveal just how much a filmic role depends on the star's physical body. The transformations of female actors may receive a slightly different treatment from viewers and the press. For example, in October 2014, Renee Zellweger attracted headlines and scorn when she appeared at the *Elle* Women gala in Hollywood with a radically different face. Cosmetic surgeries had "opened" her signature squinty eyes and removed the fullness of her cheeks, leaving the star with a sleeker, thinner visage. Such acts of physical transformation prompt consideration of the extent to which star identities are bound to their bodies in gendered ways. Is the

Academy Award winner Zellweger the same actress once she has a different face? Can she be cast in the same kinds of roles she played before, or are personality, character, and emotion simply too dependent on physical appearance, particularly in close-up shots, to tolerate such changes in the star vehicles of film?

Although change represents an unpredictable factor for star images, it also offers a potential opportunity for increasing fame or longevity. Reassessment of the iconic star paradigm problematizes what is taken for granted about the stars that viewers think they know, and it helps unfold the layers of mysterious attraction to stars who change, stumble, fall, or suffer. Our fascination with this heady mixture sometimes exposes our own private association of love with misery, nurtured by a western narrative tradition—from its beginnings in the story of Adam and Eve to the tradition of courtly love—that often conflates the two emotions. The spectacle of an actor's suffering, both onscreen and in private, gives audiences a sense of the actor's authenticity, and yet in order for the performance of suffering to accomplish its psychological goal of arousing and then displacing anxiety, it must come across as something hidden from view, beneath the obvious surface and artificiality of acting.

The public's window into the personal afflictions of stars—whether unsolicited, imposed by the media, or self-constructed—contributes a sense of depth to audience perceptions of characters. Perhaps just as important, this window allows actors themselves to use personal pain to strengthen their portrayal of troubled and troubling figures. This connection goes far beyond the well-known practice of Method acting, or inhabiting a character by using personal experience to gain insight into performance. In the lives of particular stars, personal circumstances dovetail in startling ways with the roles they perform, through the demands of typecasting and through their own initiative in actively pursuing particular roles that bear resemblance to their psychic and physical struggles. This volume considers how actors such as Daniel Day-Lewis, Hilary Swank, and Charlize Theron derive intensity and authenticity from an emotional foundation of pain, not simply in a Stanislavskian sense of calling on internal experience to perform a role, but in the everyday experience of physical discomfort, personal adaptation, evolution, and growth afforded or necessitated by suffering. Swank and Theron, like Day-Lewis, altered their bodies to the point of unrecognizability, in visual spectacles that fed into their performances and their films' publicity. In such cases, the actor is both absent and present, in a delicate balance between the actor's process of building a performance with an identifiable persona and simultaneously disappearing into the role—a sort of Freudian *fort-da* (gone/there) equation.[23] The actor's ability to fully inhabit a character results in a kind of erasure of the star, which may alienate audiences trained to expect and desire the presence of the familiar celebrity they feel they know. At the same time, the actor's extra-performative personal suffering reconstitutes viewers' sense of the existence of the actor as a real human being, not merely a pretender or faker of emotion.

Graham McCann identifies the element of suffering as a signature trait of Method actors, who "sought out roles that led to suffering, both emotional and physical," but the involvement of suffering in shaping single performances and screen identities in the world of American film acting has much older roots.[24] The stars whose lives we examine are not all Method actors, but all demonstrate the struggle to adapt and grow as an actor—or not—in the face of disruption, loss, or suffering. Although we discuss actors from the 1940s through the present, it is worth looking at a pattern of association between suffering, scandals, and celebrity models of movie stardom that began in the early days of cinema.

SUFFERING AND SCANDALS

Film historians point to connections between suffering and star celebrity as early as 1910, when Universal Studios chief Carl Laemmle took advantage of the public's curiosity about famous figures and issued a press release claiming that Florence Lawrence, who had been known only as the "Biograph Girl," had died in a streetcar accident. Until that announcement, she was an unnamed yet popular actor onscreen, but suddenly the public had a name, a purported tragedy, and a glimpse (however manufactured) into her real life (and fake death). When she appeared in St. Louis alive, in fact, her fame skyrocketed, and the phenomenon of stardom was born—or so the story goes. Richard DeCordova and other film historians counter that the birth of the star system is much more complex, pointing to the historical and economic relationship between stardom and personal identity, particularly during the early era of filmmaking. Some leaders of the industry were suppressing information about film actors in order to limit their power, while others, like Laemmle, were rapidly engineering publicity machines for what would ultimately become the most lucrative box office bait of the film industry, its stars. In a chicken-or-egg scenario, rapidly growing filmgoing audiences became obsessed in an almost romantic way with favorite actors and clamored for knowledge about figures on the silver screen, while magazines like *Motion Picture Story* and *Photoplay* just as quickly supplied sensationalized information regarding the hidden and often disastrous private lives of actors.[25]

The first half-century of film bears witness to the powerful attraction audiences had to personal details about stars—the more lurid and removed from wholesome screen personae, the better. During the teens, well-known box office draws such as United Artists' Mary Pickford, Charlie Chaplin, and Douglas

Fairbanks, or other actors and studios associated with them, like Lillian Gish and W. C. Fields, consolidated their fame through consistent screen identities and publicity pieces that struggled to cement the connection between their private lives and their acting roles. Paul McDonald contends that "star discourse picked out certain film actors as worthy of identification and desire. In contradiction to what appeared in films and sanctioned accounts of the star's lifestyle, star scandal made known what appeared to be the most intimate truths of a star's identity. Whether true or not, scandal stories were nevertheless important to an audience's understanding of the star as not only an object of desire but also a desiring subject."[26]

In spite of industry and individual attempts to fabricate coherent star images, it would be the ruptures that stuck to stars, coloring and altering the significance of their roles, sometimes more strongly in retrospect. Famed examples abound. The scandal of Roscoe "Fatty" Arbuckle caught the imagination of the public, with a grotesque, fabricated account of the overweight actor sexually attacking and fatally crushing the intoxicated starlet Virginia Rappe, in an inaccurate and sensationalized story that taints his image to this day. Arbuckle's funnyman persona disappeared, as Hollywood blacklisted the scapegoated actor in order to protect other reputations, in a frenzy of excessive image regulation and self-censorship.

Arbuckle's case was the exception rather than the rule, according to DeCordova, who sees such a rupture as something the star system can ordinarily "turn . . . around and use . . . as a selling point," with the star scandal serving as "a site for the representation of moral transgression and social unconventionality," both of which are then successfully integrated into the star persona.[27] Aside from Arbuckle's extreme and unfortunate case, scandal was clearly recognized early on as a potential asset, as demonstrated by Louis B. Mayer's attempt to manufacture a secret affair for the apparently innocent Lillian Gish, in order to change her image and increase the longevity of her star persona. Despite studio efforts to manage reputations in Hollywood, the 1930s and 1940s witnessed a string of star-related deaths, rumored murders, possible Communist and Nazi associations, sex and drug scandals galore, and even a prank that involved posing the corpse of famed actor John Barrymore in the house of his notoriously wild friend, Errol Flynn. The public responded to these and other tales with a mixture of horror, hypocrisy, fascination, and adoration.

Publicity about stars and their troubled private lives exploded as an industry in 1940s Hollywood, where our study begins. This period marked the most successful and efficient decade of the studio system managing and attempting to suppress negative information, a phenomenon detailed in Jeanine Basinger's in-depth study of how movie studios created and controlled their screen players.[28]

As typical examples, Rita Hayworth and Rock Hudson (both considered in this volume) were coerced by anxious managers who struggled to mold their private narratives. Hayworth simultaneously assisted and resisted efforts to transform her from Hispanic dancer into the bombshell whose star photo and character name, Gilda, were rumored to grace the atom bomb itself—a notion Hayworth found repugnant.[29] For his part, Hudson collaborated in segregating his homosexuality from public view, even establishing a brief married life for public consumption. Few in Hollywood or the press corps were fooled, but many fans remained ignorant of Hudson's homosexuality for decades.

A number of stars in Hollywood were not so cooperative with studio publicity machines, and yet their daring and painful exposures often proved beneficial, eventually, for their careers and star personae. Ingrid Bergman's transformation from her role as innocent and faithful Ilsa in *Casablanca* to her real-life role as an unrepentant adulterer, mother of an illegitimate child, and eventual wife to Roberto Rossellini sparked widespread controversy and vitriol that forced her into exile in Europe. Then, with a later Oscar-winning performance as the ambiguous character Anastasia, Bergman turned public sentiment from shock to sympathy, transformed her notoriety to celebrity, and revitalized her star image with even more vigor. The turnaround expanded her acting range, prolonged her career, and reflected the nation's conflicted ambivalence toward the Russian aristocracy her character represented. In a similar turnaround in 1948, Robert Mitchum was jailed for smoking marijuana, but instead of this incident spelling the end of his career, it fed into his appealing bad-boy image. Fans greeted him with open arms after his two months in jail, a reception that prefigured the public's growing infatuation with such transgressive and tortured figures as Marlon Brando and James Dean, who rose to prominence in the 1950s.

While it may seem that audiences enjoy "knowing" their comfortably predictable stars, it is ultimately even more titillating and fascinating to discover new sordid details under the whitewash, in part because it humanizes these distant figures. As Maya Luckett notes, "For an audience exhausted by perfect images of stars, nothing entrances more than the star's own public exposure of the truth."[30] The famed illicit affairs, tempestuous marriages, remarriage, and divorces of Elizabeth Taylor formed an essential part of her star identity during her long career. Even after she stopped making films, Taylor's public continued to hunger for pictures of her physical deterioration or ballooning weight, morbidly fascinating stories of her mysterious illnesses and near-death crises, and captivating news of friendships with everyone from Rock Hudson to Michael Jackson, two other stars whose lives were rocked by scandal.

While the majority of stars seem to prove the axiom that any publicity is good publicity, actors suffer varying degrees of damage from scandal (regardless of the degree of accuracy or lack thereof). For example, Joan Crawford's six-decade career received so much negative publicity from her daughter's arguably questionable accounts of child abuse that the star's carefully crafted image suffered posthumous destruction. As a result, many modern viewers know more about Crawford's alleged use of wire hangers than they do about her screen roles, and relatively few of her films received DVD release. In what many scholars argue is a gendered pattern, some stars—often male—manage to reinvent themselves and refashion their careers in order to continue working. The later films of Woody Allen, for instance, reinvent "Woody Allen" by casting other male actors in the roles he would formerly play. Proving that Allen's image has been forever tainted, some fans are careful to distinguish their appreciation of his films from their view of the artist whose reputation was first sullied in 1992, when partner Mia Farrow claimed he had molested their adopted child. Disputes over Allen's reputation continue to fuel blogs, including discussions of such minutiae as the applause level at the 2014 Academy Awards after Cate Blanchett thanked director Allen for casting her in *Blue Jasmine* (2013). Response to scandal may also depend on age, gender, or the frequency and attitude toward the offense, with the public forgiving and ribbing a charming "lad" like Hugh Grant for his prostitute scandal, yet excoriating an unrepentant Lindsay Lohan for her serial alcohol and drug violations.

Moreover, the nature of scandal and stardom altered significantly in the twenty-first century, with audiences becoming amateur paparazzi and contributing candid documentary material to stars' public images, for good or ill. Indeed, through social media sites such as Facebook, Twitter, and Instagram, we have become our own celebrities *and* our own paparazzi, posting selfies and documenting life's minutia, often in not-so-flattering ways. For example, a YouTube video—which immediately went viral—showed an apparently inebriated Reese Witherspoon challenging a police officer who had pulled her husband over for reckless driving by demanding, "Do you know who I am?" This outburst and subsequent meek apology actually improved her status in fan magazines. *Atlantic* blogger Eleanor Barkhorn asked, "Is it wrong to be charmed by Reese Witherspoon's tirade?" and observed that it reminded people she has an edge: "I wondered if part of why her recent movies have been so bad is because her personal life has been so rosy lately. New husband, new baby. Maybe this will be a kick in the pants to put a bit more work into her career."[31] This response typifies how public response to a female actor's multiple roles as wife, mother, and star is deeply embedded in gender attitudes.

Such incidents also exemplify how the offscreen exploits and scandals involving stars often eclipse the work they do on film, television, or stage, and yet they provide a boost to the actor, both personally and professionally. From the myriad revelations that blemished Michael Jackson's career to Tom Cruise's bizarre couch-jumping antics, humiliation and public scrutiny intersect in the celebrity who falls from grace. When a star experiences the embarrassment of scandal, publicity machines try to spin the events, yet it is up to fans to determine if the damaging behavior pushes the once-favored idol into the realm of the unacceptable or even monstrous, and if individual viewers can continue to identify with the suffering of that all-too-human creature. This collection explores the transaction that takes place between film industry and film audience, conducted through stars, the humans with whom we identify and empathize, as we project our desires and fears onto their mutable performing bodies and troubled personal lives.

FANTASIES OF INTERIORITY AND IDENTIFICATION

As illustrated by examples of typical celebrity downfalls, we can see how the media and consumers of popular culture pay particular attention to the private lives of celebrities when the news involves pain and suffering, but the varied effects and motivations of spectators in this regard call for further analysis of the phenomenon of viewer identification. In 1982, Lawrence Grossberger claimed in *Rolling Stone* magazine, "We love to wallow in the misfortune of others. Especially stars."[32] Critic David Denby makes the debatable assertion that audiences seventy years ago just didn't feel the need to know contradictory and unflattering details, but that today "the shift from knowing nothing to knowing everything about a star's private life puts us in an awkward funk, since it's part of our relation to stars to dream of their onscreen characters and their life as in some way unitary."[33] This comment echoes the unified star paradigm, but it also suggests important questions about why or even if we gain pleasure from witnessing the embarrassment or suffering of stars. Nitin Govil observes a similar technologically driven element in the seemingly intimate relationship between stars and today's public: "Contemporary stardom, fueled by the fiction of instantaneous access and the hyperreality of global infotainment, demands new metrics of intimacy. It is not enough that stars have a 'private' life that is both distinct from and connected to our everyday; we must know their motivations and dreams as well. Our knowledge of the personal life of the star is rooted in this engagement with the interiority of desire."[34]

This notion of the "interiority of desire" evokes Sontag's "erotics of art," relating not only to the unknown "inside" of the actor but also to the process of viewer identification, which has been exhaustively examined and theorized, early on in Laura Mulvey's "male gaze" and its successors.[35] An almost physical sense of entering the mind of the performer is an inherently filmic phenomenon, for, as McDonald notes, long before instant communication, the technology of film shifted the focus of audiences to the bodies of actors. Changing acting styles drew on "small gestures and facial expressions," combining form and performance style in a way that "constructed a greater sense of interiority in performance."[36]

The very desire for such intimate knowledge or intense identification is often framed in terms of gender, as we see in Mulvey's "male gaze" or Dyer's assertion that "particularly intense star-audience relationships occur amongst adolescents and women," adding that a similar paradigm applies in "gay ghetto culture."[37] Steven Cohan describes elements of masquerade embedded within the system of representation itself, noting that "Hollywood cinema depends so greatly on making the sexually differentiated bodies of stars visible to an audience, it invariably brings the performativity of gender to the forefront."[38] Jackie Stacey articulates such gendered dynamics in terms of the identificatory relationship between spectator and star: "In a culture saturated with images of desirable femininity, the desire to submerge oneself in an imagined ideal is constantly being reproduced. Hollywood stars offered female spectators such utopian ideals and the fantasy of becoming that ideal. The desire for transcendence can thus be fulfilled in cinematic fantasies which offer the female spectator the pleasure of temporarily merging with her star ideal."[39]

However, fantasy is at work even with images that are less than ideal, as well as with spectators and stars of both genders. Indeed, as the essays in this collection demonstrate, the power of stars' performances often derives from their ability to mine and/or project images of suffering, pain, and flaws, in body or mind, in ways that blur or obliterate gender lines.

While Stacey's "utopian ideals" may initially characterize movie stars—and how we perceive them—many stars eventually slip from their pedestals, and these falls, slumps, or changes can deepen their performances and intensify our sense of a relationship with characters portrayed and with the stars themselves. Although wish-fulfilling fantasy certainly encompasses much of the appeal of stars, empathy also helps explain why we continue to watch even after their images have shifted from idealized beings and bodies to the suffering private identities of ordinary mortals. For example, in categorizing numerous types of identificatory fantasies, from devotion to adoration and worship, Stacey chooses "transcendence" as the label for one female viewer's response to depictions of pain: "Joan Crawford could evoke such pathos, and suffer such martyrdom . . . making you live each part."[40]

Her sense of empathy and use of the terms "pathos" and "martyrdom" suggest a more aesthetic, philosophical, or even religious dimension to her response. In considering suffering and the male spectator, Kenneth MacKinnon recommends fantasy as a mode for understanding reception of a film text and viewers' identification with star identity and performance, precisely because it allows greater flexibility and fluidity in interpreting the range of emotions and types of viewer identification.[41]

In parsing fantasy identification, Mulvey and earlier theorists aligned masochistic positioning as feminine and sadistic pleasure as masculine, but more recent interpretations argue for the permeability of gender identification in both directions. Judith Mayne maintains that "the notion of fantasy gives psychoanalytic grounding not only to the possibility but to the inevitability and necessity of the cinema as a form of fantasy wherein the boundaries of biological sex or cultural gender, as well as sexual preference, are not fixed."[42] In a similar vein, Stacey contends that fantasy "signifies the world of the imagination, the inner world of idealised scenarios and wish-fulfilment and is opposed to the so-called world of 'reality'"[43] in a way that is not specific to gender. Because "sexual difference is so fluid as to have little determining significance in cinematic spectatorship," she recommends a return to "social identity," "lived experience," and "negotiated" perceptions that mediate between film theory and film history, complicated by a third category that includes social dimensions.[44]

The choice of fantasy as an avenue to understanding—like Sontag's erotics of art—guides our study toward consideration of particular stars' personal histories, careers, and filmographies. Such analysis explores the affective dimensions of viewer identification and responses to an actor's suffering and the disintegration of a powerful and unified star persona—within the context of the star's biography or social history and, in some essays, within the social context of the spectator or author.[45] In the end, the spectator helps determine the meaning of a film, just as audience identification with stars and celebrities works with gender and performance in mutually influential and sometimes transgressive ways. As an early example, Miriam Hansen cites Rudolph Valentino's persona and films, which eroticized his body in a way that oscillated between sadistic and masochistic positions, allowing for a similarly ambiguous female scopophilia at a time when such expressions were taboo.[46] Along similar lines, Steven Cohan reveals the subtle ways that Montgomery Clift, Marlon Brando, and other androgynous 1950s male stars reconfigured images of the suffering hero by constantly disrupting Cold War era monolithic American male heterosexuality and subverting gender norms and their own star images.[47] Cohan's unmasking of these stars offers another example of how the star image is hardly a matter of mere dissemination and consumption; indeed, his work highlights the interactive relationship between the disruptive or transgressive performer/performance and the viewer.[48]

STARDOM, CELEBRITY, AND SUFFERING

In addition to the overarching categories of gender identification, the commercial apparatus of public stardom and celebrity provides a mechanism that stimulates spectators' desire for intimacy with stars. While a star may be fairly easily distinguished from an ordinary actor, the difference between a star and a celebrity remains much more nebulous. In the self-reflexive *Birdman* (2014), a *New York Times* film critic (Lindsay Duncan) confronts Riggan Thomson, the has-been eponymous superhero Birdman, played by Michael Keaton, telling him with utter disdain, "You're a celebrity, not an actor." The term "celebrity" often connotes being acknowledged simply for being famous, not for having talent or working hard; virtually all stars are viewed as celebrities, a dubious accomplishment in light of the painful circumstances that often accompany celebrity status. Much of the sociological literature on celebrity has framed it as pathology or commodity, but in recent years scholars have begun to take a more nuanced view of the phenomenon. A consideration of the intersection of star performance and celebrity reveals—as Sean Redmond and Su Holmes suggest—that attempts to distinguish between the two categories of star and celebrity reflect academia's tendency to perpetuate boundaries no longer necessarily recognized in public discourse. Differentiating stardom from celebrity was a more important task before the emergence of television and Internet multimedia publicity for films stars: "In the contemporary moment, the term 'celebrity' arguably has the most popular cultural currency. This may reflect the blurring of different types of fame, . . . but the currently ubiquitous use of the term celebrity, and the connotations it carries, also suggests how these terms cannot be viewed as autonomous academic constructs, divorced from the wider historical and cultural contexts in which they circulate."[49]

Although there is a long history of scholarship on stars, celebrities, and public figures, interest in recent years has increasingly turned toward examining the relationships of viewers with celebrities they idolize.[50] At one time, movie stars viewed television work as a fall from grace that damaged their star identities, but with shifting media markets, the boundaries between movie stars, television stars, models, singers, and other celebrities have become increasingly permeable. As we put these strange and slippery interactions under the lens, we discover that a number of common assumptions about stars are simply no longer true, if, indeed, they ever were.

Far from being predictable, invulnerable, stereotypically presented idols that publicists might wish for, stars often provoke quixotic, personal, and varied responses from consumers of popular culture across an array of media outlets. The constant supply of personal information about public figures—and our continued consumption of it—creates an unmanageable series of "parasocial relationships."[51] These one-sided or imagined connections with celebrities lead us to identify, empathize, and react to the personal trials, triumphs, and tribulations of public figures, at times with an astonishing degree of intimacy—albeit a sense that is manufactured and illusory—and viewers then bring these emotions to their reception of stars' film roles. Although such behavior, when obsessive, is considered aberrant, Graeme Turner reminds us that celebrity culture serves an important social function and can offer sites of identification and pleasure.[52] Furthermore, stars and celebrities who enact both personal and fictional dramas on a public stage become potent signifiers of the human condition. "The power of the celebrity . . . is to represent the active construction of identity in the social world," writes P. David Marshall.[53] As such, the study of public figures allows for an array of responses from across disciplines, including psychology, sociology, cultural studies, film studies, and gender studies.

Attention to stardom and celebrity in the academy has clearly moved from a subdivision of cultural studies to a wide-ranging, interdisciplinary project. Redmond and Holmes argue for the scope and impact of such figures: "Stars and celebrities *do* matter: they 'house' our dreams and fuel our fantasies; they address and represent (often implicitly) some of the most important political issues of the day, and they can give us both ephemeral and lasting pleasure, even if, in the end, this is a pleasure built on artifice and the lie of the possible."[54]

This emphasis on pleasure should be broadened to include the powerful historical significance of suffering in a popular culture that regularly tosses off song lyrics like "it hurts so good" or slogans like "no pain, no gain." Claiming, "for the modern consciousness, the artist (replacing the saint) is the exemplary sufferer,"[55] Susan Sontag meditates on the universal appeal of suffering. In this volume, we suggest that stars have usurped at least a portion of that role of the artist as "exemplary sufferer." David Cronenberg's *Maps to the Stars* (2015) depicts the actor/celebrity as a hyper-psychologically distraught figure who operates in a continual state of external turmoil and emotional upheaval, with the star body oscillating between ethereally untouchable and grossly human. While the film satirizes Hollywood stardom, it captures an essential truth about how the histrionics of the celebrity machine elevate the minutiae of daily life to generate keen public curiosity and occasional empathy.

While stardom has long held an important place in film and media studies, one can observe greater, more systemic incorporations of studies of the public figure in recent education and scholarship in the academy. Examining screen icons and figures of pop culture has become the regular fodder of analytical writing courses in the undergraduate curriculum. Star-centered academic symposiums, such as the one focused on Frank Sinatra held in 1998 and on Michael Jackson in 2009, attest to the passion with which scholars from an array of fields have embraced star and celebrity studies. When the premier literary journal *PMLA* released its special topic issue on "Celebrity, Fame, Notoriety" in October 2011, it was clear that star and celebrity studies had come of age as a rich and broadly relevant field of scholarly inquiry.

Our aim is to continue the expansion of star and celebrity scholarship and enrich it by focusing on the fissures that occur when the public image is disrupted in some painful manner. At the same time, we narrow our focus by examining the details of these moments of splintering as they map onto, overlap with, and complicate our understanding of specific film performances. Although the stars considered in our collection vary from one another in terms of historical period, race, gender, ethnicity, sexual orientation, and style, they all serve as lightning rods for issues of identity, human suffering, identification, and empathy. After the disintegration of the studio system, with the advent of television, and the cross-breeding and sharing of small-screen and big-screen star identities, ever greater hybridization occurred in the mechanisms for distributing information on star identities and the triumphs, disasters, and suffering they experienced. The examples in this volume demonstrate that a remarkable variety of stars, particularly in the post-studio era, failed to maintain over a sustained period the much-vaunted stability that stardom supposedly demands. The lives and experiences of the actors considered in the pages to follow challenge us to rethink some common assumptions about the true source of star power, the ethereal nature of celebrity, and our own guilty pleasure in witnessing the misery and downfall of troubled idols. This volume adopts an eclectic approach to the suffering of stars and their shifting personae, revealing the common thread of suffering and its overarching influence, both on the lives and roles of these iconic figures and on our interpretations of their onscreen and offscreen performances.

EXTREME MAKEOVERS

The four essays of the first section, "Extreme Makeovers," consider actors who publicly undergo extreme physical transformations, some associated with Method acting techniques and others connected to aging. Studies of Joaquin Phoenix and Mickey Rourke explore the limits of fan loyalty, the dangers of self-indulgent and destructive role-playing, and the effects of drastic physical transformations on masculine star identity. Joaquin Phoenix's elaborate publicity hoax in *I'm Still Here* (2010) serves as a focus for Nina K. Martin's examination of manipulating stardom, as she asks whether the actor's ruse presents a brilliant satire of the celebrity machine or simply exposes how male privilege infuses Hollywood, both behind and in front of the camera. The star's "performance" of suffering seemed to solidify his serious actor credibility, in contrast to media coverage of various female celebrities whose meltdowns were publicly framed as women simply "letting themselves go." Colleen Glenn follows another set of extreme transformations in the spectacular figure of Mickey Rourke, whose unusual career dramatizes the collapse of the public-private binary in a star body. Looking at the two halves of Rourke's film career, interrupted by an unsuccessful attempt at professional boxing in the early 1990s and redeemed by his comeback role in *The Wrestler* (2008), Glenn considers how his personal and screen lives intersect in predictable yet also paradoxical ways, in a complicated web of authenticity and artificiality, hypermasculinity, and tortured abjection.

More calculated and painful bodily transformations present themselves superficially as legitimate tools of Method actors, yet such physical suffering emerges as a part of the actor's craft that is tempered by gender, cultural expectations, and publicity machines. Megan Carrigy's comparison of Hilary Swank and Charlize Theron demonstrates how these women inhabit the lives and personalities of their characters in films that call for drastic alteration of the body and enactment of extreme physical pain. Swank (*Boys Don't Cry* [1999]) and Theron (*Monster* [2003]) stunned viewers with their ability to mimic the unique mannerisms of real-life individuals, Brandon Teena and Aileen Wuornos, by transforming themselves from glamorous Hollywood stars to very unglamorous characters in a way that constituted part of the media hype for each film.

A similar technique for displaying painful physical performance appears in the shifting yet strategically managed and carefully engineered oeuvre of Daniel Day-Lewis. Dennis Bingham looks at the career of this British-born Method practitioner, whose acting profile demonstrates reliance on disruption rather than on the typical continuity often associated with stardom. Day-Lewis stands out as an actor who successfully disrupts his star image yet refuses to let possible disturbances in his personal life bleed into his roles in extra-professional ways, representing an alternative to the typically American way of employing Method acting.

SUFFERING IN SILENCE

In "Suffering in Silence," the collection turns to a group of stars who attempted to mask—with varying degrees of success—their private suffering. Todd Gray, who worked as Michael Jackson's photographer, offers a photo essay on Jackson's transformation during the 1980s as his pop star identity was invented and reinvented. Photography and music videos were employed to masculinize his image, yet they inadvertently revealed the scars of a stolen childhood. Gray's analysis of the connections between photographer and star—both young black men struggling to manage their images in a white world—exposes how each one negotiated personal pain as Jackson's stardom emerged, revealing the strains of a conflicted dynamic and erupting in the ground-breaking *Thriller* music video, which forever altered the relationship between popular music and film. The elusive star's handsome face morphs into that of a threatening monster, whose menacing grin expresses the pain, self-loathing, and anger Jackson had been trained all his life to conceal.

Essays on Rita Hayworth and Rock Hudson look at the masked suffering of hidden lives and the complex ways that biography may contribute to our understanding of both stardom and performance. The authors seek to locate counter texts in the two star identities in light of subsequent historical and social developments in the culture at large. Linda Rader Overman offers a personal meditation on Margarita Cansino's little recognized, grueling transformation from her Hispanic identity to the seemingly Anglo Rita Hayworth that the world would come to idolize. In looking at the marginalization of racial outsiders and the high price Hayworth paid for stardom, Overman describes her personal attachment to the Hispanic actress, thus reminding us that stars are stars because they move fans in profound ways. She details how Hayworth's transformation from "too-ethnic-gypsy-Latina Margarita Cansino" to all-American bombshell was fraught with pain, as she concealed her abusive relationships with men and endured years of painful electrolysis, hiding her true ethnicity, sexuality, and body. Overman then reveals elements of her own biography, accounting for her identification with Hayworth and inventing an alternative, empowering ending for her fantasy encounter with the star.

Considering another case of covert identity, Rebecca Bell-Metereau explores how Rock Hudson's success as a melodramatic and comedic star was ultimately overshadowed by the revelation that he was HIV-positive, altering how critics and audiences came to interpret his acting roles. Widely acknowledged in Hollywood, Hudson's secret was maintained in an era of community and coerced privacy that is almost unimaginable for audiences today, until the forced public revelation of his medical condition broadened the notion of performance into the public sphere. The creation and transformation of Hudson's public persona offers a template for understanding how both manufactured celebrity and painful exposure can deepen actors' performances and possibly expand their influence as both private individuals and cultural icons.

GROWING PAINS

The next selection of essays, "Growing Pains," deals with stars' attempts—sometimes painful—to either break out of a typecast or to maintain a type, even as one's physical or perceived identity refuses to conform. In the case of the ultimate star, Marilyn Monroe, Peter J. Bailey sees Arthur Miller's creation of the role of Roslyn Taber for his wife, Monroe, in *The Misfits* as his failed attempt to heal the fissures in Miller's own relationship with the elusive icon. The film's narrative was a desperate and doomed effort to cinematically resolve their marital conflicts and lessen the deep unhappiness he only dimly sensed in his wife. His own narcissistic vision of himself as artist or Svengali and Monroe as both his muse and Trilby remains at the center of his film. Acknowledging the difficulty of plotting the biographical and structural vectors at play in *The Misfits*, Bailey pieces together elements of Miller, Monroe, and others' statements, seeking to unearth Monroe's agency and resistance to an artistic endeavor that Miller described as his search for the "key to Marilyn's despair."[56]

Cynthia Lucia examines *Love with the Proper Stranger* as a cinematic exposé of Natalie Wood's contested star persona, including her disturbingly maturing body and the ambivalence with which her films and critics framed and perceived her sexuality. Wood's experiences as a child actor who grows up sexually onscreen, as an adolescent dominated by a powerful stage mother, as a wife to successful actor Robert Wagner, and as victim of a mysterious, unresolved death at an early age all make her a lightning rod for issues of suffering and eroticization in stardom, both onscreen and in her troubled personal life.

Harrison Ford's career is not usually associated with suffering, yet he also wished to expand his range of roles as he underplayed his struggles with the vicissitudes of aging. In interviews and onscreen, he resorted to humor to deflect attention and mask the deterioration of his dashing star persona. Virginia Luzón-Aguado examines the actor's efforts to maintain his invulnerable celebrity image, built on a considerable level of machismo, and his often unsuccessful attempts to alter his action figure persona as he moved into his late middle age and beyond. She details audience and reviewer responses in a film industry and public relations culture that are often brutally unforgiving.

DAMAGE CONTROL

The women discussed in the final section, "Damage Control," contrast with both the deliberate public display and the concealment of suffering demonstrated in the actors of the first three sections. These final three essays consider the intersection between personal quests for emotional stability and individual aspirations to artistry, as shaped by social expectations based on gender, age, or race. Conflicting sex goddess and domestic paradigms battle for preeminence in the private lives, film roles, and star identities of these and many other female actors. Sissy Spacek, Julia Roberts, and Halle Berry all represent stars who somehow reconfigure negative press or restrictive social expectations to their advantage and manage public perceptions in ways that flummox their critics.

Essays include discussion of the struggles of ingénue Sissy Spacek to establish herself as a serious actor, shedding new light on the pressures of public and personal expectations and gender boundaries in the film industry of the 1970s and beyond. Here, Alison Hoffman-Han performs a reading against the grain of Spacek's typecasting, arguing that she was paradoxically able to overcome the strait-jacket of her physique by simultaneously appropriating, exploiting, and undermining the constrictively gendered and contradictory ageist personae of the "all-American girl" versus the "girl who couldn't keep her clothes on." Spacek played the "country girl," but her star body iconically expresses exploited abjection and monstrous femininity in horror films and melodramas that highlight and problematize the New Hollywood's tentative ties to feminism.

Biographical and reception analyses of the glamorous and highly publicized stars Julia Roberts and Halle Berry demonstrate the various strategies of female actors to redefine themselves. Both Roberts and Berry sought to overcome the confinement and typecasting limitations imposed by beautiful bodies and the gender and social expectations of demanding husbands, lovers, and fans. Looking at one of the few bankable female mega-stars in recent years, R. Barton Palmer analyzes the pendulum swings between fairy tale and disaster that have characterized Julia Roberts's private life, arguing that the star both sidestepped and exploited the recurring missteps in her personal and professional life. He details how an enormous element of her appeal arises from her turbulent personal life, which was used to generate sustained interest in her career as a star and celebrity in ways that she shrewdly manipulated to her advantage throughout her most popular films of the late 1990s: *My Best Friend's Wedding* (1997), *Runaway Bride* (1999), and *Notting Hill* (1999).

The collection closes with Charles Burnetts's description of the twists and turns of another remarkably adaptable star, Halle Berry, paradoxically burdened by her refusal or perhaps inability to suffer consistently in a way that the public would perceive as sincere or authentic. Growing from her status as a top model into a tortured victim in the melodramatic *Monster's Ball* (2001), Berry became the first African American woman to win an Oscar for Best Actress, indicating the public's approval for this particular brand of suffering. However, when she subsequently played the role of coolly invincible Catwoman in 2004, she was slammed with a Razzy award for Worst Actress. Like Spacek before her, instead of hiding her shame, Berry chose to co-opt and own her critics' barbs. Burnetts explores how the fluidity and adaptability that facilitated her popular success, along with her mixed-race identity and sexual allure, undermined her position as a star, precisely because her varied roles fail to embody a single type and somehow fall short of viewers' mixed expectations for her mixed-race persona.

Star Bodies and the Erotics of Suffering employs wide-ranging approaches and considers a disparate group of stars, yet a recurring thread is the notion that our identification with stars and their suffering remains a strong source of our fascination with film, whether our reaction emerges as disgust, envy, pity, grudging admiration, emulation, or adoration. Recognition of the allure of suffering calls for a reassessment not only of individual stars, from luminous to faded, but also of the way their private pain and public displays of suffering amplify the meaning and depth in performances for an array of viewers. Those who market the erotics of suffering recognize and exploit the many ways that fans see themselves in the stars, those ethereal figures who represent who we desire to be and also who we empathize and identify with in their darkest moments of abjection. The triumph of stars has become our own, but perhaps even more important, their suffering has become ours as well, through polymorphous paths that we have only begun to explore.

NOTES

1. Susan Sontag, *Against Interpretation and Other Essays* (New York: Farrar, Straus and Giroux, 1961), 10.
2. Erika Balsom, "'One Single Mystery of Persons and Objects': The Erotics of Fragmentation in Au Hasard Balthazar," *Canadian Journal of Film Studies* (Revue Canadienne D'études Cinématographiques) 19, no. 1 (2010): 21.
3. Mary Ann Doane, *Desire to Desire: The Woman's Film of the 1940s* (Bloomington: Indiana University Press, 1987), 16.
4. Jackie Stacey, "Feminine Fascinations: Forms of Identification in Star-Audience Relations," in *Stardom: Industry of Desire,* ed. Christine Gledhill (London: Routledge, 1991), 152; and Jackie Stacey, *Hollywood Cinema and Female Spectatorship* (London: Routledge, 1994), 76.
5. Patricia White, *Uninvited: Classical Hollywood Cinema and Lesbian Representability* (Bloomington: Indiana University Press, 1999) 15, 194–215.
6. Paul McDonald, *Hollywood Stardom* (London: Wiley and Sons, 2012), 1812.
7. Karen Alexander, "Fatal Beauties," in Gledhill, *Stardom: Industry of Desire*, 53.
8. Robert Griffith, *The Movie Stars* (New York: Doubleday, 1970), 23.
9. John Ellis, *Visible Fictions: Cinema, Television, Video* (London: Routledge, 1982), 91.
10. Richard Dyer, *Heavenly Bodies: Film Stars and Society*, 2nd ed. (London: Routledge, 2004), 2–3.

11. Richard Dyer, *Stars,* new ed. (London: BFI Publishing, 2004), 47–59.
12. Dyer, *Heavenly Bodies*, 2nd ed., 2.
13. Ibid., 11.
14. Dyer, *Stars,* new ed., 26.
15. Ibid., 43.
16. Ibid., 21.
17. Dyer, *Heavenly Bodies*, 2nd ed., 9–10.
18. James Naremore, *Acting in the Cinema* (Berkeley: University of California Press, 1988), 4–5; see also 21–27.
19. Linda Ruth Williams, *The Erotic Thriller in Contemporary Cinema* (Bloomington: Indiana University Press, 2005), 39.
20. Paul McDonald, *The Star System: Hollywood's Production of Popular Identities* (London: Wallflower, 2000), 110–11.
21. Ibid., 111.
22. Richard Maltby, *Hollywood,* 2nd ed. (Oxford: Blackwell, 2003). It is difficult to know if Maltby uses "two bodies" as in "Les rois thaumaturges," the notion that the public body of the king is understood as quasi-magical. Part of the anxiety about stars would then arise from public desire for them to be unlike us—magical—but also like us, as if we are afraid of people who seem to be too magical.
23. Andrea Loselle, "Freud/Derrida as Fort/Da and the Repetitive Eponym," *Modern Language Notes* 97, no. 5 (December 1982): 1180–85.
24. Graham McCann, *Rebel Males: Clift, Brando, and Dean* (New Brunswick, N.J.: Rutgers University Press, 1991), 6.
25. Richard DeCordova, *Picture Personalities and the Emergence of the Star System in America* (Urbana: University of Illinois Press, 1990), 1–21.
26. McDonald, *The Star System*, 31–32.
27. DeCordova, *Picture Personalities*, 117.
28. Jeanine Basinger, *The Star Machine* (New York: Knopf, 2007).
29. See Cheri Chinen, *Music in the Shadows: Noir Musical Films* (Baltimore: Johns Hopkins University Press, 2014), 60, and Wesley Alan Britton, *Onscreen and Undercover: The Ultimate Book of Movie Espionage* (Westport, Conn.: Praeger, 2006), 74.
30. Maya Luckett, "Toxic: The Implosion of Britney Spears's Image," *Velvet Light Trap* 65 (2010): 41.
31. Ibid.
32. Lewis Grossberger, "The Trouble with Sylvester Stallone," *Rolling Stone*, July 8, 1982, 12.
33. David Denby, "Fallen Idols," *New Yorker*, October 22, 2007, 110.
34. Nitin Govil, "Conversion Narratives," *Media Fields Journal*, no. 2 (2011): 1.
35. Laura Mulvey, "Visual Pleasures and Narrative Cinema," *Screen* 16, no. 3 (Autumn 1975): 6–18; Laura Mulvey, *Visual and Other Pleasures*, 2nd ed. (Hampshire: Palgrave MacMillan, 2004).
36. McDonald, *The Star System*, 27.
37. Dyer, *Stars,* new ed., 32.
38. Steven Cohan, *Masked Men: Masculinity and the Movies in the 1950s* (Bloomington: Indiana University Press, 1997), xvi.

39. Stacey, "Feminine Fascinations," 134.
40. Ibid., 146.
41. Kenneth MacKinnon, *Love, Tears, and the Male Spectator* (London: Associated University Presses, 2002), 79.
42. Judith Mayne, "*Cinema and Spectatorship* (London: Routledge, 1993), 88.
43. See Elizabeth Cowie's untitled entry in *Camera Obscura* 20/21 (1989): 127–32, referenced in Stacey, "Feminine Fascinations," 30.
44. Stacey, "Feminine Fascinations," 31.
45. See Steve Neale's recommendation that in considering genre and gender, scholars should rely more on empirical evidence than on purely theoretical constructs. Neale, "Questions of Genre," *Screen* 31, no. 1 (1990): 58.
46. Miriam Hansen, "Pleasure, Ambivalence, Identification," in *Star Texts: Image and Performance in Film and Television*, ed. Jeremy G. Butler (Detroit: Wayne State University Press, 1991), 266–98; and Miriam Hansen, *Babel and Babylon: Spectatorship in American Silent Film* (Cambridge, Mass.: Harvard University Press, 1994).
47. Cohan, *Masked Men*. See also Elisabetta Girelli, *Montgomery Clift, Queer Star* (Detroit: Wayne State University Press, 2013).
48. For more on reception theory and stars, see Jackie Stacey's work on female spectatorship and consumption of Hollywood film, which details how women of the 1940s and 1950s employed movies toward empowering ends as mechanisms of escapism, consumption, and identification with female film stars who often depicted courageous suffering or amorality in ambiguous roles such as the title characters in *Mildred Pierce* or *Gilda*: Stacey, *Hollywood Cinema and Female Spectatorship*, and also her "Feminine Fascinations."
49. Sean Redmond and Su Holmes, ed., *Stardom and Celebrity: A Reader* (London: Sage Publications, 2007), 8.
50. Important works on celebrity culture include the following: Leo Braudy, *The Frenzy of Renown: Fame and Its History* (Oxford: Oxford University Press, 1986); Redmond and Holmes, *Stardom and Celebrity*; Su Holmes and Sean Redmond, *Framing Celebrity: New Directions in Celebrity Culture* (New York: Routledge, 2006); Joshua Gamson, *Claims to Fame: Celebrity in Contemporary America* (Berkeley: University of California Press, 1994); David Marshall, *Celebrity and Power: Fame in Contemporary Culture* (Minneapolis: University of Minnesota Press, 1997); Chris Rojek, *Celebrity* (London: Reaktion Books, 2004); Graeme Turner, *Understanding Celebrity* (London: Sage Publications, 2004).
51. For a survey of the scholarship concerning the "surrogate" role between celebrity and consumer, see Turner, *Understanding Celebrity*, 92–94.
52. Ibid.
53. P. David Marshall, *Celebrity and Power: Fame in Contemporary Culture* (Minneapolis: University of Minnesota Press, 1997), xi.
54. Redmond and Holmes, *Stardom and Celebrity, 8.*
55. Sontag, *Against Interpretation and Other Essays*, 42.
56. Arthur Miller, *Timebends: A Life* (New York: Grove Press, 1987), 466.

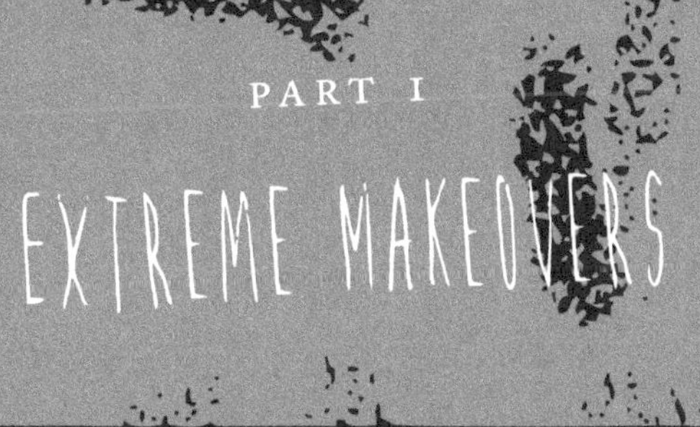

PART I

EXTREME MAKEOVERS

1

"Does This Film Make Me Look Fat?" Celebrity, Gender, and *I'm Still Here*

Nina K. Martin

FEBRUARY 11, 2009, APPEARED TO BE A TYPICAL EVENING ON *THE LATE Show with David Letterman* as the host exchanged quips with his bandleader, Paul Shaffer, before introducing Academy Award–nominated actor Joaquin Phoenix (*Gladiator*, *Walk the Line*) to the stage for a promotional chat about Phoenix's most recent film, *Two Lovers* (dir. James Gray, 2008). Following Letterman's opening salvo, Phoenix came onto the stage, looking drastically different from his formerly clean-cut, svelte persona. He had clearly gained a great deal of weight and he sported a thick, matted beard and long hair sticking up in clumps from the back of his head. Dark sunglasses hid his eyes as Phoenix sat looking at the floor or his hands, shifting and fidgety. Long silences punctuated their "interview" as Letterman, and the studio audience, laughed uncomfortably. Phoenix responded to Letterman in glazed monosyllables; when Letterman chastised him for chewing gum on the show, he pulled the wad from his mouth and stuck it under Letterman's desk. Phoenix seemed dazed, and Letterman appeared surprised and amused by

Phoenix's bizarre behavior. In the end, Letterman quipped, "I'll have to apologize to Farrah Fawcett," referring to another equally infamous moment of celebrity craziness on his show. The video of the interview immediately went viral, as the media and spectators speculated on Phoenix's transformation from photogenic actor to crazed slob.[1] Comments ran the gamut from "I don't know what to think. Is he acting?" to "Good joke if it is" to "Joaquin needs help."[2]

In October 2008, Phoenix had announced that he was retiring from acting at what seemed to be the height of his career, and that out of his love for hip-hop he would pursue a new career as a rap musician. Over the course of the next eighteen months, Phoenix became a poster-child for down-market celebrity, while fellow thespian and brother-in-law Casey Affleck "documented" Phoenix's journey in his film *I'm Still Here* (2010). Shortly after the film's release (but not a moment before), Phoenix's "train wreck" behavior and career suicide was revealed to be an elaborately staged hoax, created in order to explore the nuances of celebrity as Phoenix embodied "J.P." for Affleck's pseudo-documentary. While Phoenix's "performance" as a crazy, slovenly rapper in and out of the film is impressive, the ramifications of this journey seem only to have solidified his serious actor cred; his starring role in Academy Award–nominated director Paul Thomas Anderson's *The Master* (2012), co-starring Amy Adams and Philip Seymour Hoffman, earned him Venice's Silver Lion for acting, and his third Oscar nomination.[3]

Despite Phoenix's ridiculous behavior and appearance in *I'm Still Here*, filmmakers and the public both appear forgiving of the star's manipulation. In contrast, the press surrounding many female celebs' meltdowns suggests that something much more is at stake for women when they change their bodies for a role, when their sanity is questioned, or when they just "let themselves go." In fact, the differing attitudes toward Phoenix's physical transformation and toward Britney Spears's shaving of her head in February 2007 supports Kirsty Fairclough's claim that "female celebrities are unsurprisingly held to different and more exacting standards than their male counterparts. It seems that the female celebrity must be acquiescent to a culture that is more concerned with her physical presentation than her professional accomplishments."[4] As an example of this disparity, John Patterson claimed in the *Guardian* in March 2009 that Phoenix was "too interesting to go all Britney on us yet," making clear whose talent carried more legitimacy.[5] Even talented male actors or celebrities who are not merely playing a role but are weighed down by scandal—such as Christian Bale, Robert Downey Jr., or Tom Cruise—are given multiple chances to recover and rehabilitate themselves through a purposeful refocusing back on their "work" and away from their personal lives. This masculine privilege, along with the fact that Phoenix was only pretending to unravel, allows him to theoretically put on a fat (sloppy and ugly) suit for eighteen months, and shed its negative effects immediately afterward.

This essay explores *I'm Still Here* in conjunction with press coverage of Phoenix's "lost year" to explain some of the relationships between gender and celebrity in contemporary culture. As documented in Su Holmes and Diane Negra's excellent anthology on gender and celebrity, female stars constantly struggle to maintain their youth and beauty within a postfeminist regime that requires stringent bodily maintenance, while male celebrities frequently receive hero status for changing their appearance and gaining or losing weight according to the demands of a particular role.[6] Male celebrities' mistakes, madness, and meltdowns are still fascinating, demonstrating behavior that shores up stereotypical hetero-masculinity (promiscuity and cheating, aggression and rage, linked with drugs and alcoholism). Overcoming scandal is often treated as forgivable or even heroic for men, whereas women's attempts to overcome their foibles are viewed as signifiers of tragic instability and madness.

This pattern illustrates an apparent gendered "double standard"—a representational and cultural imbalance that informs the reception of both *I'm Still Here* and Joaquin Phoenix's star image in important ways. More significantly, analysis of this phenomenon reveals how J.P.'s "documented" lost year engages with our culture's fascination with "train wreck" celebrities, and highlights the ways in which his performance relies on and perpetuates (rather arrogantly) the same standards their film/publicity stunt claims to subvert. Strikingly, the film did not do well at the box office or critically, raking in only $570,000 worldwide, and eliciting widespread anger from both critics and audiences.[7] The film's acute audience displeasure stems from Affleck and Phoenix's unwillingness to let the audience in on the joke by not revealing the film's fictional status until a week after its release. While Affleck and Phoenix defend and describe the film as a purposeful critique of celebrity culture and the various media that fuel it, *I'm Still Here* ultimately reinforces the culture it purports to criticize. The film also serves to solidify male privilege in Hollywood, both in front of and behind the camera, by equating male celebrity meltdowns with Method acting and artistic genius rather than mental instability.

Before exploring what has variously been described as Affleck and Phoenix's "mockumentary," "performance art piece," and "an interminable movie experience," it is crucial to discuss the mutating status of Phoenix's star image prior to the screening of *I'm Still Here*.[8] Phoenix's markedly changed physical appearance during the eighteen-month making of the film inspired the most vitriol and commentary, eagerly confirming what types of celebrity bodies are appropriate and inappropriate. Commenters pointed out that "his sleek, sexy and somewhat effete persona has been replaced by a big blob," and Phoenix had "transformed himself from a chiseled hunk into a hairy, rapping hobo" who looks "like he needs a flea dip."[9] J.P.'s beard was most criticized, as one critic exclaimed "his beard is so big and tangled that I half-expected a flock of animated birds to fly out of it and sing backup," while another would "just be happy to turn him upside down and use him to brush the stairs."[10] An extended clip from *I'm Still Here* taken from the *Splashnews* gossip website has J.P. lumbering in ill-fitting clothes and matted hair toward a cameraman, and summarily "mistaken" for hirsute musician Joe Cocker. During this period, Phoenix was most frequently compared to comedic actor Zach Galifianakis, who recently starred in *The Hangover* and *The Hangover Part 2*, suggesting that, as with stars such as Chris Farley and the formerly chubby Jonah Hill, weight issues are acceptable for comedic actors.

The plethora of harsh comments regarding Phoenix's appearance, a mixture of one part concern to two parts derision, is a symptom of the rampant celebrity-bashing that is an active part of our current cultural climate. Jo Littler and Steve Cross describe this celebrity *schadenfreude* as "the taking of pleasure in celebrity misfortune. Whether mocking Michael Jackson's fall from grace, breathlessly reporting Lindsay Lohan's losses or eagerly observing Britney's meltdowns, the act of gleefully watching or pushing celebrities from their pedestals has become a major cultural trope."[11] The pleasure derived from celebrities' suffering fulfills a specific cultural function precisely because it "offers the vicarious pleasure in the witnessing of the powerful being made less powerful."[12] Further, this *schadenfreude* makes sense in a sociocultural context where the economic gap between "the haves," such as Phoenix, and "the have not" moviegoers is a chasm. Phoenix's shunning of his formerly glamorous, red-carpet persona in favor of an overweight, sloppy figure comes off as a betrayal and a visual reminder of the consequences of an out-of-control body and excess consumption (of food, drugs, alcohol). Envy over Phoenix's earlier conspicuous displays of wealth—designer suits and shoes, carefully groomed appearance—is "held in check so long as worth is *earned*, and so long as the celebrity functions as an emblem of 'making it,' in other words, as emblematic of *aspiration*."[13] Instead, Phoenix's new look epitomized loss of worth and failure, and thus inspired a degree of gleeful contempt.

Disgust with the new Joaquin Phoenix also revolved around his jettisoning of his acting career for rap; this attempt to shift his artistic focus was undermined by viral videos revealing his lack of talent as a rapper (and all replayed within *I'm Still Here*). Each performance features him rapping off beat, shambling around the stage, his pants misshapen and full of holes. In the Las Vegas clip, Phoenix lasts mere moments before he pratfalls off the stage's edge. During his Miami performance, surrounded by boisterous audience members holding cell phone cameras, Phoenix rants about his wealth, pointing out his expensive suit, and taunting, "Dude, I've got a million dollars in a fucking bank account, what do you got, bitch?" Seconds later, he suddenly hurls himself off the stage and attacks a heckler. In the middle of his infamous Letterman interview, when asked about his burgeoning music career, Phoenix suggests that he perform on the show, to which Letterman mockingly replies, "You know, that seems unlikely." Lynn Crosbie's scathing look at Phoenix's rap output sums up the criticism, albeit accurate, surrounding these performances in the most visceral way:

> In the clips and amid rumors he intends to work with Sean Combs, Phoenix looks like a filthy hog: broad and bloated, his hair virtually obscuring his face; his ruined jeans exposing, repulsively, the tip of his penis. It is ridiculous, not tragic, but vile—an attempt on his and Affleck's part to mock his credulous admirers and put one over on the kind of straight media Phoenix despises (when promoting *Walk the Line*, he would stop interviews to ask if an alien was growing out of his head, and so on).[14]

While these clips are contextualized within *I'm Still Here*, the surrounding material highlights Phoenix's overall ineptness. His raps are without inflection or rhythm, and his awkwardly worded complaints about his place in the Hollywood bubble lack passion or legitimacy; his awkwardness in front of a crowd is always palpable. He tells Edward James Olmos, "My music makes people happy, you know?" but the film provides evidence to the contrary. Phoenix's attempts to meet with Sean Combs (rapper P. Diddy) are equally misguided, and at one point, on his way to a meeting, he drives his beat-up Volvo straight into the curb like some drunken hobo. Yet no matter how poorly he performs or how badly he mistreats those around him (verbally and sometimes physically) in *I'm Still Here*, Phoenix is surrounded by an entourage of yea-sayers, eager to tell him how "good" he is. Even after the Miami altercation, and his graphic vomiting into a club's toilet (while a handler holds his tie out of his way), his friend Larry still insists, "Dude, that was a good show." As Michael O'Sullivan appropriately asks about the film, "Why doesn't Phoenix's manager—or any of his many gofers and lackeys—say anything? Yes, it's that horrifying. Maybe the answer lies in our reluctance to protect famous people from themselves. . . . Welcome to the parade of enablers."[15] While it turns out that these "enablers" were ultimately in on Phoenix's "joke," this type of blind willingness is not unfathomable when it comes to the antics of contemporary celebrities.

Phoenix's caustic reception as a hip-hop artist speaks to the difficulties celebrities encounter when they try to multitask and dip into other types of entertainment industries. As Kay Dickinson explains in her exploration of "pop stars that can't act": "If these stars are seemingly out of context, we try to put them back in their places. As we are watching or discussing [their] films, we are simultaneously considering the music industry, its workers, the artist's worth, their other oeuvre and talent. If nothing else, the dislocation of the musician-actor asks us to snap them, and ourselves, back into the world of their most reliable produce."[16] Even though Phoenix learned to play guitar and sang Johnny Cash's songs in *Walk the Line*, he had never mixed in hip-hop circles. His announcement of his retirement from acting in pursuit of his new career in rap called into question both the film and music industries, for his shift (wrongly) assumes an ease in switching from one artistic medium to the other; the immediate attention and gigs that his terrible rapping garnered ultimately implied that success could be achieved without equivalent talent. This negative attitude toward a star's attempted crossover is not new, as the contempt directed toward singing-celebrities such as Scarlett Johansson, Jennifer Lopez, and Lindsay Lohan reveals.

Still, as John Patterson's earlier worry over Phoenix going "Britney" indicates, during Phoenix's unhinged eighteen-month performance, some people were legitimately concerned for his mental health and well-being. Patterson adds, "One's first reaction was to assume Phoenix had fallen off some kind of wagon. He did time for alcoholism back in 2005, so there's a precedent. Could he now be trapped in a similar kind of narco-fuelled personal apocalypse?"[17] David Smith looked for clues in J.P.'s upbringing, reminding the public that his parents were former members, and missionaries, of the Children of God cult, and that Phoenix had changed his name to "Leaf" in order to mesh with his siblings "River" and "Summer."[18] Commenters recalled Phoenix's brother River's 1993 drug overdose, and Joaquin's panicked emergency services call that was subsequently broadcast on American TV scandal shows.[19] All this information speaks to a somewhat tumultuous past, and was trotted out in hopes of explaining Phoenix's changed behavior and appearance. The public's sympathetic reaction to Phoenix's mental distress supports

> how revelations of mental illness and excess by male stars are often constructed as courageously therapeutic acts of survival and "self-fashioning"—actively made by autonomous men. Thus, mental distress

> is reframed as indicative of essentially male attributes of creativity, uniqueness and the power to overcome life's challenges. In contrast, female celebrities' revelations of mental illness are tragedies, melodramas, and narratives of "failure" that undermine their creative agency and diminish their cultural power.[20]

The understanding and forgiveness extended toward numerous male celebrities is certainly not equivalent to the celebrity bashing released on comparable celebrity women.

Since John Patterson raises the specter of Britney Spears as a site of "celebrity meltdown," she presents a valuable gendered comparison. As Moya Luckett skillfully explains in an article devoted to Spears's star image, Spears had been hounded by the media and paparazzi for some time as she ungracefully negotiated her move from teen girl Disney moppet to sexy glamour siren to pop-singer-turned-mother.[21] Her brief Vegas marriage and her flashing the press sans underwear were not atypical gossip fodder. But as Luckett explains, "The head shaving was different. Immediately, it distinguished her from her struggles, opening up a more fascinating spectacle as well as a more troubled, even complex, interior self. Media coverage shifted from her body to her mind as the self-destructive Britney suddenly became a more interesting individual, even if, like Judy Garland, Marilyn Monroe, and others, this promised early destruction."[22] Spears's bald head and angry visage from February 2007, as she confronted paparazzi with umbrella in hand, became a meme for out-of-control female celebrity and the visual signifiers of a person struggling with mental illness. Her appearance on the September 2007 MTV video music awards garnered more vitriol, as Spears stumbled dazed onstage, missing her cues and flubbing her lip-synched performance. In January 2008, Spears was involuntarily committed to a mental ward, and her children were removed from her custody. While Spears's infamous image has been superseded by more recent celebrity scandals, her dramatically changed appearance will continually serve to anchor "all subsequent images of Spears's life and performances."[23] Spears had upset conceptions of beauty and normative femininity with a physical change that served as a marker for her lack of control, even as she momentarily attempted to regain some kind of control.

Perhaps another valuable point of comparison, one more directly attributable to the catalyst for Phoenix's place on the celebrity "meltdown" map, was the infamous May 23, 2005, *Oprah* episode when Tom Cruise visited the show and told the world about his love for Katie Holmes—otherwise known as the "couch incident." Growing increasingly and excessively excited in the telling, Cruise repeatedly jumped on Oprah's couch, hurled himself to the ground with multiple fist pumps, laughed maniacally, grasped Oprah's hands, and shook her like a ragdoll. The video is the epitome of excess; no verbal description can do it justice.[24] The response to the performance was so viral and wide-ranging that a host of parody videos ensued, including one with added stunning electrical effects entitled "Tom Cruise Kills Oprah."[25] Michael DeAngelis astutely explains the problem with both Cruise and Phoenix in terms of celebrity excess: "Unless you play it as Joaquin Phoenix did on *Late Night with David Letterman* [*sic*], proper interviewee behavior involves responding to questions posed by your host while maintaining relative positions conducive to polite verbal interchange; it is only during a sanctioned and prearranged 'performance' (singing a song, dancing a dance) that reconfigurations of spatial relations between host and guest are permitted."[26] Both Cruise and Phoenix violated the coded expectations of the entertainment industry's promotional machine by exceeding the limits of the space in which they were conscribed, disrupting what Joshua Gamson describes as a "negotiated celebration" that involves understood rules followed by agents, publicists, and producers, as well as the stars and talk show hosts who appear onscreen.[27] The virality of both incidents, perpetrated by these male stars, depends upon the surprise and shock of the hosts involved in the encounter. Oprah appears visibly stunned by Cruise's behavior, smiling yet leaning away from his aggressive movements; she does not appear to be feigning shock. Similarly, David Letterman has consistently insisted his ignorance of Phoenix's "performance" in 2009, even in light of a writer for his show providing contradictory information.[28] Still, what resonates in all three cases of celebrity meltdown are the ramifications of these moments. While Spears's career appears inordinately devastated by every scrutinized detail of her physical appearance, then and now, Cruise has bounced back, starring in films like *Mission: Impossible—Ghost Protocol*, *Jack Reacher*, *Oblivion*, and a fifth *Mission Impossible* film for 2015.[29] Phoenix's subsequent return to quality filmmaking in films by Paul Thomas Anderson, Spike Jonze, and James Gray highlights the actor's resilient career and image.[30]

Because of the differing public attitudes toward male and female celebrities' mental distress and scandals, many people, critics and fans alike, insisted that Phoenix's tale and transformation had to be a hoax—even though many found his leaked rap performances and visit to Letterman queasily compelling. (No one ever insisted that Britney was pretending.) Perez Hilton attested, "He turned the crazy switch on too quickly. If he'd been slower getting into it, then it would have been more believable," while Peter Crane at boxoffice.com decried Phoenix's attempt at career suicide: "What credibility does this joke have? People are talking about it in a way more like they did about Britney Spears's shaved hair rather than Borat's smart observations. The public are laughing at him, not with him. It's a shame, because he's a wonderful actor, but this is distracting and detracting from his brilliant body of work."[31] Crane's comments are especially telling of the media misfire that Phoenix's performance generated, and they substantiate Kirsty Fairclough's belief that "once a celebrity is considered 'out of control,' the media lament their slide into the darker side of fame, while capitalizing on the material it offers."[32]

Yet from the moment Joaquin Phoenix told *EXTRA* reporter Jerry Penacoli, on camera, that he was leaving acting for hip-hop, Casey Affleck's "documentary crew" was standing by to record every step of his journey. The ubiquitous presence of cameras following Phoenix, who was never considered an A-list actor in a league with Brad Pitt, George Clooney, or even Leonardo DiCaprio, immediately raised suspicions about the legitimacy of Phoenix's bourgeoning rap career or his physical transformation and apparent decline. Curiosity as to whether Phoenix had actually "lost it," or was merely pretending, contributed to the hype surrounding the proposed film, and its status as documentary or fiction prompted heated debate. Fairly early during the period in which Phoenix "performed" the role of a bloated, crazy retired actor-turned-rap artist, he was accused of perpetrating a hoax by *EW.com*—an interview that Affleck cannily includes in the film, with his repeated assertions that Joaquin was not faking it echoing on the film's sound track. This narrative thread continued to haunt both Phoenix's star image and *I'm Still Here* until Affleck finally admitted to Phoenix's acting "performance."[33] Significantly, Affleck's "coming clean" about Phoenix's "performance" arrived *after* numerous reviewers, including Robert Ebert and Owen Gleiberman, had admitted to believing the film's documentary claims, a calculation of timing with significant consequences.

Ostensibly, *I'm Still Here* is constructed like a fly-on-the-wall documentary, with some of the self-consciousness of reality television celebrity coverage to reinforce the form's claims to "truth" and "authenticity." As Sean Redmond points out, this documentary format suggests that stars "are free of the chains of performativity and artifice. The 'play' that viewers get to see them in is marked by their sincerity, honesty, and openness; and by their willingness to be just like us, even if this warts-and-all authenticity is a strategy to propel them to greater celebrification, far, far away from such ordinariness."[34] The film charts, through city and date titling, Phoenix's "journey" as he retires from acting and fumblingly pursues a hip-hop career. Early footage includes a scene from Phoenix's

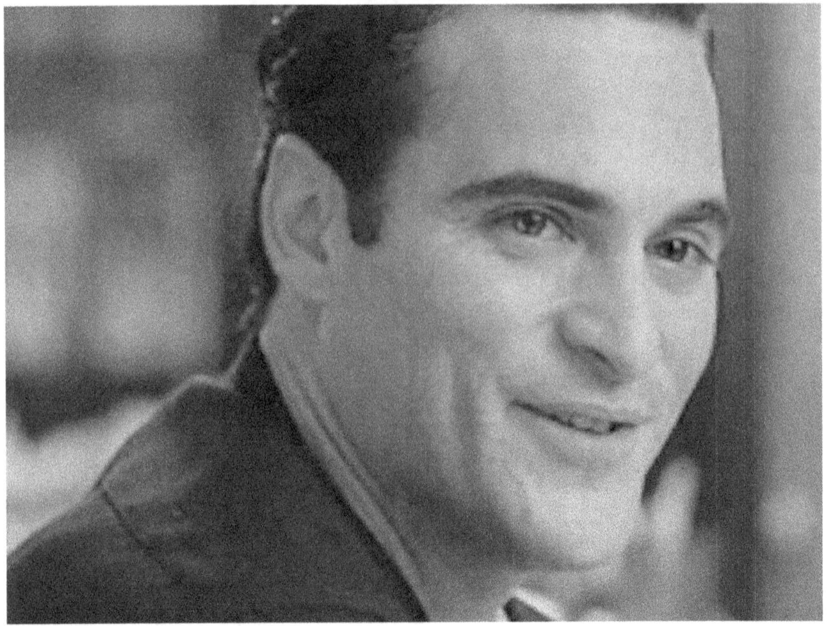

A lean and handsome Joaquin Phoenix, as Johnny Cash, charms Reese Witherspoon, playing June Carter, in *Walk the Line* (2005).

childhood, performing on the streets of Los Angeles with his siblings, onto various red carpet press ops, talk show interviews, and his Golden Globe win for his performance as Johnny Cash in *Walk the Line* (2005).

I'm Still Here initially works, through this footage, to establish Phoenix as a well-known and celebrated actor. The rest of the film graphically follows Phoenix's decline as his weight balloons, his beard grows out of control, and his public appearances become crazier and more erratic. The documenting of three separate rap "performances," combined with two meetings with P. Diddy, lends credibility to Phoenix's pursuit of a rap career. The film combines sourced footage from various media outlets with personal shots of J.P.'s experiences and interactions with friends and co-workers in order to validate the chronology of a star's life lived in both public and in private. The film's single camera hand-held footage of Phoenix makes up the majority of the film's visual material.

Scholars who study both stardom and celebrity have astutely traced the ways in which the discourses of celebrity hinge on stars being conceived as simultaneously "extraordinary" and "ordinary."[35] Images of stars without makeup and casually "snapped" or caught unprepared by cameras speaks to the push/pull tension of authenticity common to stardom. Candid images suggest that the mask of glamour hides something true or real underneath. Part of what contributes to the impression of realism in *I'm Still Here* is Phoenix's seeming ignorance of, and failure to address, the camera. In the earlier parts of the film, J.P. acknowledges that his brother-in-law (Affleck) is filming, and initially addresses the camera, explaining that the film will document his aims to escape from "this ridiculous self-imposed prison" and not "be misunderstood." He ironically claims, "I don't want to play the character of Joaquin anymore," which he describes as known for his "moody intensity" and for being entirely "fraudulent." Filming his journey to rap stardom will be a way of revealing his true identity. The film emphasizes that spectators are witnessing an "inside view" by the intermingling of private and public spaces and the camera's consistently intrusive view as it stays on top of Phoenix. As the film progresses, only characters new to the film, such as P. Diddy and Ben Stiller, comment on the presence of a documentary crew, suggesting that Phoenix no longer registers that the camera is even there. After the film's initial reflexivity, he is used to the camera's attention; and the film's audience, like the reality television audience, accepts the film's camerawork as part of its form. These techniques contribute to a sense that these moments with J.P. are not staged for a camera, but are spontaneous, ordinary experiences.

The camera proceeds to pry into multiple moments in Phoenix's life, sometimes spying on Phoenix through doorways, while at other times chasing him through the bushes of Central Park or into hotel bathrooms. Many of these scenes mimic images "captured by paparazzi," solidifying the film's realism effect. Adrienne Lai explains the lure of the celebrity caught unawares:

> Unlike the official portraits made with the celebrity's permission and input, the paparazzi images are made "on the fly," usually catching the celebrity unaware and unprepared to be photographed.
>
> These [images] are characterized by their informal, unposed, candid, grainy, and often unflattering depiction of the celebrity in his or her day-to-day activities; they stand as unmediated representations of the celebrity's "real," or "private," daily life. . . . Allan Sekula refers to this [voyeurism] as the "theory of the higher truth of the stolen image," the presumption that candid, unguarded images are more natural, and thus more truthful, reflecting more of the subject's "inner being."[36]

Still, savvy spectators are not oblivious to the ways in which the celebrity machine functions, nor are they completely duped by the reality claims the film and Phoenix make. In terms of celebrity culture, Adam Knee explains that "the audience

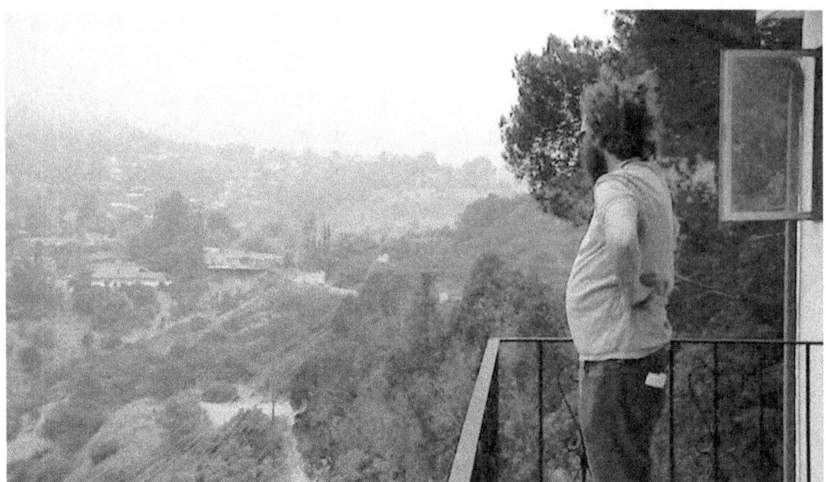

The "Private" Joaquin Phoenix.

is aware of the highly planned and constructed nature of such star imagery, but it enjoys watching the processes of industry hype at the same time as it desires a glimpse of 'authentic' aspects of the star's existence."[37] Thus, the film pointedly contrasts scenes that reveal the labor performed by Phoenix's assistants and publicists with shaky-cam moments that capture the "private" Joaquin. Significantly, these more private and personal episodes paint a vivid picture of J.P. as an ugly, narcissistic, and misogynist pig.

Scenes with Phoenix's agent, publicist, and variety of friends and assistants expose some of the work done to craft the image of Phoenix, but they usually devolve into J.P. yelling at anyone in his near vicinity; even such stars as Ben Stiller are not exempt from his withering contempt. He accuses his "friends" of selfishness and orders them to perform like trained monkeys (modeling classic "diva" behavior more commonly ascribed to celebrity women). Numerous scenes capture Phoenix on the phone with an assistant, Nicole, who struggles with the Herculean task of scheduling a meeting between him and P. Diddy; Phoenix's disgust and annoyance with her efforts reveals the ugly side of every photo-op from that time period. In one scene, he drags another assistant, Larry, to Central Park and demands he "do the fucking snow angel" in a light dusting of snow, and then laughs at his unspectacular results. He berates and towel-whips his other assistant, Antony, so frequently that the man's final grisly retaliation is to defecate on Phoenix's face while he sleeps. Still, these scenes with his male assistants, who often find reason to take their pants off, emphasize both a homosocial and homoerotic atmosphere almost entirely devoid of, and uninterested in, women; these "boy's club" shenanigans suggest that Phoenix's life, and the lives of other male celebrities, are just drawn out, exaggerated episodes of HBO's *Entourage*.

The film's most horrifying scene epitomizes the film's misogynist bent, which the female producer and cinematographer's allegations of sexual harassment and legal suits filed against Affleck during production solidify.[38] The scene opens with Phoenix on hold on the phone with an escort service while he scrolls through his options on his computer screen, hurling expletives and describing the women in the most explicit, X-rated way possible. After ordering "two girls for six" and giving a thumbs-up to his cameraman (Affleck), he proceeds to pull packets of cocaine out of his dirty, over-sized jeans, insulting Antony, who sits nearby and watches the action unfold. Phoenix cackles maniacally and bounces up and down while he sets up lines and then snorts them, first off his desk, and then off the breasts of one of the women who shows up to service him. As the scene continues, Phoenix's unclothed body sports an enormous belly that oozes over his baggy briefs, his fat rolling as he buries his face between a prostitute's breasts. His lack of respect toward his assistants mirrors the way he treats the women he purchases; their only importance is in relation to how he can use them.

This representation of Joaquin Phoenix's changing star body is oddly not about hiding this body, but displaying it for public consumption and appropriation. Instead of avoiding the limelight—as he earlier claimed to desire—J.P.'s performances were virally distributed across online, televised, and print media. Further, the footage in *I'm Still Here* frames Phoenix as unattractive physically, revealing a fat, hairy, and out-of-control body, severely in need of maintenance. These rather shocking visual revelations in the film could be read as "brave," in the sense that this star is willing to allow cameras to capture him "warts and all" (or "all warts"). If one recalls the handsome, star-dusted images of Phoenix's "better days," it becomes difficult to turn away, for, as Sean Redmond claims, the "burn-out star, wasted on pills, fat on glamour and sick on wealth is one of the most haunting and charged images in the hall of fame."[39] This imagery implies that the spectator stares "directly into the unmediated 'truth'" of Joaquin Phoenix—and this truth is very ugly.[40]

Yet there is "Method" to Phoenix's madness, as it turns out that his meltdown was all just an act perpetrated on the vindictive media and the unwitting public, and the convincing quality of his performance only serves to highlight his "talent" and abilities, or so Phoenix and Affleck assert. This gambit shifts the focus from Phoenix's inappropriate public behavior and bloated star body to his ability as an actor in masterfully inhabiting a role. The crazier he seemed, the

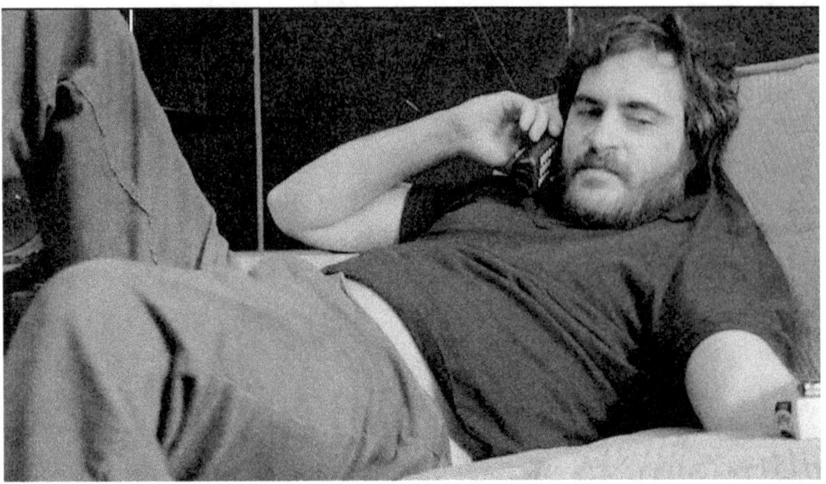

Phoenix's body in *I'm Still Here* (2010)—fat, hairy, and out of control.

more profound his acting talent. As Jason Solomons suggests after seeing *I'm Still Here* (in Venice), Phoenix "immersed himself fully in the role of an intense Hollywood actor who quit acting for a disastrous rap career," while Peter Bradshaw believes that he approached such a role "with the dedication of Robert De Niro bulking up for *Raging Bull*."[41] De Niro is well known for his employment of Method acting techniques, and Phoenix's performance is framed as equally courageous. During a Q&A for the film *Two Lovers*, when Peter Howell asks director James Gray, "Do you think this bearded rapper routine he's doing now is some kind of method actor thing?" Gray replies, "It's entirely possible. I wouldn't put it past him. . . . If it's some kind of weird method exercise, that's commitment. I'll give him that. He reminds me a bit of Brando."[42] This alignment of Method acting to male celebrities not only confers prestige on the actor "becoming his role," but excuses obsessive behavior by linking Method acting with genius. The kind of skill and control connected to Method acting is highly coded as masculine, and further perpetuates the linking of male actors to their talent, especially through their (celebrated) ability to transform their appearance to extremes. Indeed, the outrageously behaving male actor is so culturally acceptable—think Russell Crowe throwing a phone at someone's head, or Johnny Depp trashing his hotel room—that Affleck uses this trope as a way for Phoenix to stay in character. On *I'm Still Here*'s commentary track, Phoenix divulges that Affleck told him to "get angry" and "act crazy" every time someone questioned his act or thought he might be faking it.

To be fair, not everyone following Phoenix's trajectory trusted that his meltdown was only an elaborate act, fearing the residual effects of such an extended performance. Leslie Felperin at *Variety* mused that "by pretending to be crazy, Phoenix may actually have gone a little nuts by staying in character too long (Method gone completely mad)," and Mark Kermode at the *Observer* wondered, "Was Phoenix just methoding to the max? Or did he and his Boy's Own crew become rather too caught up in their own joke?"[43] Phoenix's performance creates an intriguing paradox that hinges on the way Method acting is connected to mental illness. His erratic behavior in public—making outrageous statements, dramatically altering his appearance—could be read as authentically troubled; the more effective his pose as an out-of-control celebrity, the more his star image might be affected by these associations. Even if he reminds everyone that he was only playing a role, the public image of his physical and mental meltdown, and his commitment to its outward expression, is difficult to forget; *I'm Still Here* and the Internet provide the evidence. Meanwhile, his persona as an "intense and moody" actor is further substantiated by both his lengthy dedication to the project and his investment in staying in character for a year and a half. Still, Method acting and intimations of madness are inextricably linked, even if the aftereffects of Phoenix's dance with madness come off as if he were crazy like a fox. What makes Phoenix's case striking is that he ultimately uses this "authentically" unhinged reputation as a means to garner similarly provocative acting roles.

As a result of his elaborate hoax, Phoenix's persona ingeniously, and temporarily, shifted from what Christine Geraghty terms his "star-as-performer" status, known for the roles he takes and his acting talent, into a "star-as-celebrity," someone famous for his life outside of his work.[44] This shift takes on an ironic spin when one considers that "Method acting, in particular, claims cultural status by making the celebrity trappings part of the detritus which has to be discarded if the performance is to be understood."[45] Yet in Phoenix's case, those "celebrity trappings" are intrinsic to understanding his performance in *I'm Still Here*. With his detailed embodiment of a crazed celebrity, he brings far more attention to himself than he was receiving previous to his "meltdown." In effect, while Phoenix and Affleck suggest that they are critiquing celebrity culture by testing its parameters, what their exploration actually does is reinvigorate interest in Phoenix and reconstitute his brand—a brand that, post–*Walk the Line*, was decidedly waning. As Barry King points out, "When a particular star or celebrity shows signs of market impotence, another is standing in reserve to take his or her place, or alternately, experts in spin and publicity craft another persona to restore the old vigor of commercial penetration."[46] The involvement of Phoenix's publicist and agent, who both make appearances in *I'm Still Here*, supports the notion that this career move might have been less a social experiment and more a crass calculation.

Phoenix's return to Letterman's show on September 22, 2010, eighteen months after his infamous slovenly and confused appearance, feels as if someone pressed a rewind button that erased the earlier image. Phoenix strolls onto the stage, nattily dressed in a sleek charcoal gray suit, his hair slicked back, his features chiseled, and a charming smile firmly in place. He is now cleaned up and movie star–polished. Still, Phoenix's earlier "duping" of the audience and the press through his performance has to be addressed, and Letterman jokingly chastises Phoenix for "fooling him," and reminds the show's audience that he was definitely not in on the prank. Phoenix points out that everything went better than planned, and that "we were hoping to go on a talk show. I was looking for a beatdown and I got one." Letterman then demands one million dollars from Phoenix for the extensive use of his appearance in the "documentary, claiming that 'fair use' cannot be invoked if the film is fictional and everyone was a 'paid actor.'"[47] Letterman's threats to sue might have been in jest, but his claims were accurate; he not only bumped Phoenix to celebrity status, but he served as a means of validating the film's fraudulent nonfiction status. While there is an edge to Letterman's tone on the show, the interview is surrounded by an air of good-natured, boys-will-be-boys ribbing, and Phoenix's bad behavior only incurs the usual tongue-lashing from Letterman and finger-wagging from Paul Shaffer. Then, once this interview is over and the "lost" period is explained away as a performance by an actor, Phoenix redemptively returns to his role as "star-as-performer," now heralded as an acting "genius."

During the making and throughout scenes of *I'm Still Here*, Phoenix appears to wrest control away from the celebrity machine, evading his handlers and publicists and truly letting himself go. This bizarre film and actor's bodily appearance suggest that he has simultaneously lost control (through madness, depravity, and bodily excess) and gained control (wresting it from those who work to construct his appropriate star image). Yet Phoenix's saga tells a very specific, masculinized story in which a star's agency is contingent on prevailing gender roles. Rebecca Williams outlines this contingency:

> The notion of star agency is clearly demarcated between those who have had "too much" control and those who do not possess enough. The excessively controlling star is often pathologized and demonized for their select enforcing of their public persona and is routinely typified as a "control freak" such as the characterization of the apparently controlling Jennifer Lopez as a "diva," or the endless discussions of Madonna's masculinized

> power. In contrast, stars lacking agency are caricatured as puppets, controlled by agents, managers. . . . The controlled, excessive celebrity is masculinized while the passive, powerless figure is feminized.[48]

This frustrating gendered paradox becomes further reinforced after Joaquin's "performance" was revealed shortly after *I'm Still Here*'s U.S. premiere. Phoenix starts off the journey, and the film, complaining about being a puppet, at the mercy of a media-driven world, and of audiences who are determined to strip him of power and authenticity. All appearances point to an actor suffering under the destructive weight of the star system and buckling under the pressures he faces; his escape to the rap world is presented as a means to regain control of his life by defying his movie star image. After the film's release, Phoenix and Affleck then changed the narrative into one about power rather than powerlessness, as their intentions to critique this world become clear. The story thus shifts to the "bravery" of Phoenix's transformation, emphasizing the notion of masculinized "control" as it turns out that Phoenix's agent and publicist were fully aware and supportive of this subterfuge. What Phoenix's act drives home is that for those eighteen months spectators did not glimpse the "real" Joaquin, but were fed one just as constructed as the identity of any star. However, the construction and intention of the film as satire and critique is never made clear, especially in relation to the film and filmmakers' claims to authenticity. As Michael O'Sullivan points out, "This [film] isn't *Borat*, however. If Phoenix is making fun of something—the cult of celebrity perhaps—it isn't clear what. And if it's sticking a thumb in Hollywood's eye, why are we the ones wincing?"[49] While Phoenix's behavior in the film is certainly outrageous and over the top, it is not outside the realm of possible (and passable) celebrity behavior; his humorous treatment of celebrity is far from obvious. Everyone in the film plays it straight, never laughing at Phoenix or acknowledging there might be satire at work. Indeed, the joke is not on the Hollywood system or those that enable it, since its main players—stars, directors, talk show hosts, publicists, agents—were all involved. No, the joke is on *us*.

Roger Ebert's post on September 7, 2010, nine days before Affleck's admission that the meltdown was a performance, sums up what many felt on the receiving end of Phoenix's prank: "If this film turns out to *still* be a part of an elaborate hoax, I'm going to be seriously pissed!"[50] Ebert was not the only one to fall for the film's truth claims; critic Owen Gleiberman at *Entertainment Weekly* saw the film as a "fascinating and scary documentary" and pointed to the film's "unflinching honesty."[51] The anger that Affleck's *I'm Still Here* and Phoenix's performance elicited from both critics and fans stems from the contemptuous manner with which they treated the moviegoing public. Affleck's repeated assurances that the film was "not a hoax" and Phoenix's extra-textual appearances in character created the impression, once the secret was out, of snidely pranking the audience in public, and then laughing behind their backs.

This same laughter riddles the commentary track on the DVD, which undeniably illuminates the filmmaker and star's intentions, but is only illuminating if one actually *bothers to watch* the film while this alternate sound track plays. As "assistant" Larry rightly points out, "This commentary is just going to be us laughing at the movie the whole time." What Affleck, Phoenix, and the various other players in the film—assistants like Nicole, Larry, and Antony—reveal is that almost everyone, except the public, knew and was in on Phoenix's performance; everyone is a paid actor, and the entire film is fictional. Scenes that appear to capture Phoenix at his worst, such as his diatribes against friends and actors, were scripted and planned in advance. The prostitutes were actors; Phoenix's vomiting was real, but the drugs and feces were all faked. What appears as Ben Stiller's revenge for Phoenix's ill treatment, his performance as Phoenix during the Oscar ceremony, turns out to be a ruse, as the scene where Phoenix trashes Stiller and his 2010 movie *Greenberg* was shot *after* Stiller's Oscar appearance.

The most telling scene that accompanies the commentary track is simultaneously the most poignant, and one of the only scenes that shows Phoenix in a momentarily sympathetic light. In the theatrical version of the film, after Phoenix's "disastrous" 2009 Letterman interview, he sits in shock and panic in his limo with his friend Larry, lamenting what just happened. He asks the driver to pull over, and then stumbles out of the car with Larry and cameraman in tow, crawling into the underbrush as a way to escape the camera's unwavering gaze. He then breaks down crying and moans, "I'm just going to be a goddamn joke forever—why did I do that?" The scene is pretty affecting, but on the commentary track it elicits the longest and most sustained and intense laughter. As this track reveals, this scene was shot long after the Letterman interview rather than immediately following it. Even this rare moment of sympathy was faked, intended to once more mock the viewer. While there might have been some residual concern that Phoenix's performance at times went too far in affecting his overall career, the commentary track implies that his nearly two-year "journey" was carefully crafted and bolstered by continuous emotional support. Affleck and Phoenix's masculine privilege, both behind and in front of the camera, allows them to take this kind of professional "risk" without truly jeopardizing their futures.

Part of the problem with *I'm Still Here* lies with its rather striking mimicry of reality television and celebrity documentary practices, and Affleck's refusal to admit that the film was not a documentary until after the film's release (and even after the film had been reviewed). As scholars invested in defining the term "mock-documentary" reveal, "What marks the mock-documentary out from the 'hoax' or 'fake' is this *contract* set up between producer and audience. It requires the audience to watch as if at a documentary presentation, but in full knowledge of an actual fictional status. Audiences have to be in on the joke to be able to access and participate first in the humor, then in the cultural and political critique on offer."[52] Yet Affleck and crew never honor such a contract, even when, as "with any parody, a knowing reception" is essential to effectively convey a critique.[53] Both Affleck and Phoenix insist that the over-the-top quality of the performances should tip audiences off as to the film's fictional status, yet in the same breath they speak of the film's "authenticity" and emphasize the believability of Phoenix's performance (which highlights their interest in the film's reality effect).

In a follow-up interview, Ebert points out to Affleck that "knowing that Joaquin was performing suggests a deeper level of anger against the celebrity-publicity system than a simple psychological meltdown would have."[54] Indeed, that "anger" toward a culture that holds both men in high esteem for their talent seems both ungrateful and unjustified. In terms of both mockumentary and satire, the knowing reception by the spectator is key, yet Affleck purposefully withheld the "wink." These two privileged brothers of the Hollywood elite were laughing *at* their audiences and fans, not *with* them. Instead, the film's revelation as ultimately fake, purposely devoid of any truths, emphasizes both the gullibility of audiences and the complicity that stars have with their image-making team in fooling those same audiences. What Affleck and Phoenix forget in all their fun is what Valerie Lopes reminds us in her letter to Joaquin published shortly after his appearance on *Letterman*: "Remember that celebrity and fame are a privilege and not a right. Fame is fleeting as a shooting star. Stop trying to thumb your nose at the public that's contributed to your success. Enough with the Attitude."[55]

Phoenix's risky gambit of pretending to be a repulsive, unhygienic, sexist nutball in *I'm Still Here* initially had more repercussions than he might have anticipated; the damage to his image was not so easy to shake, even if he actively worked at reclaiming his "celebrated actor" status. As Heather Nunn and Anita Biressi explain: "The scandalized celebrity, then, even if rehabilitated through confession and abject self-exposure, remains an ambivalent public figure: initially set up as the idealized emblem of successful individualism, then cast out from idealized status, although they may return to public favor they must remain open to constant observation for signs of setbacks, recidivism, subterfuge, or deceit. Celebrity status, then, is an endless project to achieve, sustain, and manage."[56]

While director Casey Affleck could easily slip back into his former role as actor, Phoenix had to work with, and against, the representations that virally circulated during the time of his supposed breakdown. Initially, Phoenix "was no longer being offered A-list scripts," and his "bank account was running dangerously low."[57] Yet his out-of-control performance was a catalyst for Paul Thomas Anderson to choose Phoenix for the equally unhinged starring role of Freddie Quell in *The Master*, a man gifted at making hooch out of paint thinner. For Anderson, Phoenix's reputation for blurring his life with his acting made him all the more appealing: "He's the kind of actor who doesn't have a barometer, whatever that gauge is that can stop you from going into the red."[58] One of *The Master*'s standout scenes has Phoenix, as Quell, violently exploding with rage in his jail cell; Phoenix managed to destroy the cell's antique lavatory in the scene's first take.[59] While Stephen Rea suggests that "Phoenix presented a Master class in being a Method hambone," Christopher Goodwin points out that Phoenix's "performance is so fierce and raw and disturbing, his physical appearance so shocking . . . his body so wracked and tormented, that audiences have come away wondering how much of the actor himself it reflects."[60] Both of these descriptions could just as easily be about his performance in *I'm Still Here* as in *The Master*.

By all indications, Joaquin Phoenix has resettled into the Hollywood firmament with bad attitude intact. What lingers after his provocative "craziness" is Phoenix's penchant for a borderline-dangerous slippage between actor and role, where the taint of madness always underlies his genius; yet this type of behavior continues to be enabled by his directors and lauded by those who designate status and awards. Two years after *I'm Still Here* premiered at the Venice Film Festival, Christopher Goodwin paints the following picture:

> [Phoenix's] public reappearance in Venice, where *The Master* premiered, only cemented those worrying impressions. I was shocked when the fidgety, sweaty, chain-smoking Phoenix disappeared in the middle of the press conference, walking off the stage. When he came back, he managed to mumble a reply to just one question, about where he found inspiration for his character. "I don't know where it comes from, and I don't care," he snapped, taking another deep drag on his cigarette. At the photo call, he was roundly booed when he stomped off after fifteen seconds. This seemed to be a man who had taken method acting past

> the point of no return, who had lost the ability to discern the boundaries between his characters and himself.[61]

This complete absorption into a role, accompanied by remarkable physical transformations (such as extreme weight gain or loss), is often held up as evidence of a "consuming talent" comparable to "the greats of American film acting: Marlon Brando, Montgomery Clift, Robert De Niro."[62] Drawing boos at the Venice Film Festival during *The Master*'s premiere, or venomously declaring to Elvis Mitchell after winning the Volpi Cup for Best Actor at the same festival that any award is "a carrot, but it's the worst tasting carrot I've ever tasted in my whole life. I don't want this carrot," only solidified Phoenix's reputation as an acting genius/rebel.[63] His painstakingly constructed persona reminds us that Phoenix is no sellout, and that he truly cares about the craft of acting. In light of his attitude toward accolades, Phoenix was destined for another Oscar nomination, supporting those "who believe the actor who scoffs at the awards and all the frippery is actually the one who's most deserving because he's 'so gosh darn authentic.'"[64] Yet ironically, what Phoenix has made clear through *I'm Still Here* is that this "authenticity" is just as much a sham as any other role he might play.

Indeed, Phoenix is now held up as a yardstick for other celebrity meltdowns, designating the difference between an act that garners publicity and one that represents an actor's descent into actual mental illness. The furor over actress Amanda Bynes, known for her work in teen films such as *What a Girl Wants* (2003) and *She's the Man* (2006), as well as starring in a slew of *Nickelodeon* television shows, serves as an important contrasting and cautionary tale to Phoenix's ascension back into our culture's good graces.[65] After retiring from acting at the age of twenty-four in June 2010 and un-retiring in July 2010, Bynes has been documented in the last two years exhibiting increasingly bizarre and dangerous behavior.[66] Following her arrest for DUI in April 2012, Bynes was involved in six other vehicular incidents, causing her license to be suspended and her car impounded. Beyond her legal run-ins, she has shaved part of her head, pierced her cheeks, and tweeted pictures of herself clearly under the influence, then threatened to sue tabloids for reporting these exploits.[67] Yet reporters and fans do not believe that Bynes is "Joaquin Phoenix-ing" the public, for people do not believe that "she is that great of an actress to pull off something like this."[68] Unlike Phoenix, Amanda Bynes and most Hollywood women are held to entirely different standards, and when "we're used to seeing actresses, pop stars and models as part of an assembly line of real-life Barbie dolls, it becomes all the more interesting to see one go by with her head popped off."[69] While actors like Phoenix are ultimately celebrated for their daring in displaying Method intensity or overcoming physical and mental unhealthiness, "women we use as morality tales. It's a sort of superiority to be able to take to Twitter or any tabloid pages and remark how *sad* a woman's behavior is."[70]

The consequences of Phoenix's "crazy act" have been mostly positive: he seems to have been able to mine this unsavory chapter in his career to procure more unhinged, morally corrupt, socially isolated, or crazy roles, and in critically acclaimed films, too. After *The Master*, he appeared in Spike Jonze's film *Her* (2013), where he plays a lonely writer, Theodore, who falls in love with his computer operating system. The nerdy vulnerability with which Phoenix plays Theodore almost seems to serve as an olive branch for his previous bad-boy behavior. In *Inherent Vice* (2014), Paul Thomas Anderson's adaptation of Thomas Pynchon's novel, Phoenix once again channels the sort of madness that undeniably appeals to Anderson, turning in a credible performance as Doc, the perpetually stoned private detective caught up in a chaotic, hilarious, and sometimes tragic caper.

With *The Master* and *Inherent Vice*, Phoenix's acting reputation seems firmly reestablished, even if he "behaves badly." As Betsey Sharkey states, "Should at some point in the coming years, Phoenix need a break from it all again, to go a little nuts, so be it. All I would ask is that he come back. And keep coming back—to the screen, or the stage—where he can move us, enlighten us, unsettle us, entertain us. He has a gift. To waste it, or walk away from it, or rap about it—now that would be crazy."[71] His booing at Venice notwithstanding, Hollywood and celebrity culture seem intent on forgiving male stars such as Phoenix for their tantrums, experiments, and missteps, whether real or feigned. He may be a little tainted and tattered, but Joaquin Phoenix is probably far from "retiring," or saying goodbye. He continues to remind us that *he's still here*.

NOTES

1. "Joaquin Phoenix on Drugs, on Letterman (Full, HD)," YouTube video, February 12, 2009, www.youtube.com/watch?v=zVg-c9P2CKc&feature=related, accessed July 15, 2012.
2. "93vrss" comment, "bat2032005" comment, and "Lumiger" comment, all on "Joaquin Phoenix on Drugs, on Letterman (Full, HD)."
3. "Joaquin Phoenix," Internet Movie Database, www.imdb.com/name/nm0001618, accessed June 1, 2013.
4. Kirsty Fairclough, "Fame Is a Losing Game: Celebrity Gossip Blogging, Bitch Culture and Postfeminism," *Genders*, no. 48 (2008), www.genders.org/g48/g48_fairclough.html, accessed March 1, 2012.

5. John Patterson, "What's Up, Joaquin?" *Guardian*, March 17, 2009, www.guardian.co.uk/film/2009/mar/17/joaquin-phoenix-letterman-show, accessed March 1, 2012.
6. Su Holmes and Diane Negra, eds., *In the Limelight and Under the Microscope: Form and Functions of Female Celebrity* (New York: Continuum, 2011).
7. "I'm Still Here (2010)," Box Office Mojo, boxofficemojo.com/movies/?id=imstillhere.htm, accessed August 1, 2012.
8. Jay Stone, "The Fine Line between Reality and Hoax," *Gazette*, September 24, 2010, final edition; Manohla Dargis, "Running Away from the Circus," *New York Times*, September 10, 2010; and Steve Persall, "Phoenix Isn't Rising," *St. Petersburg Times*, September 16, 2010.
9. Peter Bradshaw, "Keeping It Real," *Guardian*, September 17, 2010; and Myrddin Gwynedd, "Joaquin Phoenix Makes a Shocking Debut . . . as a Rapper," *New Zealand Herald*, January 19, 2009, www.nzherald.co.nz/entertainment/news/article.cfm?c_id=1501119&objectid=10552547, accessed March 1, 2012.
10. Shari Low, "Overgrrown Chaps Give Me a Hairy Fit," *Daily Record*, February 5, 2009, www.dailyrecord.co.uk/news/politics/overgrown-chaps-give-me-a-hairy-fit-1008336, accessed March 1, 2012; and Matt Zoller Seitz, "I'm Still Here: Joaquin Phoenix's Fascinating Performance Art," *Salon.com.* September 10, 2010, www.salon.com/2010/09/10/im_still_here_joaquin_phoenix/, accessed March 1, 2012.
11. Jo Littler and Steve Cross, "Celebrity and Schadenfreude: The Cultural Economy of Fame in Freefall," *Cultural Studies* 24, no. 3 (May 2010): 396.
12. Ibid., 399.
13. Ibid., 406–7.
14. Lynn Crosbie, "Complex? Yes. Odd? You Bet. Rapper? Uh . . . ," *Globe and Mail*, January 2009, www.theglobeandmail.com/arts/joaquin-phoenix-complex-yes-odd-you-bet-rapper-uh/article1146837/, accessed March 1, 2012.
15. Michael O'Sullivan, "Is He Putting Us On? Maybe," *Washington Post*, September 2010, www.washingtonpost.com/gog/movies/im-still-here-2010-i,1168087/critic-review.html#reviewNum1, accessed March 1, 2012.
16. Kay Dickinson, "Pop Stars Who Can't Act: The Limits of Celebrity 'Multi-Tasking,'" *Mediactive*, no. 2 (2004): 77.
17. Patterson, "What's Up, Joaquin?"
18. David Smith, "People: Is Joaquin Phoenix Just Another Actor in Meltdown, or Is This a Hoax?" *Observer*, February 15, 2009, www.guardian.co.uk/film/2009/feb/15/joaquin-phoenix-letterman-behaviour, accessed March 1, 2012.
19. Patterson, "What's Up, Joaquin?"
20. Emma Bell, "The Insanity Plea: Female Celebrities, Reality Media and the Psychopathology of British Pop Feminism," in *In the Limelight and Under the Microscope: Form and Functions of Female Celebrity*, ed. Su Holmes and Diane Negra (New York: Continuum, 2011), 203.
21. Moya Luckett, "Toxic: The Implosion of Britney Spears's Star Image," *Velvet Light Trap*, no. 65 (Spring 2010): 39–41.
22. Ibid., 40.
23. Ibid., 39.

24. "Tom Cruise Goes Crazy on Oprah (Danger)," YouTube video, posted by "ApprovedbyChuck," September 8, 2008, www.youtube.com/watch?v=frI_BUk-H5OY, accessed August 15, 2012.
25. "Tom Cruise Kills Oprah Extended Version," YouTube video, posted by "maxishine," September 21, 2006, www.youtube.com/watch?v=CRbhE3GRiUE, accessed August 15, 2012.
26. Michael DeAngelis, "Tom Cruise, The 'Couch Incident', and the Limits of Public Elation," *Velvet Light Trap*, no. 65 (Spring 2010): 42.
27. Joshua Gamson, "The Negotiated Celebration," in Gamson, *Claims to Fame: Celebrity in Contemporary America* (Berkeley: University of California Press, 1994), 79–107.
28. PopEater Staff, "Writer: David Letterman Faked Interview with Joaquin Phoenix," PopEater, www.popeater.com/2010/09/20/david-letterman-faked-interview-joaquin-phoenix/, accessed March 1, 2012.
29. "Tom Cruise," Internet Movie Database, www.imdb.com/name/nm0000129/?ref_=sr_1, accessed June 1, 2013.
30. "Joaquin Phoenix," Internet Movie Database, www.imdb.com/name/nm0001618, accessed June 1, 2013.
31. Smith, "People: Is Joaquin Phoenix Just Another Actor?"
32. Fairclough, "Fame Is a Losing Game."
33. Josh Rottenberg, "Joaquin Phoenix's Rap Career: An Elaborate Hoax?" *Entertainment Weekly*, January 27, 2009, insidemovies.ew.com/2009/01/27/joaquin-phoenix-2/, accessed March 1, 2012.
34. Sean Redmond, "Intimate Fame Everywhere," in *Framing Celebrity: New Directions in Celebrity Culture*, ed. Su Holmes and Sean Redmond (London: Routledge, 2006), 28.
35. John Ellis, "Stars as a Cinematic Phenomenon," *Film Theory and Criticism*, 6th ed., ed. Leo Braudy and Marshall Cohen (New York: Oxford University Press, 2004), 598–605.
36. Adrienne Lai, "Glitter and Grain: Aura and Authenticity in the Celebrity Photographs of Juergen Teller," in Holmes and Redmond, *Framing Celebrity*, 219.
37. Adam Knee, "Celebrity Skins: The Illicit Textuality of the Celebrity Nude Magazine," in Holmes and Redmond, *Framing Celebrity*, 162.
38. PopEater Staff, "Casey Affleck Calls Sexual Harassment Lawsuit a Case of Sour Grapes," PopEater, www.popeater.com/2010/07/24/casey-affleck-lawsuit-blackmail-amanda-white, accessed March 1, 2012.
39. Redmond, "Intimate Fame Everywhere," 42.
40. Ibid.
41. Jason Solomons, "Observer Review: Venice Film Festival," *Observer*, September 12, 2010, www.guardian.co.uk/film/2010/sep/12/venice-film-festival-vincent-gallo-joaquin-phoenix, accessed March 1, 2012.
42. Peter Howell, "Pity If Phoenix Packs It In," *Toronto Star*, April 10, 2009, www.thestar.com/news/2009/04/10/two_lovers_pity_if_phoenix_packs_it_in.html, accessed March 1, 2012.
43. Leslie Felperin, "I'm Still Here: Review," *Variety,* September 19, 2010, www.variety.com/review/VE1117943443?refcatid=31; and Mark Kermode, "The Year Hollywood

Made a Mockery of the Documentary," *Observer*, January 9, 2011, accessed March 1, 2012.

44. Christine Geraghty, "Re-examining Stardom: Questions of Texts, Bodies, and Performance," in *Rethinking Film Studies*, ed. Christine Gledhill and Linda Williams (London: Arnold, 2000), 183–201.
45. Ibid., 192.
46. Barry King, "Stardom, Celebrity, and the Money Form," *Velvet Light Trap*, no. 65 (Spring 2010): 7.
47. "Joaquin Phoenix on Letterman 9/22, Full Interview," YouTube video, posted by "Jamie767," September 23, 2010, www.youtube.com/watch?v=xl3c_L2sy90&feature=related, accessed March 1, 2012.
48. Rebecca Williams, "From Beyond Control to In Control: Investigation Drew Barrymore's Feminist/Agency/Authorship," in *Stardom and Celebrity: A Reader*, ed. Sean Redmond and Su Holmes (London: Sage Publications, 2007), 111–12.
49. O'Sullivan, "Is He Putting Us On? Maybe."
50. Roger Ebert, review of *I'm Still Here*, directed by Casey Affleck, RogerEbert.com, September 7, 2010, rogerebert.suntimes.com/apps/pbcs.dll/article?AID=/20100907/REVIEWS/100909992, accessed March 1, 2012.
51. Owen Gleiberman, review of *I'm Still Here*, directed by Casey Affleck, *Entertainment Weekly*, September 17, 2010, www.ew.com/ew/article/0,,20419430,00.html, accessed March 1, 2012.
52. Steven N. Lipkin, Derek Paget, and Jane Roscoe, "Docudrama and Mock-Documentary: Defining Terms, Proposing Canons," in *Docufictions: Essays on the Intersection of Documentary and Fiction Filmmaking*, ed. Gary D. Rhodes and John Parris Springer (Jefferson, N.C.: McFarland, 2006), 17.
53. Alexandra Juhasz and Jesse Lerner, eds., *F is for Phony: Fake Documentary and Truth's Undoing* (Minneapolis: University of Minnesota Press, 2006), 10.
54. Roger Ebert, "Casey Affleck Levels about *I'm Still Here*," RogerEbert.com, September 22, 2010, blogs.suntimes.com/ebert/2010/09/casey_affleck_levels_about_im.html, accessed March 1, 2012.
55. Valerie Lopes, "Joaquin Phoenix—Screw You Too . . . A Letter from a Lingering Fan," Open Salon, February 13, 2009, open.salon.com/blog/valerie_lopes/2009/02/13/joaquin_phoenix_screw_you_too_a_letter_from_a_lingering_fan, accessed March 1, 2012.
56. Heather Nunn and Anita Biressi, "'A Trust Betrayed': Celebrity and the Work of Emotion," *Celebrity Studies* 1, no. 1 (2010): 53.
57. Martyn Palmer, "In Private, I Live a Quiet Life. My Extreme Sport Is Acting," *Mail Online*, October 20, 2012, www.dailymail.co.uk/home/moslive/article-2219521/Joaquin-Phoenix-In-private-I-live-quiet-life-My-extreme-sport-acting.html, accessed June 1, 2013.
58. Christopher Goodwin, "Is Joaquin Cracking?" *Sunday Times*, November 4, 2012, www.thesundaytimes.co.uk/sto/culture/film_and_tv/film/article1157610.ece, accessed June 1, 2013.
59. Ibid.

60. Steven Rea, "Funny, Filthy, Careful, Compassionate," *Philadelphia Inquirer*, December 23, 2012, articles.philly.com/2012-12-23/news/35983981_1_skyfall-james-bond-magic-mike, accessed June 1, 2013.
61. Goodwin, "Is Joaquin Cracking?"
62. Ibid.
63. Elvis Mitchell, "Joaquin Phoenix," *Interview Magazine*, October 18, 2012, www.interviewmagazine.com/film/joaquin-phoenix, accessed June 1, 2013.
64. Lauren [pseud.], "Joaquin Phoenix Rejoins Hollywood Just to Complain about Hollywood," Crasstalk, October 2012, crasstalk.com/2012/10/joaquin-phoenix-rejoins-hollywood-just-to-complain-about-hollywood/, accessed June 1, 2013.
65. "Amanda Bynes," Internet Movie Database, www.imdb.com/name/nm0004789/?ref_=sr_1, accessed June 1, 2013.
66. Tracie Egan Morrissey, "Amanda Bynes: Breakdown of a Meltdown," *Jezebel*, September 18, 2012, jezebel.com/5944292/amanda-bynes-a-breakdown-of-a-meltdown, accessed June 1, 2013; and Jill Filipovic, "Amanda Bynes' Public Meltdown Says More about Us Than about Her," *Guardian*, May 29, 2013, www.guardian.co.uk/commentisfree/2013/may/29/amanda-bynes-meltdown-why-we-watch, accessed June 1, 2013.
67. Morrissey, "Amanda Bynes," and Filipovic, "Amanda Bynes' Public Meltdown."
68. Ent Lawyer, "The Amanda Bynes—Joaquin Phoenix Theory," *Crazy Days and Nights*, www.crazydaysandnights.net/2012/10/the-amanda-bynes-joaquin-phoenix-theory.html, accessed June 1, 2013.
69. Filipovic, "Amanda Bynes' Public Meltdown."
70. Ibid.
71. Betsey Sharkey, "Joaquin Phoenix Can Leave Hollywood—As Long as He Comes Back," *Los Angeles Times*, October 24, 2012, articles.latimes.com/2012/oct/24/entertainment/la-et-mn-joaquin-phoenix-essay-20121025, accessed June 1, 2013.

1

BEAUTY TO BEAST: THE REBIRTH OF MICKEY ROURKE

Colleen Glenn

> Acting is the least mysterious of all crafts. Whenever we want something from somebody or when we want to hide something or pretend, we're acting. Most people do it all day long.
>
> Marlon Brando

> Hollywood is a very unforgiving place.
>
> Mickey Rourke

ONE OF THE MOST PROMISING ACTORS OF THE 1980S, MICKEY ROURKE surprised everyone when he quit acting at the height of his film career to pursue professional boxing. Like Marlon Brando, to whom Rourke was often compared in the early days of his career, Rourke was known for his boyish beauty, rebellious attitude, soft-spoken voice, and an intense corporeal onscreen presence. Rourke, like Brando, exhibited self-loathing and self-destructive tendencies, often related to discomfort with his star status. Rourke once cut off his own finger in a fit of rage, suffered a nervous breakdown after time on a particularly frustrating set, and has now evolved into an odd figure on the red carpet, clinging to his dogs, his sunglasses perched over a mask of his former self.

By the time Rourke left acting to fight in 1991, his reckless behavior had rendered him nearly unemployable in Hollywood. Claiming he was "self-destructing . . . [and] had no respect for [himself as] an actor," Rourke returned to the boxing ring, where he had competed as an amateur during his high school years in Miami, Florida.[1] He boxed in the professional circuit for five years until his doctor ordered him to quit after failing to pass a neurological test.[2] In addition to suffering significant short-term memory loss, Rourke broke several ribs, a toe, and his nose multiple times; he split his tongue, sustained a shattered cheekbone, and required numerous cosmetic surgeries to repair these various injuries.[3]

Rourke's redemption in Hollywood in 2008 with the release and widespread critical acclaim of Darren Aronofsky's *The Wrestler* was made all the more dramatic and strange by Rourke's radical physical reincarnation. Not only had the Golden Globe winner aged twenty years; he was virtually unrecognizable, in face and body.[4] The handsome, almost effeminate face and slender build had been replaced by a bumpy, scarred mask sitting atop a hulking, muscled physique. Even his soft voice had shifted to a low and gravelly register.

Rourke's career has become the ultimate "before and after" story, ranking as one of the most drastic cases of all time in movie star transformations. Of course, disruptions are part of the natural ebb and flow of stardom: any star who survives in the business long enough will be judged by any sort of deviation from his or her iconic image. However, Rourke's career remains an arresting example of a metamorphosis so extreme that he has had essentially two different acting careers, one for each body and face. While other stars have reinvented themselves with new physiques or different screen personae, Rourke's resurrection in Hollywood marks not so much a return but a completely new entrance with a different body, face, and voice.[5] Indeed, were he not attached to his name, the second Rourke would not be a star at all.

In his transformation from leading man to grizzled action player, Rourke provides us with an intriguing figure through which to explore the link between the ethereal movie star and the vulnerable physical body to which it is attached. Rourke's badly damaged face and hyper-developed body read like a map of suffering, excess, and violence, yet Rourke has managed to exploit his emotional and physical instability with great success onscreen. Indeed, suffering, excess, and violence have now become the primary vehicles through which we understand the characters played by the "second Rourke," raising questions about the degree of masochism that his comeback career has required.

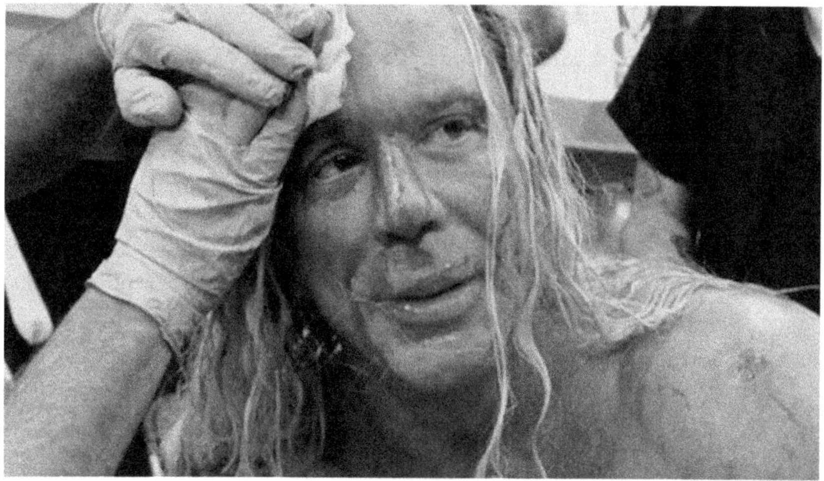

Mickey Rourke's shocking, real-life transformation and suffering are inseparable from his performance in *The Wrestler* (2008).

In addition to his two "separate" acting careers, Rourke's dual careers as actor and boxer, while seemingly drastically different occupations, are inextricably linked. Acting made him feel like a fraud, so he returned to the ring; unsuccessful in the ring, he returned to acting. The cycle continues. Recently, at age sixty-two, after his acting career petered out (again), Rourke has once more returned to professional boxing, a pursuit that feels intensely more meaningful to him than filmmaking. Yet his approach to boxing has always been highly performative and public, just as his film performances have always felt genuine and private, almost as if he is letting us intrude on his personal space. As a star, Rourke confounds the distinction between performance and authenticity: it is never clear when he is acting versus when he is being "real." This slippage of public persona/private self has defined Rourke, and that definition is seen not only in his remarkably curious career, but also in his strange and extraordinary body.

Epitomizing the extremes and contradictions of Hollywood stardom (talent, beauty, wealth, success, loss, failure, garishness, plasticity), Rourke dramatizes the machinations of stardom and provides a fascinating spectacle of instability contained within the hypermasculine body. Moreover, Rourke offers a compelling figure through which to explore the blending of fact with fiction as a way of conceptualizing embodied and disembodied stardom. The fact that he played a wrestler (an athletic profession noted for the slippage between fact and fiction) in the comeback role of his film career locates Rourke's star image at the intersection of masculine performance, authenticity, and masochistic obsession.

LIFE IMITATES ART

Real-life backstories are hardly inconsequential when it comes to stars. The "how the star became a star" narrative can be instrumental in shaping an actor's public image. This phenomenon is particularly magnified in a comeback situation, when a star garners audience empathy for suffering in his personal life. This is certainly the case with Mickey Rourke, whose tumultuous offscreen life has conjured as much attention as his filmic roles, if not more. Rourke is, as so many have called him, a "character," an appellation that highlights the artificiality and constructedness of his identity.

Rourke's dramatic biography, circulated widely in the second phase of his career, helped elevate him to cult status in Hollywood, making his offscreen history a potent component of his public persona. If celebrity is characterized by a tension between extraordinary and ordinary, then Rourke's extraordinary talent, as well as his all-too-human series of mistakes, writ large on his scarred and swollen face, embodies the inherent contradictions that constitute celebrity. As Joshua Gamson claims, "Contemporary celebrity has been composed of two major, often competing narratives about the relation between celebrity status and merit. . . . In the first, they are successful because they are extraordinary, unlike us, and more powerful than we are; in the second, they are ordinary people, just like us, only luckier, prettier, and better marketed."[6] Rourke's path to stardom reflects this dichotomy with striking clarity, given his meteoric rise to fame, precipitous decline, and just as sudden comeback.[7] Furthermore, the contradictions of celebrity are evidenced not only by his unique history, but also by the two drastically different bodies of Mickey Rourke, one exceptionally beautiful and the other extraordinarily damaged.

Indeed, it may be argued that Rourke is now cast in films as much for his well-known painful history as for his acting ability; since 2008 he is increasingly, if not exclusively, understood to be "playing himself." Like any compelling star, he brings a particular set of associations to his films that informs our understanding of his screen character. Mickey Rourke epitomizes rebellion, regret, and hard living, among other things, but, perhaps most importantly, the second version of Rourke powerfully projects a sense of authenticity. Audiences sense that Rourke seems not to possess a public self that is separate from his private self, an accessibility that accounts, in large part, for his appeal and cult following.[8]

His macho "what you see is what you get" swagger actually masks a highly unstable male star body and persona. Rourke regularly becomes too emotional to speak during interviews when asked personal questions about his mother or about his battle with serious depression and suicidal urges over the years.[9]

Indeed, Rourke's interviews seem more akin to confessionals, acts of public contrition not unlike the private ones he admits he regularly conducts over a bottle of wine with his Catholic priest friend. Under the scrutiny of his interviewers, Rourke seems to not possess that protective veneer that other stars do; he appears exposed, contrite, and uncomfortable, smoking cigarette after cigarette, struggling to make eye contact with his interviewers.

However, a number of inconsistencies pepper his public appearances and his biography, complicating his powerfully "real" persona. While most interviews since 2008 feature a humble and contrite actor who is grateful for a second chance, decidedly unassuming in his unpolished demeanor and candor, other public appearances reveal a narcissistic star with a potentially nasty edge, insensitively flubbing his co-star's name or brusquely ordering some low-level staff member to fetch his glasses or cigarette lighter. Rourke remains curiously secretive about his age, sometimes refusing to disclose it to journalists, yet given his current appearance, this concern seems oddly misplaced.[10] On some occasions, Rourke vows that he never heard of Brando before he was so often compared to him, but at other times he has asserted that *Mutiny on the Bounty* (specifically, Brando's suffering in it) inspired him to try acting. His stepfather calls Rourke's "street cred" an exaggeration, and goes further to claim Rourke "never spoke the truth in his life."[11] Rourke denies the blackest mark on his record—allegations of physical abuse toward now ex-wife Carrie Otis; yet she has remained consistent in her accusations for nearly two decades. Finally, his boxing career and winning fight record have been the subject of considerable dispute and ridicule, with some claiming fights were fixed or that Rourke fabricated much of his history in the sport.[12] Such inconsistencies only serve to further obscure the line between the "real" Rourke and his onscreen characters, especially now given how heavily his onscreen roles draw on his offscreen life.

Rourke's biography contains all the highs and lows of filmic melodrama, and yet, as with most stories that tap into the mythos of the American Dream, his history is steeped in gritty realism, further exploding the line between fact and fiction. Born into a working-class family in Schenectady, New York, Rourke traveled a road to Hollywood that was unplanned and unlikely. His mother, having left her alcoholic husband, moved Mickey and his siblings to Miami, Florida, to live with her new husband, a policeman. Growing up in Liberty City, Rourke avoided home, where his stepfather was abusive and his mother was "checked out." He spent a good deal of time at the Boys Club of Miami, which gave him his first exposure to boxing. As a teen, Rourke trained at the famous Fifth Street Gym, intending to pursue boxing professionally, but a concussion altered that plan. While taking a small break from the ring, he tried his hand at acting—at a friend's suggestion—in an amateur production of Genet's *Death-Watch.*[13] According to Rourke, he chose acting because he didn't "like to work" and because being a gangster (an occupation he tried briefly) was too dangerous.[14] Deciding to try and make a career of it, Rourke left for New York City with only $400, a gift from his sister.[15]

His transition from Miami to New York and from boxer to actor created considerable uncertainty for Rourke, who struggled to understand and control his changing identity. To pay the bills, he worked as a bouncer at transvestite clubs, an experience he sometimes found disorienting. His good looks and lack of employment also made him an object of attention for men who assumed he was hustling. Rourke's account of this confusing period indicates a time in which he was split between his old self and his new one:

> Yeah, that whole scenario went on for a few years. If you're back hanging with your boys you'd act a certain way in those situations. But when you're alone and trying to change yourself anyway, you don't know what to do. Or you don't know what you are, even. It was real confusing. . . . I remember sitting in Sheridan Square Park one day and a fucking construction worker—a guy like forty years old, all-American-looking dude—walked up to me. 'How ya doin'?' he said. 'Got a smoke? Whatta you doin'?' 'Just hangin',' I told him. 'Lookin' for work?' 'Yeah.' 'I live in Jersey,' he said. 'I got to get home to my wife. How 'bout a quick blowjob and I'll give you fifty bucks.' Back home I was supposed to punch a guy in the mouth for saying that. Yet it kept happening over and over.[16]

His recollection highlights the undetermined and mutable nature of his identity, suggesting, early on, an uncertainty of self, as well as a proclivity to perform roles as the situation demanded, perhaps as a method of survival. Thus, the lines between onstage and offstage (or on- and off-camera) seem to have blurred for Rourke from a young age. Later, some of his memorable film roles would portray him as unmoored, anxious, and in a confused state regarding his identity (*Rumble Fish*, *9½ Weeks*, *Angel Heart*, and *The Wrestler*).

Despite his early uncertainty about the direction his life was taking—or what his boundaries now were—Rourke displayed a readiness to adapt to his new circumstances. His actions during this time continue to illustrate an indecisive, unstable nature, as he undermined the very steps he was taking to better himself. For instance, feeling that acting was "pussy shit," he refused to get out of his seat for an entire year in an acting class in which he had enrolled.[17] Nevertheless, for an uneducated, unskilled actor from Florida, Rourke made some savvy decisions during his first few years in New York City. He may have lived in low-rent hotels, but he chose the right ones in Greenwich Village, where he was befriended by people "in the business," such as an older homosexual man in theater who became a mentor to Rourke and loaned him countless books as the struggling actor worked to educate himself. Recounting this time, Rourke explains, "I had no social life at all. I was very shy and had low self-esteem. I wasn't very good at picking up girls. The highlight was picking up a fat girl in a fur coat."[18]

Rourke's training in the prestigious Actors' Studio encouraged the slippage of boundaries between personal and private, genuine and performed. Method acting required Rourke to dig through his personal feelings—often painful memories—in order to convey realism in his characters. In fact, Rourke attributes his admission into the Actor's Studio to acting coach Sandra Seacat, who, when he was having difficulty relating to a father-son scene in *Cat on a Hot Tin Roof*, told him that he would have to seek out his estranged father in order to perform the scene. In a story that resembles a scene from a movie, he describes how two days before his big audition, having no information whatsoever concerning the whereabouts of his derelict biological father, Rourke started his search. He decided to go to a White Castle restaurant in Schenectady that he recalled his dad frequenting twenty years earlier. There, he found his father, and the two walked across the street to a bar, where his father bought him dinner, drank twenty-two screwdrivers, and gave him fifty dollars. The next day, able to tap into his own feelings regarding his father when he played the scene from Williams's play, Rourke nailed his audition. Gaining membership into the Actors' Studio is notoriously difficult: to offer some comparison, Harvey Keitel auditioned eleven times before being accepted, Jack Nicholson five times, and Dustin Hoffman six. Rourke was accepted on his first try. Elia Kazan, founder of the Actors' Studio, called Rourke's "the best audition he'd seen in thirty years."[19]

As Rourke began his acting career, he continued the habit of personalizing his roles, bringing characters to life by imagining a life for them outside of the page. He took risks with his characters, and they paid off. He describes his approach:

> For one role, there's going to be fifteen to twenty-five people reading the same shit. So . . . I used to think, can I give myself an activity? How can I do it not in the way it's written, yet make it interesting because I think the whole burden or responsibility is to take a chance to fail. Maybe you're going to make a bad choice but you got a damn better chance

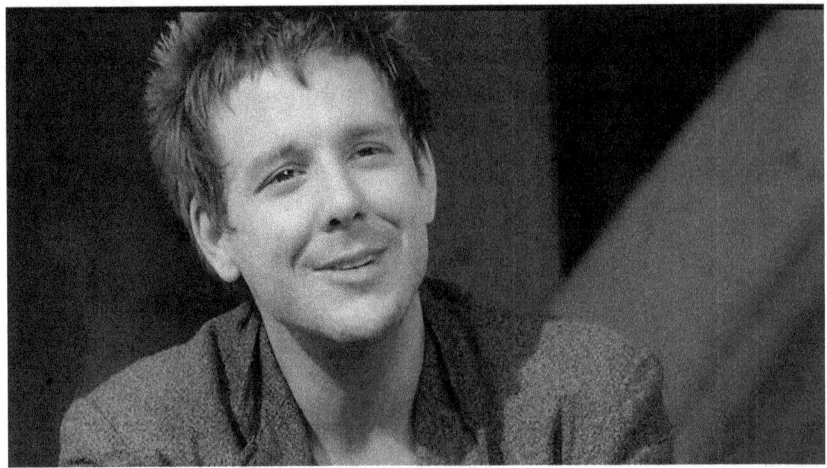

In his early years of acting, Rourke was often compared to Marlon Brando and James Dean. Here, as "The Motorcycle Boy" in *Rumble Fish* (1983), Rourke exudes an alluring combination of toughness, sensitivity, and tenderness.

> when there's that many people up for same part than if you make the safe choice or the obvious choice that somebody would make.[20]

Rourke's inclination to "give [himself] an activity" to flesh out his characters resulted in performances that drew attention to his body, often in comical and sometimes in humiliating ways. Sporting a ridiculous-looking nose guard on his sunglasses (*Angel Heart*), talking with his mouth full (*9½ Weeks*), lurching stiffly in boxer shorts in a bowlegged gait (*Barfly*), dancing on the mound before pitching a baseball (*The Pope of Greenwich Village*)—Rourke developed an acting style that was distinctively corporeal and instinctual.

His acting prowess, passion for motorcycles, working-class roots, along with his tousled hair, dark eyes, delicate facial features, trim but muscular build, and soft feathery voice all made the frequent comparisons to Brando apt and inevitable. Like Brando, Rourke's early roles solidified his screen persona as a sensitive, streetwise rebel. Yet Rourke's linkage to the iconic actor went beyond superficial similarities. Both actors developed an edgy, hypermasculine image that relied heavily on the eroticization of their bodies onscreen. As with Brando, Rourke's early films identified his body as a paradoxical site of sexual power and vulnerability, continually engaging in a process of fetishization that alternates between appreciation and exploitation. Over and over again, Rourke's body is introduced as powerful, virile, only to be damaged or degraded and gradually revealed as powerless and vulnerable.[21]

This process of fetishization and punishment of Rourke's body carries over into his characters in other ways as well: his 1980s movies feature him as a young man who is naturally smarter and more highly skilled than those around him, but who is doomed to fail. A self-destructive streak, more existential than violent, tethers him to an unscrupulous existence. In his breakthrough part in Lawrence Kasdan's sexy noir film *Body Heat* (1981), Rourke plays Teddy Lewis, an ex-con, who warns William Hurt's character to abandon his insidious plan to commit arson: "Any time you try a decent crime, you got fifty ways you're gonna fuck up. If you think of twenty-five of them, then you're a genius . . . and you ain't no genius. You remember who told me that?" Yet, after the sage advice to his ex-attorney, Lewis casually offers to do the crime himself, repaying a favor that results in his return to jail.

Though it is not Rourke's body that is referred to in the title, it might just as well be. He manages to dominate the screen in his two scenes, bringing a quiet intensity that derives from an electricity in his movements and an apparent intense kinetic awareness of his own body. The first of his scenes opens on Rourke, casually perched on the back of a sofa, while he studies William Hurt below him, clumsily fumbling with the arson mechanism. Tapping his hands to the rhythm and lip sync-singing to Bob Seger's angsty rock 'n' roll hit "I Feel Like a Number," Rourke immediately evokes an earthy and sensual blue-collar sensibility. Finally exasperated, Rourke, dressed in the 1950s greaser garb of snug blue jeans and a plain white T-shirt, gracefully crosses the room and demonstrates with the flick of a finger how to set the switch. Speaking in a gentle lilt, hinged by a strong Brooklyn accent, he chides Hurt for his incompetence ("What's-a-matta, can't take a little music?") and stops the lawyer in mid-motion when he authoritatively announces, "There's no smoking in here." Though edgy, the character of Lewis is more nice than dangerous: like many of Rourke's hoods, this bad boy has an inherent sweetness that undercuts his posturing and bravado. As Keri Walsh argues, the scene is fascinating precisely because having established himself as in command, he suddenly throws it all away, chucking his common sense and his freedom:

> There was a reason Rourke wasn't Rourke until *Body Heat*: if it gave him his rock persona, it also crystallized his way of playing a scene. As an actor, his strongest fascination was the capital he made out of his seemingly bottomless bottomhood. He had a way of reading and responding to other actors, an openness, a curiosity, an empathy so extreme that he seemed to become the other. It overcame all self-protection or self-interest, leading him to acts

> of extraordinary renunciation. The compulsion to watch him, it seemed, came from this casual throwing away of the self.[22]

Roles in *Diner* (1982), *Rumble Fish* (1983), and *The Pope of Greenwich Village* (1984) extended his stint as the gentle rebel, featuring him as an edgy, sexy, charismatic working-class young man who becomes a reluctant and wayward leader of his peers. Rourke's signature close-lipped smile and manner of hesitating slightly before speaking infuse these characters with a sense of bemused detachment from the drama in which other characters are embroiled.

For instance, in *Diner*, as his buddies struggle with decisions concerning marriage, children, family, and careers, Boogie (Rourke), whom the other boys clearly look up to, passes the days working at a beauty salon. Again, Rourke is feminized, even as he represents the masculine ideal. Although he tells potential girlfriends he is going to law school, he appears to have no clear direction—or options—for his future. Boogie is at once the leader of the gang yet also separated from their juvenile games and antics. Absent during Eddie's silly, sexist football quiz and Fenwick's drunken Christmas manger romp, Boogie opts for more "adult" activities, like gambling and sex. When Eddie (Steve Guttenberg) and Moddell (Paul Reiser) try to settle one of their puerile nightly debates at the diner by consulting Boogie—this time, the touchy subject of whether Frank Sinatra or Johnny Mathis provides better make-out music—Boogie confidently responds, "Presley," sending all the boys into an uproar and marking Boogie (and, by extension, Rourke) as the group's nonconformist.

In a similar vein, in the more melancholy *Rumble Fish*, Rourke, as the cool and enigmatic martyr-figure, Motorcycle Boy, stumps his younger, dull-witted brother (Matt Dillon) and his friends repeatedly by retorting to their questions and accusations with such poetic quips as "If you're going to lead people, you have to have somewhere to go," and "Even the most primitive societies have an innate respect for the insane." The latter statement provokes a comment by Steve (Vincent Spano), who expresses wonder that Motorcycle Boy hasn't been murdered yet. It foreshadows his eventual tragic death, which occurs when a policeman shoots the unarmed Motorcycle Boy while he is trying to release tropical fish into the river. Steve's comment also acknowledges that he may be psychologically unstable, a label that circulates around the character from the moment of his screen entrance. According to his father (Dennis Hopper), though, Motorcycle Boy isn't crazy: "He's merely miscast in a play. He was born in the wrong era, on the wrong side of the river. . . . With the ability to be able to do anything that he wants to do and . . . findin' nothin' that he wants to do. I mean nothing."

ART IMITATES LIFE

Such "rebel without a cause" roles early in Rourke's career accentuated his status as the most intriguing and desirable bad boy in Hollywood in the mid-eighties. Offscreen, Rourke was taking the moniker to a new level, riding motorcycles up and down the Strip with his entourage and behaving like the party would never end. According to Kevin Sessums, "Rourke literally translated [his street] sense into his roaming posse of Harley riders, who roared with him down Sunset and Santa Monica at all hours of the night. 'Chasing chicks and racing dicks' is how one observer describes it."[23] Sounding as if he were describing Motorcycle Boy from *Rumble Fish*, Matt Dillon described Rourke's magnetic personality: "The thing that's unique about Mickey's appeal is that both women *and* men are attracted to him—and I don't necessarily mean in a sexual way. Mickey is very 'street,' but at the same time there is a nobility about him."[24]

As with other aspects of Rourke's life and film career that obscured the line between fact and fiction, Rourke's egocentric and erratic offscreen behavior could be increasingly witnessed onscreen. If questions had been raised regarding his character's sanity in *Rumble Fish*, the next several roles that Rourke tackled left no room for ambiguity. Rourke embarked on a raft of psychotic performances in the late eighties: an obsessive Vietnam veteran and Chinatown detective in *Year of the Dragon* (1985); a seductive sociopath in *9½ Weeks* (1986); a traumatized, amnesiac, violent World War II veteran in *Angel Heart* (1987); a lewd, self-destructive, alcohol-fueled poet modeled on Charles Bukowski in the semi-biopic *Barfly* (1987); and a deformed gangster in *Johnny Handsome* (1989) who undergoes reconstructive facial surgery in prison but who ultimately cannot shake his criminal desires.

Over the top, darkly funny, and often crude, this series of movies veers heavily toward camp, an aesthetic to which Rourke gravitated from the beginning of his career, according to Walsh. "Rourke's method camp," she writes, consists of "his combination of intense, psychologically complex, gut-fuelled performances with a variety of mannerisms, flourishes, and poses. If Brando was method's answer to Elvis Presley, then Rourke was its David Bowie. Just as his youthful idol Bowie had playfully undone the 'authenticity' of rock with eye shadow and sequins, Rourke brought an under-the-radar glam edge to the raw performance style of the Actors' Studio."[25] The "satisfying tension" between realism and artifice that Walsh describes in Rourke's acting style could also be applied to the actor's body, which seems at once highly realistic, human, and vulnerable, and highly contrived or altered.

Indeed, this grouping of films is remarkable for the drastic physical transformation Rourke undergoes from film to film. From gray-haired, unkempt, middle-aged detective in *Year of the Dragon,* Rourke next appears as the handsome, svelte, well-dressed, kinky Wall Street seducer in *9½ Weeks*. Less than a year later, Rourke sweats through his shirts in the New Orleans heat as the sleazy but sympathetic private eye in *Angel Heart* before appearing longhaired, bloody, and unshaven in *Barfly*, careening loosely in the frame complete with soiled underwear and a large belly hanging out. Having achieved the status of Hollywood sex symbol, Rourke seemed determined to reverse that process by making himself as ugly and distasteful as possible. In that regard, *Barfly* not only marks a tremendous performance but also signals an early attempt to employ body modification to assert his deeply disturbed sense of identity. Interestingly, *Johnny Handsome*, in which Rourke undergoes reconstructive facial surgery to the point of unrecognizability, seems almost prescient now, uncannily "foreshadowing" the trauma that would occur to the actor's face. These films emphasize his body, at times eroticizing it, but more often revealing it as an unstable entity, a male body out of control.

Strangely enough, Hopper's description of Rourke's character in *Rumble Fish*—as a young man who could do anything he wanted but could not find anything he wanted to do—applied at this time to the real Rourke, who possessed an incredible talent for acting but demonstrated little respect for the proprieties of the business. Ill at ease with his fame, Rourke began acting out and developing a reputation, apparently warranted, for being difficult on set.[26] Acting came easy for him, and, Rourke, feeling like a fraud as the accolades rolled in, managed to offend everyone when he referred to his profession as "woman's work," i.e., not respectable or physically challenging. The episodic nature of filmmaking—shooting short, unconnected scenes over a series of days, weeks, and months—makes it understandable how any actor might have difficulty finding meaning in such fragmented activity. Given Rourke's claims that he never viewed the finished product, he may have found his work particularly unsatisfying. More tellingly, though, Rourke's disdain for his success as an actor was rooted in his need to feel powerful, masculine, and legitimate, qualities that, for him, were at odds with the art of performance.

At the very moment his career was poised to evolve into truly distinguished stardom, the actor, consumed with self-loathing and at the same time brandishing unchecked levels of vanity, set about destroying it. In one of the greatest backslides in Hollywood history, Rourke turned down the most important leading male roles of the 1980s, including *Top Gun, Platoon, Rain Man,* and *The Untouchables,* gravitating instead toward sleazy, poorly written, box office disasters like *Homeboy* (1988), *Wild Orchid* (1989), and *F.T.W.* (1994), B-grade movies that allowed Rourke to play a sexy, misunderstood loser, a role that seemed more and more to denote his offscreen sense of identity as well.[27] Eventually, having burned all of his bridges in Hollywood, he stopped receiving offers altogether. Overextended financially, his reputation sullied by allegations of spousal abuse, and having purchased a huge house and multiple vehicles for his posse of friends, Rourke hit rock bottom. When asked whether it was at this time that he lost his passion for acting, Rourke later reflected thoughtfully: "I think what it really was is that I lost myself. I could blame it on this studio guy or that director or this bad movie, but I had some screws loose. I had some broken pieces that I didn't have the knowledge of how to fix. So I had to fall."[28]

At age thirty-four, when most fighters were retiring, Rourke left Hollywood and returned to the ring. Rourke's decision to leave acting for boxing, while singular in the history of Hollywood, can be understood as sheer necessity or as a rejection of the veneer of stardom in order to locate his authentic pre-star self. Boxing pal Ray "Boom Boom" Mancini asserts: "I think by boxing Mickey is trying to legitimize himself. . . . I think he's tired of the world of pretend and wants to be in the world of reality—which is what boxing is. I think it is quite honorable work: to create. But Mickey has been beaten down by it. He needs to feel in control of his life, and that's what boxing gives you."[29] That Rourke's search for authentic selfhood entailed getting relentlessly pummeled by professional fighters seems particularly masochistic for a star who would, under normal circumstances, be spared such grueling—and permanently damaging—physical punishment. It was masochistic on emotional levels as well. Not taken seriously as a boxer, he faced crowds chanting "Mickey sucks," to which he responded by jeering back and parading around the ring, still playing the part of the defiant bad boy.[30] Indeed, the real-life descriptions of his fights could be lifted from *Homeboy*, a film he wrote in which he plays a washed-up, aging, "coulda been a contender" fighter who engages in juvenile antics in the ring in a masochistic desire to provoke the crowd's rage.

Despite his attempt to legitimize himself by boxing, and thus achieve authenticity, Rourke's boxing career seemed more of an extension of his acting career than an actual break from it. And here is why: his quest to become "real" again through boxing was already problematic because what is real about Rourke *is* the performance. "Mickey Rourke" represents, literally, the role of a lifetime. His comeback role he so convincingly inhabits in *The Wrestler* years later would prove this: the "real" Mickey Rourke cannot be represented as a boxer, but as a wrestler, in a sport that combines the physicality of boxing and the theatricality of performance.

Ultimately, Rourke not only traded in his remarkably good looks during his time in the boxing ring, but he also sustained brain damage, including what would become permanent short-term memory loss. Along the way, though, as disappointed fans and friends watched with varying degrees of disappointment, pity, and disgust, Rourke did learn something important about himself: he wanted to be an actor.

Although Rourke claims he was out of work for fourteen years, more accurately he was out of *important* work from roughly 1990 to 2000, acting in straight-to-video movies and forgettable films that had no American distribution. Gaining admission back into the business proved to be much more challenging than Rourke had expected. He had considerable difficulty repairing the bridges he had burned during the mid- to late eighties. Humiliated, he returned to Hollywood and slowly began to work his way back into decent pictures, yet he still proved himself capable of poor decision making when it came to choosing projects, turning down the role of Butch in Quentin Tarantino's *Pulp Fiction* (1994) and extending his own exile from stardom for another fourteen years. But other young male directors seemed willing to gamble on the now middle-aged actor, and a series of supporting roles in films such as *Get Carter* (2000), *The Pledge* (2001), *Spun* (2002), and *Once Upon a Time in Mexico* (2003) proved that Rourke still had "it." A starring role as the mangled hardbody hit man Marv in *Sin City* (2005) earned Rourke recognition, and, as with other subsequent roles, capitalized on his drastic physical transformation from sex symbol to almost monstrous freak.

Sin City's use of CGI exploited and heightened the exaggerated and grotesque elements of Rourke's new physique, with the CGI blending of fact and fiction, growling hard-boiled voice, hulking hard body, and mask of a face. The masochistic role he plays in *Sin City* prefigures his role in *The Wrestler*, as he manages to steal the entire show, though his sequence occupies only a portion of the movie. In a line that could come from *The Wrestler,* the aging warrior briefly exposes his psychological wounds when he says, "Hell's waking up every goddamn day and not even knowing why you're here." A mentally unstable anti-hero, Marv/Rourke occupies the wrong side of the law but is morally good. Demonstrating a weakness for women, Marv ultimately becomes a tortured tragic hero when he goes to prison for attempting to avenge a woman's murder and is electrocuted unjustly at the hands of a corrupt politician. Dwight's (Clive Owen) description of Marv/Rourke reinforces this picture of sacrifice, when he compares him to a gladiator: "Most people think Marv is crazy. He just had the rotten luck of being born in the wrong century. He'd be right at home on some ancient battlefield swinging an axe into somebody's face. Or in a Roman arena, taking his sword to other gladiators like him. They woulda tossed him girls like Nancy back then." The flashy, highly fictional *Sin City* essentially marked his initial comeback picture, containing nearly all ingredients that would define the second Rourke, but it would be the realistic, quasi-biopic *The Wrestler* that pulled the actor from the margins of Hollywood celebrity back to its A-list.

THE WRESTLER

That Rourke should regain his footing in Hollywood with *The Wrestler* seems more than fitting, given the parallels between his life and that of the aging, washed-up athlete he plays in Aronofsky's 2008 film. Yet Rourke's potency in the film goes beyond the powerful link between Rourke's two lives as the has-been actor and failed professional athlete and the character of Randy the Ram. *The Wrestler* capitalizes on all the complexities and contradictions that define Rourke an actor, including his hypermasculine/feminine persona, his vulnerable/bad boy quality, the blurring between authenticity and artifice, and his proclivity toward self-exploitation and masochism onscreen.[31] Rourke's low pay and reportedly tough treatment by Aronofsky on the set, eagerly recounted by the actor in interviews surrounding the film's release, make issues regarding Rourke's masochism almost impossible to avoid. Photographs of the actor-director pair in *Vanity Fair* emphasized the "S&M" dynamic of their relationship.[32] Clearly recognizing what the film role would demand, Rourke states, "When Darren wanted me for the role, I instinctively knew why he had set his mind on me. And deep inside I knew what he wanted from me: to go to a dark and painful place of my own life. He wanted—literally—my flesh and blood."[33]

Rourke's striking performance as the aging and remorseful athlete was punctuated by an intense focus on his muscular and manufactured physique. He reportedly gained forty pounds of muscle in order to play the part, going from one hundred and ninety pounds to two hundred and thirty, and frequent shots of his chiseled abdominal muscles and bulging biceps testify to hours of fitness training and steroid use. Aware that Rourke's facial and bodily transformation would incite gasps, Aronofsky and director of photography Maryse Alberti, who employs documentary-like cinematography, film the first few scenes with the camera directly behind Rourke's back, delaying and, finally, accentuating the "screen entrance" of the actor. Only diegetic sound is used once the film begins, creating a minimalist, intensely realistic feeling to these scenes.

The Wrestler tells the story of aging pro wrestler Randy "the Ram" Robinson, whose abuse of his body has taken its toll over twenty years of grueling matches in the ring. Not unlike Rourke's real-life exile into acting obscurity, Randy's once headliner status at Madison Square Garden has descended to matches in veterans' halls and community recreation buildings, earning him so little pay that he can't afford his rent at a trailer park. The end of the opening scene features Randy returning home after a match to find a padlock on his trailer; defeated, he sleeps in his van for the night. He has sacrificed his personal life to a career that leaves him alone and needy, with no stable support network. After a heart attack nearly kills him, Randy tries to reestablish a relationship with his estranged daughter, Stephanie, while he also attempts to connect meaningfully with a stripper named Pam (Marisa Tomei), whom he genuinely adores.

The jarring contrast between Randy's imposing physical presence in the ring and his impotence in life outside the ring presents itself immediately. He is, at once, the epitome of masculinity and its failure, a strange contradiction that makes Randy's incredible bulk an almost clownish prop of manliness. Indeed, in the first shot of Randy's exposed body as he dresses before a match, his overly developed muscles cannot diminish the overwhelming sense of vulnerability that his body language exudes. Sitting in his underwear, breathing heavily and clearly in chronic pain, Randy wraps his knees and arms for protection and tapes a razor blade against his wrist to later cut his forehead in order to create a bloody battle for his fans.

The film is remarkable for its investment in focusing on the male body enduring pain and exposure in its fragility. Gruesome bouts in the ring, including a grisly sequence in which Randy's prop-happy opponent inserts large staples all over his body with a staple gun, create a sickening display of violence for the sake of entertainment. Randy's strutting bravado in front of the crowd shifts to a frightening vulnerability, as he nearly dies attempting to please his S&M opponent and the bloodthirsty crowd. When Randy vomits and collapses back in the locker room after this match, the scene reveals that the staged match induced real pain, providing an uneasy portrait of masculine masochism. It also, like many other moments in the film, reveals the real consequences of pro wrestling, staged though it may be. The character's self-exploitation can barely be separated from that of Rourke's: interviews in 2008 and 2009 include the actor's recountings of Aronofsky's harsh directing style, but they also include Aronofsky's recollections of Rourke punishing himself far beyond the call of duty, when, not satisfied with the basic moves the script called for, he insisted on learning and shooting the "fancy," physically grueling moves of pro wrestlers.[34]

The film undermines both the character and actor's masculinity over and over, even as it pays close attention to his hard physique. For example, Aronofsky includes several humiliating moments for Randy, such as a shot of Rourke's bare buttocks in a hospital gown when his character struggles to stand after his heart attack, or, a short time later, a heartbreaking shot of him standing alone in the hospital parking lot, with no one to call for a ride home. Other vignettes show Randy similarly isolated, pulling his suitcase into and out of rec halls, or collapsing in the woods after attempting a jog too soon after his heart attack. Earlier in the film, one of the kids from the trailer park, who appears to be his only company, turns down his request to play another round of the Ram Jam video game, an embarrassing moment that highlights the impotency of the Ram's celebrity status. Most disconcertingly, Randy's verbally and emotionally abusive manager at the grocery store where he works part-time constantly berates him, making crude remarks about Randy's wrestling tights and forcing him to wear a nametag that states his hated real (feminine) name "Robin," rather than the stage/masculine name by which he goes.

Other scenes quite consciously unmask the hypermasculine wrestling persona as contrived and feminized theatrics, further undermining Randy's masculinity: Randy tans in a salon, shaves his armpits, gets blonde highlights in his long hair, and injects steroids in his butt in order to maintain his "stage" persona. Even the weightlifting sessions in the gym lack the typical machismo of the standard action-film training montage. Rourke painfully completes heavy reps, breathing heavily, fully clothed in ratty sweatpants. Not only is the carefully groomed and developed male body already at odds with notions of normative masculinity, but also, in Randy's case, this disturbing display of physical vulnerability is accentuated by the utter lack of power in his emotional life.

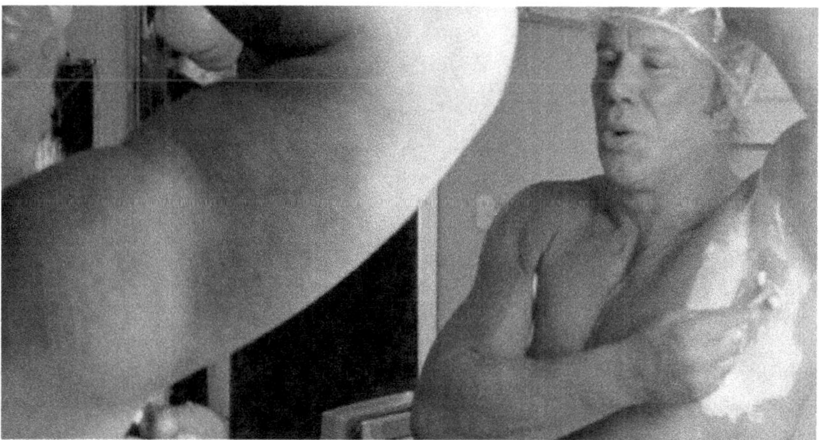

Throughout *The Wrestler*, Rourke/Randy provides a curious spectacle of hypermasculinity versus femininity; here, he dyes his hair and shaves his armpits to maintain his macho stage/wrestling persona, "Randy the Ram."

Dialogue also focuses on Randy and other characters' uneasy relationship with their bodies. In an early scene, after receiving a lap dance from Pam, Randy lifts his shirt and recounts the story behind each hideous scar, as Pam comments on how his tortured body resembles Christ's crucified body. This exchange foreshadows Aronofsky's somewhat heavy-handed comparison between a wrestler's career and a stripper's—how each exploits his or her own body to entertain for money—but it also establishes Randy's body as a site of traumatic experience as well. As he later tells his daughter, "I'm just a broken down piece of meat," a statement that makes clear Randy's imprisonment within his own disintegrating body. Like Pam, who is ridiculed by young men at the strip club for being "like their mom," Randy experiences age as his worst enemy. There is no retirement plan or health insurance for pro wrestlers or strippers, and typically little longevity in careers (and life, for wrestlers).

The excessive and overdetermined presentation of Randy's strength and physique match the excess of punishment he suffers in and out of the ring. Indeed, this relationship reminds us of a trope common to the hardbody film: the hardbody hero must undergo physical pain, whether through torture or a strict training regime.[35] Of course, Aronofsky's melodramatic film does not really belong in the action/hardbody genre, but the discussions surrounding the function of masochism and spectacles of the male body are useful in understanding Aronofsky's film and Rourke's role in it. However, *The Wrestler* complicates these theories concerning spectatorship and the male body by portraying a tortured male body that is gradually faltering and will ultimately fail completely. Unlike *Rambo* or *Bloodsport*, where we see the male warrior's body repeatedly punished before it finally triumphs in an incredible display of power, *The Wrestler* offers no reward or magical redemption for its suffering protagonist or for his empathetic spectators: there is no payoff. Without the hero's reward, the film ultimately becomes a relentless exposition of male suffering and humiliation.

What exactly are we looking at, then, when we look at—and can't look away from—Rourke's hyper-developed and suffering body in *The Wrestler* (and *Sin City*, *Iron Man 2*, and *The Expendables*), and why does Rourke form such a compelling and sympathetic figure in these movies? In discussing the hardbody/action film and its appeal to male spectators, Susan Jeffords asserts that the erotic content of the male gaze in this genre is diverted by the sadomasochistic elements of the narrative. Therefore, the torture of the male body negates or displaces any homoerotic threat, and the pain the hero undergoes becomes a source of pleasure rather than discomfort.[36] While Rourke does not denote the type of beautiful, slick, hard body of which Jeffords speaks (e.g., Sylvester Stallone, Jean-Claude Van Damme), perhaps the very abjectness of his appearance and plight becomes its own kind of taboo yet pleasurable content, in the vein of a compulsive fascination with something repugnant or strange. In other words, the curious and pitiful spectacle of tormented and overblown masculinity that Rourke provides triggers a sort of can't-look-away desire to peer at the macabre. And, as with any train wreck, the audience responds to the most extreme gruesome moments of his physical torture with groans and gestures of disgust—and more compulsive viewing. However, the overwhelming response to Rourke must be pity, for it's impossible to not feel sympathy for him, whether it is for the regretful, overgrown, isolated, and disempowered Randy, or whether it is for Rourke himself, a star whose drastic, unsightly metamorphosis invites scrutiny at every instance he appears in public or onscreen.

The most telling scene in this regard takes place at the deli counter in *The Wrestler*, when a former fan recognizes Randy and mentions he looks "just like the wrestler from the '80s, only older." Randy—who has reluctantly accepted the position out of financial desperation, even though he prefers loading boxes, out of sight from customers—severs his own thumb in the slicer in a moment of self-loathing. It is as if Randy cannot bear the exposure. Becoming the pitiful object of the gaze—one over which he has no control—causes him to snap. With its echoes of Rourke's own finger-slicing experience, the actor can relate to this humiliating scene, as he admits in commenting on his own rollercoaster career: "[*The Wrestler*] reminded me of my own life, how I had achieved so much success in my career and then had this spectacular fall from grace that left me unemployed and living in a town, Los Angeles, that is built on envy. Once you fall, people don't really root for you to come back again."[37]

Randy's only control and feelings of self-worth come when he is in the ring, performing and publicly suffering under his assumed wrestler/stage persona. In the end, despite his doctor's warning that another match could be fatal, he returns to the ring for what will be his final performance. Adding to the tragic dramatic irony of this scene, Pam, who has not reciprocated his feelings thus far, appears at the arena, finally ready to pursue a relationship with him. She cannot dissuade Randy from stepping into the ring, though, and as he makes his entrance, swaggering to the Guns N' Roses song "Sweet Child O' Mine," it is clear that, having neglected his real life for twenty-odd years, only his "stage life" holds any value for him at this point. Randy's death/suicide proves that he identifies so closely with his public persona that his play-acting has overwhelmed his actual life.

Just before Randy begins his last match, he thanks his fans for their loyalty:

> I just want to say to you all tonight I'm very grateful to be here. You know, when you live hard and play hard and you burn the candle at both ends, you pay the price for it. In this life you can lose everything

> you love, everything that loves you. Now I don't hear as good as I used to and I forget stuff and I ain't as pretty as I used to be but goddamn it I'm still standing here and I'm The Ram. A lot of people told me that I'd never wrestle again. They said, "He's washed up," "He's finished," "He's a loser," "He's all through." You know what? The only ones that are going to tell me when I'm through doing my thing is you people here . . . you people here. You're my family.

Composed by Rourke himself, this monologue represents not only the melding of Randy and Rourke, but also of Rourke's onscreen and offscreen identities.[38] It also dramatizes the tragic end—like Norma Desmond's in *Sunset Blvd.* (1950)—that follows when a performer finds more self-worth in a stage persona than in his real life. If Rourke highlights the slippage between authentic self-presentation and artificial performance in the star image, then his presence in *The Wrestler* epitomizes the powerful collusion of actor, character, and star. Just as Randy the Ram's real demonstrations of athleticism—and pain—cannot be distinguished from his planned performance of them in the ring, Rourke's real-life acts of bravado, scandal, and suffering cannot be separated from his staged gestures of martyrdom, dejection, and misery. Making it impossible to sort fact from fiction, Rourke's star image, finally, achieves what may be the highest (back-handed) compliment in stardom: the sense from the audience that he is merely playing himself, and not acting at all.[39]

As James Lipton describes him, Mickey Rourke is a "man whose personal and professional path that for drama, risks, highs and lows rivals any movies in which he has ever appeared."[40] Yet, after *The Wrestler*, Rourke's career has actually leveled out, with his ups and downs flat-lining into a state of regular film appearances without major distinction. Movies like *Iron Man 2* (2010), *The Expendables* (2010), and *Sin City: A Dame to Kill For* (2014), arguably the most successful pictures he has made since *The Wrestler*, employ Rourke's star persona as narrative shorthand for suffering and remorse to flesh out his characters, but this seems to exhaust his potential as an iconic figure in the post-*Wrestler* phase of his career. One could, of course, imagine Rourke playing more dramatic roles such as the one he played in Aronofsky's film, but any role would have to incorporate his obviously disfigured body and face as part of the narrative. *Sin City: A Dame to Kill For* restores the actor to the made-for-Rourke role of Marv, whose physical beastliness and ability to endure severe physical punishment works to express his toughness—and his charm. In the second installment of the adapted graphic novel that is marked by its extreme violence, Rourke's character once again bears—and inflicts—the brunt of it as the self-destructive hit man who has a superhuman threshold for pain. If, as Mark Gallagher states, "proof of masculine power lies in the male body's ability to withstand pain,"[41] then Marv should epitomize masculine power. Yet Marv complicates Gallagher's assertion: his body displays the scars of tremendous pain, but also the scars of tremendous (and horrendous) damage and loss, a fact that complicates any reading of him as stoic and powerful. Like Randy, Marv lacks intelligence; his only asset is his body, which will inevitably age and weaken.

Dramatic physical changes typically belong to the realm of female stars, whose bodies and faces are the topic of intense scrutiny on a daily basis. Weight gain, weight loss, plastic surgery, Botox, haircuts, and fashion choices are all items of "news" most often associated with female actors. Indeed, the public has witnessed many a female star (Elizabeth Taylor, Oprah, Meg Ryan, Jennifer Grey) become closely identified with and in some cases ruined by their physical transformations. It is hard to imagine a female film star managing to successfully mine a detrimental facial physical alteration, yet Rourke has done exactly this by playing tough guys, hit men, athletes, special ops agents, and villains, all macho characters that benefit from a scarred appearance. Of course, accomplishing this feat has required an extreme degree of self-exploitation, which has included punishing roles and countless contrite interviews.

Rourke's now apparently permanent place on "Worst Celebrity Plastic Surgery" lists (where he often ranks #1) and "Worst Dressed Celebrity" lists, and the jeers that accompany before-and-after shots ("Hey Mickey, you're not so fine anymore"), suggest that—for all his swaggering machismo and desire to assert his manhood—his altered face and body have emasculated him. He is now unable to escape his body or—more accurately—the public scrutiny of his body as a site of pain and humiliation. Trouper that he is, Rourke seems to take his damaged looks in stride, shrugging off the issue in interviews. But in true Rourke fashion, he speaks candidly about his fears of aging:

> Getting older sucks. You know, I hear all this crap about, oh, you can age with dignity. Really? That means like you're aging gracefully or something? No, you're dying, man. . . . Everything is dropping, falling. In the beginning, it's . . . harder, faster, stronger. Then it's softer, slower, older. I never heard somebody say give it to me, baby, older, slower, softer. . . . So it is like—it's a process of I'm not—I'm not accepting it, you know, laying down or standing up. It's like there's nothing I can do about it. And it's like—I mean, you look in the mirror and it is like, hmm, it is all going to hell.[42]

Rourke's endearingly frank admission, one all of us can acknowledge as true, underscores the particular difficulty of aging for "bad boy/badass" type, whose appeal stems directly from his (assumed) virility (youth). Yet if Rourke's ability to make his damaged physical transformation bankable is any indication, it is more than possible to imagine that he could manage to mine his aging in a similarly successful vein. The question will be whether directors offer him the kind of roles that allow Rourke to act and not to simply play a prop.

The comparison often made in the 1980s between Rourke and Brando proved to be more accurate than anyone could have predicted: both men struggled with tragedies in their personal lives; both actors, disgusted by their star status, imploded in spectacular fashion during their peak, resulting in temporarily truncated careers; and finally, both, in their second bodies, became spectacles onscreen, shocking objects always subject to constant comparison to their desirable former selves.

For a star who detested stardom but behaved like a celebrity-gone-wild, perhaps it is fitting that Rourke destroyed his star image by radically altering the body to which his stardom was attached. His comeback in the mid- to late 2000s, though, gave birth to a second star, also named Mickey Rourke, one who is infinitely more complex and emotional. His cult following of fans faithfully support him, finding irresistible his candidness (however contrived), his charismatic personality, but, above all, his suffering.

NOTES

I am indebted to Rebecca Bell-Metereau and Jonathan Sircy for their insightful comments and suggestions on this essay—thank you.

1. Harry Haun, "Rourke Mania: Darren Aronofsky Directs Portrait of Aging Wrestler," *Film Journal.com,* November 25, 2008, www.filmjournal.com/filmjournal/content_display/news-and-features/filmmakers/e3ifcb7b0c6e00764408fab87945d105104, accessed June 5, 2013.
2. Kieran Mulvaney, "The Manny/Freddie/Mickey Story," March 8, 2010, sports.espn.go.com/sports/boxing/news/story?id=4974064, accessed June 5, 2013.
3. By his own admission, Rourke "went to the wrong guy" for his cosmetic surgeries, which arguably did more damage to his face than boxing. See Chris Sullivan, "I've Hacked Off So Many People in Hollywood: Who the Hell Would Give Me an Oscar?," Mail Online, last updated February 20, 2009, www.dailymail.co.uk/tvshowbiz/article-1150506/Mickey-Rourke-Ive-hacked-people-Hollywood-hell-Oscar.html, accessed May 1, 2013.
4. Rourke won the Best Actor Golden Globe in 2009 for his performance in *The Wrestler*, and was nominated for an Oscar (he lost to his friend Sean Penn).

5. To offer some support for this comment regarding other star transformations, consider Alec Baldwin's reinvention as a comedian in his bulkier physique or James Stewart's turn to darker, more complex roles after World War II.
6. Joshua Gamson, "The Unwatched Life Is Not Worth Living: The Elevation of the Ordinary in Celebrity Culture," *PMLA* 126, no. 4 (2011): 1063.
7. Rourke's comeback was really not sudden at all: it was a long process, but the media and the moviegoing audience experienced it as sudden.
8. For instance, see his uncensored acceptance speech at the Spirit Awards from February 22, 2009. "Mickey Rourke's Spirit Award Speech: Hilarious and Curse-Laden," *Huffington Post.com*, March 25, 2009, www.huffingtonpost.com/2009/02/22/mickey-rourkes-spirit-awa_n_168965.html, accessed August 15, 2014. Furthermore, see the fan responses to these types of Rourke's unbridled public appearances by scanning comments under the video posts of his interviews and appearances.
9. For example, see Carole Cadwalladr, "I've Been to Hell. I'm Not Going Back There," *Guardian/ Observer*, November 22, 2008, www.theguardian.com/film/2008/nov/23/mickey-rourke-interview
10. Most sources indicate Rourke was born in 1952, which puts him at sixty-two at the time of the writing of this essay.
11. Given Rourke's assertions that his step-father was abusive, it would be problematic to accept his step-father's claims; however, the contradictions between Rourke's account of his childhood and his step-father's account further support my point concerning the inconsistencies in Rourke's biography. In yet another instance of controversy, his step-father claims that Rourke grew up in a white middle-class neighborhood in Miami and not the impoverished, predominantly black neighborhood of Liberty City, which Rourke claims. For these claims from Rourke's step-father and for more information on his controversial boxing career, see "Mickey Rourke," *Boxrec*, www.boxrec.com/media/index.php/Mickey_Rourke, accessed March 5, 2015.
12. Ibid.
13. Kevin Sessums, "Fighting Irish," *Vanity Fair*, July 1991, www.vanityfair.com/hollywood/features/1991/07/mickey-rourke-199107, accessed April 15, 2013.
14. Rourke's comments regarding his distaste for work specifically deal with his aversion to manual labor, such as digging ditches for the electric company in the heat of Florida. See Rourke's interview with James Lipton on *Inside the Actor's Studio*, Bravo, August 31, 2009.
15. Ibid.
16. Sessums, "Fighting Irish."
17. Ibid.
18. Ibid.
19. Rourke's account of reconnecting with his father and his audition can be found in his interview with Lipton on *Inside the Actor's Studio*.
20. Ibid.
21. While this is true early in his career, Rourke's "impotence" becomes literalized in *Bullet* (1996); sexual dysfunction also becomes a temporary issue for him in *Wild Orchid* (1989).

22. Keri Walsh, "Why Does Mickey Rourke Give Pleasure?," *Critical Inquiry* 37, no. 1 (2010): 135.
23. Sessums, "Fighting Irish."
24. Ibid.
25. Walsh, "Why Does Mickey Rourke Give Pleasure?," 134.
26. *Barfly* co-star Faye Dunaway claimed that Rourke was a terrific improvisational actor, and was "never malicious" on set. Yet Rourke admits to disrespectful behavior, which typically entailed his short temper and sharp tongue. Sessums, "Fighting Irish." See also *Inside the Actor's Studio.*
27. Some have asserted that Tom Cruise owes his career to Rourke's bad decisions in the late 1980s. For roles Rourke turned down, see "Mickey Rourke: Trivia," Internet Movie Database, imdb.com.
28. *Inside the Actor's Studio.*
29. Sessums, "Fighting Irish."
30. Rourke's record includes ten wins, two draws, and zero losses over the course of his time in the ring. But there are conflicting reports on his record—some indicate nine wins; some indicate two draws; some say only one draw—but of more significance is the fact that his advanced age (he was between thirty-four and thirty-eight when he began boxing professionally, depending on the source) kept Rourke from fighting top-level opponents. See Harry Haun, "Rourke Mania" and *Inside the Actor's Studio.* His most recent fight, at age sixty-two, has likewise been mired in scandal, with accusations that his victory over a man less than half his age was fixed. See Hugo Daniel, "Mickey Rourke Boxing Opponent Was Paid to Throw Fight," *Daily Mail Online*, November 30, 2014, www.dailymail.co.uk/sport/boxing/article-2854855/Mickey-Rourke-s-opponent-paid-throw-fight-against-62-year-old-actor-sources-reveal-Elliot-Seymour-sleeping-rough-California-park.html, accessed December 7, 2014.
31. For an insightful discussion of Rourke's BDSM qualities and status as an unruly "bottom," as well as a more lengthy reading of his masculine/feminine qualities, see Walsh, "Why Does Mickey Rourke Give Pleasure?"
32. For more on Rourke's self-exploitation/masochism in publicity promoting *The Wrestler*, see Walsh, "Why Does Mickey Rourke Give Pleasure?"
33. Julian Schnabel, "Ring Free," *Vanity Fair* (Germany), January 2009, reprinted in *The Fashion Spot,* forums.thefashionspot.com/f50/mickey-rourke-77485-10.html, accessed April 5, 2014.
34. A number of interviews around the time of *The Wrestler* quote Rourke describing Aronofsky as being very hard on the aging actor, particularly in terms of shooting physically demanding scenes repeatedly. Yet, as stated, Rourke seems more than complicit in his own "punishment." See, for example, Josh Horowitz, "Mickey Rourke Explains His Preparation for 'The Wrestler': 'I Had Some Demons,'" MTV.com, www.mtv.com/news/articles/1594599/mickey-rourke-talks-about-training-wrestler.jhtml.
35. See the following works: Yvonne Tasker, *Spectacular Bodies: Gender, Genre and the Action Cinema* (New York: Routledge, 1993), and Drew Ayers, "Bodies, Bullets, and Bad Guys: Elements of the Hardbody," *Film Criticism* 32, no. 3 (2008): 41–67.

36. Susan Jeffords, *The Remasculinization of the America: Gender and the Vietnam War* (Bloomington: Indiana University Press, 1989), 13.
37. Piers Morgan, "When Piers Met Mickey Rourke," *GQ,com* (UK), July 22, 2010, www.gq-magazine.co.uk/entertainment/articles/2010-07/22/gq-film-piers-morgan-interviews-mickey-rourke, accessed December 7, 2014.
38. Rourke actually rewrote many of his scenes and dialogue in the film.
39. Though Richard Dyer does not speak of this phenomenon as a compliment or an insult, he does explain that successful stars, by virtue of their powerful sense of authenticity, inevitably fall prey to this charge—that the star is merely playing himself. See his *Heavenly Bodies,* 2nd ed. (London: Routledge, 2004), 9–10.
40. *Inside the Actor's Studio.*
41. Mark Gallagher, *Action Figures: Men, Action Films, and Contemporary Adventure Narratives* (New York: Palgrave Macmillan, 2006), 187.
42. "Piers Morgan Tonight," CNN, November 19, 2011, transcript accessed at transcripts.cnn.com/TRANSCRIPTS/1111/19/pmt.01.html.

3

HILARY SWANK AND CHARLIZE THERON: EMPATHY, VERACITY, AND THE BIOPIC

Megan Carrigy

HILARY SWANK LAUNCHED HER HOLLYWOOD CAREER IN 2000 WHEN SHE won her first Academy Award for Best Actress for her performance as Brandon Teena, a well-known victim of transgender hate crime, in Kimberly Peirce's *Boys Don't Cry* (1999). Charlize Theron's portrayal of convicted serial killer Aileen Wuornos in Patty Jenkins's *Monster* (2003) also earned her an Academy Award for Best Actress in 2004. In the case of both young women, their Oscars were distinguished by the fact that these were their first nominations. Academy recognition helped them break into the arena of celebrity and affirmed their status as stars. Both performances were marked by dramatic physical transformations; indeed, it has become customary for cynical commentaries to suggest that these wins are part of a trend toward awarding actors for taking on unflattering roles that require them to "get ugly."[1] Theron's weight gain and elaborate latex makeup in *Monster* placed her performance at the top of surveys suggesting that difficult and unflattering physical transformations give actors an "edge" in the Oscars race. Swank's decision to cut her hair, lose weight, and strap her breasts with tension bandages to play Teena also places her high in the ranks of such surveys. Yet unflattering "extreme makeovers" and difficult physical transformations merely gesture toward why Swank and Theron were so successful in these roles. The connections between transformation, veracity, empathy, and suffering that amalgamate in the star performances of Theron and Swank hinge on strategically negotiating the tension between private and public life, a tension similar to the ones that inspired the making of both biopics.

Certainly, the physical transformations that Swank and Theron underwent to play Brandon Teena and Aileen Wuornos did require considerable suffering and endurance. In an interview to promote a more recent movie, *Conviction* (dir. Tony Goldwyn, 2010), Swank admitted that as she gets older she is less inclined to radically reshape her body for a role because "when you change your weight it has an impact on your health. For *Boys Don't Cry* I went down to nine per cent body fat so that I would look kind of sunken, but I was 24 and I bounced right back."[2] For Theron, there were lengthy preparation times in hair and makeup throughout the twenty-nine-day shoot, including liquid latex applied to her face and dried with a hair dryer to achieve a leathery texture, as well as layers of tattoo paint with a spray gun to give her skin a mottled look. Gelatin was applied to her eyelids to make them droop, her eyebrows were plucked and bleached, and she was fitted with sculpted fake teeth. Gaining thirty pounds in three months to play the role, she reportedly maintained a diet of potato chips, soy sauce, and miso soup to attain a bloated look during filming. As Robert Blackwelder describes it, Theron made the decision to "trash her own body and beauty for a $2 million movie."[3]

Emphasis on the mechanics of the difficult physical transformations Theron and Swank underwent for these roles risks overshadowing the fact that the suffering Aileen Wuornos and Brandon Teena both experienced in their inescapable real lives was far greater than that endured by Theron and Swank in order to portray them. By the age of fifteen, Wuornos had been abandoned by her parents, abused by her grandfather, forced to give away a baby for adoption, and left homeless. At the time of her arrest in 1991, she had accumulated a long history of charges for assault, armed robbery, and forgery and worked as a prostitute on the streets around Daytona Beach, Florida. After a series of high-profile court cases that began in 1992, she was convicted of killing six of her clients. Wuornos claimed that these men had either raped or attempted to rape her and that the killings were committed in self-defense, but she later recanted this claim in 2001 after twelve years on death row. Despite concerns about her mental health and her capacity to meet the requisite competency evaluation, she was executed by lethal injection on October 9, 2002.

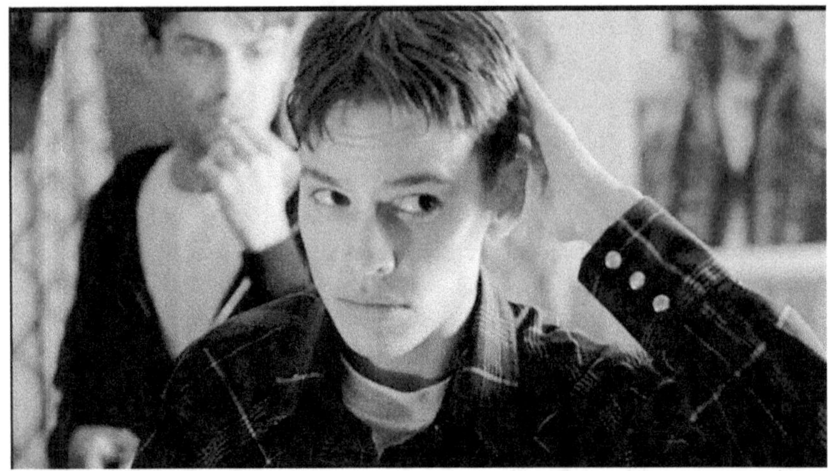

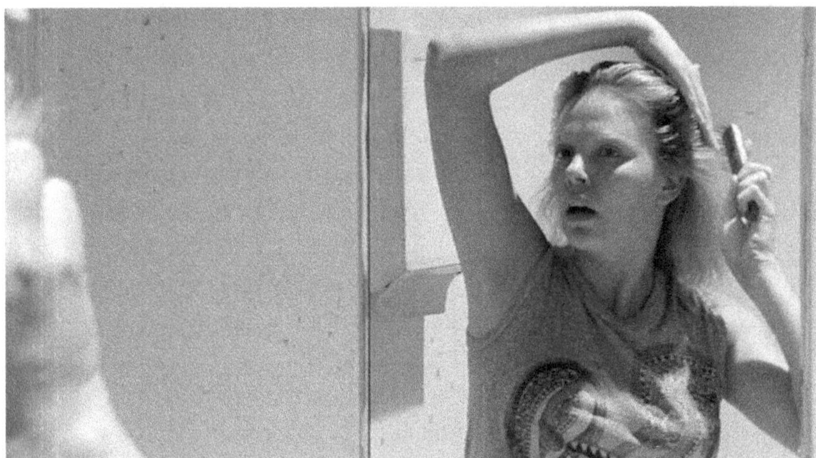

Unlike the suffering experienced by Brandon Teena and Aileen Wuornos in real life, the difficulty Hilary Swank and Charlize Theron experienced in bringing their characters to life was temporary. However, the actors' transformations helped them foster empathy for their real-life counterparts. *Left*: Swank in *Boys Don't Cry* (1999); *right*: Theron in *Monster* (2003).

Brandon Teena, born Teena Renae Brandon in Lincoln, Nebraska, was dating girls and calling himself Billy by the time he was in high school. After getting into trouble with the law for theft and forgery, he moved to Falls City, Nebraska, in 1993 at the age of twenty-one and found a new girlfriend, Lana Tisdel. He passed successfully as male before his transgender identity was discovered and he was raped by John Lotter and Tom Nissen, two men from Tisdel's circle of friends. He reported the rape to the police but several days later was shot and killed on New Year's Eve (along with Lisa Lambert and Phillip DeVine) by Lotter and Nissen, who had tracked him to Lambert's house in Humboldt, Nebraska. Teena's violent rape and murder have become an enduring symbol in public mobilization against transgender hate crimes in the United States.

The physical suffering that Swank and Theron endured to transform themselves for their roles was not only designed to achieve an accurate physical likeness to their subjects. Theron and Swank's physical transformations were also closely associated with their emotional and psychological connections to Wuornos and Teena. For example, Theron describes her concerted efforts to gain weight for her role as driven by her desire for empathetic engagement with the suffering Wuornos had endured throughout her life: "She'd lived a homeless life, so nutrition was the lowest thing on her priority list—whatever food she was going to get, that's what she was going to eat. . . . It wasn't about getting fat. Aileen wasn't fat. Aileen carried scars on her body from her lifestyle, and if I'd gone to make this movie with my body—physically I'm very athletic—I don't know that I would have felt the things Aileen felt with her body. It was about getting to a place where I felt closer to how Aileen was living."[4]

Swank spent six weeks doing vocal training to deepen her voice and worked with a trainer to sculpt her body into Brandon's lean shape. She also spent four weeks before production started trying to live and pass as male, which helped her to better understand what it was like to be Brandon Teena: "Sure enough, people talked to me as if I was a boy. I was fascinated by their reactions, always looking into their eyes to see how they were reading me, if they were seeing through me. It was intense. It gave me a real insight into Brandon because this wasn't just a role for her. It was her life."[5] Physical transformations were directly connected to Swank's and Theron's ability to portray the visceral physicality of their subjects, their bodies, but also their gestures, mannerisms, voices, body language, and temperament—their ways of being in, and relating to, their worlds—convincingly and with empathy.

In both cases, the emphasis on the veracity of the women's performances did not stop with accurate or even empathetic reproduction of their subjects' physicality. The authenticity and truthfulness in their performances is also directly connected to their capacities to make empathetic connections between their own personal experiences of transformation and suffering and those of Teena and Wuornos. Indeed, the promotion of *Monster* and *Boys Don't Cry* emphasized not only the challenging physical transformations Theron and Swank endured to play Wuornos and Teena but also connections to the suffering they had experienced in their personal lives. As a teenager Theron saw her mother shoot dead her physically abusive alcoholic father in self-defense, an experience that helped her empathize with Wuornos, who originally claimed to have shot her clients in self-defense. Swank (who actually was born in the same town as Brandon Teena but grew up in the Pacific Northwest) explained how her impoverished childhood living in a mobile home attracted her to playing outsiders "who have to struggle against the odds": "I learned what class was. . . . They wouldn't want me to come round to their house to play. It was like, 'Well, what's wrong with me?' . . . When I was ostracised by my friends I felt like an outsider. Everyone feels like an outsider at some point, but because it happened to me in those formative years I related to characters in movies, outsiders like the Elephant Man, ET, and the Wizard of Oz."[6] By emphasizing the similarities between Theron's and Swank's personal experiences and those of the women they were portraying, the publicity for *Monster* and *Boys Don't Cry* implied that the actors had the capacity to connect with and be touched emotionally by the lives of their subjects. These suggestions promoted the idea that Theron and Swank could reenact the struggles of their subjects authentically, contributing to the perceived veracity of each biopic.

Significantly, the personal experiences that Swank and Theron drew upon to identify with Teena and Wuornos are also connected to some of the stories that have been central to the construction and promotion of them as stars. Richard Dyer writes that "star images are always extensive, multimedia, intertextual," and particular elements of a star's image will predominate at particular moments in that star's career.[7] Swank's and Theron's performances in *Boys Don't Cry* and *Monster* interact with, indeed contribute significantly to, narratives of personal transformation, suffering, and empathy that have been integral to the production, continuity, and success of their own star personae. Typically, stories about Swank's and Theron's success as actors and stars imply that their achievements are the result of their ability to overcome the great hardships that they endured early on in their lives. The fact that Theron saw her mother shoot dead her father is often referred to in stories about her rise to stardom. For example, a biography of Theron published online for *Hello! Magazine* states, "The road has not always been a smooth one, however, and the actress has had to overcome trauma and tragedy before finding happiness. . . . 'When you're 15 and your father suddenly dies, you realise life is very short,' she says. 'He was only 43. I know that if I die tomorrow I'll have at least tried everything I wanted to try. In some ways that's sad, but it's also been why I never give up.'"[8]

For Swank, overcoming poverty is conceived as a key factor in her success as an actor. In her Oscar speech for *Boys Don't Cry*, Swank referred to her mother in the audience, declaring that "it looks like living out of our car was worth it." In her speech after winning another Academy Award for Best Actress in a Leading Role, this time for her work in *Million Dollar Baby* (dir. Clint Eastwood, 2004), she claimed, "I'm just a girl from a trailer park who had a dream." Statements about Swank such as this one from the *Daily Mail* are also common: "From trailer park to two-time Oscar winner, Hilary Swank is a woman with determination and drive."[9] These stories about Theron's and Swank's rise to stardom help present them as role models and contribute to what Dyer describes as the "success myth" that "anyone can make it in America," a trope that Dyer sees manifesting in "several contradictory elements" in relation to movie stardom: "that ordinariness is the hallmark of the star; that the system rewards talent and 'specialness'; that luck, 'breaks,' which may happen to anyone typify the career of the star; and that hard work and professionalism are necessary for stardom."[10]

For Swank especially, *Boys Don't Cry* marked the beginnings of an ongoing narrative central to her star persona. Stories about her rise from poverty to success in Hollywood also featured prominently in the promotion of *Million Dollar Baby*, based on the life of Maggie Fitzgerald, a working-class woman who tried to turn her life around through her boxing career. They also appeared in the promotion of *Conviction* (dir. Tony Goldwyn, 2010), in which Swank plays Betty Anne Waters, a high-school dropout and single mother who put herself through law school to try to overturn her brother's murder conviction. Swank's early difficulties are regularly described as giving her "real empathy with the characters she's portrayed—women who have to struggle to overcome prejudice and discrimination, whether because of their sex or their blue-collar backgrounds. She feels a bond with these women."[11] In the promotion of her movie *Conviction*, for example, she continues to point to her early struggles to explain her capacity to play Betty Anne Waters successfully: "Growing up in a lower-income family, you don't have the resources to make ends meet and you have to find creative ways to get by. That infuses your character with a lot of drive and determination and yes, I share that with Betty Anne. She was easily judged as a kind of castoff, and that's part of her story that I can relate to."[12] Swank's star image has been consistently built on personal experiences of deprivation, discrimination, fortitude, and grit as they relate to the real-life stories of characters she has portrayed.

An emphasis on close proximity between the experiences of a star performer and the experiences of their subjects has a history stretching back to the studio era. Dennis Bingham points out that the promotion of Susan Hayworth's Academy Award–winning performance as Barbara Graham in the biopic *I Want to Live!* (dir. Robert Wise, 1958) emphasized her strong-willed, working-class, no-nonsense "girl-from-Brooklyn" background, constructing her as a star who "embodied both the glamorous and the ordinary."[13] Graham, whose life has a number of similarities with that of Aileen Wuornos, was caught in a cycle of crime since her youth and vilified for her participation in robbery, forgery, perjury, and prostitution before she was convicted for murder and executed. In *I Want to Live!* Hayworth identifies with Graham as she foregrounds "the complex humanity of a woman whom the press caricatured in her own time."[14]

Like Barbara Graham, Brandon Teena and Aileen Wuornos also became celebrities in their own right when the media first brought the tragedies in their lives to public attention. It was Wuornos's arrest on the charge of multiple murders that led to her life becoming widely publicized and sensationalized. She became the subject of intense media fascination and attained notoriety under the label of the nation's first female serial killer. Only after Brandon had been murdered did his alter ego Teena attain celebrity status, quickly becoming the focus of public debate about transgender hate crimes, with coverage ranging from tabloid television to true-crime paperbacks to intellectual analysis of Brandon's cultural meaning.[15] "Certain careers and types of people become the prime focus of public curiosity in each generation and the biopic reflects these shifts in the public notion of fame," writes George Custen.[16] He suggests that fame is not created through a standard or stable set of practices but a shifting set of relationships tied to communication technologies that have continued to broaden and transform the category of fame itself.[17] In his view it was made-for-TV biopics, broadcast from 1971, that first drew inspiration from tabloid news and created a different kind of famous person, "everyday people to whom unusual things had happened."[18] Bingham also sees an emphasis on suffering and victimization starting to become prevalent in biopics about women as early as the late 1940s.[19]

Boys Don't Cry and *Monster* both attempt to reveal the private person behind the public figures of Teena and Wuornos and interrogate the ways in which their fame circulated and what it represented. The films are used as a means of getting inside the lives of people whose celebrity was fueled by an intense fascination with their vilification for failing to adhere to gender expectations. In Fox Searchlight Pictures' press kit for *Boys Don't Cry*, Kimberly Peirce describes what drew her to Brandon Teena:

> Here was a character who was already becoming an icon within months after being killed. Brandon Teena represented so many strands of our culture—he was a female to male, he was a petty thief, he was the victim of a hate crime—he was being written about by true crime writers, journalists and feminists. There was no disputing that his story was dramatic and tragic, but the real challenge in telling it was finding the human

> being underneath it all, discovering what it was like to be inside Brandon's skull the very first night he passed as a boy. When you think about who he was and begin to see how extraordinary what he did was, just how powerful his spirit, imagination and creativity had to have been.[20]

As a transgender male and a lesbian prostitute, Teena and Wuornos existed on the margins, both of them outcasts from their homes and victims of violence. As Bingham proposes, "Biopics about female subjects highlight the contradictions between the public positions—positive and negative—women have achieved and the 'unladylike activities' that have landed them there."[21] The relationship between private suffering and public notoriety is a key theme in *Monster*. Patty Jenkins makes it clear that she created *Monster* to challenge the ways in which the mainstream media sensationalized Wuornos's life, especially its labeling her as "the first female serial killer." The title of the biopic refers to the image the media made of her.[22]

By publicizing the private sufferings of Theron and Swank, the promotion of *Monster* and *Boys Don't Cry* mirrors the public circulation of the private sufferings of Wuornos and Teena, a phenomenon that originally inspired the making of each biopic. Public discussion of the suffering that both actors endured and summoned for the roles necessarily becomes interlaced with public narratives about the suffering of the "real" Brandon Teena and Aileen Wuornos. In "Historical Fiction: A Body Too Much," Jean-Louis Comolli draws attention to an interplay between absence and presence in historical films that occurs in the game between the body of the historical subjects and the actors who play them.[23] This interplay is central in the biopic, one of the most popular subgenres of the historical film, distinguished by its explicit emphasis on depicting the life of a historical person, past or present, whose real name is used.[24] The biopic must constantly manage the tension generated by a performing body whose presence cannot help but signal the absence of the historical body it represents.[25]

In *Change Mummified: Cinema, Historicity, Theory*, Philip Rosen argues that the use of factual details—which emerge out of the research undertaken in preparation for a film and are based in securing the referential claims of fictional narrative—constitutes one of two main forms of referentiality associated with cinema. The other is based on documenting reality, cultivated from the idea that a trace of the pro-filmic field is inscribed into the photochemical image and that its imprint on the film image remains as a form of testimony to that past interaction. The historical film and its subgenres, including the biopic, are heavily invested in this kind of research labor. Rosen therefore defines the historical film precisely in terms of its relationship to researched detail, constituted by the combination of "a 'true story' (or elements of a 'true story') plus enough profilmic detail to designate a period recognizable as significantly 'historical,' that is, as signifying a generally accepted minimum of referential pastness."[26] The biopic's focus on the life of a particular historical figure makes the actor portraying the main "subject" a central site for the accumulation of researched details: not only the settings, props, and costumes that she inhabits, or even the details of her resemblance, manufactured or actual, to the real person she is portraying, but also the actions that she undertakes.

The tensions that Comolli identifies between presence and absence, between actor/star and historical body, make themselves felt more strongly as the circulation and documentation of our public and personal lives multiplies with increasing frequency across media platforms—which will continue to exist in accessible form long after we die. As Mary Ann Doane points out, we have reached a point in the history of our media environment where "the imprint of a moment, a person, an object, a movement could now be detached and circulated, repeated without perceptible difference far from its original time and place. Both the intimacy of that relation to a unique and contingent reality, and the detachability and circulation of its representation, have had enormous cultural consequences."[27] Today, of course, much documentation previously difficult to access is available to researchers and also to the wider public. The increasing accessibility of archive materials and audio-visual documentation has meant that biopics manage an increasingly complex set of referential, textual, temporal, and spectatorial relations between document and diegesis.

When *Monster* and *Boys Don't Cry* were released, feature documentaries about the lives of Wuornos and Teena, already released or in production, served as key reference points for Theron's and Swank's performances. The Teddy Award–winning documentary *The Brandon Teena Story*, directed by Susan Muska and Greta Olafsdottir, was released in 1998 while *Boys Don't Cry* was in production. Nick Broomfield's first documentary about the exploitation of Wuornos, *Aileen Wuornos: The Selling of a Serial Killer*, was released in 1992, and his second documentary, about her life on death row, *Aileen: Life and Death of a Serial Killer* (2003), was released in the United States just a few months before *Monster* appeared on cinema screens. *The Brandon Teena Story, Aileen Wuornos: The Selling of a Serial Killer,* and *Aileen: Life and Death of a Serial Killer* incorporated much of the existing research and media drawn from books, photographs, television coverage, and news reports in wide circulation as well as other documents less widely circulated and otherwise unavailable to general audiences.

They also incorporated interviews with friends, family, colleagues, and eyewitnesses to particular events in their subjects' lives. These documentaries offered a counterpoint to Swank's and Theron's performances, helping to establish their veracity through comparison with existing image and audio recordings of their subjects, thereby underscoring the tensions between presence and absence that were at work. This has contributed significantly to the critical reception given to the actors' work and to the success and acclaim they have attained in these roles.

Interestingly, the critical reception of Chloë Sevigny's portrayal of Lana Tisdel, Brandon Teena's girlfriend, in *Boys Don't Cry*, which earned her an Academy Award nomination for Best Actress in a Supporting Role in 2000, is also tied to the release of *The Brandon Teena Story*. Tisdel is a central figure in the documentary, in which she appears frequently in interviews. Sevigny successfully reproduces the unique mannerisms, actions, behavior, gestures, and intonations Tisdel displays in the documentary (as well as in her brief appearances on the television news coverage of Teena's murder, some of which is also incorporated into *The Brandon Teena Story*). Sevigny's skill in her performance matches those of Swank and Theron in her successful embodiment of details that make the material traces of Tisdel perform for the biopic. At the same time, it is notable that Sevigny's Lana strikes a much more sympathetic figure than her real-life counterpart in *The Brandon Teena Story,* and Peirce acknowledges that this was part of her decision to make all the characters in *Boys Don't Cry* "as empathetic and understandable and human as possible."[28] Lana Tisdel actually filed a lawsuit on October 19, 1999, charging that *Boys Don't Cry* uses her name without permission and portrayed her in a false light. Fox Searchlight Pictures settled the matter out of court in March 2000. Significantly, among a range of details related to her depiction in the film, Tisdel argued that the film falsely portrayed her continuing a relationship with Brandon after she discovered Brandon was not anatomically male and falsely implied that she is a lesbian.[29] Fidelity to these details would have undermined the love story Peirce built at the center of *Boys Don't Cry*.

As with *Boys Don't Cry*, the central love story of *Monster* is essentially fictionalized. Christina Ricci's performance as Wuornos's girlfriend in *Monster* was not received the same way that Sevigny's was. Ricci plays a character called Selby, who looks nothing like Wuornos's actual girlfriend, Tyria Moore. Unlike Tisdel, who cooperated with both the documentary and the biopic about Teena, Moore did not want to participate or be depicted in either: in order to dissociate herself from Wuornos and avoid incrimination, she had collaborated with the police. Accordingly, she is hardly visible in any of Broomfield's documentary footage or the television footage of Wuornos. The main television footage that exists of Moore shows her as a witness against Wuornos in court. Ricci's performance as Selby was therefore not substantiated or measured by the documentation, participation, or association of Moore, and her performance of an essentially fictionalized character did not require her to cultivate authenticating and measurable details within the film as did Theron, Swank, and Sevigny. Although Ricci's performance was generally well received, she did not garner any major award nominations.

Selby is integrated into the reenactment of a well-documented event in the Wuornos-Moore relationship: the tape-recorded telephone call that Moore made, in collaboration with the police, to try to get Wuornos to confess. The resultant conversation was played in the courtroom at Wuornos's trial, and Broomfield included footage of it in both documentaries. The events related to the phone conversation are reenacted on two occasions in *Monster*. The actual conversation (for which there is only audio documentation) is reperformed, with Selby in a hotel room surrounded by police and Wuornos on a prison pay phone in police custody. In Ricci's performance, she repeats a number of the phrases spoken, as well as the emotions and sentiment expressed by Moore in the actual phone call, saying, "They've been up to see my parents asking all kinds of questions," and "You're going to let me go down for something you did." Rosen argues that researched details in the historical film are "always hybridized with some degree of narrativized diegesis."[30] A researched detail embodies a hybridized temporality because it both "claims to have its own previously documentable 'reality,' that of researchable historiography," and operates according to the "virtual time" created by the narrative hierarchies of the fictional world. Rosen argues that researched detail manifests a complex referential and temporal tension by being able to "simultaneously propose some extra supplement of referential truth, but one that can only be signified as diegesis."[31] The phone call operates with this hybridity. It is integrated into the fictional world of Selby and Moore and into the temporality of the fictional narrative but at the same time resonates very strongly with the documentation and circulation of Wuornos's life.

The phone call is a key moment in Wuornos's private life that was made public as a result of her trial. While listening to the recorded conversation as it replayed in the courtroom, Wuornos broke down and wept in front of the cameras, an incident included in both Broomfield documentaries and was also broadcast on television in the United States at the time of her trial. What is more, Jenkins has described how watching Wuornos weep during the playing of this tape was the television event that first touched her emotionally and inspired her to make *Monster*.[32] Jenkins includes reenactment of the phone call and Wuornos's weeping in the film in part to validate her own empathetic response to Wuornos and to encourage the audience of the biopic to recognize precisely what this television footage made her feel in the first place—that there is a different, more sympathetic human beneath the "monster." While Jenkins experienced this breakdown as a television event, Broomfield's documentaries, available now on DVD, provide easy access to the televised footage of this event, giving it extra circulation and longevity. Like Jenkins, Broomfield clearly expressed his desire to challenge the media's portrayal of Wuornos as a "monster." His first documentary, which represented Wuornos as the victim of media frenzy, deals head-on with the grotesque manner in which Wuornos was exploited by those whose object was to sell her story to the media. His second documentary, released the same year as *Monster*, painted a nuanced and sympathetic portrait, including interviews with Wuornos's friends and supporters, focusing on the struggles she faced in her childhood. Broomfield also argued vehemently against the execution of Wuornos on the grounds that she was not mentally competent.

Both of Broomfield's documentaries, but especially *Aileen: Life and Death of a Serial Killer*, became very important for authorizing Theron's performance as Wuornos in the critical reception of *Monster*. Theron has also acknowledged her debt to Broomfield's documentary in interviews: "Fortunately enough I had met Nick Broomfield, or ironically enough, maybe six months prior to this movie coming to me. He was telling me he was making a documentary, and then I found out it was about Aileen, and he was still in the editing room. And I called him and I said, 'I know you're still cutting and you're not ready to show your movie, but I'd love to see any footage you have.' He sent an early cut of his film."[33] *Monster* and *Aileen: Life and Death of a Serial Killer* were regularly cross-promoted and discussed together. One of the ways to access *Monster* now is as a DVD box set with the 2003 documentary. Tanya Horeck argues, for example, that two freeze-frame shots of Wuornos, her head tilted back and her handcuffs framing her face, which were used extensively in the promotion of *Aileen: Life and Death of a Serial Killer*, are central to the visual iconography on which *Monster* draws. Many scenes in the documentary, Horeck continues, of "Wuornos raging against the world, shouting to reporters as she is bundled into cars," also played "a pivotal role in the reception of *Monster*."[34] In particular, Horeck points to a review in which Roger Ebert claims: "There were times, indeed, when I perceived no significant difference between the woman in the documentary and the one in the feature film. Theron has internalized and empathized with Wuornos so successfully that to experience the real woman is only to understand more completely how remarkable Theron's performance is."[35] Clearly, Theron's capacity to "disappear" into Wuornos was key to her success in the role.

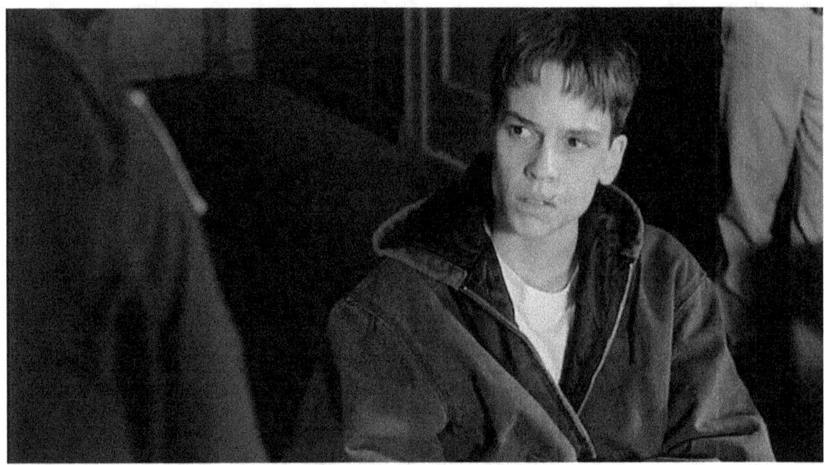

A double disappearance: Teena's transformation into Brandon, followed by Swank's disappearance into Teena/Brandon in *Boys Don't Cry*.

The critical reception of both *Aileen: Life and Death of a Serial Killer* and *Monster* became "reliant not only on how they relate to actuality but also how they relate to each other," according to Horeck. She goes so far as to argue not only that "the 'real' Wuornos found in Broomfield's documentary is scrutinized to see how the performance of the stunning actress in *Monster* matches up," but also vice versa: "Wuornos is found to be as good or less good and either more or less real than Theron."[36] This statement suggests, intriguingly, that Theron's performance can be compared to Wuornos's own performances as herself, and as a celebrity in her own right—the first female serial killer—in front of the cameras at her trial and in front of Broomfield's camera in both his documentaries. Interestingly, Hilary Swank's performance is also measured against Teena Brandon's performance as Brandon Teena. Swank essentially underwent the same physical transformation as Teena by clipping her hair into a butch cut, flattening her breasts, putting on boys' clothes, and changing her body language in order to pass as male. The success of Swank's performance as Teena hinges on her ability, through the cultivation of Teena's mannerism and gestures, to pass as male, a feat that marked Teena himself as a successful performer. This is a double disappearance because Teena himself first performed that radical disappearance of his female body into a male identity.

In contrast to *Monster*, *Boys Don't Cry* does not make any explicit reference to the film's relationship with the documentary of its subject's life in the promotion or credits for the film. The DVD commentary emphasizes Peirce's independent research efforts, reporting that she "set off on a five-year journey researching the life of Brandon Teena."[37] *Boys Don't Cry* and *The Brandon Teena Story* were made at the same time and draw on much of the same research materials and subjects, but each is the result of separate research. Furthermore, in the absence of video and television footage of Teena, the sources Swank had to use for her reenactment of Teena were audio recordings and still photographs made available by police, friends, and family members, which were subsequently circulated widely in media reports about his murder as well as incorporated into *The Brandon Teena Story*. Julianne Pidduck notes that the close-up in the opening scene of *Boys Don't Cry*, in which Brandon looks at himself in the mirror, simultaneously positions the audience in a traditional relationship of identification and "rubs up against the residue of photographs widely reproduced in news reports, on the internet, or in the documentary *The Brandon Teena Story*," because it mimics the framing of another photo of Teena frequently used in media reports.[38] And one of the photographs that Brandon carries in his duffle bag in the film is actually of Hilary Swank dressed as a gangster in imitation of a photograph of the "real" Brandon Teena that appeared frequently in media reports after his death. This correspondence demonstrates the high level of attention paid to real-life details in the mise-en-scène of *Boys Don't Cry*.

Manifestations, associations, and conceptualizations of research details are historically specific and shaped by frequent changes in the media landscape. Factors include the recording capacities of the photochemical process and the circulatory capacities of technical media, from the dominance of photography and cinema during the late nineteenth and early twentieth centuries to television, DVD, and the Internet of today, all of which have accelerated and diversified this circulation. Acts of referencing across different media and genres have always been central to the ways in which the biopic makes its claims to truth, and the authenticity of the biopic's fictional world depends upon convincing reenactments of events that are known to its audiences. In the current media environment, what certifies a reenactment as historically accurate is not so much adherence to the events it reenacts as much as their media representations. Thus, the most frequently reenacted events are those that have already been well documented or widely circulated in the public domain as film and media events. Reenactment of a known or accessible media representation signals the performance of a preexisting event, the veracity of which can be easily verified.

The documentation of the violent rapes—extremely significant events in the personal and public lives of Teena and Wuornos—played a critical function in the production and reception of *Boys Don't Cry* and *Monster*. *Boys Don't Cry* reenacts the tape-recorded police interview during which Teena reported his rape by Lotter and Nissen, the original audio of which is included in *The Brandon Teena Story.* Teena's rape was a major turning point in his life in Falls City: it violated the gender identity he had been living out since his arrival there. The failure of police to prosecute the rape case quickly also put his life at risk, and was a central point in subsequent campaigns against transgender hate crimes: it meant Nissen and Lotter were free to track Teena down on New Year's Eve and murder him, ostensibly to punish him for reporting the rape to the police.

The tape-recorded police interview in which Teena reports being raped by Nissen and Lotter is one of the most significant reenactments in *Boys Don't Cry*. First, it provides an accessible comparison between Teena's testimony as it appears in the documentary and Swank's performance of it in the Hollywood film. Swank speaks the testimony word-for-word and reenacts very closely Teena's delivery in the audio recording. What is more, Sheriff Laux, the officer who interviewed Teena at the police station and the other voice on the audio tape, is also interviewed in *The Brandon Teena Story*, commenting on his thoughts, feelings, and responses to the events described in the recording. This interview provides us with further documentary material by which to corroborate the authenticity of both Lou Perryman's performance as the sheriff in *Boys Don't Cry* and the reenactment of the report of the rape. Second, the reenactment of Teena's testimony frames the reenactment of the actual rape in *Boys Don't Cry*, which is presented as a flashback. The testimony spoken by Swank becomes a narrational device for the reenactment of the rape itself. Horeck argues that this emphasis on flashback in *Boys Don't Cry* is designed to "echo the trauma of the rape itself."[39] It foregrounds the trauma of testifying to police and of Teena being obliged to name his female genitalia in violation of his own gender identity, and it connects this with Nissen and Lotter's desire to violate Teena's gender identity as a motivation for the rape itself. Furthermore, the interaction between these two reenactments, based on the same document, successfully incorporates the audio recording into the dramatic world of *Boys Don't Cry*, framing the rape from the point of view of Teena.

In *Monster*, the rape of Wuornos by Richard Mallory (who becomes Wuornos's first victim) occurs in a scene early on in *Monster* in which she breaks loose and shoots him dead after he has tied her to the front seat of the car, raped her with a tire iron, and poured cleaning fluid over her genitals. The scene is based on Wuornos's courtroom testimony, which was aired on American television and is included in both Broomfield documentaries. The television footage of Wuornos's courtroom testimony was first incorporated into *Aileen Wuornos:*

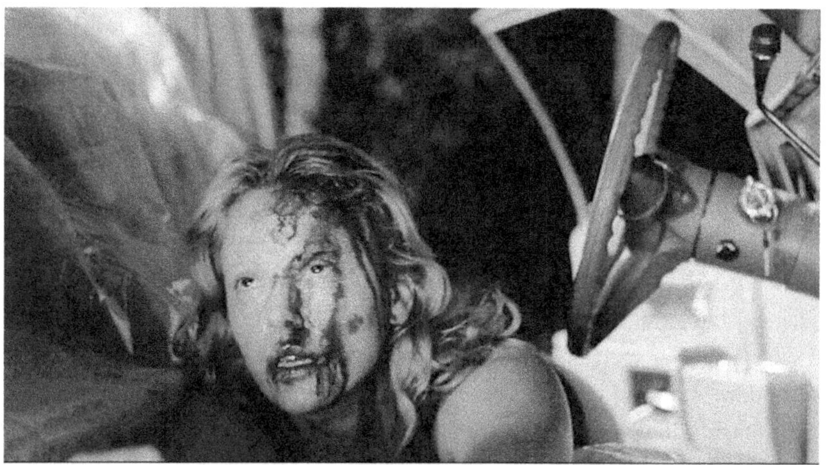

Charlize Theron in *Monster.* The documentation of the violent rapes in *Boys Don't Cry* and *Monster* played a critical function in the production and reception of the film.

The Selling of a Serial Killer, released in 1993, and was only about a year old at the time. It is used as a part of sequence showing the lead-up to Broomfield successfully obtaining an interview with Wuornos for that first documentary. *Aileen: Life and Death of a Serial Killer* was made eleven years later; there, the footage of the testimony is inserted almost like a flashback immediately following an interview with a much-aged, wearied, and more cynical Wuornos, who has since spent twelve years on death row.

In contrast to *Boys Don't Cry*, the connection to the courtroom testimony in *Monster* is not self-evident because the testimony itself is not reenacted. Regardless, Tanya Horeck contends that the rape scene in *Monster* still "derives its dramatic charge from its close association with Wuornos's powerful testimony . . . rendered here in visual detail and offered up to us as a truthful spectacle of the real."[40] Horeck describes this rape as the "defining trauma of the film."[41] It works to set up a commonly held argument that this rape was the "primal scene" for Wuornos's subsequent murders. This line of reasoning proposes that she was so traumatized by Mallory's brutal and humiliating rape and by having shot him as he prepared to rape her again that she relived both actions in her subsequent shootings of later clients who either raped or attempted to rape her.

Such devastating and harrowing scenes were emotionally challenging for Theron and Swank to perform, primarily because of their empathy with Wuornos's and Teena's suffering, but also because of the scenes' dramatic narrative significance and their importance in certifying the veracity of their performances. At the same time, analyzing these rape scenes subtly underscores the fact that the suffering of Wuornos and Teena was far greater than the suffering Theron and Swank endured to play them. The distinctions between what suffering meant for Wuornos, Teena, Theron, and Swank, as well as how that suffering circulated and was received, are significant.

Both Wuornos and Teena were vilified by their communities and sensationalized by the mainstream media for failing to adhere to expectations for their gender. That Teena lost his life because he dared to live out his preferred gender identity is the tragedy that dominates his representation across media. Wuornos's enduring public image is that of the first female serial killer. While Theron and Swank were praised for their bravery in transgressing gender norms in their performances, the physical transformations they underwent were both reinforced and undercut by their appearance as glamorous Hollywood stars on the award and publicity circuits after the films were released, ultimately reaffirming gender norms. Robert Blackwelder, for example, describes Theron's appearance during a publicity tour to San Francisco "where she was certainly back to her old self—drop-dead gorgeous and curvy in a lace-striped tank top, snug jeans, fashionably comfy UGG boots and a short velvet jacket."[42] For many commentators, Swank's beauty seemed all the greater for the contrast: "The fact that she came off so convincingly butch is a testament to her talent, because except for having such slim hips that it's a wonder her low-riding slacks stay on, in person she exudes femininity."[43] Indeed, this other self-conscious and conscientious transformation into beautiful and graceful film stars is perhaps as important to the success of each film as their capacity to transform themselves into Wuornos and Teena.

This reappearance of Theron and Swank as fashionable, heterosexual, feminine stars serves to emphasize the distance between Theron and Wuornos and Swank and Teena. Swank, in particular, is acutely aware that while the revelation of Teena's performance as male was punished with rape and murder, her own successful transformation to pass as male earned her accolades. In an interview with "The Movie Show," she explicitly points out this contrast: "Here I am living my dream. . . . I wanted to be an actress, and I'm accepted for it. She went off to pursue her dream and she's condemned for it."[44] The dynamic negotiations between closeness and distance, presence and absence, public and private that have played out in relation to these two performances ultimately expose the different ways in which all four women's lives have been constructed, contested, and valued. Both films were an attempt to intervene in public perceptions of Wuornos and Teena, with Theron and Swank as vehicles that enabled audiences to get closer to their emotions, their experiences, and their unique points of view.

Ultimately, however, the complex associations between transformation, suffering, empathy, and veracity central to the promotion and reception of Theron's and Swank's performances as Wuornos and Teena have contributed most significantly to the production, continuity, and success of their own star personae.

NOTES

1. Ellen A. Kim, "Getting Ugly for Oscar," *NBN News Today*, February 26, 2004, today.msnbc.msn.com/id/4113650/ns/today-entertainment/t/getting-ugly-oscar/, accessed March 10, 2013.
2. Martyn Palmer, "'I Know What It's Like to Be the Outsider': Hilary Swank on Her Journey from Trailer Park to Tinseltown," *Daily Mail*, January 7, 2011, www.dailymail.co.uk/home/you/article-1341187/Hilary-Swank-journey-trailer-park-Tinseltown-I-know-like-outsider.html, accessed March 10, 2013.
3. Robert Blackwelder, "Respect from Theron Out," SPLICEDwire, splicedwire.com/03features/ctheron.html, accessed March 10, 2013. After the shoot ended, Theron also had to lose the weight quickly—at a rate of six pounds per week—in preparation for her next role in the film *Head in the Clouds*, which started shooting a month after production for *Monster* wrapped.
4. Ibid.
5. Press kit, *Boys Don't Cry*, directed by Kimberly Peirce (Fox Searchlight Pictures, 1999), 12.
6. Palmer, "I Know What It's Like to Be the Outsider."
7. Richard Dyer, *Heavenly Bodies: Film Stars and Society*, 2nd ed. (London: BFI Publishing, 1986), 3.
8. "Charlize Theron profile," *Hello Magazine*, www.hellomagazine.com/profiles/charlizetheron, accessed March 10, 2013.
9. Palmer, "I Know What It's Like to Be the Outsider."
10. Richard Dyer, *Stars*, new ed. (London: BFI Publishing, 2004), 42.
11. Palmer, "I Know What It's Like to Be the Outsider."
12. Ibid.
13. Dennis Bingham, "'I Do Want to Live!': Female Voices, Male Discourse and Hollywood Biopics," *Cinema Journal* 38, no. 3 (Spring 1999): 3–26.
14. Ibid., 6.
15. Press kit, *Boys Don't Cry*, 8.
16. George Custen, *Bio/Pics: How Hollywood Constructed Public History* (New Brunswick, N.J.: Rutgers University Press, 1992), 6–7.
17. George Custen, "The Mechanical Life in the Age of Human Reproduction: American Biopics, 1916–1980," *Biography* 23, no. 1 (Winter 2000): 137.
18. Ibid., 215.
19. Bingham, "I Do Want to Live!," 5.
20. Press kit, *Boys Don't Cry*, 4.
21. Bingham, "I Do Want to Live!," 3.
22. "Interview with Patty Jenkins and BT" and "The Making of *Monster*," *Monster*, directed by Patty Jenkins (Dej Productions, 2003), DVD.

23. Jean-Louis Comolli, "Historical Fiction: A Body Too Much," *Screen* 19, no. 2 (1978): 41–53.
24. Custen, *Bio/Pics*, 5–6.
25. Comolli, "Historical Fiction," 41–53.
26. Philip Rosen, *Change Mummified: Cinema, Historicity, Theory* (Minneapolis: University of Minnesota Press, 2001), 178.
27. Mary Ann Doane, "Indexicality: Trace and Sign: Introduction," *differences* 18, no. 2 (2007): 2.
28. Kimberly Peirce, interview by Scott Tobias, *A.V. Club*, October 27, 1999, www.avclub.com/articles/kimberly-peirce,13626/, accessed March 10, 2013.
29. "Fox Settles Lawsuit with Woman Depicted in Film," *McCook Daily Gazette*, March 22, 2000.
30. Rosen, *Change Mummified*, 183.
31. Ibid., 179.
32. Jenkins, "Interview with Patty Jenkins and BT."
33. Carlo Cavagna, AboutFilm.com (2004), www.aboutfilm.com/features/monster/interviews.htm.
34. Tanya Horeck, "From Documentary to Drama: Capturing Aileen Wuornos," *Screen* 48, no. 2 (Summer 2007): 147. Horeck also points out that on April 30, 2005, Channel 4 in the UK screened *Monster* and *Aileen: Life and Death of a Serial Killer* as a double bill, explicitly foregrounding their relationship to each other.
35. Roger Ebert, review of *Aileen: Life and Death of a Serial Killer*, directed by Nick Broomfield, RogerEbert.com, September 7, 2010, www.rogerebert.com/reviews/aileen-life-and-death-of-a-serial-killer-2004, quoted in Horeck, "From Documentary to Drama."
36. Horeck, "From Documentary to Drama," 142, 150, 153–54.
37. Kimberly Peirce, "Featurette," *Boys Don't Cry*, directed by Kimberly Peirce (Twentieth Century–Fox, 1999), DVD.
38. Julianne Pidduck, "Risk and Queer Spectatorship," *Screen* 41, no. 1 (Spring 2001): 98.
39. Tanya Horeck, *Public Rape: Representing Violation in Fiction and Film* (London: Routledge, 2004), 112.
40. Horeck, "From Documentary to Drama," 157.
41. Ibid.
42. Blackwelder, "Respect from Theron Out."
43. "Hilary Swank Interview," Contactmusic.com, www.contactmusic.com/interview/hswank, accessed May 6, 2013.
44. "The Movie Show," Special Broadcasting Service, www.sbs.com.au/films/video/11682371946/interview-with-kimberly-peirce-and-hilary-swank, accessed March 10, 2013. *Boys Don't Cry* led Swank to become a spokesperson for the Hetrick-Martin Institute, a New York charity that offers counseling and support to young gay, lesbian, and transgender people. Swank worked with the charity for eight years, visiting regularly and helping to raise funds to build a school, before finally relinquishing her role in 2006.

4

BROKEN NOSE AND ALL: DANIEL DAY-LEWIS AND THE PERFORMANCE OF DISRUPTION

Dennis Bingham

HISTORY WAS MADE IN 2013 WHEN DANIEL DAY-LEWIS BECAME ONLY the second performer in history to win three Academy Awards for leading roles.[1] Day-Lewis has enjoyed a singular career, taking roles only when he feels that he shares the filmmaker's "madness";[2] he has never to date played a villain in a superhero franchise or taken a role for obvious commercial reasons. At the same time, he eschews (again, to date) the stage despite—or because of—his conventional English stage training and apprenticeship with the Royal Shakespeare Company.[3] Since his first Academy Award, for *My Left Foot* (1989), Day-Lewis has exercised a perhaps unparalleled prerogative to define and control his roles and performance choices. A review of *The Last of the Mohicans* (1992) in the United Kingdom called Day-Lewis "the only [British] actor of his generation whose move to Hollywood seems to involve no compromise."[4]

Scholars of stardom have seldom considered Daniel Day-Lewis. None of the editors of the ambitious Rutgers University Press Star Decades series thought to slot in an essay on the dominant Irish-English actor, who is best known now for playing American characters in films with historical settings. In the 1990s, Day-Lewis was in a total of five films; in the 2000s he appeared in only four. Indeed, Day-Lewis won his three Oscars over a twenty-three-year period on five nominations, in a twenty-seven-year film career totaling, at this writing, sixteen films, from his breakout roles in *My Beautiful Laundrette* and *A Room with a View* (both 1985) to *Lincoln* (2012).[5] His often combustive power onscreen comes from an intense process of discovering the character in pre-production combined with a total insistence upon keeping the character with him when the film is in production. Each film in which Day-Lewis has appeared has produced its own story about the presence of the character on the set, inspiring articles with titles such as "The Craziest Ways Daniel Day-Lewis Prepared for Roles" and headlines that strike ever more clever combinations of the words "madness" and "method."[6]

The career of Daniel Day-Lewis has continued by disrupting continuity in the usual sense—except for his famous off-camera continuation of character during a shoot, which does continue, predictably, from film to film. What Day-Lewis deliberately disrupts is the idea of a career itself. Furthermore, the seeming lack of continuity between one character and another, and especially between Day-Lewis's gentle, charming offscreen personality and his powerful performances, frustrates the continuity of a "real person" whom spectators can feel they know. This is what leads Paul McDonald to assert that Day-Lewis is a star who rejects stardom.[7] Perhaps Daniel Day-Lewis is the actor who, by dint of a grounded personal life to go with his great talent, has completed the project begun by Marlon Brando in the 1950s of shattering the principle of Hollywood stardom as a brand that changes only a little from one film to the next.

CONTINUITIES AND THEIR DISCONTENTS

Representing the culmination of sixty years of Method acting on film, Daniel Day-Lewis combines a process of living the role with an offscreen insistence on privacy that is counterintuitive in the age of 24/7 celebrity news. So many times has Day-Lewis disappeared from public view after promoting the release of a film and soldiering through the following awards season that the entertainment press treats a report that he has signed on for a new film as more surprising than an announcement of his retirement would be.

Day-Lewis can be taken as an antidote to end-of-cinema syndrome, a reassurance that there is still a "there there," to borrow from Gertrude Stein, when it comes to cinema. He is a flesh-and-blood artist whose specialty is creating historical authenticity in front of the camera with effects that cannot be simulated by digital technology. The craft of acting may not even be required in an era of computer-generated imagery (CGI), as the actress Jessica Alba has noted: "When I was dying in [*Fantastic Four: Rise of the*] *Silver Surfer* [2007] . . . the director [Tim Story] was like, 'It looks too real. It looks too painful. Can you be prettier when you cry? Don't do that thing with your face. Just make it flat. We can CGI the tears in.'"[8] In the pre-CGI 1980s, however, a different aesthetic was still extant. J. Hoberman advised his students not to be distracted by special effects and costly production values. "Movies," he said, "always come down to actors in front of a camera."[9]

Our belief in that simple axiom has been shaken in the end-of-film, digital, CGI era, yet Daniel Day-Lewis reassures us that it can be true after all. He presents himself as a throwback to the values of "the work," the term he uses most often in interviews about his acting process, and of the cinematic—not the digital—signifier. If the twenty-first century sees the survival of the theatrical feature film as a place to see actors in front of a camera, Day-Lewis may be remembered as one of the leading figures in keeping alive the human drama, real and theatrical at once, in cinema.

Whether or not Day-Lewis is a star has itself often been in dispute, although the unexpected success of *Lincoln* may have finally settled the question. Day-Lewis came in at number seven on the 2012 Quigley Poll, his first-ever appearance on the American exhibitors' annual listing of the top ten moneymaking stars, published since 1933.[10] His early successes (and first two Oscars) came in manifestations of indie cinema in its formative years (before indie became its own institution). Categorizing him as an "anti-star star" and a "prestige star," Paul McDonald notes: "His fame positions him on a hierarchy which grants him more power, influence, and profile than the vast majority of film actors working in Hollywood. He is a marketable figure: on posters his name appears above the film title and trailers emphasize his presence in films. Although a figure in the symbolic commerce of Hollywood, Day-Lewis's status is formed around his overt rejection of the market. . . . Day-Lewis has never appeared in a 'hit,' if that term is measured purely in commercial terms."[11] Based on the standard industry threshold of $100 million at the box office as defining a "hit," this is true, although it is worth noting that *A Room with a View* returned $20 million in the United States on a $3 million investment,[12] *My Left Foot* grossed $14 million domestically following production costs of $2 million, and Day-Lewis's first post-Oscar Hollywood film, *The Last of the Mohicans*, made $75 million in the United States on a budget of $40 million. Day-Lewis's ability to avoid being an actor for hire has nonetheless exposed him to a high degree of risk. His four later films in the 1990s were commercial failures of one degree or another. The $100 million *Gangs of New York* (2002), one of the most gaudily publicized films of its era, essentially broke even. The extravagantly acclaimed *There Will Be Blood* (2007), a polarizing film that, more than any other, earned Day-Lewis his anti-market credentials, did make a substantial profit worldwide, earning $75 million on its $25 million investment. On the other hand, *Lincoln* became an undoubted popular hit against almost all projections, grossing $182 million domestically against $65 million in production costs, ranking thirteenth in box office among films released in 2012.[13] *Lincoln* was the most successful of Steven Spielberg's films since *Saving Private Ryan* (1998) that wasn't a science fiction summer blockbuster (*War of the Worlds* [2005]) or didn't have *Indiana Jones* in the title. After *Lincoln,* Day-Lewis's first genuine mainstream hit since *The Last of the Mohicans* twenty years earlier, the actor may have scored some measure of public affection to go with his accolades.

Instead of asserting, as McDonald does, that Day-Lewis is a star who refuses the tenets of stardom, Jack Avery, in a blog post that appeared the day after the 2013 Oscars, argued that Day-Lewis offers an apt persona for these times: "His positioning as an enigmatic, mysterious star gives audiences a sense of pleasure. In an age where knowledge and information is so readily available, Day-Lewis offers the audience the unknown, he defies definition. He has a complex identity, such as the ambiguity surrounding his identity as Irish or English. He keeps his personal life secretive and rejects discussing both his films and acting methods."[14] A perusal of Internet videos, however, uncovers a rich literature of Day-Lewis on acting. Indeed, the actor often talks in detail about his characters and his methods, even, comically, after he has prefaced his remarks by saying that what he does cannot be described. For instance, asked by Charlie Rose to explain his character Daniel Plainview in *There Will Be Blood,* the actor hesitates: "I'm kind of the worst person to ask, because you're inviting me to objectify him in a way that I haven't even begun to try and do." Then he proceeds to provide an incisive, detailed character analysis that might be the envy of any critic.[15] This is typical of his television interviews. He starts out a bit inarticulately, but by midway through he is giving a master class on acting, which, especially when the camera cuts to a live audience, one senses may be over the heads of many of his listeners.

Seeing him on one of the Oscar roundtables that *Newsweek* held from 1998 to 2012 is instructive; alongside performers like George Clooney and James McAvoy, who play to the audience and feed off it, Day-Lewis appears recessive and ruminative but at the same time unfailingly polite and respectful.[16] In his charming acceptance speeches and as he makes the rounds of awards shows, one gets the sense of Day-Lewis as a gentle, even a nice man, as well as an unfailingly modest one who appears to have no idea why others consider him the greatest actor in the world. The "mystery" then comes in realizing that this same man has embodied the venomous Bill the Butcher and the volcanic Daniel Plainview. Where does the power of a scene like the "I drink your milkshake!" finale of *There Will Be Blood* come from? "It's funny. My mother said the same thing to me," Day-Lewis told Richard Schickel.[17] Herein may lie the mystery. It is hard to see continuity between the calm, civilized, charming person Day-Lewis is in public and his intensely charged characters, especially those he has played since 2002. In discussing preparation for these roles, he frequently uses the expression "to feed the work."[18]

TAKING PAINS

Day-Lewis's acting technique is the sort often described in reviews as "painstaking." Pain may also have stemmed from the lengths to which the actor has gone in allowing a character to "find" him, as he has put it. These techniques range from forcing his body to become contorted so as to play the poet and painter Christy Brown, who was born with cerebral palsy, in *My Left Foot*, to cracking two ribs and getting his nose broken while living the life of a middleweight who tries to bring peace and normalcy to war-torn Ulster in *The Boxer* (1997). Watching the more popular Johnny Depp in *Sweeney Todd* (2007), wrote David Thomson, "leaves you wishing you were seeing Daniel Day-Lewis as the demon barber. Can Day-Lewis sing? I don't know, but I believe he would have tried harder than Depp does. And when Day-Lewis tries, the ground shakes."[19] Thomson charges Depp with standing back from a role, not fully letting it inhabit him. This choice of words—the character inhabits the actor, lives in him—is probably the best way of characterizing Day-Lewis's particular application of the Stanislavsky system and the Method.

The mystique surrounding the actor's preparations, which sound extreme but "make complete sense" to him, and his insistence upon privacy obscure the essence of Day-Lewis as an actor of exceptional power and subtlety, one who has created a gallery of some of the most complex and confounding characters in film history.[20] Day-Lewis adopts the Stanislavsky system and the Method's theory and practice of acting, the original aims of which were greater realism. However, in the view of the media (though not in his own opinion or that of his collaborators), his working methods often overshadow what the methods actually achieve. "Theatricality," as opposed to the naturalistic acting styles that are supposed to typify post-studio cinema and contemporary stage acting, is a charge that has followed the twenty-first-century Day-Lewis like a spotlight. Aaron Taylor, fixing on the "infamous final fifteen minutes" of *There Will Be Blood,* claims that the actor's performance spins out beyond the realistic boundaries of the story and the character, a pioneering early-twentieth-century oilman, landing on a flat, two-dimensional "presentationalism."[21] An actor defined by extremes—both in terms of an acting school known for its goals of greater psychological and emotional realism and for performance mannerisms summarized as "playing to the balcony"[22]—might be working on a level that no one quite knows how to respond to, except to praise him and fill his house in Ireland with awards. These opposites—character realism and anti-realistic "theatricality"—are associated with Day-Lewis consistently. No one can embody such opposites. Can he?

Heights of realism in preparation were identified with Day-Lewis ever since he learned Czech in order to play a Prague doctor in *The Unbearable Lightness of Being* (1988), or since he confined himself to a wheelchair and refused to break character off-camera during the shooting of *My Left Foot.* However, Day-Lewis was not said to be given to flights of theatricality until fairly recently—in the third phase of his career, the period following his absence from filmmaking after *The Boxer,* a return that saw a difference in the types of roles the actor took on. Day-Lewis had made it plain that he is interested not in "a career" but in playing roles that interest him.

Daniel Day-Lewis is the son of Cecil Day-Lewis, who was Irish-born but eventually became a poet laureate of England. Daniel's mother, Jill Balcon, an actress, was his father's second wife. Daniel's grandfather was Michael Balcon, the preeminent British producer who worked with Alfred Hitchcock in the 1930s and headed up Ealing Studios in the 1940s and 1950s. Day-Lewis has often spoken of himself as "a middle-class Englishman," causing biographers and profilers to take him at his word. "Yet this is hard to believe," writes Jim Cullen, citing the nannies who raised him and his sister Tamasin, the boarding school to which he was sent only after his Socialist parents, who first enrolled him in public school, realized he wasn't being well educated, and the literary and show business personalities who streamed in and out of his home as he was growing up.[23]

Day-Lewis's point in claiming his class background is nearly always to express his disdain for the English class system. "The thing that I've been least interested in myself, I suppose, is the fact that I'm a middle-class Englishman," he said on a talk show on British television, pointedly, in 2006.[24] After *Lincoln* was released in the United Kingdom, amidst a quite instructive interview on the BBC about his year-long process of research and character discovery before filming began, the reporter, Sophie Raworth, asked him, "Does it irritate you, the way that [the process of staying in character] is often portrayed?" "Funny enough," Day-Lewis answered, with the tiniest hint of Bill Cutting or President Lincoln working up a climactic froth, "they don't really ask me about that in America. . . . It's in England [where] I tend to be asked that because it's almost as if you're not playing by the Queensbury rules or something. It's as if you're involved with something that takes itself a little too seriously and is a dark ritual of some kind, because there's more a tradition of that kind of work in America." Then he took pains to mention that he was trained in Stanislavsky and the Method in England, not the United States.[25]

His distaste for English traditions provided motivation in both his personal and professional choices, leading him to obtain an Irish visa and later Irish citizenship. After his early BBC movies, made between 1980 and 1985, followed by *My Beautiful Laundrette,* a middle finger to Thatcher's Britain, and *A Room with a View,* Day-Lewis never again appeared in anything that could be called "an English film." His early star period, following his Oscar for *My Left Foot,* is marked by the completion of his "Irish trilogy," with his friend, writer-director Jim Sheridan. At the same time, an attraction to things American, especially American film and the acting of such idols as Montgomery Clift, Marlon Brando, and Robert De Niro, moved him to assent to certain American film projects, historical films as they turned out. He began with *The Last of the Mohicans,* directed by Michael Mann, a seemingly out-of-character move itself, given Mann's identification with contemporary crime films and the 1980s TV series *Miami Vice.* While preparing the role of John Proctor with Arthur Miller on the film version of *The Crucible* (1996), Day-Lewis met the playwright's daughter (by Inge Morath), Rebecca Miller, whom he married in 1996. The actor and his wife live with their two sons, plus his older son, Gabriel (from a relationship with Isabelle Adjani), dividing the year between a home in New York and one in the remote Wicklow Mountains of Ireland.

McDonald finds there to be no genre associated with Day-Lewis except for what he terms "prestige," a label that refers to values attached to films by those who, it is assumed, will not take movies seriously unless they can be defined as important in a social, historical, or literary sense.[26] Others, however, have seen more specific meaning in the actor's body of work. Historian Jim Cullen made a startling discovery after he devised a high school history course strategically dotted with movies to illustrate certain historical periods and movements: "All of them starred Daniel Day-Lewis. . . . His characters are essentially frontiersmen, even if they happen to be a gang member or a lawyer on a New York street."[27] This Irish/English actor has amassed a gallery of American historical figures that few Americans have approached. A complex ideological and philosophical completeness rounds off his characters, American or not, embodying moral and historical journeys traveled by the films themselves, as narratives and as cinema. Daniel Plainview's quest for oil, for success, for riches, and for the accomplishment of his goals leaves him a specimen of human devolution, a troglodyte in a Tudor-style mansion. Christy Brown's story might lend itself to a hackneyed "triumph-of-the-human-spirit" melodrama, but in Day-Lewis's performance, Christy's cerebral palsy cannot keep him from expressing simple humanity as well as extraordinary gifts. It also allows him no excuse for Christy's often selfish, boorish behavior, even if pain, loss, and childhood resentments lie behind much of it.

Day-Lewis saves his power for the screen; he does not own a production company and has actually never initiated a film project, waiting for others to come to him with characters and story ideas. Once he is involved in a film, he is a full partner, shaping not just the theme and the story but also experiencing the character's pain. There must have been a wicked subtext beneath Day-Lewis's Oscar 2013 jokes about the "straight swap" that took place between himself and the role of Lincoln and Meryl Streep, the prior year's Best Actress, who presented the award for Best Actor. Streep had won for playing Margaret Thatcher in *The Iron Lady* (2011), a mindless film that ignored the prime minister's politics and tried to create sympathy for her dementia and her grief over the death of her husband, Denis. An American playing a controversial British politician, Streep cares only for the character distinct from her contexts, and she accepts the fraudulent contexts concocted by the filmmaker, Phylinda Lloyd. Streep delivers a pristine impersonation of Thatcher in a safe, disingenuous portrait. The comparison is stark: granting for a moment the ludicrous idea of Day-Lewis playing Thatcher, Day-Lewis would not have signed on until there was a script that said something complete and coherent about Thatcher and her conservative "revolution"; his rejection of *Lincoln* scripts prior to the one penned by Tony Kushner is a case in point.[28] Day-Lewis moved to Ireland during the Thatcher years, as the prime minister was taking a harder line toward the IRA fighters in Northern Ireland than most of her predecessors had done. He made *My Beautiful Laundrette,* written by Hanif Kureshi and directed by Stephen Frears, a subversive turn on the free market avarice brought on by Thatcher's policies.

NOT FAZED BY PHASES

Whether he acknowledges having a career or not, Day-Lewis's career, as of this writing, can be said to have played out in four distinct phases.

1.

His formative period as an actor began with his walk-on role at the age of fourteen as a London street urchin in John Schlesinger's *Sunday, Bloody Sunday* (1971). He then trained at the Bristol Old Vic Drama School (1975–1979), followed by a one-year contract with the Bristol Old Vic Repertory Company (1979–1980); alternating periods of early work and unemployment—a stint with the traveling Royal Shakespeare Company; parts in BBC television dramas; a triumph as a replacement in a West End drama, *Another Country* (1982); and his first featured film role, in *The Bounty* (1984), with Anthony Hopkins and Mel Gibson.

2.

His early film star period coincided with a renaissance of the British cinema in the mid-1980s. Day-Lewis won Best Supporting Actor in 1986 from the New York Film Critics Circle for two performances that scarcely appeared to have been given by the same twenty-eight-year-old actor. The simultaneous appearance of *My Beautiful Laundrette* and *A Room with a View*, which made their American debuts in New York on the same day, March 7, 1986, is probably one of the things Day-Lewis had in mind in his 2013 Oscar speech when he referred to having enjoyed "more than my fair share of good fortune." Had either film appeared without the other, it might have been enough to typecast the actor for some time. The priggish, unbearable Cecil Vyse in *Room* could have cemented him into upper-class roles (it took Helena Bonham Carter, who made her debut as Lucy Honeychurch, fourteen years to break out of her Merchant-Ivory corsets, which occurred when Brad Pitt gave David Fincher the idea to cast her as Marla, the love interest in *Fight Club* [1999]).[29] *Laundrette*, seen without its opposite, might have made it difficult for the actor to find work at all. A lower-class ruffian, Day-Lewis's Johnny becomes the lover, bouncer, and handyman for Omar, the Pakistani scion in Thatcher's Britain, who is put in charge of his businessman uncle's laundromat and turns it into a fashionable establishment. The character might have typed its portrayer in "gay roles" in the homophobic 1980s. It is easy to see in these roles two sides of a younger Day-Lewis: the rebellious punk and the poet's son who knows his way around a book-lined study. "One of the great privileges of having grown up in a middle-class literary English household," he said in 2007, "but having gone to school in the front lines in Southeast London, was that I became half-street-urchin and half-good-boy at home. I knew that dichotomy was possible."[30]

On the other hand, both roles cross and blur character types. In this respect they foretell the actor's coming career the most. While most writing on

Day-Lewis emphasizes his "mysterious" Methodologies, what Cecil and Johnny reveal is the actor's ability to find in his characters facets that might escape even their writers and directors. As Johnny, the actor strictly avoids any mannerisms that would remind us that the character is gay; like Johnny himself, Day-Lewis clearly wants us to give "fuck all" what anybody may think. Reportedly, what his colleagues on *Room* found amazing was that Day-Lewis made pitiable a character who is simply a repellent caricature in the E. M. Forster novel.[31] In this respect we see the actor's ability to show human beings even in monstrous specimens like Bill the Butcher and walking nightmares like Daniel Plainview.

The up-and-coming actor performed his first starring film role in the movie version of Milan Kundera's *The Unbearable Lightness of Being*. As Christy Brown in *My Left Foot*, he first earned his reputation as an actor who does not break character off-camera; for it, he won his first Oscar for Best Actor at age thirty-two. The period of his first great success coincides with the division of the American film industry into two—major studio, blockbuster-oriented Hollywood; and low-budget independence and semi-independence. *My Left Foot,* a hand-to-mouth independent production picked up for U.S. distribution by Harvey and Bob Weinstein's Miramax Films, won two of the company's first three Oscars (Brenda Fricker, who played Christy's mother, won Best Supporting Actress)[32] and also was Miramax's first film nominated for Best Picture. For a company whose reputation for procuring nominations and Oscars would become legendary, this was significant.[33]

3.

The films of Day-Lewis's first period as a star with the freedom to pick and choose roles (1990–1997) were not for independent companies but for Twentieth Century–Fox (*The Last of the Mohicans*; *The Crucible*), Universal (*In the Name of the Father* [1993]; *The Boxer*), and Columbia (*The Age of Innocence* [1993]). These films were made in the last period when human-interest dramas were still regularly produced by the major Hollywood studios, rather than their indie subsidiaries. Day-Lewis forged on as a committed, risk-taking actor who made every role his own; he turned Nathaniel/Hawkeye in *Last of the Mohicans* from a role that presumably any action star could have played to a character only he could have created (which Michael Mann, who considered no one else for the part, understood from the beginning).

Day-Lewis's American films of the 1990s have about them the inevitable touch of the conventional stalwart male lead, as if the nobility the actor resented lending to the Royal Shakespeare Company were now being imported by

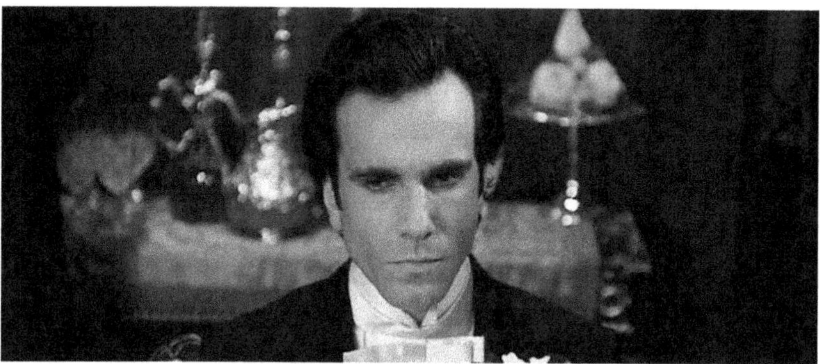

"The right nose for classical theater"—or for playing trapped upper-class Americans in deceptively gilded costume dramas. Daniel Day-Lewis as Newland Archer in *The Age of Innocence* (1993).

Hollywood. Had Day-Lewis not exiled himself for those five years at the turn of the millennium, he might have perpetually gotten mired in hollow prestige projects like *The Crucible,* proving Paul McDonald's point. Day-Lewis said that he would not have accepted his role as Newland Archer in *The Age of Innocence*—"too English"—had Scorsese not been the director.[34] Day-Lewis's Newland is necessarily self-conscious about the role he must play in Edith Wharton's gilded prisons, which Scorsese recreated for film. Everything about Newland's behavior appears studied; his gallant bows to the many women in his life look as if he had been carefully trained since childhood in the chivalrous arts, and repeating them returns him to the twelve-year-old within him, performing by rote.

The two Universal releases were made in Ireland by Jim Sheridan (*My Left Foot*); low-budget and modest in scale, these look as though they could be independent films. Day-Lewis's style from *My Beautiful Laundrette* through *The Boxer* is essentially realistic. Indeed, he starts often with characters who are caricatures—like Johnny the punk in *My Beautiful Laundrette* and Cecil the prig in *A Room with a View*—and makes us accept their reality. In the Jim Sheridan trilogy, the characters he plays struggle to live like ordinary men, even or especially when that means the freedom to be a horse's ass. Day-Lewis, like any great film actor, meshes with the director's vision.

What the characters he creates in his Sheridan trilogy have in common is a spare, sharp simplicity. As many shadings as Day-Lewis gives to those characters, they stay between the lines of ordinary behavior, even Christy Brown, whose disability forces him to struggle to live as an ordinary person (or man—*My Left Foot* is ultimately concerned with Christy's manhood as his defining trait), much less the extraordinary artistic soul who dwells inside a tortured body. Like Christy, *The Boxer*'s Danny Flynn, who comes out of prison having served a fourteen-year sentence for IRA-related terrorist activities, struggles to live an ordinary life according to his gifts. Danny is a man for his time; his resolve to maintain a boxing gym in Ulster just as the historic peace accord with Tony Blair's Britain is reached puts him on the right side of history, but the wrong side of a desperate conflict with hardliners in the IRA who refuse to let go of The Cause.

Christy and Danny are heroes, while *In the Name of the Father*'s Gerry Conlon is an anti-hero, a young fool who gets himself, his whole family, and practically everyone else he knows arrested and put away for life. Conlon is at the mercy of 1970s British authorities, who are desperate to destroy the IRA and make examples of anyone they suspect of being terrorist bombers. Conlon, whose father actually died in prison years before the entire family was cleared of their alleged crimes, is practically stomped into the ground. In preparation for his role, Day-Lewis famously lived in a prison cell and arranged to have himself subjected to an hours-long interrogation by actual police officers. Even though *In the Name of the Father* is a Hollywood-style melodrama about an innocent person persecuted by the legal and prison systems, it doesn't seem like one. This is because Day-Lewis pushes elements of the script that demonstrate Conlon first digging his own grave and, once in it, shoveling out more and more dirt. The result is one of Day-Lewis's most problematic films dramatically. Day-Lewis and Sheridan make Conlon increasingly irredeemable at the same time that Conlon's attorney, played by Emma Thompson, works earnestly to free her clients. The antagonists, like the unyielding IRA terrorist played by Gerald McSorley in *The Boxer,* are eminently hissable villains.

Day-Lewis was off the screen for five years following *The Boxer.* Reports, which Day-Lewis refuses to confirm, have it that the actor apprenticed with a master cobbler in Florence, adding shoemaking to the expertise in carpentry that he picked up as a teenager.

4.

When he returned, it was in his second film for Martin Scorsese, *Gangs of New York*, a dream project of Scorsese's for three decades, realized for him by producer Harvey Weinstein, who knew Day-Lewis since *My Left Foot.* It is telling that Day-Lewis, after breaking his nose amid his strenuous training for *The Boxer*, never got the nose fixed. A persistent Internet rumor has it that Leonardo DiCaprio busted Day-Lewis's nose in rehearsing a fight for *Gangs,* making for juicy celebrity gossip, though it isn't true. The once noble nose points sharply to the left throughout *The Boxer*, a fact Sheridan and cinematographer Chris Menges emphasize by lighting the nose from the left so as to show it in all its slanting glory. On the poster for *The Boxer*, however, Universal shadowed Day-Lewis's face half in darkness, as if nervous about what audiences would think about the star with his newly imperfect face. "His broken nose," writes Christopher Goodwin, "adds to, rather than detracts from, his beauty," a factor the journalist calls "inexplicable."[35]

On the face of it, literally, Day-Lewis might have been almost happy to break that Romanesque nose, which he has sardonically called "the right nose for classical theatre," a proscenium-pleasing proboscis that moved his producers at the Royal Shakespeare Company to be "always trying to throw a cloak over me."[36] One senses that the broken nose is an inadvertent victory of the disorderly punk over the middle-class literary lad. The busted nose, moreover, is *reality*; it's life, an example of the kind of happenstance that cannot be planned for. In an era when the public scrutinizes the faces of public figures for telltale signs of facelifts, nose jobs, and Botox injections, Day-Lewis goes forth bearing evidence of life's hard knocks. When this actor speaks of "the work," he isn't describing the services of a plastic surgeon.

After returning from his five-year absence with an altered instrument, he played to theatrical traditions whereby evil crosses from stage right to stage left. A left-leaning nose hardly gets in the way of creating a sinister character. As with *Last of the Mohicans* a decade earlier—for which Day-Lewis learned to shoot with a longbow and slept with his rifle throughout filming—Day-Lewis now prepared for *Gangs of New York* by making butchers' knives his trusty tools, learning how to carve up a side of beef and throw knives on target. The scene in which Bill uses Jenny (Cameron Diaz) as his "lovely assistant" for a sadistic show of knife-throwing prowess in front of a raucous crowd seems gratuitous and riveting at the same time. It features an improvisation, "Whoopsy Daisy," typifying Bill's use of archaic, innocuous phrases that one's great-great-grandmother might have spoken to a child. Day-Lewis strengthened his acuity by sharpening knives between takes, while on his headphones the angry stylings of Eminem circa 2000, a white rapper from the racial war zone of Detroit, strafed his ears like high-velocity knives hurtling toward their target.

Richard Schickel, doubtless speaking for many, remarked to Scorsese, "I find it fascinating that you would even think of the same actor [who played the courtly uptown Newland Archer] for Bill the Butcher."[37] The actor is able to "feed himself" into fearsome roles without noble good looks to distract the audience or the false noses employed at times by the likes of both the Methodical Dustin Hoffman

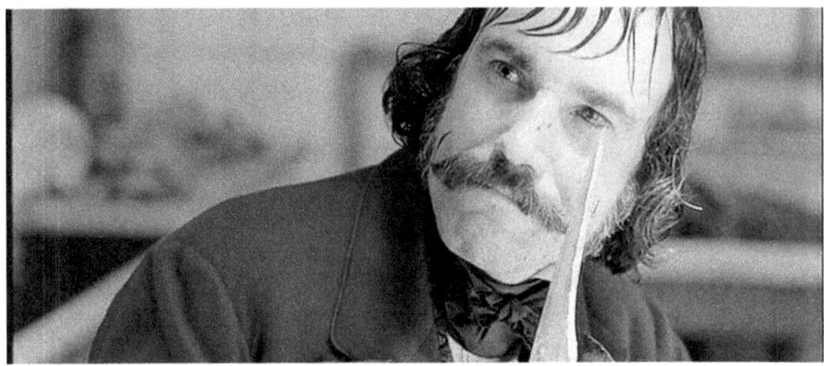

Day-Lewis as Bill the Butcher in *Gangs of New York* (2002), splattered with blood, tapping his glass with his carving knife. Did Day-Lewis's left-leaning nose give him a new life playing melodramatic villains, sans the melodrama?

and the traditionalist Laurence Olivier. The films in between *Gangs, There Will Be Blood,* and *Lincoln* are not easily generalized, for they include a quirky independent drama, *The Ballad of Jack and Rose* (2005), written and directed by Rebecca Miller, and *Nine* (2009), the film version of a 1982 Broadway musical based on Fellini's *8½*, directed by Rob Marshall (*Chicago*) for the Weinstein Company. Day-Lewis might have taken the singing role in *Nine* as an answer to the dare David Thomson's 2008 *Guardian* piece inadvertently laid down. Day-Lewis appears to take a role only if it presents an insuperable challenge, if "I knew it couldn't be done," as he said about *My Left Foot*,[38] or if it seems "preposterous," as he said about the idea of himself as Lincoln.[39] He can certainly sing, and better than Johnny Depp's half-throated efforts in *Sweeney Todd.* The ground did not shake, however, mostly because Marshall's frenetic staging of Day-Lewis's numbers doesn't allow the camera or the mise-en-scène to stay still for more than an instant. It is the camera and some of the production design that shake, never the "ground." These artistic and commercial failures, in which Day-Lewis gives realistic, perfectly well-proportioned performances, are easily forgotten in contrast to his showy and acclaimed work in the large-scale works *Gangs of New York, There Will Be Blood,* and *Lincoln,* all set in epochal periods of American history. They amply demonstrate the impact of Day-Lewis on the cinema of the early twenty-first century.

VOICES OF THE PIONEERS: THE GANGSTER, THE PROSPECTOR, AND THE PRESIDENT

Martin Scorsese has said of Day-Lewis's process that "the character has to find him, has to make himself be known to him."

> So after two or three weeks, you find that whatever moves he's making, suggestions for improv, [and so on] are coming from the character who is . . . permeating his being in a way. So when he's talking to me, it's no longer as Daniel. . . . I was talking to Bill more often than to Daniel . . . and it's not some magical process. It just happens to be the way he goes through it. I think it pulled together when he started trying on the clothes, and working out his moustache, and also the hairstyles.[40]

Bill the Butcher is probably the most fanciful, outlandish character in Scorsese's oeuvre. Scorsese, the cineaste-auteur, creates inside a dialectic of influences, with realists such as Cassavetes and Kazan on one side and formalist fabulists like Minnelli, Visconti, Leone, and Michael Powell on the other. Scorsese is a match for Day-Lewis's own dialectic, swinging from twentieth-century realism and—beginning with *Gangs*—to nineteenth-century melodramatic theatricality. Only the high-wire Paul Thomas Anderson has made as explosive a collaborator.

Gangs of New York contains striking similarities in performance, scene structure, positions of the all-powerful but doomed characters, and the way Scorsese composes them in his mise-en-scène, between Day-Lewis's Bill and Jack Nicholson's Frank Costello in *The Departed* (2006), which came out four years later. In *Gangs of New York* Day-Lewis enters a character-actor-as-star period—less Montgomery Clift of the *A Place in the Sun–From Here to Eternity* period, and more akin to Charles Laughton's Javert in *Les Miserables* (1935, directed by Richard Boleshevsky, a disciple of Stanislavsky) and Captain Bligh in *Mutiny on the Bounty* (1935), to name the acting idols Day-Lewis most often cites (along with Robert De Niro, whom he must have felt looking over his shoulder as he played a proto-gangster for Scorsese).

Not only had Day-Lewis broken his nose, but he had entered middle age; he was forty-three when *Gangs* began production in the summer of 2000 and forty-five at its release in December 2002. The broken nose made it easier yet to throw off the romantic lead mantle—or is it a cloak?—that age would relieve him of eventually anyway. Day-Lewis may be a flamboyant actor, but it is certainly flamboyance of a more inward and realistic kind than Nicholson's. While Day-Lewis is a more premeditated type of actor than Nicholson, both know how to build intensity with a role and in a scene by making the unexpected choice. In *Gangs*, in short, Day-Lewis gives the kind of performance Nicholson might give, although Nicholson doesn't have Day-Lewis's gift for voices and for total immersion in a character.

In *Gangs,* also, Day-Lewis performs the sorts of improvisations Nicholson and De Niro are known for. The improvised monologue of Bill the Butcher, in a short-lensed medium close-up facing the camera and waving his hands in the foreground, crying crocodile tears and pretending to mourn "the murder of this poor little rabbit," strikes me as a Nicholson moment, similar to Jack's monologues to the imaginary Lloyd the bartender in *The Shining* (1980). Scorsese sets up the camera the same way, for example, in the "I smell a rat" scene in *The Departed* in which Costello suddenly pulls a gun on Billy Costigan (DiCaprio), a moment that Nicholson improvised on the set.[41]

In a related way, the three towering performances of Day-Lewis between 2002 and 2012 are distinguished first by voices that situate the character unshakably in a particular historical place and time. Bill "The Butcher" Cutting was based on an actual personage named Bill "the Butcher" Poole (1821–1855), a criminal big fish in the small pond of the Five Points neighborhood of Lower Manhattan, and a member of the Know-Nothing movement, a nativist, anti-Catholic party that opposed the massive influx of immigrants. Because Scorsese's Bill lives until 1863, he is folded in with the Civil War opposition, which peaked after the Battle of Gettysburg, in which terrible casualties caused Lincoln to initiate the second draft of the war. This action led to the Draft Riots of July 1863, which play out in the film at the same time that Bill's nativist gangs and the Irish gangs of Amsterdam Vallon (DiCaprio) meet for their final battle. Bill speaks in a voice that is peculiarly appropriate. "Surrounded by Irish brogues and deracinated British accents," writes A. O. Scott, "Mr. Day-Lewis has the wit to speak an early version of Noo Yawkese, making the Butcher the butt of a marvelous historical joke: this bigoted, all-but-forgotten nativist, it turns out, bequeathed his speech patterns to the children of the immigrants he despised."[42]

Scott pinpoints something highly significant about Day-Lewis as Bill; he captures the parochialism of many native New Yorkers. Bill insists that America is only for those who were born here, and yet he scarcely knows anything outside his Five Points neighborhood, which he oversees like a Roman emperor. The other point that Scott makes is that in *Gangs,* as in *Lincoln,* no one else in the film talks the way Day-Lewis's character does. Scorsese actually covers this by having the major characters on Bill's side be fallen away Irishmen who have, from Amsterdam's point of view, sold out. Thus, exempting the WASP powers-that-be uptown, played by English actors such as David Hemmings and Patrick McGoohan, Bill's merchant-class WASP appears to be a constituency of one.

Day-Lewis's vivid performances as American historical figures lead Cullen to wonder if it could "make sense to think of actors as historians."[43] Day-Lewis's work from 2002 and after might make one ask if actors can be linguists, especially pre-Saussure historical linguistics. The voices that have "found" Day-Lewis are specific to regions of the United States. In *Gangs,* Day-Lewis, lured back to acting by the chance to play a gangster in a Scorsese film, speaks like Charlie (Harvey Keitel) and Johnny Boy (Robert De Niro) in *Mean Streets* (1973), or Jimmy Conway (De Niro) in *Goodfellas* (1990)—that is, if those characters lived 110 to 125 years earlier. Day-Lewis's historical voices are not twenty-first-century vocalizations of nineteenth-century speech, as, for instance, Charles Portis's comic conceit in his novel *True Grit* (1968) and both its film versions (1969, 2010), that having characters speak without contractions will make them sound more nineteenth century. Day-Lewis matches, with period pronunciations and mannerisms, the archaic language the screenwriters have supplied. Bill the Butcher, a gangster, is a dandy; his costuming is Dickensian. He could be the Artful Dodger at age forty-seven. Bill's gestures are theatrical, oratorical, and at times almost prissy; in a scene in which he threatens Boss Tweed, Bill makes a "tsk-tsk" motion while holding his fingers up to Tweed's face, the sort of motion that a chiding grandmother would make.

The most astonishing voice that "finds" Day-Lewis (as hard as it seems to beat Bill the Butcher and Abe Lincoln) is that of Daniel Plainview in *There Will Be Blood.* Anderson said that the cast and crew repeatedly watched John Huston's *The Treasure of the Sierra Madre* (1948) for its story about prospecting fever.[44] Day-Lewis's way of catching the fever was to pick up Huston's unforgettable voice itself, a voice that literally carries, from the measured voiceover he performed for his U.S. Army documentary, *The Battle of San Pietro* (1944), to his own performance in the New Hollywood revisionist noir masterpiece *Chinatown* (1974), in which he plays the rapacious tycoon Noah Cross with the future of Los Angeles in his fist. Plainview is a primitive whose years coaxing oil up out of the ground have left him unfit for human relationships—Richard Schickel calls him "perhaps the most misanthropic character in film history."[45] Oil becomes a valuable commodity, produced in California, at the same time as the rise of the movie industry. Thus Daniel Plainview has somehow developed a Hollywood voice, clear, resonant, declamatory, and accentless.

Almost like Christy Brown, to whom speech does not come naturally, Plainview must cultivate a voice. Anderson and Day-Lewis create this impression with the film's first twenty minutes, which are totally without dialogue. When we finally hear Plainview speak, it is to a public gathering, and it seems as if the measured, sing-song cadence of his speech does not belong to him. This is because it actually doesn't. To the ears of a 2007 audience, in indie art theaters, in a film dedicated to the late Robert Altman (another prolific maverick), it is a voice that resonates through Hollywood history. Plainview abuses it, and when he loses his carefully crafted but fraudulent control, the meticulous rhythms of the voice fall away. When he is brought to the church of his nemesis/doppelgänger Eli Sunday (Paul Dano) and made to confess his sins, the voice is driven out of him, and what is left is an inarticulate howl, which, freed from the voice's calculation, expresses truth. Daniel cannot let that stand, cannot allow truth about himself to be at large in the world.

In the film's double climax, Plainview first renounces his adopted son, and then finally and gratuitously conquers his nemesis, Eli, bellowing words, "I drink your milk shake," that come from congressional testimony in 1924 about the Teapot Dome scandal during the administration of Warren G. Harding.[46] I disagree that with Aaron Taylor that "the actor abruptly abandons the absorptive restraint of a classical realist performance for the disruptive ostentation of theatricality."[47] Like Bill the Butcher, Daniel progressively isolates himself personally. Day-Lewis creates a chronicle of meltdown and of devolution. In mid-film, when Daniel talks to the man he thinks is a long-lost brother, but who turns out to be an imposter, he launches into a *Richard III*–like soliloquy on his own hate-filled soul, a theatrical moment where the protagonist unveils his character and intentions. Increasingly, any action off the oilfield is a public display; Daniel has no capacity for a private life. With his Hollywood voice and delivery and his audiences of either townspeople on whose land he hopes to drill for oil or Eli's crazed faith-healer congregation in a church that doesn't even appear to be scripture-based, Daniel's declamation signifies his increasing insanity.

Day-Lewis's performance of Daniel's character arc is not classical; it is continuous as is Daniel's upward mobility/downward trajectory. Anderson cuts suddenly from Plainview's oilfield habitat to his Tudor-style mansion where he lives, apparently alone, unfurnished and impersonal except for a bowling alley, the absurd epitome of conspicuous consumption. Plainview is a twentieth-century frontiersman, pulling up out of the ground fuel for the new mechanized era. But Plainview is in no way modern. In a film that has been likened to numerous genres, including horror, Anderson and Day-Lewis end the film like a deranged kind of western.[48] Like the hero who makes the frontier safe for civilization but is too savage to join it, Plainview completes his corruption and suggests that of the society his oil enables. The last line of the film, "I'm finished," is declared in a normal tone to a house servant, whose job it presumably is to clean up the mess. Once the annihilation of religion by capitalism is completed Plainview has no "unfinished" business; like Charles Foster Kane, he has finished off any meaning in life except consumption.

The lively rondo of the third movement of Brahms's Violin Concerto, which Anderson kicks to twice in the film—just after Plainview's last line and much

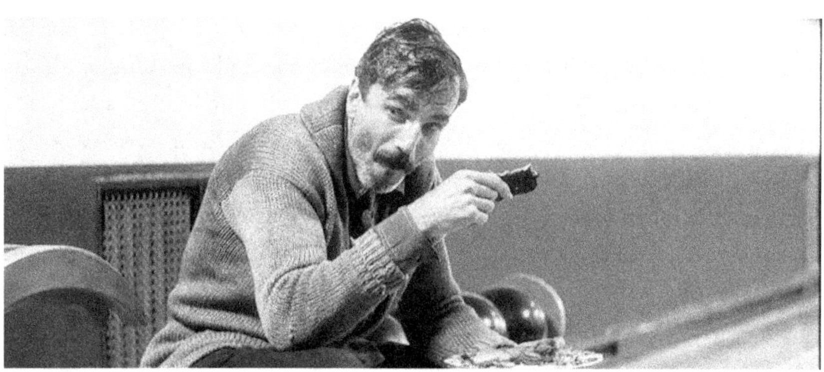

The famous final scene of *There Will Be Blood* (2007). The leathery, weather-beaten Daniel Plainview lives like a wolf in the wild in his mansion. Eating a steak with his fingers, drinking gin out of the bottle, sleeping on the hardwood floor as the only way to relax his back, which he had injured in a fall down a mineshaft thirty years earlier, Daniel is in no way fit for civilization. Except that he owns it. This is Day-Lewis's most expressionistic and least naturalistic performance.

earlier, at the opening of the oil derrick, which also inaugurates Plainview's unspoken feud with Eli—suggests the complexity of Daniel's hollow victories, with their ominous implications for American society in the future. The musicologist Kelly Dean Hansen calls the rondo "gypsy-inspired," which may explain the film's use of it.[49] Plainview, for all his success and wealth, remains a gypsy, treating his mansion (the actual Doheny mansion) like another encampment, and all relationships as competition. Nothing is his own, in Day-Lewis's rendering, not even his voice.

Abraham Lincoln's voice is also an act of historical linguistics. For this actor, a high-pitched voice issuing from Lincoln is not only historically accurate according to nearly all the many accounts that exist of what the sixteenth president's voice sounded like; it is also unexpected and intriguing, and thus good drama. Lincoln contains multitudes, and Day-Lewis's Lincoln, like earlier cinematic Lincolns, gives us the Great Emancipator the way Americans of a particular period care to remember him. In the age of Obama, he is the best result of the American experiment—plus, he is a politician as well as a statesman, a reminder that in a democracy a leader not only has to be both, but that there is no shame in being both.

He speaks as a rube who knows by heart bulky passages from Shakespeare, the Bible, Greek scholars, and American law. In short, he speaks like Abraham Lincoln. This Lincoln is capable of mortifying a group of congressman and cabinet secretaries who try to tell him on the eve of the vote on the Thirteenth

Amendment that the final two votes for passage cannot be had. Telling his listeners that they "grousle and heckle and dodge about like pettifogging Tammany Hall hucksters," he rises and seems to gather up unto himself a rhetorical cyclone: "I am the president of the United States, clothed in *immense power.*" His voice having risen in a crescendo, he then lowers it to a dramatic hush, declaiming confidentially, "You will procure me these votes." Seconds before that, however, tired of listening to the excuses of short-sighted politicians, and already having shown himself willing to engage in nitty-gritty political horse trading to "procure" the votes, "procure" not being a word associated with high-minded statesmanship, he says of the two votes, "You've got a night and a day and a night, several perfectly good hours," his speech speeding up, his delivery sounding like that of a leader of any organization or committee, trying to get his troops to deliver. Suddenly his voice raises impatiently, his arm flourishes out: "Now git the hell outa here and git 'em." In one speech, Lincoln goes from a Roman emperor gathering his toga about himself (Laughton again, this time in *Spartacus* [1960]) to the backwoods with Kentucky, southern Indiana, and Illinois in his voice.

Day-Lewis's Bill the Butcher and President Lincoln are characters who do everything with an awareness of audience and a sense of theater. What makes these characters most authentic—and realistic—is the way their characteristics fail to match, thereby disrupting audience expectations. A six-foot-four-inch frame with a matching stentorian voice is found in the movies, but probably not in actuality. Day-Lewis understands, as Stanislavsky did, that life is full of incongruities, and that art is richer if it portrays them. Paul McDonald writes that the star's task is partly "to provide a prism through which the film could be viewed."[50] It is intriguing, then, that Day-Lewis uses the same word to describe the actor's relation to the character he/she plays. "It's *utterly delusional,*" he says, "to say you become some other person. You don't. But you do get to know yourself in a different way, through the prism of that other life."[51] The remarkable thing about Day-Lewis's Lincoln is that it almost instantly supplanted not only most other actors who played Lincoln (reducing the lead performance in John Ford's immortal 1939 *Young Mr. Lincoln* to Henry Fonda's trademark voice and lanky frame, plus a prosthetic nose), but most visual images of the sixteenth president of any kind that have appeared over the past 175 years. "You will never think of Lincoln from now on without seeing Daniel Day-Lewis," said Lesley Stahl on *60 Minutes,* which is not so remarkable considering that Lincoln was a pre-modern figure who lived before the invention of sound reproduction media or the motion picture.[52]

As "Abraham Lincoln" himself remarked:

> After some days of wandering around in his skin,
> I found myself imitating his spikey voice, his iconic
>
> glazed look. His crooked nose fit my face when he
> scratched his scraggy chin. When he got down on
>
> his hands & knees, crawled to stir the logs in the drafty
> White House fireplace, I felt the creak in his battered bones
>
> from years ago when he'd trained his body to deal
> with a typing left foot. O, I cannot say just how many
>
> times I felt Godawful, day after day, night after night
> of the movie making because the sumbitch kept
>
> pushing and pushing himself to get my stoop,
> my lumbering gait just so . . . [53]

So says "Abraham Lincoln on Daniel Day-Lewis." In poet Earl J. Wilcox's conceit, the actor "becomes" the historical character so much that Lincoln starts to think of himself as Daniel Day-Lewis, or as himself in Daniel Day-Lewis, or Daniel Day-Lewis in him, certainly a new spin on the "body too much." The poet imagines Lincoln standing outside Day-Lewis, looking in and finding himself—beholding a Lincoln that is more Lincoln than Lincoln. The poem also gives new meaning to Day-Lewis's frequent insistence that the character finds him.

His Lincoln is serene, a peculiar man in every physical sense. One can see in him, the original trickster, the slow-talking backwoodsman who shows up the unsuspecting sharpies, the slick, silver-tongued orators and educated statesman. This Lincoln is crafty, often keeping his designs even from his secretary of state, William Seward (David Strathairn). Seward becomes enraged at hearing of Lincoln's back-channel overtures to the Confederates, in a scene that Strathairn plays fast, loud, and out of breath. Day-Lewis's Lincoln is calm and still, in contrast. Moreover, Lincoln calls Seward "Willum," one of numerous little results of the year of study for which Day-Lewis asked Spielberg after he accepted the role. "Get me thirteen votes. Them fellers from Richmond ain't here yit." It is not clear what accent—far more backwoodsy than his own—Lincoln is mimicking, but whatever the source of this private joke, we believe it is Lincoln's secret, not the actor's (even if both pronunciations are in the published script).[54]

The crucial early scene in which Lincoln lays out for his cabinet his rationale for passing the Thirteenth Amendment, outlawing slavery before the impending war and the restoration of the Southern secessionists to statehood, cuts at one point to a close-up of his hands, whittling a piece of wood with a knife. But we soon forget this rough-hewn folksy woodshaving as the scene turns to a conversational but fiery speech to the president's war cabinet. Is the serene, smiling, almost passive presence cloaking the iron-willed leader? Is this tightly coiled president the embodiment of a leader in a democracy, who must take action and then wait for others, who must persuade but not dictate? This Lincoln *is* the archetypal hero of the Great Man biopic, the singular man who sees the right—John Ford's young Mr. Lincoln, who stretches out his long limbs under a tree, closes shut a law book, and declares, "By jing, that's all there is to it: Right and wrong." And yet he is so often awkward, garrulous with his jokes and stories, bottled up and weary, that we must realize that this is the sainted Abraham Lincoln as he very well might have been in life.

CONCLUSION

Daniel Day-Lewis now has done what no other male actor has done, but there remains Katharine Hepburn's record to scale—four Oscars in lead performances. Hepburn makes a good comparison. Seldom truly popular, winning the bulk of her Oscars and acclaim in the last fifteen years of her career, Hepburn, like Streep, beat the game for actresses just by surviving. Like Day-Lewis as of this writing, Hepburn made the Quigley Poll only once. She ranked number nine in 1969, following her back-to-back Oscars for *Guess Who's Coming to Dinner* (1967) and *Lion in Winter* (1968). Day-Lewis may be the inverse of Hepburn, playing "monsters sacred or profane"[55] in middle age, whereas the beloved actress's roles, with the exception of Eleanor of Aquitaine in *Lion,* became domestic, if not domesticated—and even Eleanor is a wife, sort of. It would not be surprising if, someday, Day-Lewis matched Hepburn's achievement. Unless he retires from acting instead. Could a man with Day-Lewis's passion and commitment, so often projected onto the screen, walk away from performing? Does a man who just as self-evidently has little need of acting and can just as easily withdraw into the hills of Eire to indulge his love of carpentry and shoemaking have the fire to return again to the crucible? Day-Lewis appeared serene at the Academy Awards ceremony of March 2, 2014, as the previous year's Best Actor, gallantly presenting the Best Actress Oscar to Cate Blanchett, giving no sign of future plans.

Disruptions are part of the continuity of the film industry. Day-Lewis has had the luxury of acting when the work beckons him, of orchestrating his own disruptions. What he could not control or predict—what no one could—is the warm audience response to his Abe Lincoln, a performance that appears to embody for Americans what is best in their own past, even as it reminds viewers of the most painful disruption in the nation's history. Here is an anomaly: an Englishman-turned-Irishman-turned portrayer of American icons. Few of them, with the notable exception of Lincoln, are actual historical figures. Most of them are fictional characters—John Proctor, Bill the Butcher, Daniel Plainview, hewn from personages who lived, but all distinguished by their anguish, their menace to an established order. The artistry of Daniel Day-Lewis—with *Lincoln*, one that a broader American public has finally come to appreciate—rests in his ability to internalize and then portray the eternal struggle of disruption.

NOTES

1. Day-Lewis was voted Best Actor for *My Left Foot* (1989), *There Will Be Blood* (2007), and *Lincoln* (2012). The redoubtable Katharine Hepburn won four for Best Actress (1932–33, 1967, 1968, 1981). Three performers won two for lead roles and one for a supporting part. They were Ingrid Bergman (Best Actress of 1944 and 1956, and Best Supporting Actress of 1974); Jack Nicholson (for Best Actor of 1975, Best Supporting Actor of 1983, and Best Actor of 1997); and Meryl Streep (Best Supporting Actress of 1979, and Best Actress of 1982 and 2011). Walter Brennan won Best Supporting Actor three of the first five years it was given (1936, 1938, 1940).
2. "Movies 101 with Richard Brown," AMC-TV, June 16, 2005, www.youtube.com/watch?v=RKfGU3vKjvc&list=UUjQlZNrqfumK3lIR-9ZRpzg&index=11, accessed March 11, 2013.
3. Daniel Day-Lewis has not acted onstage since a fateful evening near the end of a National Theatre run as Hamlet in October 1989. He fled the stage during the scene in which Hamlet confronts his father's ghost and left the production, which included Judi Dench as Gertrude. As this happened a month before the U.S. release of *My Left Foot*, for which he won his first Oscar the following March, it was easy for him to commit himself to a life as a film actor thereafter.
4. Adam Mars-Jones of the *Independent*, quoted in Garry Jenkins, *Daniel Day-Lewis: The Fire Within* (London: Pan Books, 1995), 330.
5. To show how extraordinary Day-Lewis's Oscar record is, Susan Hayward, Jack Nicholson, Susan Sarandon, Kate Winslet, and Julianne Moore all won for the first time on their fifth nominations. Nicholson's three Oscars and Hepburn's four emerged out of twelve nominations, and three-time winner Streep has been nominated nineteen times as of 2014. Day-Lewis's other Best Actor nominations were for *In the Name of the Father* (1993) and *Gangs of New York* (2002).
6. Mark Lankester, "The Craziest Ways Daniel Day-Lewis Prepared for Roles," Yahoo UK Movies Features, January 28, 2013, uk.movies.yahoo.com/

the-craziest-ways-daniel-day-lewis-prepared-for-roles-171013867.html, accessed April 11, 2013.

7. Paul McDonald, *Hollywood Stardom* (Malden, Mass.: Wiley-Blackwell, 2013), 224.
8. Qtd. in Thomas Fisher, "Acting Disaster," *Celebrity Studies* 3, no. 3 (November 2012): 344.
9. J. Hoberman, lecture delivered at New York University, November 1983.
10. www.quigleypublishing.com/MPalmanac/Top10/Top10_lists.html.
11. McDonald, *Hollywood Stardom*, 224.
12. Jenkins, *Daniel Day-Lewis*, 199–200.
13. www.boxofficemojo.com, accessed March 11, 2013.
14. Jack Avery, "The Construction of Daniel Day-Lewis's Star Persona," in *Strange Enlightenments*, February 25, 2013, strangeenlightenments.wordpress.com/2013/02/25/the-construction-of-daniel-day-lewis-star-persona.
15. "A Discussion of the Film *There Will Be Blood* with Paul Thomas Anderson and Daniel Day-Lewis," *Charlie Rose*, December 21, 2007, www.youtube.com/watch?v=6tTw24Jt4AY, accessed March 11, 2013.
16. See "*Newsweek*'s 2008 Oscar Roundtable," January 18, 2008, www.youtube.com/watch?v=Hbm9KgdLk9s&list=PLA1F8BE3AADAFA035, accessed April 19, 2013.
17. Richard Schickel, *Conversations with Scorsese* (New York: Alfred A. Knopf, 2011), 231.
18. *The Andrew Marr Show*, BBC, January 28, 2013, www.bbc.co.uk/news/entertainment-arts-21227022, accessed January 31, 2013.
19. David Thomson, "Biographical Dictionary of Film, No. 29: Johnny Depp," *Guardian*, January 10, 2008, www.guardian.co.uk/film/filmblog/2008/jan/11/biographicaldictionaryoffil9, accessed December 30, 2012.
20. *Andrew Marr Show*.
21. Aaron Taylor, "Playing to the Balcony: Screen Acting, Distance, and Cavellian Theatricality," in *Stages of Reality: Theatricality in Cinema*, ed. André Loiselle and Jeremy Maron (Toronto: University of Toronto Press, 2012), 185.
22. Ibid., 185.
23. Jim Cullen, *Sensing the Past: Hollywood Stars and Historical Visions* (New York: Oxford University Press, 2013), 58.
24. "Daniel Day-Lewis on Parkinson," www.youtube.com/watch?v=oLRdyqSoiSo, accessed March 15, 2013, taken from *Parkinson*, season 28, episode 4, BBC, March 25, 2006.
25. *Andrew Marr Show*.
26. McDonald, *Hollywood Stardom*, 225.
27. Cullen, *Sensing the Past*, 3, 60.
28. Spielberg made the rejections public at the 2013 New York Film Critics Circle Awards dinner by reading the 2003 letter Day-Lewis wrote to the director, turning down the role based upon an early version of the script, which told Lincoln's story in a much more sprawling frame. The actor rejected a second script two years later; finally, Tony Kushner, the Pulitzer Prize–winning playwright who had collaborated with Spielberg on *Munich*, wrote a new 500-page first draft, severely paring it down after the writer and director settled on a narrative focused on the passage of the Thirteenth Amendment. Only then did Day-Lewis say yes. An actor who cared only

for the character and not for the overall film might have agreed much sooner. Jordan Zakarin, "Spielberg Reveals Daniel Day-Lewis' Original Lincoln Rejection Letter," *Hollywood Reporter,* January 8, 2013, www.hollywoodreporter.com/news/steven-spielberg-reveals-daniel-day-409709, accessed April 3, 2013.

29. Sharon Waxman, *Rebels on the Backlot: Six Maverick Directors and How They Conquered the Hollywood Studio System* (New York: HarperCollins, 2005), 181–82.

30. Lynn Hirschberg, "The New Frontier's Man," *New York Times Magazine,* November 11, 2007, www.nytimes.com/2007/11/11/magazine/11daylewis-t2.html?pagewanted=all&_r=0, accessed April 3, 2013.

31. Jenkins, *Daniel Day-Lewis,* 176.

32. *Cinema Paradiso* (dir. Giuseppe Tornatore, 1989), which Miramax distributed in the United States, won the award for Best Foreign Film.

33. Alisa Perren, *Indie, Inc.: Miramax and the Transformation of Hollywood in the 1990s* (Austin: University of Texas Press, 2012), 41–42.

34. Hirschberg, "The New Frontier's Man."

35. Christopher Goodwin, "What Makes Daniel Day-Lewis Tick?," *The Week,* January 21, 2008, www.hollywoodreporter.com/video/q-a-lincoln-team-403077, accessed March 7, 2013.

36. "Movies 101 with Richard Brown."

37. Schickel, *Conversations with Scorsese,* 233.

38. Hirschberg, "The New Frontier's Man."

39. Scott Feinberg, "Q and A with the Lincoln Team," December 14, 2012, www.hollywoodreporter.com/video/q-a-lincoln-team-403077, accessed March 30, 2013; Charles McGrath, "Abe Lincoln as You've Never Heard Him: Daniel Day-Lewis on Playing Abraham Lincoln," *New York Times,* November 4, 2012, www.nytimes.com/2012/11/04/movies/daniel-day-lewis-on-playing-abraham-lincoln.html?pagewanted=all, accessed March 30, 2013.

40. "Director Commentary," *Gangs of New York,* directed by Martin Scorsese (2003; Santa Monica, Calif.: Miramax Lionsgate, 2011), DVD.

41. Schickel, *Conversations with Scorsese,* 265–67.

42. A. O. Scott. "To Feel a City Seethe," *New York Times,* December 20, 2002, www.nytimes.com/2002/12/20/movies/film-review-to-feel-a-city-seethe.html?pagewanted=all&src=pm, accessed March 20, 2013.

43. Cullen, *Sensing the Past,* 3.

44. Georgiana Banita, "Fossil Frontiers: American Petroleum History on Film," *A Companion to the Historical Film,* ed. Robert A. Rosenstone and Constantin Parvulescu (Malden, Mass.: Wiley-Blackwell, 2013), 323.

45. Schickel, *Conversations with Scorsese,* 231.

46. Banita, "Fossil Frontiers," 319–20.

47. Taylor, "Playing to the Balcony," 185.

48. Banita, "Fossil Frontiers," 317.

49. Kelly Dean Hansen, "Listening Guides to the Works of Johannes Brahms: Opus 77," www.kellydeanhansen.com/opus77.html, accessed April 20, 2013.

50. McDonald, *Hollywood Stardom,* 78.

51. Jessica Winter, "Hail to the Chief," *Time*, November 5, 2012, 40 (emphasis in the original.).
52. "Daniel Day-Lewis on Playing Lincoln," *60 Minutes Overtime*, November 14, 2012, www.cbsnews.com/8301-504803_162-57536809-10391709/daniel-day-lewis-on-playing-lincoln/, accessed March 11, 2013.
53. Earl J. Wilcox, "Abraham Lincoln on Daniel Day-Lewis," *New Verse News*, November 29, 2012, newversenews.blogspot.com/2012/11/abraham-lincoln-on-daniel-day-lewis.html, accessed January 31, 2013.
54. Tony Kushner, *"Lincoln": The Screenplay* (New York: Theatre Communications Group, 2012), 48.
55. Mike Hale, "Before an Actor Became an 'Actor,'" *New York Times*, March 17, 2013, 2:18.

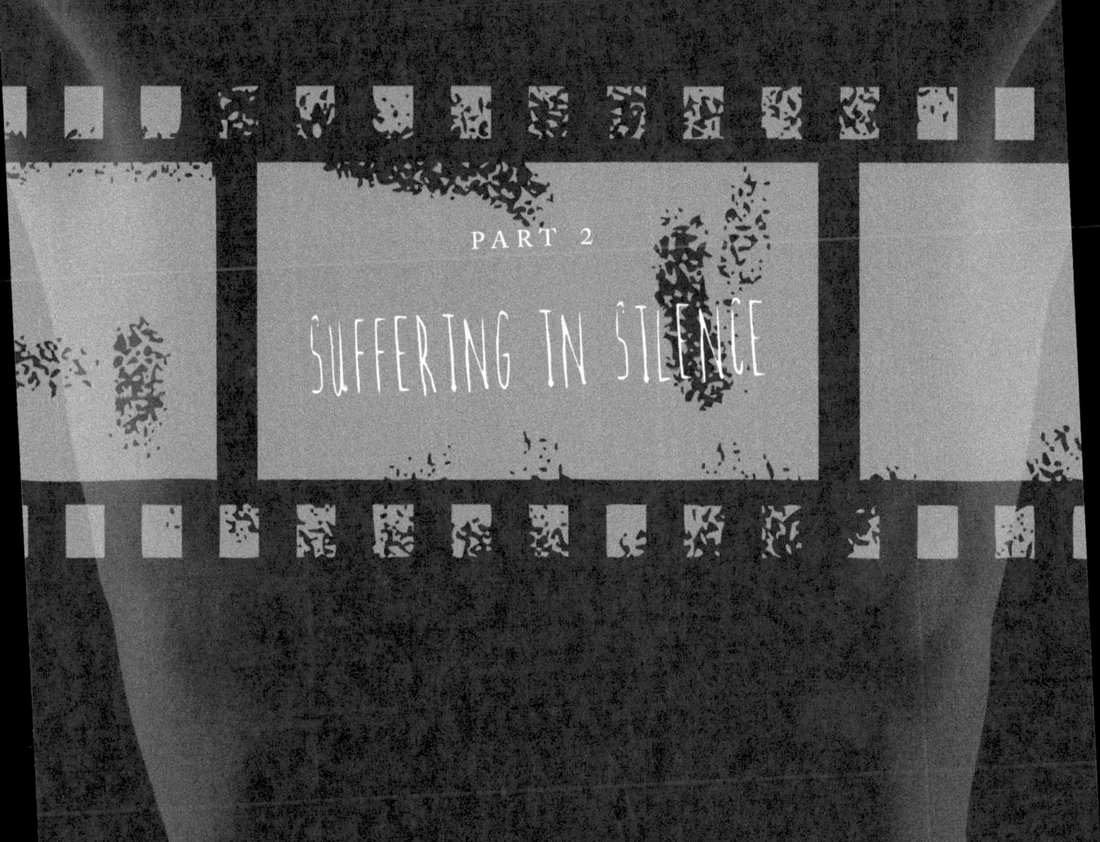
PART 2
SUFFERING IN SILENCE

5

Michael Jackson and the Pain Behind the Mirror: A Photo Essay

Todd Gray

> Neither child nor man, not clearly either black or white and with an androgynous image that is neither masculine nor feminine, Jackson's star-image is a "social hieroglyph," as Marx said of the commodity form, which demands, yet defies, decoding.
>
> Kobena Mercer, "Monster Metaphors: Notes on Michael Jackson's Thriller"

It's a bit of a shock to recognize a description of one's self in a text while researching the phenomenon of Michael Jackson's stardom. In such a moment, cathartic confusion and denial replace objective thought and reason. Frantz Fanon was to blame. While reading Fanon's *Wretched of the Earth,* I discovered there was a name for my state of being, one that captured the experience of many African Americans: mental colonialism.

> When we consider the efforts made to carry out the cultural estrangement so characteristic of the colonial epoch, we realize that nothing has been left to chance and that the total result looked for by colonial domination was indeed to convince the natives that colonialism came to *lighten their darkness*. The effect consciously sought by colonialism was to drive into the natives' heads the idea that if the settlers were to leave, they would at once fall back into barbarism, degradation, and bestiality.[1]

I came to think more and more about this concept when I began working as Michael Jackson's personal photographer in the 1980s. I had no desire to be chosen as Jackson's photographer. But I was. Truth be told, I would have rather worked for Patty Smith, Iggy Pop, or even Elvis . . . Costello. I'd just gotten out of art school and I was ready to rock 'n roll with all the excesses that accompany that white-dominated world.

I did not realize at the time that the reason Epic Record hired me to photograph the Jacksons at a backstage event was because of my age and color. They might have reconsidered if they had known more of my past: I was an acid-dropping surfer who had no interest in team sports, who shared a house with Iggy Pop for a while, and received a Marxist education from an elite institution, the California Institute of the Arts. Unimpressed by the Jackson style, I felt overqualified and overeducated for this job. Within a week's time I photographed Michael and his brothers on three occasions and said nothing more than hello and goodbye to Michael at each event. I assumed we had little in common. My quiet reserve drew Michael's attention and fueled his decision to hire me as his personal photographer, but it was only later that he told me why I was chosen for the job. He summed up his reasons for choosing me to capture his star image in four words: "You don't talk much." It was not until much later that I began to understand the pain beneath the surface of Michael Jackson's carefully managed stardom, the hidden loneliness that both spelled his downfall and ensured his lasting stardom and the public's fascination with his celebrity.

I gradually saw that Michael's experience mirrored my own in significant ways. We were both in our twenties, shared family histories, and had a similar upbringing. Both of our families were part of the great black migration from the agrarian rural South to the industrial urban North. My family settled in Chicago, Illinois, and his in Gary, Indiana. Our parents nurtured bourgeois dreams and desires for themselves and their children, and they wanted to emulate the pictures they saw on billboards and magazines of normal white families and, more importantly, of famous white stars, both filmic and musical. To do so we had to follow a strict code: speak the Queen's English; don't bring attention to yourself in public; dress in neat and clean attire appropriate for the social occasion; keep your nappy head in order; and maintain the Right Attitude.

The first rules of appearance were superficial and easy enough to achieve, but maintaining the Right Attitude took some time and effort to understand, internalize, and eventually master. The Right Attitude was an intangible veneer that took a considerable amount of practice, skill, and, eventually, self-deception. It was vital to understand this principle if we wanted to increase our value and succeed in the labor market. Simply put, we would need to work twice as hard to get half as far. Thus, we had to work four times as hard to reach parity by burying the blatant unfairness of the workplace deeply within our consciousness, all while maintaining a pleasant disposition as our labor was being exploited. The exceptionally ambitious would need to work eight times harder than whites to get ahead, and perhaps at that point they would have the liberty to reveal something beyond what W.E.B. Du Bois called "the talented tenth," as long as the climb to the top did not lead one to forget their place on the ladder of race and class.[2]

As a result of these rules we both knew how to act when outside of our own home or community, and we also realized an added responsibility that accompanied our success. As the first wave to hit the shores of this newly integrated society of the 1960s, we shared a common burden: the first impression. As the first blacks through the door, we had to make sure it didn't close behind us in a way that would keep others from following. Our presence often afforded the first live impression on a society whose primary attitudes about "blacks" were formed by stereotypical images in mass media. Michael often told me, "Be careful; they are just waiting for us to mess up."

My first big assignment was to photograph Michael taping a Disney television special at the theme park in Anaheim. The record company directed me to make images that accentuated and helped define Michael's masculinity. Meanwhile, Michael wanted playful pictures of himself having fun with Mickey, Donald Duck, and the crew. Jackson was receiving an exceptional amount of media attention and speculation about his sexuality, due to the success of his *Off the Wall* album. CBS Records planned to use photographs as part of their media campaign, prompted out of fear that any question about his sexuality might have a negative impact on record sales. Michael was not part of the conversation; I was frequently and covertly instructed to capture the moments that would masculinize his star image.[3]

The best I could manage to make Michael look manly, given the situation, was to direct him to give Minnie Mouse, the only female character on the set, a kiss on the cheek. At that time, during the 1980s, Michael was not one to convincingly contort his face into a scowl or squint his eyes into a cold gaze toward the camera for the macho shot. In any case, no photograph was released without Michael's final approval. He controlled and defined his own star image, and if anyone suggested he broadcast a more masculine image, it would reflect his interpretation of the word.

MASCULINIZING MICHAEL

The project of masculinizing Jackson was easier in the more adult, professional setting of the American Music Awards ceremony, held in Los Angeles on January 18, 1980. In a picture that again places the star in the midst of being kissed, Michael stands with his right hand in his pocket, body shifted in toward Patti LaBelle, who is about to kiss his cheek. He smiles almost demurely, staring into the camera, exposing a small portion of teeth, his face calm, his composure cool, as if he is unaware of the kiss about to be planted on his face. But he knows. I was the one who asked LaBelle to kiss Michael's cheek and she complied without hesitation. His shirt sparkles and glitters, covered with thousands of rhinestones. The sleeve of the shirt peaks out just above the right wrist of the tuxedo appearing like a diamond bracelet, a sparkling contrast to the black material of his coat and his dark skin. But it is not a bracelet; Michael is *not* pictured wearing jewelry, and he doesn't wear it privately.

LaBelle's dress is also sparkling, resembling a costume more than a dress—highly reflective and provocatively cut into a V-line from the neck to below her waist with a sheer material, making her skin both visible and covered. As in Botticelli's painting *The Birth of Venus*, LaBelle's collar creates a visual V-line as it sits atop her body, similar to the clam shell Venus (Aphrodite) stands upon; her pearls reference the sea and the provocative plunging neckline stops just above her genitals, while the rest of her body is fully covered in opaque material, a playful reversal of modesty. Venus is depicted as naked, born from the sea, using her hands to cover her breasts and vagina. Smoke enters the scene on the left side of the photograph; in the painting white lines are coming out of an angel's mouth, though the reference is actually the wind. The partial profile of a woman in a white dress cinched at the waist with a glittering material similar to Patti LaBelle's dress occupies the left side of the photograph. She is standing close to Michael in an attempt to be captured in the frame of the photograph. In the background, between her and Michael, a man wearing dark glasses looks on, smiling as he gazes onto the two objects of desire. This creates a delicate balance that places Michael in contrast to the love goddess and yet suggests that he is a sort of love god himself, simply

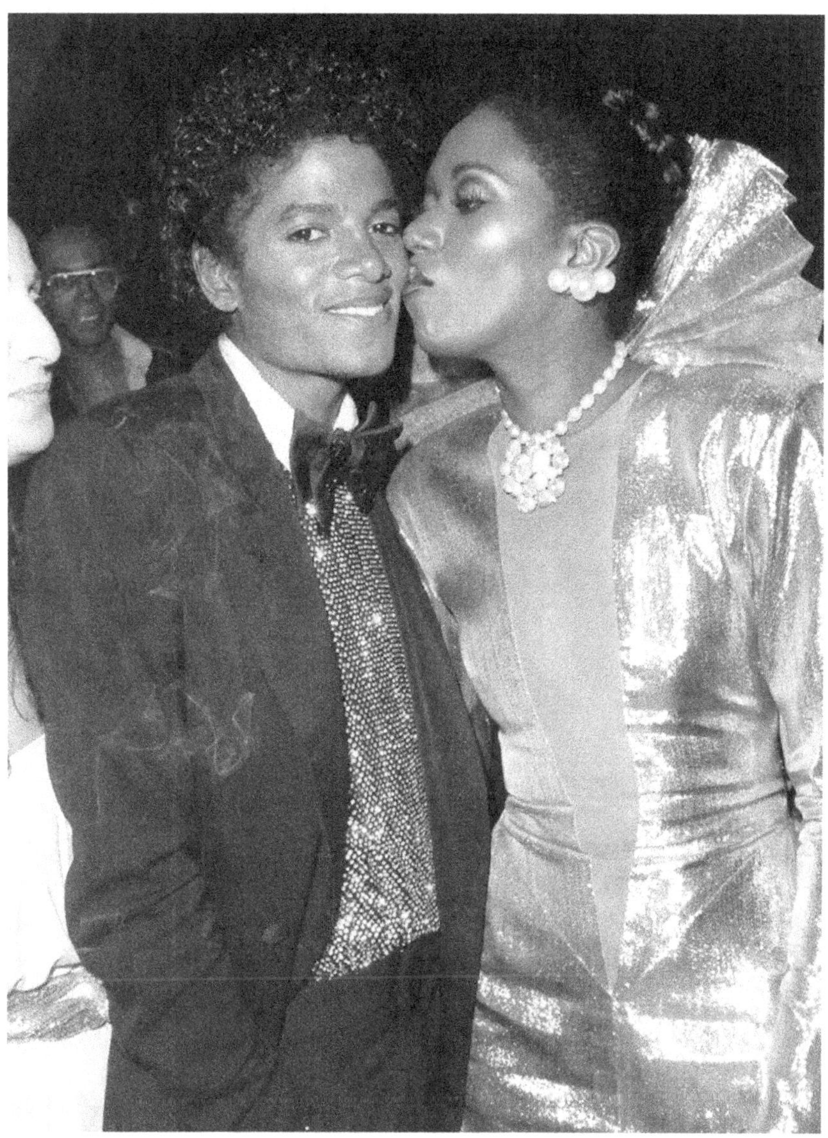

Copyright Todd Gray.

because she chooses to kiss him. This framing places him as the object of desire, ordinarily a feminine position, and yet the positioning of a man gazing into the camera eye is typical of advertisements directed at females.

While Michael gets a kiss from the Black Venus, his eyes appear cool. He is relaxed and has the grace of a young Adonis. I requested the kiss from Patti, the sexy lead singer whose international hit "Lady Marmalade," with the French refrain *Voulez-vous coucher avec moi (ce soir)?* (Do you want to sleep with me tonight?) had made her the Madonna of the 1970s. This photograph typifies the kind of image that his management had asked me to create in shots to accentuate Michael's effortless masculinity. It was necessary to walk a fine line between giving him masculine sex appeal yet not violating the unwritten rule against oversexualizing—and thereby rendering threatening—this "lightened" version of the black man.

Another staged pose of Michael with a prestigious woman—this time, Donna Summer—reveals the odd emotional tension and hidden pain at the root of the image. At this music awards event, Michael had won every category in which he was nominated: Favorite Soul / R&B Male Artist, Favorite Soul / R&B Single ("Don't Stop 'Till You Get Enough"), and Favorite Soul / R&B Album (*Off the Wall*). He was pleased, but not satisfied, perhaps because he always perceived his victories and accomplishments as tenuous, short-lived.

"Congratulations!" I said at the party afterward held next door, on another stage. "You swept every category. A perfect record. You got the most awards of anyone here."

"No I didn't. Donna Summer got three also, and more important ones too. She got Best Female Artist in Pop / Rock and R&B and Best Pop / Rock single." His life in the spotlight drove him to be the best at all times, second to none, but his satisfaction was rarely fully savored for fear it might lead to complacency.

"Yes, but she didn't sweep every category she was nominated in. Only you did that, Michael."

"*Bad Girls* is a disco album just like mine. It's a dance album. What makes mine R&B and hers Pop / Rock and R&B. It's not fair." Shaking his head, he repeated, "It's not fair." Just then Donna Summer was walking by with her publicist, who asked Michael for a photo. Neither showed much enthusiasm. In the photograph Donna isn't smiling and she appears withdrawn, wearing a black jacket resembling a man's tuxedo with a black vest underneath in a sophisticated, androgynous style. A cross hangs low from her neck, her hair hangs in long, flowing, braided tresses. The smile on Jackson's face appears almost forced, apologetic, or artificial, especially given his previous comments.

The two competitors were forced together by the camera lens, each communicating, signaling their position in the photo by their lack of emotion, although Michael gave ground by displaying a polite, perfunctory smile while she maintained the aloofness of a queen. Neither one shows any hint of deferring to the other, unlike the photos I had taken moments before with Patti Labelle, Sly Stone, and Rick James. Each of those artists, although peers, showed emotion, or

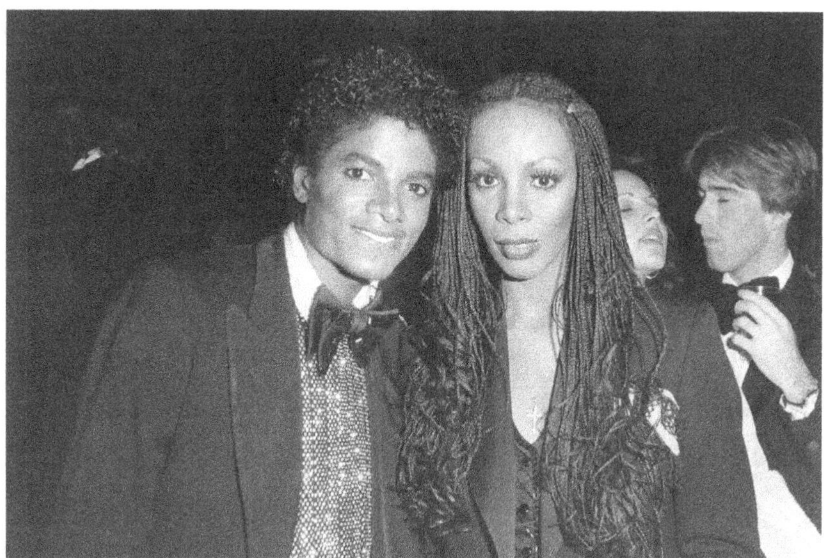

Copyright Todd Gray.

some form of consideration of the achievement Michael had accomplished that evening, while Michael maintained his cool. Not so with Donna Summer on this night. She triumphed over Barbra Streisand, Olivia Newton-John, and Rod Stewart. Michael's only claims were Rick James, Teddy Pendergrass, Kool and the Gang, The Commodores, and Peaches & Herb. He was still in the chitlin' circuit and desperately wanted to escape.[4]

On this evening, I remember spotting Chuck Berry, sitting alone near the buffet table, and dragging Michael over for a picture. I asked Chuck if Michael could sit on his lap. I wanted to show the intergenerational kinship, grandson and grandfather. He complied. With no prompting, their hands met in a Black Power handshake. Nowadays this handshake is ubiquitous in sport and pop culture, but the handshake emerged from the black struggle for civil rights in the 1960s and from black soldiers serving in Vietnam. It was both secret code and pronouncement of political struggle and solidarity.

In this photograph, the younger man sits on the lap of the older one, both wearing tuxedos, the older man's jacket velvet, finely dusted with glitter, while the young man's jacket is classic, made of wool, breast pocket stuffed with a white rhinestone-studded handkerchief. Jackson wears his glitter beneath his jacket, only to be seen from a frontal position, slightly more concealed than his elder's. Jackson's brilliant white teeth signal privilege, good dental care, and youth. The

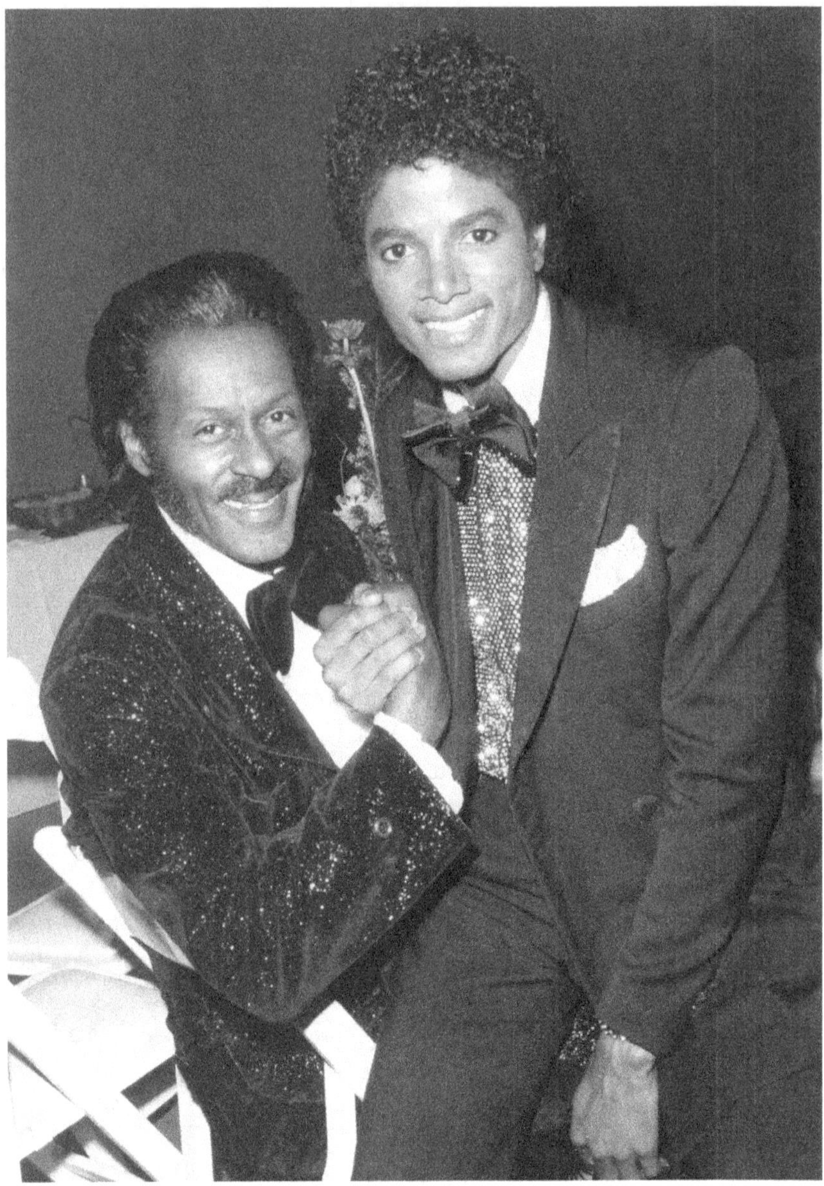

Copyright Todd Gray.

men's contrasting hairstyles also telegraph two generations, the older man with a shock of white in the front of his straight coiffed hair, Jackson's hair in shiny, tight curls, piled high on his head, revealing the generational shift to a belief that more natural black hair is beautiful.

DEVELOPING THE IMAGE

Kobena Mercer observes that Michael Jackson's image took on the iconic status of classic film stars, representing cultural tensions in a way that transcended the world of music:

> In "The Face of Garbo" Barthes sought to explore the almost universal appeal of film stars like Chaplin, Hepburn and Garbo by describing their faces as masks: aesthetic surfaces on which a society writes large its own preoccupations. Jackson's face can also be seen as such a mask, for his image has attracted and maintained the kind of cultural fascination that makes him more like a movie-star than a modern rhythm and blues artist.[5]

As Michael's fame grew, after a while a bond formed between us, and he started seeking out my help with the creation of his photographic image. Over time we discovered that we had separate yet complementary goals for the photographs to fulfill. Michael needed the images to communicate his effortless stardom and boyish, naive innocence. He had spoken with Kate Hepburn and Jane Fonda, who advised him to study the classic Hollywood photo books from the 1930s and 1940s so he could understand the visual nuance that constitutes the aura of the star. These were the same books I had looked at when I was younger, in order to learn about lighting. I used my knowledge of photo history and referred Michael to Lewis Hine's moving images of child factory workers taken at the turn of the century, which outraged the public and resulted in our first child labor laws. During these sessions, Michael would choke up nearly every time he saw those photographs. He repeatedly told me to look at their eyes, to look at their incredible sadness.

In the next photograph, Michael is standing in a room, leaning on a column that extends out of the camera frame. His arms are gathered around the column, left hand clasping right. The fingers on his right hand curve delicately inward. His head tilts toward the camera as he looks into the lens, unguarded, vulnerable. A chair is in the background situated against a wall with patterned designs on the surface. The chair casts a long shadow on the wall, indicating the low position of the sun. Three chairs are in the photograph, suggesting a room of social exchange, yet he is alone in the room. It is late in the afternoon.

I had arranged to photograph Michael in the largest suite of the hotel, the President's Suite. It is reserved for the wealthy and powerful. American presidents have slept there. In this photo, Michael is wearing a white T-shirt, jeans, and black belt. Although he is a millionaire, he looks like he is from the black working class, save for the studded belt. Michael told me he wanted to

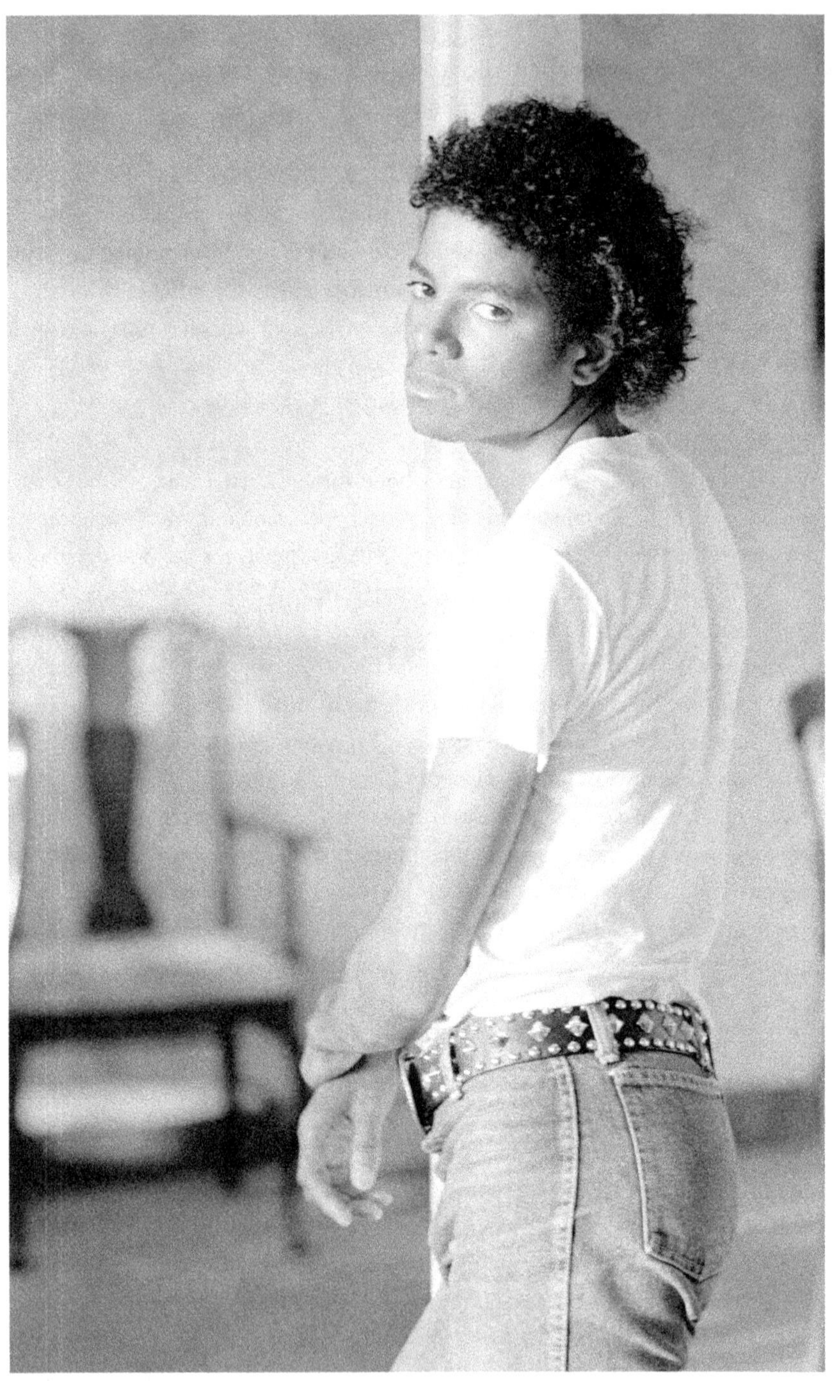

Copyright Todd Gray.

wear expressions similar to the children's faces he saw in Lewis Hines's early twentieth-century photographs of exploited child labor working in factories. The exhaustion and sadness in the faces of the children were undeniable. Michael did not smile once in the forty-five minutes we spent making photographs that day in the President's Suite. We barely spoke, not wanting to break the quiet of the moment. I made minimal gestures with my head and hands to give him direction and would nod and hum approvingly when I was certain of capturing a particularly melancholic image.

In his own quiet way he was instructing me on how he wanted to be portrayed. I wanted to show him and the world a thoughtful, reflective portrait, a counterpoint to the usual image of a grinning black entertainer. Looking back now, I realize I was actually making a portrait of myself, with Michael as my stand-in. Odd: over the years through the study of these images, I've learned more about myself than I care to admit.

In contrast to the somber melancholy of this photograph, Jackson's star image was being pulled increasingly in the direction of glamor and glitz, even as the haunting sadness of Michael's face shines through the sophisticated veneer. I could relate to this duality. Like Michael Jackson, I found myself filled with romantic fantasies and desires fueled by the faces on my television screen: Ginger and Mary Ann from *Gilligan's Island,* Sue Ellen on *The Beverly Hillbillies,* and Pussy Galore in the film *Goldfinger.* During my school years I never listened to the black rhythm and blues radio station, instead opting for "white" rock 'n' roll. Growing up, I worshipped at the altar of The Doors, Jimi Hendrix, and Led Zeppelin, all playing music my father loathed. He was a jazz and blues man, a race man. Not I.

I eventually came to recognize the African American roots of the supposedly white music and stars that I idolized. During a drunken backstage conversation with Led Zeppelin's lead singer, Robert Plant, he ranted on to me about his heroes, Leadbelly, Howlin' Wolf, Willie Dixon (names I only vaguely remembered from my father's generation), about how black music was the best in the world. Was he kidding me? I nodded my head knowingly, but in my mind I was still convinced that bands like the Rolling Stones, Zeppelin, and The Doors were the best. He blurted out that Zeppelin made millions by co-opting the Mississippi Delta blues. Was this his confession? Why was he telling me? Was I missing something? Couldn't he understand that I was a rocker, in spite of my appearance?

Eventually, with the help of theorists such as bell hooks, Fanon, and Du Bois, I grew to understand the self-loathing that had made me want to be like the white stars I worshiped. Then, as I looked at other photographs I'd made of Michael and saw how his hair, nose, and skin color had gradually transformed, I thought to myself that, indeed, his racial self-loathing was becoming apparent. It was at this same moment that I began to understand my own racial self-hatred. While playing in the streets and alleys on Chicago's South Side as a child in the 1960s we would sing out the phrase, "If you're white, you're all right. If you're brown, stick around. If you're black, step back," innocently sowing the seeds of self-loathing and nihilism. Michael grew up in Gary, Indiana, thirty miles away. His overbearing father, Joseph, forced his sons, the Jackson Five, to rehearse incessantly, and he beat them when they erred. Michael was not allowed to play after school or have friends over at the house, depriving him of the joys of a normal childhood. Joseph commanded him to come home and rehearse, and if beatings weren't enough to quell dissent, then he would brandish a 38mm revolver to legitimize his authority. Joseph viewed Michael as his ticket out of Gary, Indiana.[6] I also wanted to escape the constant reminders and restrictions of my second-class status. Black pride was both dream and oxymoron.

This kind of experience and attitude emerged in Jackson's descriptions of his own upbringing. He recounted how he had to be careful of his actions and be on his guard ever since he was a child, because the press and racist society "were just waiting for us to mess up. Waiting to jump on any mistake we make." I understood the immense pressure required to be a model citizen and to keep oneself in check, or suffer the consequences of being labeled a "bad Negro"—uncouth, ignorant, and criminal. We both made adjustments and spoke in softer tones and minimized aggressive behavior, which, by default, softened our personae. We were less threatening young black males, thanks to the vigilance of our internalized wardens, policing and under self-surveillance as described in Foucault's Panopticon: "He who is subjected to a field of visibility, and who knows it, assumes responsibility for the constraints of power; he makes them play spontaneously upon himself; he inscribes in himself the power relation in which he simultaneously plays both roles; he becomes the principle of his own subjection."[7]

Because of Michael's celebrity, his overseer was much harsher than mine. As a black pubescent child star he learned that if signs of carnal desire were broadcast and distorted by the press, white parents would stop buying his records for fear of corrupting their daughters. He knew firsthand the pain a family suffers when sales drop and layoffs occur, since it had happened to his own father at the Indiana steel mills. Michael did not want to let this happen to his family and friends at Motown Records—a lot of weight to bear on his delicate twelve-year-old shoulders. In order to escape the negative stereotype of blackness, Jackson overachieved and overcompensated to show that he was different, in a logical response to a corrupt cultural assault.

THE PAIN OF PERFORMANCE

Both the pain and sheer physical effort of Jackson's performances come across throughout his career, particularly in those that recall the experiences of his youth. In a photo during the J5 medley of their earliest hits, his fatigue is evident. Michael's eyes are cast down, mouth open and chest glistening with sweat. His pants sparkle from the reflection of thousands of rhinestones. Light is falling on his body from multiple directions—left, right, behind, low, and high. In back of him below his waist are three large objects, numerous high lights reflect off their surface, and further below are several more cylindrical objects, much smaller in size. A bright light is at the upper right corner of the frame.

This image reveals the almost mechanized work and energy expended during performance. The glitter pants weigh in around ten pounds. A bank of lights come on periodically during the performance, shining a blinding light directly into the eyes of the audience and performer, unleashing a burst of heat on anyone within ten feet. The expression on Michael's face looks as if he is exhausted, going through the motions, working for a living. Perhaps he wants to be someplace else—maybe in his mind, at this precise moment, he is. A glaring spotlight is trained on his every move, 40,000 eyes watching, but he's not there. Meanwhile, he performs the same dance moves to the same song at the same precise moment as he had been doing since he was a child.

When we were in Disneyland Michael told me that Mickey Mouse was the most successful and beloved star in the world and he wanted to be just like him—not another human being, not even another living being, but a cartoon animal. Mickey was an international star, but his persona was a commodity as well as an entertainment character. The price Michael paid in his quest to transform into commodity and character was high. In his quest for such fantastic stardom, he had to repress almost all his carnal desires and impulses, indeed, much of his humanity, to achieve his goal.

Consequently, Jackson maintained an immense degree of self-control to differentiate himself from performers like Rick James, Sly Stone, and even James Brown. All these artists had served time in jail and perpetuated a public perception of the black male as pathological and criminal. Jackson policed his desires and repressed his id in order to, as Fanon put it, "lighten [his] darkness" and become the model minority representative, the Good Negro.

In the pre-civil rights era, black mothers taught their boys at an early age to be quiet and demure in public to ensure their survival. White southern culture viewed these boys as wild and untamed animals. It was not uncommon to see a mother give her son a yank on the collar or smack on the head in the Jim Crow South.

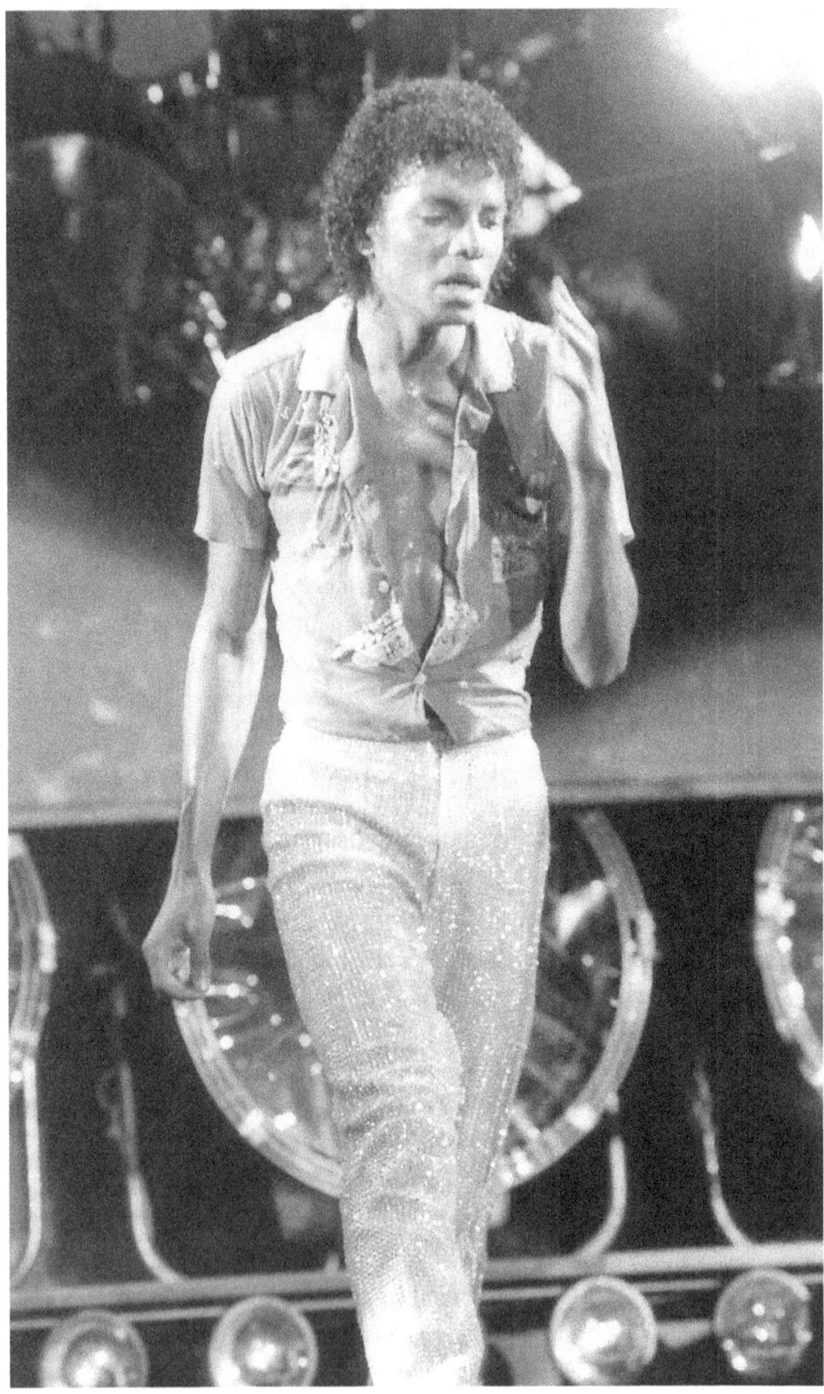

Black boys could be savagely beaten or worse for the (mis)perceived insult to a white woman caused by a smile, laugh, or gaze. A neurotic pattern of internalized suppression would often develop in children as the result of a mother's loving instinct to protect and help her child survive. As blacks moved from the South to the North these parenting methods persisted. Michael Jackson's family exercised the extremes of such practices, as his youth was taken from him, both by a culture that inhibited his movement and action and by parents who recognized him as a valuable economic resource, a magical tool for escaping the bounds of racial and economic oppression.

Michael was famous for loving animals and children, perhaps as extensions of his own image of himself. In this photograph, Michael stands facing right, in a stoic profile, wearing a sweater with a family seal or emblem embroidered over his heart. He holds the harness of a white llama facing him with his right hand, while his left hand rests on top of the llama's head. Bright sunlight illuminates the scene and reflects off the steel chain link enclosing them.

Michael Jackson had a private zoo in his backyard, perhaps in an attempt to establish his own domain or perhaps a connection to his African ancestry. The zoo has its earliest beginnings in Mesopotamia and Egypt, as a way for monarchs and rulers to exhibit their conquests and spoils of war. Private zoos were symbols of power, wealth, and authority. Michael's coat of arms or family crest on his sweater confirms his own historical aspiration to class affiliation, and yet one wonders: Is this the crest of Gary, Indiana? The photograph shows both Michael and llama sharing space in a chain link cage, one trapped by the force of man, the other trapped by the seduction of capital, culture, and stardom.

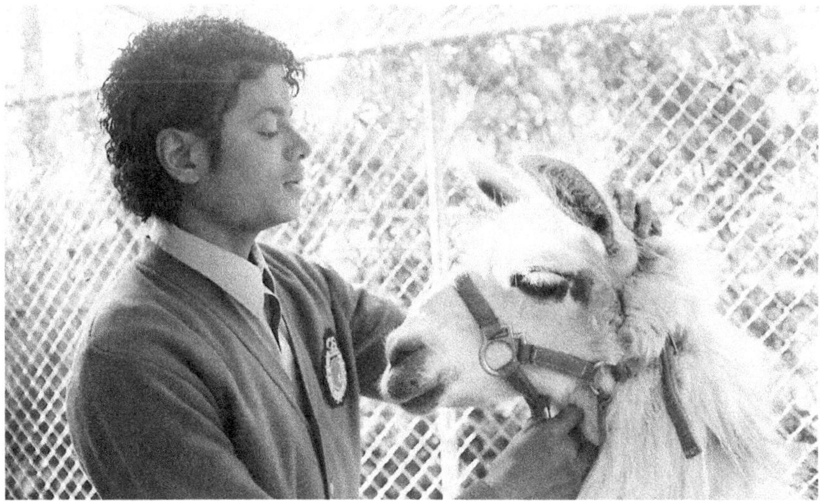

Copyright Todd Gray.

"THRILLER" AS PARABLE

Much of Michael Jackson's meteoric rise to superstardom occurred with his breakout music and dance performance in "Thriller," which revolutionized, indeed, created, the modern music video. Instead of a stagey performance of a song accompanied by awkward dance moves, appropriate to *American Bandstand* or *The Ed Sullivan Show*, "Thriller" was more of a short film, enacting a zombie uprising through Jackson's riveting choreography and music. This music video resonated profoundly with viewers because behind the dance, it was a parable for a larger social conflict.

The cultural perception of the black male as a wild and untamed animal expresses itself and contributes to the anxiety at the beginning of the "Thriller" video, as Michael Jackson watches an image of himself morph into a beast—a werewolf—onscreen while sitting in the audience at a movie theater. A short while later he leaves the theater only to turn into a zombie in the "real world" outside.

These two mutations, beast and zombie, convey the suffering of mental colonialism and self-loathing, materialized and come to life onscreen. "Thriller" serves as a way for Jackson to exteriorize and exorcise his demons of internalized cultural oppression and self-repression. The historical roots of this dichotomy are evident in the antebellum South's division of "Negroes" into two categories: house slaves and field slaves, one good and the other bad. House slaves were viewed as good docile servants, while field slaves were seen as potentially violent beasts of labor. Jackson unleashes his inner "bad Negro" on the movie screen as the growling, howling werewolf, and he takes an immense amount of pleasure in

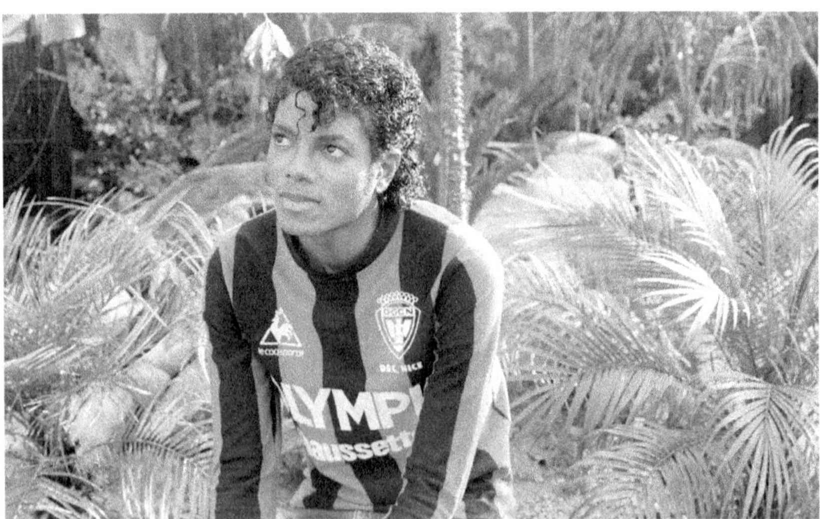

Copyright Todd Gray.

doing so. He is the only person in the audience pictured onscreen who smiles and happily munches popcorn while others around him are terrified of the image. In a sadistic twist he takes pleasure in the suffering others experience as they are repulsed by the image of his cinematic doppelganger. Better to laugh than to cry.

During the zombie segment of the video, mindless bodies lacking souls move in sequence. This is the final tragic outcome signifying a lifetime of suppression that ultimately destroys the spirit, along with any glimmer of independent thought. For the zombie, the internalized thought police have finally won the battle and successfully subdued his free will and consumed his humanity. Michael expresses this condition with syncopated choreography befitting a military drill team. All the dancers hit their marks in unison with sharp precision. Michael Jackson is no longer the sole focal point of our attention, as the whole troupe of dancers turn into a unit with Michael at the helm. We can join in the march of the zombies, forgetting ourselves in order to become something significantly bigger, an army. In later years Jackson adopts the uniform of a decorated military leader. For a while he only ventured out in public wearing some form of uniform. His sole source of warmth and security is found in the cold embrace of the military uniform. Zombie.

Capturing this notion, Nigerian singer Fela Kuti wrote a song entitled "Zombie" and equates this state of mindless being to that of a soldier in the military:

> Zombie no go go, unless you tell am to go
> Zombie no go stop, unless you tell am to stop
> Zombie no go turn, unless you tell am to turn
> Zombie no go think, unless you tell am to think.[8]

Public space is seen as battlefield and he is ready for another attack. Jackson's superstardom laid siege to his psyche and sense of well-being, leaving him a seeming automaton. This impression of Jackson's psychological position came to me at the moment that I was also losing my place as insider. I now see that at some point Michael ceased being a mere mortal and morphed into the mythical world of hero and demi-god. He became a star. He had taken a sip from the philosopher's cup, entering the pantheon of the artist, as described by Thomas Carlyle:

> The meaning of Song goes deep. Who is there that, in logical words,
> can express the effect music has on us? A kind of inarticulate
> unfathomable speech, which leads us to the edge of the
> Infinite, and lets us for moments gaze into that![9]

Unfortunately for me, my photos did not reflect this transformation in his new star image. I still saw him as a man in this world, similar to myself, and I was caught unaware that he had shape-shifted like an African trickster or shaman. I suppose my photos anchored him to this world while he was blasting off into the cosmos. On my first critical search through these photographs I was looking for proof of his shame and betrayal, but found only my own. Frantz Fanon, Foucault, Du Bois, and other theorists sat on my shoulder, pointing out clues as I sifted through my archive. I had previously thought the place for theory was only in the classroom, not in my home, but true knowledge cuts both ways and knows no boundaries. Traces and signs of mental colonialism and self-commodification were apparent in both my object of study and in myself.

Michael's transformation of hair and facial features and my own history of hair straightening both demonstrate aspects of Fanon's theory of race and racism. Michael spoke softly and did not dress in the style of other black youths his age or mimic street culture, careful not to be mistaken for the ethnic stereotype of the criminal black man, behavior that embodied Foucault's theory of self-policing. I was often called an "Oreo" because of my purging of blackness in grooming, speech, and dress, an indication of the kind of inferiority complex Toni Morrison writes about in her book *The Bluest Eye*, when the narrator observes how "it was as though some mysterious and all-knowing master had given each one of them a cloak of ugliness to wear and they had each accepted it without question."[10]

RETURN TO AFRICA

In order to understand Michael Jackson's ceaseless and progressively more desperate attempts to hide his self-perceived ugliness and whiten his image, I sought a global perspective and began to explore perceptions of Michael among people in black-dominated countries. I began to travel to Ghana, so often that I now maintain a studio there. When I first visited Ghana I experienced what it was like to be in the racial majority for the first time in my life. My blackness did not stick out there; it was commonplace. In late 2008, several months before Michael's death, I took photographs of Michael with me to Africa. I wanted to see if people in a remote fishing village, off the grid, would know who he was and tell me what they made of him. Everyone I approached immediately recognized his face without me saying his name. I asked them to pose with the photograph as if he were their brother, lost in the city, and they were attempting to call him back home to the village. Everyone I approached in Ghana claimed this star as theirs, as African.

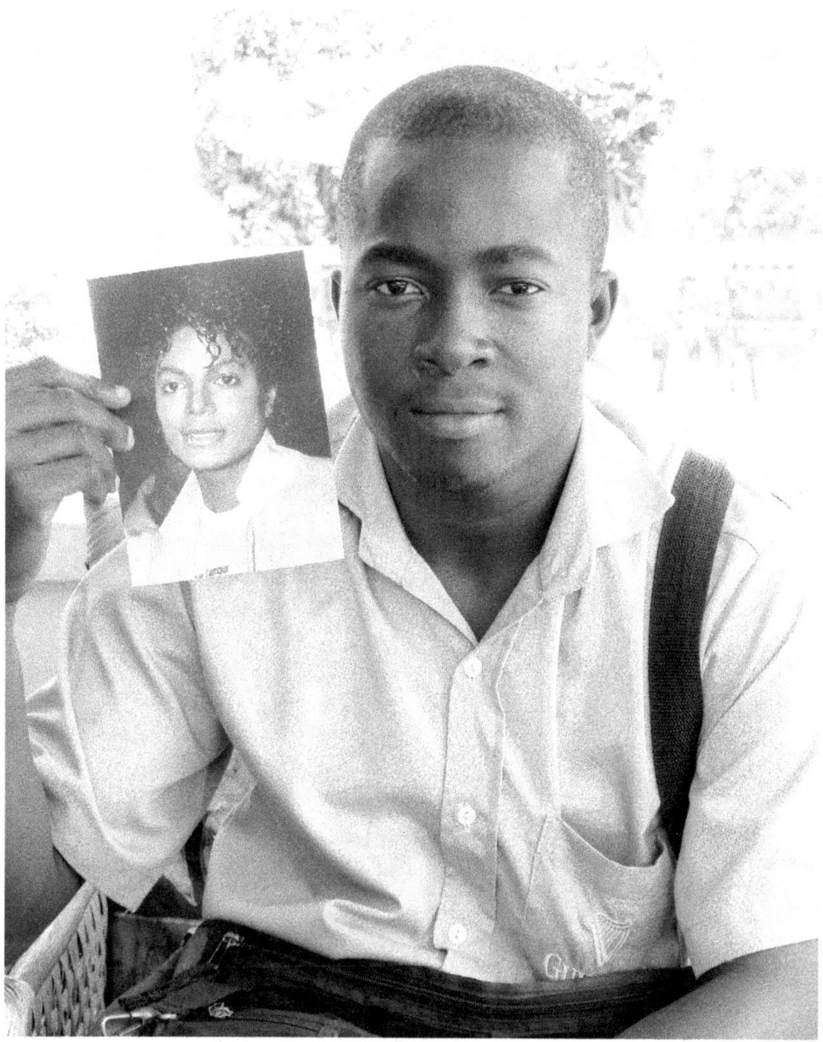

Copyright Todd Gray.

Even though the images of Michael Jackson elicited expressions of brotherhood from everyone I encountered, I did not experience the same sense of homecoming, perhaps because I was perceived as an ordinary person, not an icon or a star. My ancestors left Africa as a physical commodity, and now I had returned as the Other, Western on the inside, in spite of my dark skin. I was called "obruni" in the Twi language of Ghana. "Obruni, obruni," the children called out to me as I passed through the village. Obruni is what they call

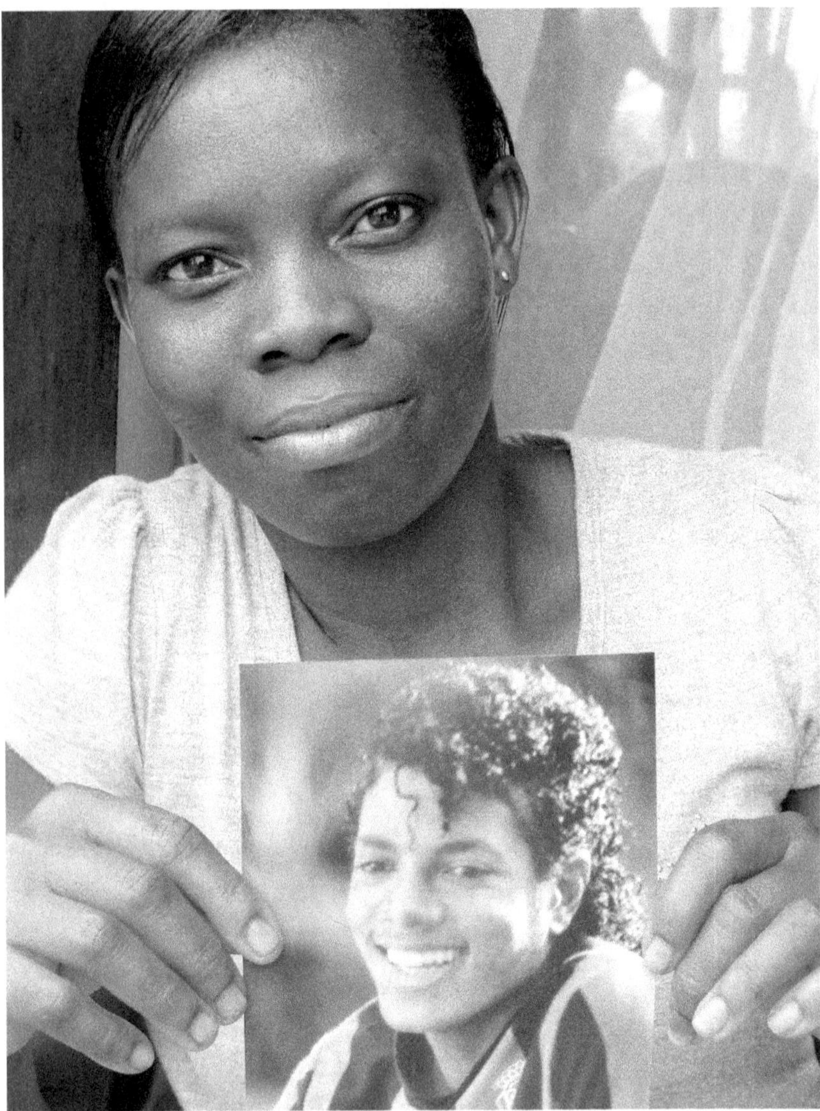

Copyright Todd Gray.

Westerners. Obruni means white man. In talking with people in Ghana, my impression was that they were drawn to Michael Jackson not so much because of his stardom as they were moved by a sense of pity for a man whose ancestors were forced to leave Africa. I cannot know if they were simply trying to follow my directions, but to my eyes, their pictures tell the story of a genuine and sympathetic longing to bring Michael Jackson back home.

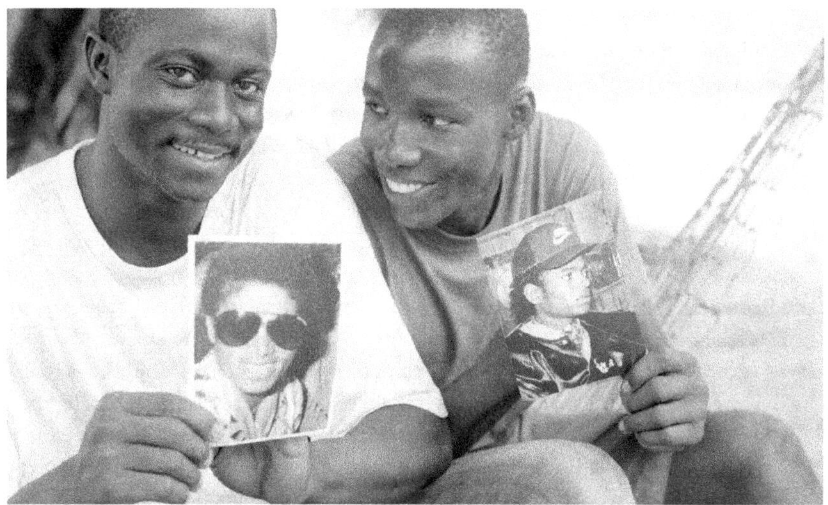

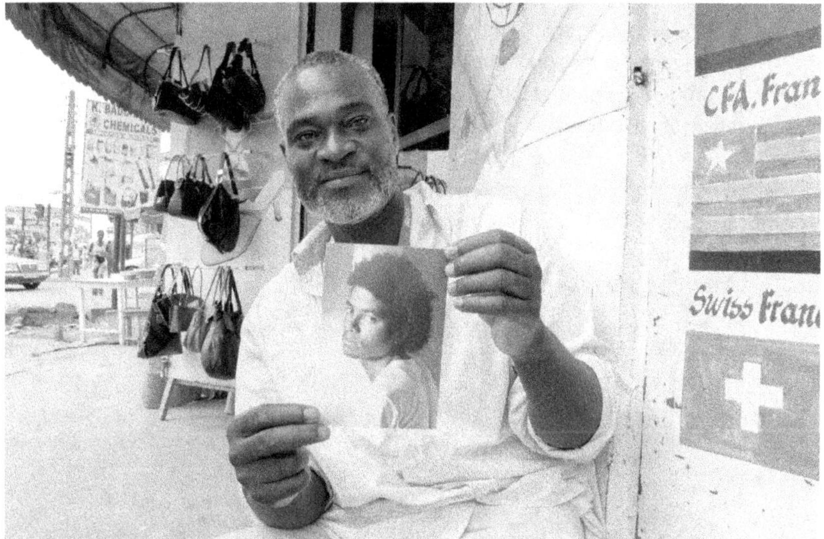

Copyright Todd Gray.

NOTES

1. Frantz Fanon, *Wretched of The Earth* (New York: Grove Press, 1963), 210–11.
2. W.E.B. Du Bois, "The Talented Tenth," in *The Negro Problem: A Series of Articles by Representative Negroes of To-day* (New York: James Pott and Company, 1903), 31–76. Du Bois states that "for three long centuries this people lynched Negroes who dared to be brave, raped black women who dared to be virtuous, crushed dark-hued youth who dared to be ambitious, and encouraged and made to flourish servility and lewdness and apathy" (43).

3. Management asked me to be alert for photo ops accenting Michael's masculinity and manhood whenever they appeared. When I first heard these words I almost blurted out, "I ain't no sissy," as I had done to my father, years ago, before realizing this was not aimed at me or my work. I never revealed this directive to Michael.
4. Margo Jefferson, *On Michael Jackson* (New York: Pantheon Books, 2006), 57.
5. Kobena Mercer, "Monster Metaphors: Notes on Michael Jackson's Thriller," in *Stardom: Industry of Desire*, ed. Christine Gledhill (London: Routledge, 1991), 302.
6. Christopher Andersen, *Michael Jackson Unauthorized* (New York: Simon and Schuster, 1994), 21.
7. Michel Foucault, *Discipline and Punishment* (New York: Vintage Books, 1995), 202–3.
8. Fela Kuti, "Zombie," www.youtube.com/watch?v=Q76UngzHX5Y, accessed February 23, 2015. Ten years later, I found myself in a similar situation in a meeting with Bobby Brown's manager and the Creative Director of MCA Records, finalizing the image I would produce for his *Don't Be Cruel* album cover, his first solo project after leaving the teen heartthrob boy band New Edition. The manager described the photo he wanted: "Bobby's wearing all black leather and looking tough on top of a Harley Davidson motorcycle in the desert at dusk. He's revving the engine and spinning the rear tire, kicking up rocks and dirt on a hot young babe he's just done, lying on the ground near the rear tire as he is about to roar off into the sunset." Although I needed this job, I could not ethically make this image. I asked two questions: What percentage of teenage girls will buy Bobby Brown's album? If you were a teenage girl, would you enjoy a fantasy of Bobby using you and then discarding you alone in the desert, showering you with dirt and rocks? Point made.
9. Thomas Carlyle, *The Best Known Works of Thomas Carlyle* (Rockville, Md.: Wildside Press, 2010), 209.
10. Toni Morrison, *The Bluest Eye* (New York: Plume, 1994), 39.

6

ADIÓS MARGARITA CANSINO, HELLO RITA HAYWORTH

Linda Rader Overman

WHEN I WAS TEN YEARS OLD, I WOULD STAY UP LATE AND SNEAK INTO MY *abuelita's* bedroom where Mom hid the old black-and-white TV set; the living room was no place for such a thing, she said. *Abuelita* could sleep through an earthquake, so while she slept, I sat at the foot of her bed, mesmerized by old films from the thirties and forties on *Million Dollar Movie*, with their fantasy figures projected in gradations of gray. If Mother caught me and sent me to bed after a fierce scolding in Spanish, I could always sneak another peak on the local station, KHJ, which repeated the same movie every night for an entire week. The one that captured me was Charles Vidor's *Gilda* (1946).

I watched it in pieces, out of order. The first night, Rita Hayworth's Gilda sang "Put the blame on Mame, boys, put the blame on Mame," in that sleek, black, Jean Louis strapless gown, with mid-arm gloves, torturing Johnny (Glenn Ford) by doing a mock striptease for the enthusiastic and supposedly Argentine casino audience. Tuesday night, just after 11:30, I saw smack, smack, smack, smack, four

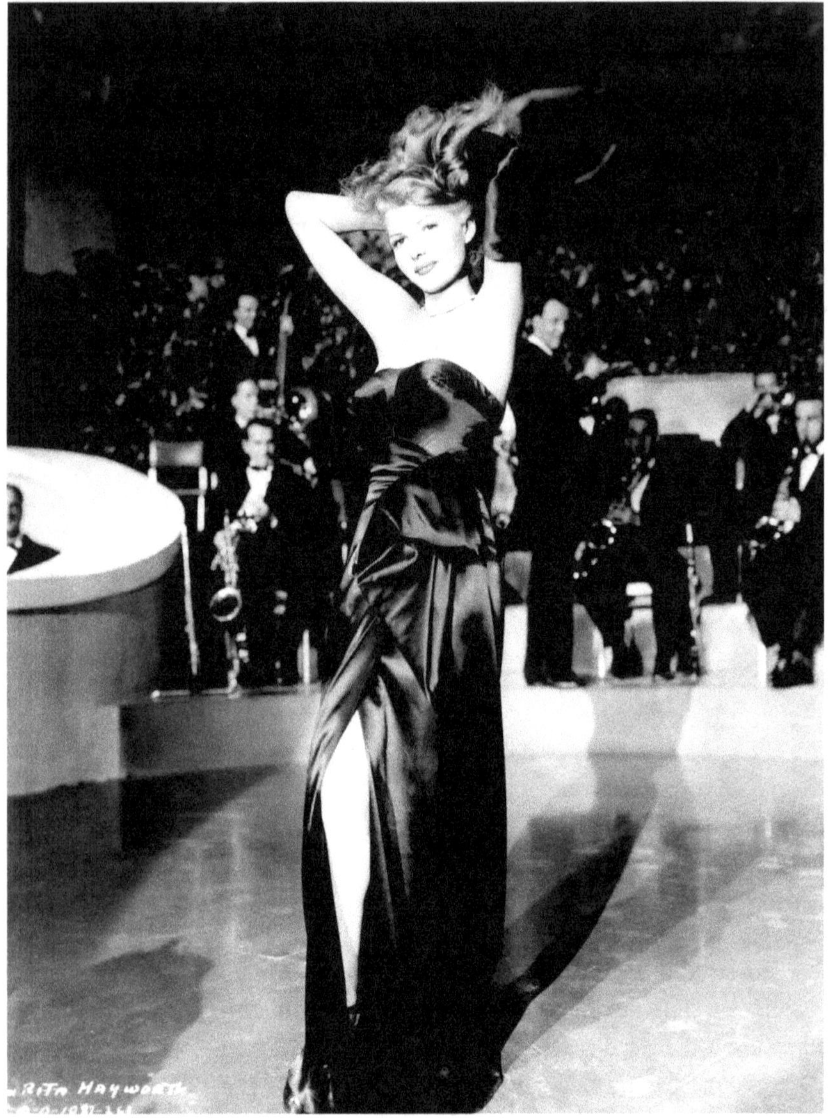

Rita Hayworth puts the blame on Mame in *Gilda* (1946). Collection of the author.

times across Johnny's face, as Gilda collapses against his chest, falls down onto the floor clutching his leg, sobbing, "Johnny, let me go." Wednesday night just after 10 o'clock, Gilda's voice softly sings to herself off-camera. She flares onto the screen, languidly shaking back her mane of soon-to-be-famous red hair, and the Gilda glamour of Rita[1] appears in her first scene: "Are you decent, Gilda?" "Me [pause] sure I'm decent." Smoldering is more like it. Oh, yes, I almost forgot. Thursday night, just after 10:45, Mother became particularly annoyed with my repeated late-night infractions, so I only managed a nanosecond of Hayworth and Ford dancing together closely while Gilda suggestively proclaims, "I have to keep talking, Johnny, as long as I have my arms about you, or else I might forget to dance. Push my hat back, Johnny." As I was wondering what her hat had to do with anything and why Johnny should push it any which way, and how that scene worked with the ending where Gilda and Johnny go off together, Mother came in, snapped off the TV, and yanked me back to the bedroom I shared with her, threatening "*vas a ver*" with a small, horizontal slicing-the-air-motion of her hand. That usually meant a spanking was imminent. But the important point for me was that I knew Johnny and Gilda were living happily ever after, so my peripatetic viewing and threat of punishment were well worth it. However, Gilda and the tortured Rita Hayworth who played her did anything but live happily ever after.

Although nothing like Gilda, the "evil, conniving . . . best remembered of the bad-bad women,"[2] Rita—or as she was born, Margarita Cansino—traveled her road to female stardom surrounded by others, mostly men, who could have been labeled as similarly evil. The vamp she played onscreen was in deep conflict with the innocent young Spanish girl who began dancing at four years old and never really stopped. The evolution of the too-ethnic gypsy-Latina Cansino into the Anglicized product of the all-American girl-next-door was fraught with the

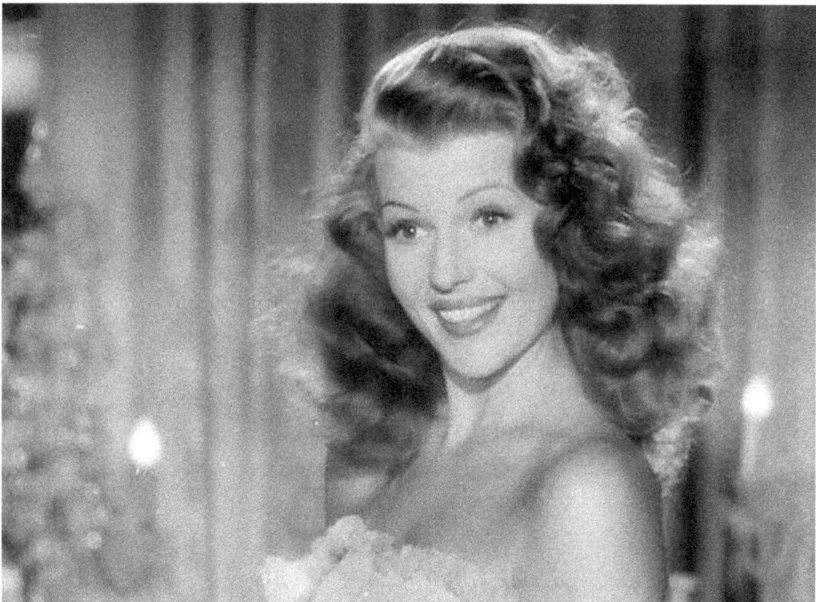

Hayworth plays the evil, conniving, best of bad women in *Gilda*.

same pain Rita endured when an inch of her hairline was gradually removed over many years of electrolysis. This was but one mandatory alteration, among many, in the construction of a Hollywood princess. This *white* Hollywood princess, who was then objectified in films like *Gilda* and *Cover Girl* (a story about the search for the appropriate Golden Wedding Girl for *Vanity Fair* magazine), showed "what 1940s Hollywood was all about . . . where the process of glamorization is done."[3] Every trace of a black-haired Margarita was obliterated in life and onscreen, enabling a bleached redheaded "goddess like star, Rita Hayworth," to erupt into "quite possibly the definitive sex goddess . . . served up to the public as a gorgeous physical specimen."[4] This fake, fiery Anglo was much more appealing to a mass audience coping with World War II and its aftermath than a shy Latina would have been. The moviegoing public relied on Hollywood studio power brokers to provide a beautiful, enviable, and desirably exotic creature who nevertheless appeared wholly American and, more importantly, Caucasian.

Margarita Dolores Carmen Cansino[5] was part Latina and part Anglo (born to Irish mother Volga Haworth, former showgirl in the Ziegfeld Follies),[6] although the image movers and shakers responsible for Margarita's career resculpted her to look anything but Latina. In *Cover Girl*, Hayworth's "hair is unwrapped and her hundreds of red curls are pulled out, combed and teased. Lights are rushed forward and carefully positioned while the photographer studies her intently. Everyone inside the frame focuses on Hayworth, who smiles, dimples, poses, and has her picture taken. Soon the screen is filled with literally hundreds of reproductions of this image, all of which appear on magazine covers all over town."[7] Of course, she couldn't have gotten there until the magazine publisher, in the film, commands that she "climb aboard [his] magic carpet."[8] This metamorphosis at the behest of the many men who abused and used her, on and off the screen, was to remain an unrelenting pattern starting with the first man in her life.

At first, her controlling father, Eduardo Cansino, emphasized Margarita's Spanish heritage. A former Spanish dancer, Eduardo shared fame with a dancing partner, his sister Elisa, on the renowned Orpheum Circuit around 1915. It was only four years earlier that the two of them emigrated from Spain to dance and cash in on vaudeville's halcyon days.[9] Eduardo and Elisa were headliners when another brother and sister dancing duo, Fred and Adele Astaire, were a small act on the same bill.[10]

Eduardo used his thirteen-year-old daughter, Margarita, as a dance partner when reviving the old act in 1931, at the height of the Great Depression. Eduardo's dancing school in Hollywood was operating at a loss, and the family,

Volga, and the two young boys, Eduardo Jr. and Vernon, needed money to survive. Thus, in her early adolescence, gone were "the two long pigtails that hung down Margarita's back when she was allowed to attend school. She now wore her dyed black hair parted severely in the center and pulled back into a knot at the nape of her neck."[11] She looked so mature that she was often confused for her father's sister, and when performing, he led people to believe she was his young wife, forbidding her to call him "father." Since Margarita was still a minor and California laws prevented minors from appearing where alcohol was sold, Eduardo and Margarita's first engagement was at the Foreign Club Casino in Tijuana, "a favorite watering spot for cinema bigwigs."[12] Following that commitment, they performed for two years at Agua Caliente, an opulent Tijuana resort.

The deliberate emphasis of Margarita's Spanish features led to her being "mistaken for a Mexican and singled out for extra work as a street dancer outside a bullfighting arena."[13] Since the Dancing Cansinos went over so well in Mexico, the family temporarily moved nearby to Chulavista, in San Diego. During this time Margarita's parents lied about her age so she did not have to attend school along with her brothers. In her biography of Hayworth, Barbara Leaming writes, "She was the family income. For Rita there was no life, no school, no friends, no girlfriends. . . . She often sat on the front porch staring silently ahead or seeming to watch" her brother and the neighborhood children play, something Margarita was not allowed to do.[14] When one of the boys in the group attempted to speak with her, either Eduardo or Volga called her into the house on some pretense.

A former Cansino childhood friend interviewed by Leaming recalls when Eduardo and Margarita practiced their dance routines in the afternoons: "We'd watch through the window. . . . He'd scream and holler at her, 'Don't do that! Don't be so stupid! Don't do that!' Just *screaming* at her. He was kind of a small man, like a little banty rooster. . . .When she made a mistake, he would shout at her—I never heard her answer him back, not ever. She would simply do the routine again, until he was satisfied. She was always quiet, sweet, obedient."[15] Following these rehearsals, the quiet, painfully shy, fourteen-year-old Margarita, who wore simple dresses or skirts and blouses while sitting on the porch, would enter her parent's car around four o'clock looking "suddenly much older,"[16] wearing "high heels, a dress or a suit, and a hat" and leave for Tijuana to do twenty shows a week. There, a paralyzingly shy, self-conscious, and barely audible Margarita would project a "fiery and sensual stage presence"[17] aflame with adult sexuality. It was all a façade, however, for she would no sooner complete her dance routine than be overcome by her timidity, avoid eye contact, and return to her usually withdrawn self.

Many patrons thought Margarita did not even speak English. Most had no idea that Eduardo locked Margarita in her dressing room to protect her from the riffraff in late night Tijuana. After all, he was a strict, old-fashioned parent who wished to keep his daughter out of harm's way, or so he claimed.[18] Patrons did not know of the beatings Margarita received if she displeased her father in any way during their nightclub dancing engagements, especially when Eduardo got drunk and proceeded to gamble away their weekly salary.[19] Unknown to those around them "during this period her father . . . repeatedly engaged in sexual relations with her"[20] in the afternoon, prior to dancing with her in the evenings. Naturally, after a performance, Eduardo would insist that his daughter sit and be photographed at the various tables with producers who would give her an "entrée into film-industry inner circles."[21]

Ultimately, as Eduardo hoped, schemed, pushed, and manipulated, his "family income" succeeded in obtaining the appropriate screen test. After several disappointments, sixteen-year-old Rita Cansino signed a contract and emerged onto the screen as a bit player. Much later, as a fledgling actress, her big break eventually came when she was twenty-one, in Howard Hawks's *Only Angels Have Wings* (1939) opposite Cary Grant.[22] This came after Columbia Pictures boss Harry Cohn remarked that "she really ought to change her name," since *Cansino* was "too . . . well . . . Spanish-sounding."[23] Consequently, each new film brought a different, more homogenized and Anglicized version of Margarita to the moviegoing audience, ultimately culminating in the breakout film for the star Rita Hayworth (her mother's maiden name plus the "y"), a full-blown "love goddess . . . everything a man could desire,"[24] projected on the giant Hollywood screen in *Gilda* (1946). By then, Rita was twenty-eight.

The "love goddess" image was another façade, set in motion, long before *Gilda*, by forty-five-year-old Eddie Judson, eighteen-year-old Rita's first husband when they eloped in 1937. Judson, a former luxury car salesman and huckster, "helped her see that being a Hispanic limited her work as a cinematic loose woman."[25] He then successfully orchestrated the transformation of the overly Spanish-looking Rita Cansino into a beautified Anglicized commodity. Through two years of painful electrolysis to raise her hairline almost one full inch, cutting her long, black, dyed hair shorter, bleaching it, and finally settling on an auburn shade that became her trademark, Rita's physical assets finally fit a white paradigm.[26] The studios and filmdom could then capitalize on Hayworth's heritage considering "the fact of her ethnicity, [which] serves both as a set of origins to be transcended and as the guarantor of her authenticity as a star. . . . Rita Hayworth's Spanish-Irish background represents the out-of-date but still valuable stock from which she is refined, as is provided as evidence that Hayworth's stardom, her talent, and her eroticism are genuine rather than artificial. "[27] Margarita kept silent and smiling with a look of "things pent up in her which she was controlling,"[28] in spite of the domination and incestuous demands of her father. She kept smiling as if a volcano might blow any minute through the fabrication of her Latina self into an Anglo self. Her genuine desire to please was consistent with her professionalism "as a punctual hard-worker."[29] Even when the "star treatment" Columbia Pictures and Harry Cohn gave her during a picture was dismissive and disdainful, Rita remained smiling and hard-working. Jack Cole, her choreographer on *Gilda* recalls, "She never had anything to say about the script or when she was going to work. Harry Cohn could say: 'This is the script, be there Monday 10 a.m. to have your costume fitted.' And that was it. He never asked her if she wanted to do it or whether she liked the script or how she felt about the part. Just do it! As if you were some kind of horse."[30]

Rita's superficial tameness and dutiful compliance are not surprising, considering her victimization at the hands of a rigid taskmaster at such a young age, which set the stage for a lifetime of ill treatment at the hands of the men she fell in and out of love with so easily. Indeed, her behavior underscores her upbringing in a culture that is described as supporting "male dominance beginning in the home . . . [with] female children often [finding] themselves in positions of complying with the male hegemony even when it [is] detrimental to themselves. Their socialization [does] not include learning 'assertive social skills and self confidence' . . . therefore, they [cannot] distinguish when it [is] not only proper but essential to contradict the authority of an older male. Thus, the young woman unwittingly cooperat[es]."[31] From this perspective, Margarita Cansino was a trapped voiceless creature who always cooperated, reenacting her initial submissiveness to her father even after she became the star, Rita Hayworth. The pattern of male exploitation would recur with her adherence to the "male-decision-making"[32] of all five of her husbands, as well as that of the megalomaniacal Cohn. This was her star image, according to the popular conception of Hayworth, yet Adrienne McLean uncovers a more complex and powerful woman in her 2004 study of the star's career. McLean unearths a gifted figure who was ambitious and talented enough to create ground-breaking performances and choreography with Fred Astaire, Gene Kelly, and Valerie Bettis (among the first female choreographers in the Hollywood system), and savvy enough to create her own production company in the late 1940s. Given her work history, McLean wishes to reclaim Hayworth's reputation from ideological feminists who, in their zeal to expose sexism in Hollywood, leave an image that tends to "collapse the meaning of the very vital Hayworth."[33]

The star was in a constant struggle, however, with the men in her life, for, as she observed, "men fell in love with 'Gilda' but they woke up with me."[34] Her second husband, "boy wonder" Orson Welles, wanted to marry "that" (as he called her) pin-up girl when he saw a photograph of a negligee-wearing tease, kneeling in bed, looking over her shoulder suggestively, which appeared in *Life* magazine. In a larger cultural enactment of this kind of objectification, it was variously rumored that Bob Landry's famous 1941 photo of Hayworth eventually graced the nose of the first atom bomb detonated in 1945 or that the name "Gilda" was painted on the weapon.[35] Hayworth despised the thought, but the powerful legend persisted. Welles first objectified and then altered his prized "still photo" by having her long red locks cut and dyed topaz blonde, a procedure witnessed by sixteen press photographers at Columbia. This media event was publicity for her role as Elsa Bannister, the young seductress married to an older man in *The Lady from Shanghai* (1948), written and directed by Welles. Here is a Rita completely shorn of any hint of the Latina-esque. Welles's aim was to foreground her as the bad girl, a seductive (and completely Americanized) amoral goddess transforming the archetype of the Gilda femme fatale (who is really a good girl) to the ultimate cool and calculating killer. At the film's conclusion, her character dies after trying to kill the film's protagonist, Michael O'Hara (Welles). Shortly after, the real-life couple divorced.

Rita's third husband, Prince Aly Khan, legendary Casanova, horse breeder, soldier, pilot, racer, and Muslim, whose family claimed direct descent from the Prophet Mohammed's daughter, fell in love with Rita, or rather, the Gilda archetype.[36] He reportedly screened *Gilda* over and over for himself alone or for friends. The real Hayworth (who left her film career and moved to Europe for him) could never measure up to her onscreen persona and did not try to. After the birth of their daughter, Princess Yasmin, Rita's non-Gilda self—unable to live the frenetic jet-set life of her playboy husband—left Aly and the French Riviera, taking two-year-old Yasmin and six-year-old Rebecca (fathered by Welles) back home to Hollywood in 1951.

An apparently masochistic and self-effacing fourth marriage followed, this time to singer/actor Dick Haymes, a high-living crooner who "was reported to have squandered as much as $4,000,000 in earnings from recordings, nightclub appearances, and film . . . [and who] already had the reputation of a loser, a man on the way down, a deadbeat—'Mr. Evil,' as he was called by the Hollywood community."[37] He took control of Rita's career and most of her assets, forcing her to sell her potentially lucrative production company in order to help cover his enormous debts. Haymes also induced Rita to dance through a "Kafka-esque maze of lawyers and lawsuits,"[38] racking up huge legal fees. In addition, he drove her to leave her girls for long periods of time under improper care with an inadequate nanny, as Rita traveled around the country with Haymes non-stop. For this foolish and lamentable act of misjudgment, Rita almost lost custody of both her daughters on grounds of neglect. Haymes, too, knocked Rita about in abusive behavior witnessed by friends and associates during nightclub outings. These brutal reminders of life with her father became intolerable, and Rita left Haymes in 1955.

During all these unions, Rita was under contract to Columbia Pictures. Directly or indirectly, Cohn attempted to play the evil puppet master, pulling strings to exacerbate her disastrous marriages and excoriate her husbands. Rita had rejected Cohn's casting couch early on in her career, an amazing and uncharacteristic stance considering her background, but for that rejection he would make her pay. Any time she was dating or married, in Cohn's view, Rita was distracted from a film. He even had her dressing room bugged. Cohn wanted total control over her, how she spent her time, how she behaved, and with whom she slept. He also made sure her salary was usually below what she would earn at a rival studio whenever possible.[39]

Rita's last husband, film producer and writer James Hill, who was in love with her long before he met her, documents Cohn's ritual degradation of Rita one afternoon when Hill found himself at her home in Beverly Hills, where she mistook him for a Hollywood cleaning man on Christmas Eve. At the time, she was just dating Aly Khan. In his memoir, Hill describes playing doorman for "Miss Hayworth" and mistaking Cohn for an autograph seeker. Cohn was outraged at Hill for not recognizing him and then ordered his chauffeur to "cream this goddamn crumb, Louie!"[40] Hayworth, however, stopped Hill from being clobbered. Hill then records the ensuing conversation between Cohn and Hayworth:

> "I'm going to give you one last chance, Hayworth. You can join me and the family at the Springs for the holidays. You'll have your own bedroom, where you can sleep alone for a change." The way he laughed made it obvious he planned on visiting that bedroom. "And don't give me that bullshit about being busy, because that prince of yours is fucking his brains out with some model in the Alps."
>
> She paled at this, because he had really hit her where it hurt, but she didn't fold. "He's skiing."
>
> "If you can fuck on skis, then he's skiing. So get your goddamn diaphragm and get your ass in my car."
>
> I thought for sure she was going to break then, because of the way her lower lip trembled. "I'm busy, Mr. Cohn."

> "How many times have I told you not to call me Mr. Cohn!" he bellowed. "I've tried to be nice to you. I've tried to treat you like a lady, but you've done nothing but piss on my efforts of friendship. And don't think it's not going to affect the parts offered you!"[41]

At this point Hill states that Rita "turned back into the living room" and rushed up the stairs.[42] Interestingly, this scene resonates with the very same chords of abusive control she experienced more than twenty years earlier from her father, Eduardo, and in every subsequent intimate relationship. As a producer and writer, Hill was certain that he could remold a new image for Rita as a serious actress when he cast her in *Separate Tables* (1958) opposite Burt Lancaster (her last major film for which she received high praise). Hill married Rita, but the abusive union lasted only two years.

Hill's obituary of January 16, 2001, describes the eighty-four-year-old deceased as "once married to Rita Hayworth" and who, like his wife, died of "complications of Alzheimer's disease."[43] It is ironic that Rita died of the same disease fourteen years earlier at age sixty-eight. Hill had admitted in his memoir that their marriage "fell apart because he forced Hayworth to continue making movies when she wanted both of them to retire from the Hollywood hubbub, enabling her to paint and him to write."[44] Not one man she loved could accept her on her own terms, nor did she ever insist upon them. Her last decades of anguish were diluted into a haze by an illness that, during her lifetime, had no real acknowledgment or recognition from those Hollywood power brokers who quickly lost interest in this star who could no longer labor for them.

Under the influence of Alzheimer's, Rita's behavior became unpredictable as early as 1960, and Hill's head was bloodied more than once due to her temperamental and unexplainable rages. During her later years, she often appeared confused and terrified: "She claimed to hear things in the Beverly Hills house and would insist someone was breaking and entering. No one could convince her that nothing was wrong, and she would call for the police"[45] needlessly. She stopped working in film because she simply could not remember her lines anymore. People mistakenly attributed her violent and emotional outbursts in public and private over the next twenty years to alcoholism, but she was not an alcoholic.

Hayworth's daughter Yasmin commented in an interview that when she would try to approach her mother about her erratic behavior, Rita would deny that anything was wrong.[46] No wonder, considering that a strong denial mechanism had been a way of life for Margarita. Hayworth's condition went undiagnosed until 1981, when Rita was only sixty-two. It was then that Yasmin moved her to New York in an apartment next door where she could provide round-the-clock care for her mother. Rita's death and dementia were the final indignities and suffering she endured.

Her life had indeed endured an unwilling transformation from "ethnic Spanish dancer to all American Love Goddess,"[47] as Priscilla Peña Ovalle writes in *Dance and the Hollywood Latina* (2011), a work that attempts to "unpack the myth of the Hollywood Latina and its role in mitigating tensions surrounding nonwhiteness and gender/sexual equality."[48] The necessity of assimilation "for Latino performers aiming to become mainstream stars with leading roles and far-reaching careers"[49] is one of the frames through which Peña Ovalle views Cansino's cosmetic renovation, yet one cannot help but focus on the painful price Cansino/Hayworth paid for "the exoticism that underscored her Hollywood career as a Love Goddess."[50] Other scholars such as Mary Beltrán and Beretta Smith-Shomade have noted that celebrities, particularly of Hayworth's generation, often avoided acknowledging their ethnic backgrounds because "a noticeable Hispanic accent" led to "a marked and permanent reduction of casting possibilities."[51] Representations of women of color (a phrase not even in the cinematic consciousness in the Hayworth's time) "have been stereotyped, vilified, underserved, ignored, or absent"[52] until the advent of television talk shows hosted by powerful women like Oprah Winfrey, who openly shared her own stories of abuse to the public. But no such forum was available for women like Cansino/Hayworth: "Rita's racial mobility—transition toward whiteness—was ultimately affiliated with Irishness"[53] and becoming "de-ethnicized."[54] The transition from an innocent Margarita Cansino into hot-blooded Rita Hayworth was initially escalated by her pedophiliac father, who enslaved her into no other possible moneymaking role but that of a "fiery temptress."[55] Although this publicized eroticized identity was the antithesis of the person she wanted to be away from the camera, the powerful screen image encouraged and enabled studio heads like Cohn to debase her with seeming impunity. Ultimately, recent feminist critics argue that such tactics were common in Hollywood but not fully successful in breaking the spirit of female stars. For example, Jeanine Basinger comments: "Having interviewed dozens of female stars of the 'golden era' (not Rita Hayworth, although I discussed her with both Gene Kelly and Fred Astaire), I can attest that the majority definitely did not view themselves as victims. They believed themselves to be pioneer career women who accepted studio transformations to further what they thought of as their *own* work."[56]

Basinger attests to McLean's finding that "no secret was ever made of the way in which Margarita Cansino had her name changed, her hair dyed, and her hair-line raised on her way to becoming Rita Hayworth."[57] Studios and publicity magazines were eager to use various forms of rags-to-riches stories to convince women spectators that they, too, could become stars. For those who have followed the details of her life, the makeover from little-known Margaret Cansino to Rita Hayworth's smoldering star persona has struck chords with fans for myriad reasons, from sympathy to admiration. For me it was always my personal identification with her secret suffering that drew me to her story.

CONNECTING WITH A STAR

My ninety-year-old aunt Terri (a devout Rita fan) and I sip tea one afternoon at her home in the Hollywood Hills and flip through photographs of Margarita and her transmutation into Rita Hayworth. We discuss our family's French pastry shop, which used to be on Vine Street just a short walk south of Sunset Boulevard. As we often do in my family, we speak in Spanish and English, switching back and forth rapidly wherever the syntactical structure leads us. Given that Terri and her siblings moved to Los Angeles from Mexico (escaping the revolution) in 1924, they consistently spoke Spanish with my indigenous Mexican grandmother and French with their French Basque father in the home and in the shop. In its heyday in the 1930s and 1940s, my grandfather's patisserie, Balagué Bakery, provided countless gourmet cakes, pastries, and desserts to the major film studios and the stars of the period. My aunt loves talking about those days because she waited on most of the famous customers who came in to buy goodies, as she called them. Rita was one of them.

We begin looking at photographs in various biographies of Rita. We pause on one taken of her dressed in that erotically black strapless Gilda-glam-gown.

"But here her hair was lightened . . . *pero,* she had an affair with her father, you know that?"

"Well, tell me what you remember? What do you recall about dealing with her, if anything?"

"Very charming, she came in *con su papá*, Eduardo Cansino, *pero la trataba groseramente* [but he treated her rudely]. He would be wearing a hat, something like a Gaucho hat almost. He wasn't very nice to her."

"Was he stern?"

"Not stern, just crude."

"Crude?"

"Crude. He would say '*¡Bruta! ¿Que te pasa? ¡Eres tan burra! ¿No sabes caminar?' Y cuando se metían al carro, él se metía primero.* [Stupid, what is wrong with you? You are such an ass, don't you know how to walk?]"

"You saw him speak to her like that in the bakery?"

"When she was a little girl. . . . This was in 1931. *Estaban en* Tijuana. [When they were in Tijuana.] He saw a way of making money."

"Right, the dancing. Here she is dressed as a dancer. She looks quite Spanish."

Terri and I stare at the photo of Eduardo and Margarita posed in a faux kiss for one of their dance routines. We examine an early black-and-white studio still of Margarita before she underwent electrolysis treatments to alter her hairline. She looks fifteen or sixteen. Her hair is raven, parted in the center, combed straight back and knotted at her neck. She stares off into the distance, camera left. Her hands are folded in front of her, relaxed, fingers elegantly extended. She wears a wide-striped, long-sleeved dress. The dress looks cream, the stripes the color of mercury. There are two roses sewn onto the front of the dress, level with her covered breasts. Her hands barely brush against these roses—one black, the other white. Her lips are in a slight pout with dark lipstick that looks the color of smoke. What is she thinking? Terri and I look up from the photograph.

"Oh you know she was fatter than that. When she came into the shop, she spoke in Spanish. *'Y con éstas cosas me voy a poner gorda.'* [Eating these will make me fat.]"

"So she would come in occasionally to buy some things?"

"Yes, like in Europe, you go and buy this and that."

"Would you ever chat with her a little?"

"Ohh, a little bit. *Y decía 'Sabe usted, parece que me van a dar una parte.'* [You know, they are going to give me a part.] *'Hay magnífico señorita, magnífico.'* [How magnificent, Miss, magnificent.] *Pero no era elegante. Caminaba, pero no tenía la gracia.* [But she really was not that elegant when she walked.]"

"Did she ever come in with Rebecca or with Yasmin?"

"Solamente con Yasmin. Yasmin la cogía y la besaba [Only with Yasmin. She would hug Yasmin and kiss her] and the nurse would tell me, 'They're so close.' *Era una señora . . . como . . .* [She was a lady . . . but] she was afraid. She was shining when she went in the movies, but otherwise she'd be afraid of her own shadow."

"So how many times did she come into the shop?"

"*Con su papá la vi como cuatro veces. Y siempre estaba parada detrás de él* [She came in with her father four times, but she always walked behind him]. . . . If you think she got beaten up by her father, this guy Haymes was worse. When she would come in she looked so beautiful all in blue, but . . . I knew she was hiding something."

"Did she have a scarf on, or a hat?"

"No, no, no a scarf."

"She had a little bruise? And you just figured it out?"

"*Es que no hablaba mucho* [She didn't talk much]," Aunt Terri said softly. "Howard Hughes wanted her too. They all abused her. They all did. Rita, though, was social looking but she never flashed herself. Courteous, but never pushy."

"Not a glamour queen?"

"She was humble in a way. She would talk softly. Answer nicely. *Y le decía una o dos veces* [And she would say, a couple times] to her daughter, 'Ma petite.'"

Terri and I continue to flip through the photographs of Margarita and her transfiguration into Rita Hayworth by a variety of photographers. I recognize and understand that look of posing, because I grew up around a photographer. My father was an excellent portrait photographer who began his career as a stand-in and an extra in the 1930s, when he became a photographer's apprentice. Just as Eduardo did to Margarita, my father also looked upon me with a similar sexually perverse intent, something he made known to me in secret at a similarly young age. I, too, remained silent about this agonizing secret for most of my life.

My father was not a Latin, but my mother, Henriette, was. She was determined to be just the opposite of the silent and suffering male-dominated Latina. Typically fiery, sensuous, beautiful, and flirtatious, my mother was a Dolores Del Rio lookalike, as the photographs my father took of her in the late 1940s reveal. Her independent, peremptory nature squelched any hope for a successful long-term marriage to my father—a handsome, Tyrone Power clone. He was charming, adulterous, and he refused to be pushed around. He enjoyed spending money, but not necessarily the effort involved in making it.

My mother was more of a Gilda, at least Rita Hayworth's characterization in *Gilda*. Mother was a model of outspokenness and confrontation, so much so that I usually veered in the direction of avoidance. I would avoid confrontation, avoid stirring up anything that would make my father angry, avoid upsetting parents who were already embroiled in fallout from a tense divorce. I finally confessed to Mother how my father liked taking nude photographs of his fifteen-year-old daughter, throwing sexual commentary in to make me *relax* under the hot lights (among other things). My mother went on a rampage and called her ex-husband "a dirty old man," a phrase he detested. He disliked growing old and rejected the notion that anything to do with any form of sex was dirty. She threatened legal action and all the incriminating photographs immediately arrived overloaded with apologies and puerile explanations.

It was not until I was middle-aged that I was ready to reveal the whole truth to anyone willing to listen. Mother had fought for me *como una tigresa*. Hence, unlike Rita, I did not suffer in silence, hating my father as Rita did. I did not recall this period merely "with a shudder"[58] as Rita did of her own childhood; as a grown woman I refused to suppress my painful experience any longer. I came out with my feelings and finally let the truth be known, to my father and my family. This was something Rita could never do because no one fought for her. Rita could never have borne the

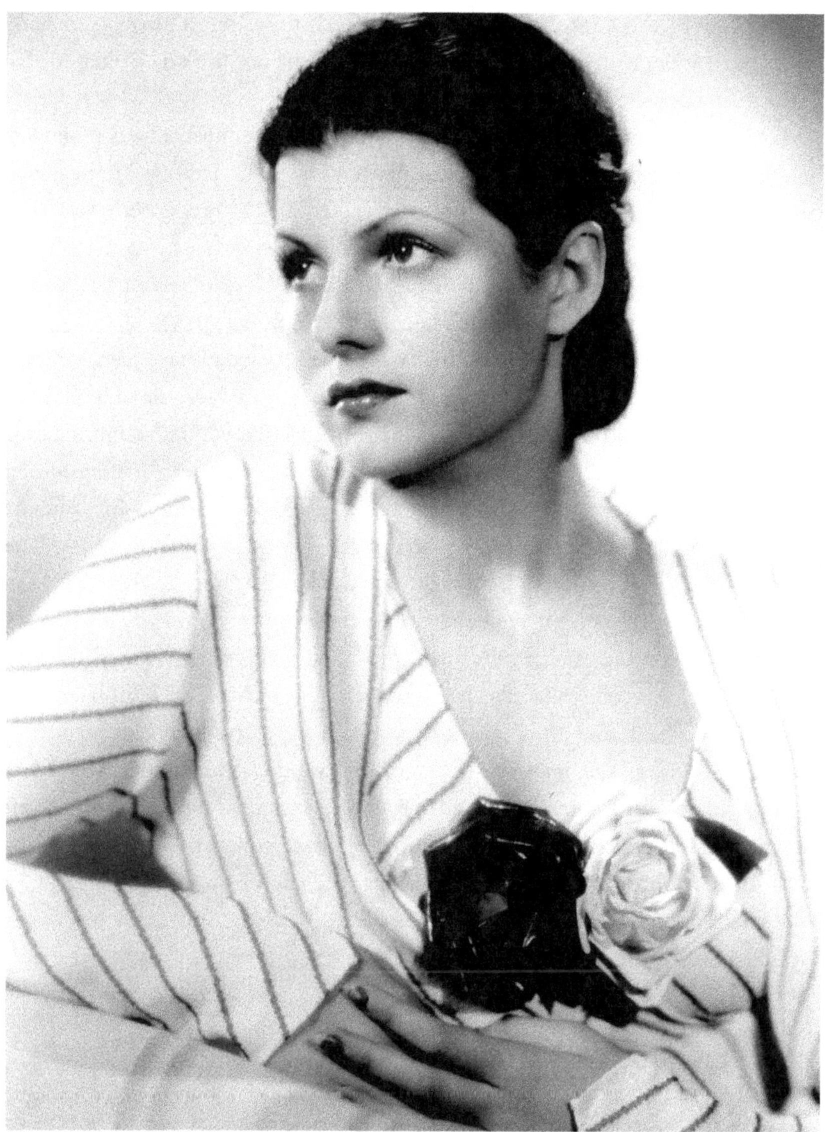

A young Margarita Cansino, date unknown. Collection of the author.

outrage of her family members as I had to—not from my mother's family, but from my father's Anglo family. They and my father chose to react with stereotypical denial, refusing to accept any responsibility for my father's egregious behavior. It was far easier for them to justify my father's behavior or put the blame on my misremembered youth, or on the bitter retaliation of a divorced, histrionic Latina mother.

I think of these intertwined stories as Terri insists on getting up to make more tea. I gaze at that one photograph of Rita, but not the one in her famous black satin strapless, inspired by John Singer Sargent's painting of Mrs. X for the "Mame" number in *Gilda*. No, the one that compels me most now is pubescent Margarita in the photographer's studio, posing. She looks nervous, but in silence she does what she is told—a response I recall from my own experience. Margarita's photographer does not even realize she speaks English, she is so mute. I want to walk in there and say: Don't. Don't do it. *No lo haces, mija*. Walk away. Leave. Now. While you still can. It's not worth it, not really.

She has that look like a frightened fawn—the very look I have seen of myself in those photos that my father took of me decades ago, nude, vulnerable, and terrified. I want to hold that young girl that I was, and that young Margarita, until I cry, until we both cry. I want to reassure her that she's done nothing wrong, that she does not have to stay under the hot lights and keep on posing. She can ignore the man behind the camera who directs: Rest your hands this way. Place your chin that way, turn your body a little to the left, no, more to the right, stop. Stop. Yes that's it. Look off camera. Just like that.

No, not just like that, I say. Turn, stand, and walk out that door. Yes, that one over there, the one marked exit. It's okay. Really. I know you want happiness. Doesn't every girl? But there's another way. I swear there is, *mijita. Andale, ya es tiempo. Vamanos*. Go, it's time. Let's go. And we do. We walk out slowly. She hesitates. I reach for her lengthened, elegantly manicured nails. Our hands are almost identical in size. We wear the same color nail polish: million-dollar red. I push the door open. Margarita looks back at the studio. She wonders aloud, "If this was supposed to be happiness, what will the happy ending really be?"

I smile.

NOTES

1. Rita Hayworth (formerly Marguerite [Margarita] Cansino) is referred to here as "Rita," in part to acknowledge her original Hispanic name and the close emotional attachment of the essay's author to her subject, and as "Hayworth," her professional name throughout.
2. Jeanine Basinger, *A Woman's View* (Middletown, Conn.: Wesleyan University Press, 1993), 72.
3. Ibid., 144.
4. Ibid.
5. John Kobal, *Rita Hayworth: The Time, the Place and the Woman* (New York: W.W. Norton, 1978), 18.
6. Barbara Leaming, *If This Was Happiness* (New York: Viking, 1989), 6.
7. Jeanine Basinger, *The Star Machine* (New York: Vintage Books, 2009), 145.

8. Ibid., 144.
9. Leaming, *If This Was Happiness*, 4.
10. Kobal, *Rita Hayworth*, 24.
11. Leaming, *If This Was Happiness*, 16.
12. Kobal, *Rita Hayworth*, 44.
13. Ibid., 48.
14. Leaming, *If This Was Happiness*, 17.
15. Ibid., 20.
16. Ibid.
17. Ibid., 25.
18. Kobal, *Rita Hayworth*, 47.
19. Leaming, *If This Was Happiness*, 15.
20. Ibid., 17. Orson Welles, Hayworth's second husband, revealed this to Leaming in 1983, when she was researching for her biography of Welles.
21. Ibid., 25.
22. Kobal, *Rita Hayworth*, 95.
23. Leaming, *If This Was Happiness*, 37.
24. William Vincent, "Rita Hayworth at Columbia: The Fabrication of a Star," in *Columbia Pictures: Portrait of a Studio*, ed. Bernard F. Dick (Lexington: University Press of Kentucky, 1992), 128.
25. Valerie Menard, "Luscious Latinas," *Hispanic* 10, no. 5 (1997): 22.
26. Adrienne L. McLean, "I'm a Cansino: Transformation, Ethnicity, and Authenticity in the Construction of Rita Hayworth, American Love Goddess," *Journal of Film and Video* 44, no. 3–4 (1992–93): 23.
27. Ibid., 12.
28. Kobal, *Rita Hayworth*, 70.
29. Ibid., 203.
30. Ibid.
31. Elizabeth Rodriguez Kessler, "Language, Nature, Gender, and Sexuality: Theoretical Approaches to Chicana and Chicano Literature" (Ph.D. diss., University of Houston, 1998), 267–68.
32. Ibid., 269.
33. Adrienne L. McLean, *Being Rita Hayworth: Labor, Identity, and Hollywood Stardom* (New Brunswick, N.J.: Rutgers University Press, 2004), 4.
34. Ibid, 1.
35. Kobal, *Rita Hayworth*, 130.
36. Leaming, *If This Was Happiness*, 153.
37. Ibid., 237.
38. Ibid.
39. Joe Morella and Edward Epstein, *Rita: The Life of Rita Hayworth* (New York: Delacorte Press, 1983),
40. James Hill, *Rita Hayworth: A Memoir* (New York: Simon and Schuster, 1983), 21.
41. Ibid.
42. Ibid.

43. Myna Oliver, "James Hill; Producer-Writer Married Rita Hayworth, Teamed with Burt Lancaster," *Los Angeles Times*, January 16, 2001, B12.
44. Ibid.
45. Albin Krebs, "Rita Hayworth, Movie Legend, Dies," *New York Times*, May 6, 1987.
46. Yasmin Aga Khan, "Remembering Rita," *People Weekly*, June 1, 1987, 72.
47. Priscilla Peña Ovalle, *Dance and the Hollywood Latina* (New Brunswick, N.J.: Rutgers University Press, 2011), 3.
48. Ibid.
49. Ibid., 20.
50. Ibid.
51. Lisa Jarvinen, Review of *Latina/o Stars in U.S. Eyes: The Makings and Meanings of Film and TV Stardom* by Mary C. Beltrán, *Journal of American Ethnic History* 31, no. 3 (2012): 72–76.
52. Sharon D. Johnson, "Shaded Lives: African-American Women and Television," *Black Issues Book Review*, no. 44 (2002): 52–53.
53. Peña Ovalle, *Dance and the Hollywood Latina*, 75.
54. Ibid., 76.
55. Ibid., 81.
56. Jeanine Basinger, Review of *Being Rita Hayworth: Labor, Identity, and Hollywood Stardom* by Adrienne McLean, *Film Quarterly* 60, no. 1 (Fall 2006): 61.
57. Ibid., 60.
58. Kobal, *Rita Hayworth*, 47.

7

Baby, It's Cold Out in Hollywood: Rock Hudson's Multiple Masculinities

Rebecca Bell-Metereau

> It could be claimed that Rock Hudson was one of the greatest actors who ever lived: a gay man who became an unassailable international symbol of heterosexuality.
>
> Keith Howes, *GLBTQ Encyclopedia*

WHEN ROCK HUDSON SANG "BABY, IT'S COLD OUTSIDE" WITH MAE WEST at the 1957 Academy Awards, Hollywood insiders saw the irony of their pairing as a camp couple.[1] Few fans from the general public of that era would have recognized anything unusual about this duo, other than the reverse December-"Mae" aspect of their age difference. Even this disparity would have made sense in the context of West's reputation for indiscriminant naughtiness and Hudson's performance as the much younger love interest in Douglas Sirk's successful 1955 melodrama, *All That Heaven Allows*. Throughout the following years, rumors about Hudson's sexuality simmered, but, as he told Boze Hadleigh in 1982, "America does not want to know" about homosexual stars.[2] Hudson's manager,

Henry Willson, and the publicity engines of stardom all worked to keep Hudson's (and others') sexual orientation hidden from the public for fear of damage to their star products.

Once Hudson was forced out of the closet as a man with AIDS in 1985, everyone around the world saw the man behind the screen, and the general public's relation to the star—and indeed to stardom itself—was irrevocably altered. The revelation of his illness was one of the most dramatic instances in Hollywood history of when the façade of stardom fractured, revealing a gap between public and private identities, disturbing fans who had difficulty reconciling the familiar narratives of an iconic star with a strikingly different private life. Although the popular narrative is one of disbelief, Richard Dyer contests the notion "that it was surprising to think that Rock Hudson was gay, that there is a contrast between how he seemed in public appearances and how he was in private, that there was nothing gay about Rock as performer or image."[3] In his reading of Hudson's film performances, Dyer sees a "parade of the signs of masculinity without any real assertion of it," presenting "endlessly deferred gratification."[4] The continually evolving case of Hudson's contested public personae and personal selves offers an opportunity to investigate the delicate balance between image and identity in stardom and the constant tensions at play in an actor's performance in public and in private, particularly in the realm of sexual orientation in all its mercurial Hollywood glory.

Although much of the fan and critical literature describes Rock Hudson in monochromatic terms, the development of his persona and his growth as an actor constantly morphed throughout his career, as his roles migrated from adventure to melodrama and comedy, moving from commercially successful tear-jerkers with Jane Wyman and light comedic roles with Doris Day to an Oscar nomination for his performance in George Stevens's lavish Texas epic, *Giant* (1956). Further expanding his range later in his career, Hudson took on his most challenging role in the offbeat John Frankenheimer film *Seconds* (1966), which went from utter flop to cult favorite, in a film and performance that merit serious reconsideration. Early in his career, Hudson's personal appeal as a handsome gay man had attracted the devotion of Willson, an agent who catapulted him from an obscure life as wannabe actor to star status, if accounts of the casting couch are to be believed. The hidden identity that contributed to Hudson's stardom from the beginning problematized his performance and reception of his work by exposing a disruption that continues to fascinate viewers.

The ultimate shattering of Hudson's star image was famously connected with his covert homosexuality, but according to many in Hollywood, Hudson's story before 1985 was typical in that he expended almost as much acting energy managing his star persona as he did performing his dramatic roles. When publicity about his medical condition brought about the ultimate demise of his previously heterosexual star image, the public was suddenly forced to reevaluate social attitudes toward homosexuality and the AIDS epidemic. The news also prompted an ongoing reassessment of Hudson's performance as actor and icon of traditional masculinity. When the star was finally forced by his illness to come out as a gay man, American viewers were suddenly privileged to witness the hidden struggles of an actor whose publicity and acting roles had once seemed to embody the ultimate in conventional masculinity. This revelation exposed stardom as a public display that simultaneously belies and enhances performance. Because Hudson was a beloved star, his admission and his plight put a human, sympathetic face on a disease that had initially caused panic and hysteria, but Dyer maintains that the star's death "has also been used to reinforce venerable myths about gay men."[5] Even if one accepts Dyer's argument, fans and the public at large ultimately experienced a profound and relatively rapid transformation in the way they saw the disease and the star.

Examination of the hidden spectacle of Hudson's efforts to conceal his forbidden and stigmatized sexual orientation—in conjunction with a consideration of how Hudson's personal life affected his roles and how his roles affected him—promises new insight into the performance of an actor who was considered simple, even flat, during his heyday. The creation of Rock Hudson as a star and the disintegration of his iconic reputation as he neared the end of his career merit discussion because his experience serves as a template for a number of other stars whose personal identities clash with their star images and public careers in various ways. With minor variations, his is the story of countless other gay actors, who simultaneously concealed their homosexuality and exploited the personal lessons learned from having to live at least two distinct lives to deepen and problematize their performances.

TWO BODIES AND MULTIPLE MASCULINITIES

The Midwest truck driver born Roy Fitzgerald (later Roy Scherer Jr.) owed his screen name, Rock Hudson, and much of his physique and style to Willson, an agent and image coach who was known in inside circles as the "fairy godfather of Hollywood."[6] Hudson's career came into being under the guidance of a mentor who lavished as much attention on the hairstyles and color, gestures, speech, and clothing of his largely gay male clients as the studios generally did on their female stars. Willson transformed Roy's body and manners from those of a blue-collar laborer with poor teeth and unpolished diction to the image of one of the hottest leading men in Hollywood. Although many stars of the 1950s were rigidly typecast, Hudson managed to demonstrate a remarkable range over the span of his career, suggesting a subtle depth that was unusual for the so-called beefcakes Willson brought to fame, such as Troy Donahue, Tab Hunter, and Rory Calhoun. Willson was able to spot talent as well as beauty, and he served as agent to a bigger mix of more substantial stars, including Olivia de Havilland, Lana Turner, Natalie Wood, and her husband Robert Wagner, all part of a stable that gave Willson a reputation as one of the most powerful agents in Hollywood.

From the beginning, Hudson's potential as a putative star was predicated on the beauty of his body, a potentially feminizing element in his public persona. Early public attention came from Willson's brilliant and daring exhibition of that physique at two consecutive Press Photographers Balls. First Rock was paired with Vera-Ellen, both wearing nothing but skimpy bathing suits and gold paint (which made Hudson sick afterward), impersonating twin Oscars. The next year, Hudson's body was again on display as the Wild Man of Borneo, wearing only a tiny loincloth, his skin painted black. This dazzlingly over-the-top and arguably racist gesture, which would later be seen as outrageous high camp, laid the groundwork for his arrival as an up-and-coming figure on the Hollywood scene. Willson had an eye for raw sex appeal—male and female—but he found himself at a disadvantage in jockeying for power and influence against aggressive alpha males such as David O. Selznick, who rejected his ideas for luring people like Montgomery Clift, Frank Sinatra, and James Whale to the studio.

Given all these factors in the Hollywood hierarchy, both Willson and Hudson had to transition the actor from flagrant displays of his body (in a flashy way that was distinctly feminine) to an extreme version of masculine "drag." His acting potential was not immediately apparent, however, as he delivered early wooden performances that could have condemned him to the worst actors' Hall of Fame. Initially infamous for his difficulty in delivering lines, Hudson needed thirty-eight attempts to get an acceptable take for a single sentence in *Fighter Squadron* (1948). Despite this unpromising debut, he eventually responded well to coaching, not just in acting but also in an array of other activities required for action films, from sword fighting to horseback riding. Hudson reinvented himself when he snagged the role of John Wesley Hardin in *The Lawless Breed* (1953), with coaching from the homophobic director Raoul Walsh. The actor played a convincing Hardin as a brash young man and then a hard-bitten father, who ages twenty years in the course of the narrative.

Just as Hudson's adaptability in acting revealed itself to Walsh, the malleability of the actor's body struck director Douglas Sirk: "Rock Hudson was not an educated man, but that very beautiful body of his was putty in my hands."[7] Beyond Hudson's physical attributes, Sirk spotted something he claimed only the camera could highlight: "It sees things the human eye does not detect. And ultimately you learn to trust your camera. And it was not wrong about Hudson."[8] The actor blossomed in his ability to emote, once he began working with Sirk, who saw a sweet, natural quality in Hudson that he nurtured in a series of melodramas. Sirk didn't foreground his awareness of Hudson's sexual orientation, but he may have empathized with the role of a man obliged to hide a secret identity. Sirk himself was no stranger to subterfuge, having emigrated from Nazi Germany, where he had been an intellectual leftist in a second marriage to a Jewish woman. Mark Rappaport has noted the apparent father-son element of Douglas Sirk's relationship with Hudson, born the same year as Sirk's own son, who had died fighting for the Nazis in 1942.[9]

The themes of deception and transformation, which mark a number of films of the fifties,[10] are at the core of Hudson's breakout film, *Magnificent Obsession*, Sirk's 1954 remake of the 1934 film adaptation of Lloyd C. Douglas's popular novel. The film features a secret mentor (Otto Kruger) who bears a remarkable physical resemblance to Sirk, and who also parallels the real-life relationship between actor and director. Kruger plays an artist who guides Hudson's character, wealthy and selfish Bob Merrick, to a life of professional expertise and genuine sacrifice. Jane Wyman portrays Ellen Phillips, a widow whose selfless husband, Dr. Phillips, died because Merrick was being treated with the only medical equipment that could have saved her husband's life—exactly when he needed it, of course. Compounding unlikely plot twists, Merrick then inadvertently causes a car accident that results in Ellen's blindness. Hudson manages to play his character's improbable transformation from playboy to secular saint somewhat credibly, as Merrick realizes what he has done and eventually converts to Phillips's selfless philosophy. In order to save Ellen's sight, Merrick returns to his own abandoned medical studies to transform himself into someone who may be able to cure her and prove himself worthy of her love. Years later, when he is called on to perform a complicated surgery to save her life, he freezes, until a glance up into the gallery reveals his mentor's face, smiling down and conveying the self-confidence that Merrick needs to perform.

Although Sirk's melodrama is a bit more implausible than Hudson's real life, the actor's personal experience resembles the character's position in an essential way when he is unable to perform. The young Hudson lacked confidence, a notion that both Sirk and Hudson mention repeatedly in interviews. Sirk's patient direction provided the reinforcement he needed to succeed, as the actor explains: "Without saying so, he said, 'Come on, you can do it.' . . . Douglas Sirk took me under his wing; he was like old dad to me and I was like his son, I think. When you're scared and new and trying to figure out this thing and suddenly an older man will reach out and say, there, there, it's ok; that was Sirk."[11] The actor and his roles function in perfect consort, solidifying and amplifying each other, in a model of the symbiotic star and publicity dynamic.

This pattern of a repeated real-life story that mirrors film roles is a common feature of publicity pieces, but what is notable is the effectiveness of Hudson's delivery of these anecdotes. From one decade to the next, even from one continent to the next, Hudson talks in interviews about this relationship with a casual sincerity, as if he were recounting favorite family stories. The standard way to explain such a match between the actor's film roles and personal life is that it simply typifies the workings of Hollywood publicity and the celebrity machine in general, in a time-honored technique. Ever since the sixteenth century's doctrine of the king's two bodies, iconic celebrities and leaders have both intentionally and accidentally melded publicity about their private and public lives, with both celebrities and society confabulating historical, personal, and fictional events, in a pattern noted by Michael Rogin and other critics.[12] In modern Hollywood, as Anne Helen Petersen argues, "The way to win the publicity game is to look like you're not playing at all."[13] Another more nuanced interpretation of Hudson's growth as an actor is that he was not merely role-playing, nor was Sirk. Rather, both men may have been participating in the sort of transference that often occurs in relationships. Sirk treated Hudson as a surrogate for his lost son, and Hudson reacted to Sirk as a replacement for the father who had abandoned him in his early childhood. This version of the story may be viewed with skepticism as mere wish fulfillment for fans, or it may be seen as a more complicated function of the actor in society, as a figure whose heightened fictional crises mirror and crystalize real-life struggles for the actor and for viewers who identify with their film dilemmas and real (if slightly distorted) personal lives.

Within this matrix of relationships, *Magnificent Obsession*'s combination of sympathetic stars and sappy story hit emotional pay dirt with fifties' audiences, hungry for narratives of self-reinvention. The impact for Universal studios was enormous, delivering the second highest box office of 1954. The relatively underpowered Universal was one of the most successful studios in diversifying their offerings and tying television and magazine promotion to their films, saturating women's outlets for all ages, as well as general publications, to create a "date" movie as well as a family film that would draw in both women and men. The effect on Hudson's career was similarly smashing, establishing his star profile and creating a particular type of identity that seemed to recur across genres. As Dyer and others have noted, even in a movie era notable for narratives of secret lives, Hudson had more than his share of roles that called on him to hide his identity, to take on a false personality, transform himself, or impersonate a different character in order to accomplish his goals.

Instead of seeing Hudson's remarkable adaptability as a feature of his persona, critics—particularly those writing before 1985—tend to see in Hudson a consistency and lack of complication or depth, arising perhaps more from a unified-image conception of stardom than from evidence of the actual performances and career of the actor. Barbara Klinger suggests that Hudson "functioned defensively against changing conceptions of masculine power and sexuality in the post–World War II era. In a society obsessively concerned with the problem of male 'weakness,' posed as a result of such social specters as the 'modern woman' and the 'homosexual menace,' the media developed Hudson's image as proof of the widespread appeal and endurance of uncomplicated virility."[14] While this paradigm might apply to some of his films, reading his appeal in this way doesn't fully account for his breakout success in *Magnificent Obsession* and the follow-up popularity of *All That Heaven Allows*, or, for that matter, his effectiveness in comedies that called on him to alter his personality and behavior—often to abandon unfettered masculinity and choose a very non-masculine domesticity.

Far from representing "uncomplicated virility," Hudson often serves not so much as a model of masculinity for males as he functions as the object of fantasy for middle-aged women, particularly those trapped in the gender and social constraints of 1950s domesticity. Richard Meyer observes that, "as the object of

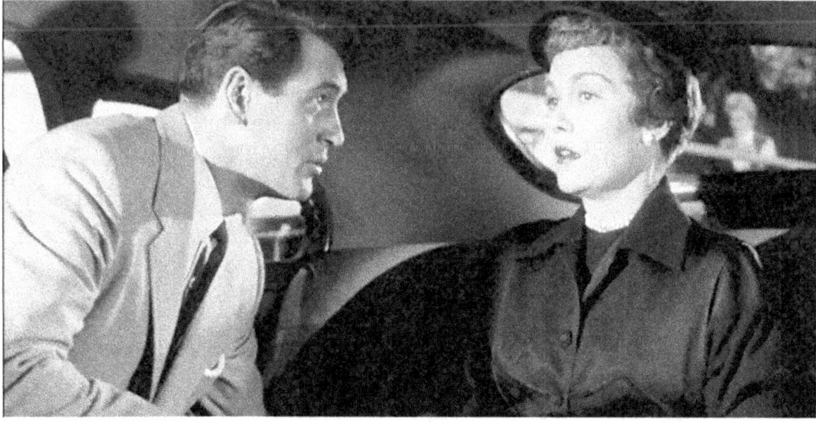

Rock Hudson's body and face appear restrained and gentle as he interacts with Jane Wyman's "older woman" character in *Magnificent Obsession* (1954).

a desiring, implicitly female gaze, Hudson's masculinity is at once less aggressive and more eroticized than that of the conventional male hero of Hollywood film."[15] Sirk comments on the age difference in *Magnificent Obsession* as "no big deal; she was 38 he was 29," but clearly the handsome young Hudson was cast to appeal to older women.[16] Such leading women as Jane Wyman and Doris Day, often paired with Hudson in his most successful roles, are not ingénues. They are attractive in particularly non-threatening and almost asexual ways, with short hair, turned up noses, and baby doll faces that carry elements of the matron combined with the infant. The restrained relationships with these women and Hudson's controlled body language naturally conform to the demands of the restrictive Hays Code, but his combined towering height and the graceful way he carries his body also give the impression of someone who is at once protective yet docile, powerful yet obedient. Meyer claims that "part of the appeal of Rock Hudson's body, then, was that it seemed somewhat immobile, available as an object of erotic delectation but without the threat of male action," during a "cultural moment when young women were often reminded of their 'duty' to rebuff the erotic advances of their male companions."[17] I would argue that a slightly different dynamic occurs for an intended audience of older women, who are not virgins but who may identify with the actor, who plays characters that appear less than confident in aggressively displaying their sexuality. Meanwhile, he exhibits an open easiness in expressing affection for male father figures, again diminishing the potential menace of such a large physique, for both men and women, through a set of caretaking mannerisms that appears in a number of his films.

Tamar Jeffers McDonald argues that during Hudson's comic performance of masculine sexual restraint or virginity—far from signaling what Dyer identifies as a less "manly" identity—"the men are at their most priapically heterosexual."[18] She goes on to complicate Dyer's reading of Hudson's roles by arguing that the actor's performance of comic masculine virginity gives him "the chance to perform troubled characters, albeit in comic mode," permitting a "range of aberrations at that, as virginity shades into homosexuality and impotence," suggesting that pairing "comedy with the new Hudson personae and their introduction of new possibilities of male subjecthood thus relieves some of the tensions and anxieties" of "non-normative masculinities."[19] While McDonald's interpretation provides a depth and resonance different from the points of Dyer or Meyer, it still neglects consideration of the allure of such figures for 1960s (or later) females, in favor of a focus on male reception of the star text. But what, exactly, constitutes the appeal for *women* of Hudson's performance of ambiguous masculine figures? Dyer and Meyer seem to assume and argue that women—trained to be virginal—are relieved at the prospect of avoiding sex altogether. Overlooked is the possibility that women find exciting the prospect of being the aggressor in a way that actually does result in having sex, but a version of sex that is on their terms, at their pace. Another and not mutually exclusive possibility is the notion that some women enjoy seeing a man enact (even in a feigned way) the same kind of anxiety or hesitance that women themselves may experience in regard to sexuality—fears of frigidity, abnormalcy, or inadequacy—precisely because women do not follow the aggressive, often speedy, self-confident model of masculine sexual behavior. The very act of presenting a deceptive sexual stance may also appeal to women, who are culturally encouraged to behave in a way that masks their own desires. Women may also take pleasure at identifying with a female character—socialized in the arts of sexual deception—who outsmarts a male at the game of masquerade, offering, as Jackie Stacey argues, "the qualities of confidence and power."[20]

Hudson's restrained, unassuming body language fits neatly with the publicity picture of Hudson as non-threatening, appreciative, humble, yet polished, a combination of traits socially encouraged among women, both for themselves and their male partners. Just as Hudson's portrayed relationship with Sirk has a narrative arc, so do his relationships with Wyman, Day, and Elizabeth Taylor, among other female co-stars. He explains that Wyman, like Sirk, was incredibly generous during filming of *Magnificent Obsession*.[21] When the beginning actor thanked her for being patient with him, he reports that she told him it was given to her and she was just passing it on to him, a concept that is echoed in the plot of the film. No doubt, these similarities are manufactured correspondences, story lines learned in the same way that politicians learn to repeat their messages in a consistent, disciplined fashion. However, does it necessarily follow that these "actors" don't ever believe in what they are saying? They may, indeed, find themselves affected and shaped by the messages they deliver and the roles they play. Hudson's apparent malleability defies the supposedly stable image of "virility" or fixed identity we associate with male stars of the fifties. Hudson performs both sincerity and its apparently opposite quality of changeability in a convincing way, perhaps because these attributes conform to those he learned in order to survive as a star.

Another element that feminizes Hudson's persona, the imagery of architecture and interiors associated with Hudson's characters, also merits examination. In an attempt to discover a similarly "uncomplicated" consistency in the domain of melodrama, Thomas Elsaesser describes how the careful placement of objects in the interior sets of melodramas signals the "characteristic attempt of the bourgeois household to make time stand still, immobilize life, and fix forever domestic property relations as the model of social life."[22] The showy bourgeois trappings of Wyman's first husband's house in *All That Heaven Allows* conform to Elsaesser's description, but overall Hudson is placed in interiors that are in the midst of transformation, sometimes throughout the entire narrative. The confinement and stuffiness of Wyman's husband's house contrasts with the rustic interiors of Hudson's small greenhouse cabin and the mill house. The closing of the film has Wyman commenting on how beautiful the mill house is, and a mutual friend says that he had been working on remodeling it for her. In Michael Gordon's *Pillow Talk* (1959), Doris Day plays an interior decorator, and the end of the film features her redesigning the playboy apartment in garish brothel style, taking a jab at Hudson's predatory playboy character by making a seductive nest for him. He then explains that he hired her as a decorator because he wanted to create a place that would make her truly happy, not to update his bachelor's seduction chamber. His willingness to transform domestic space and align it with female wishes at the film's resolution goes counter to the stereotype of fifties stagnation and unbending masculine domination, in a fantasy rejection of conformity that may be interpreted as reflecting resistance against gender stereotypes.

The domestic "interior decorating" motif that runs through a number of Hudson's films goes well beyond the stereotype of preferred gay career choices. Rather, it echoes repeated themes of interiority, safety, comfort, and security. Hudson mentions in an interview that the element that empowered him as an actor working with George Stevens on *Giant* was the director making him feel secure, as if he could have whatever he wanted, particularly when Stevens consulted with him on what the house in Texas should look like. Instead of a dull, white, Victorian mansion, Hudson wanted tan and maroon, a colorful and personal option. The actor also comments on how Stevens would make him feel as if he had thought of ideas, even though Stevens had been the one who knew all along what he was looking for. Reading against the grain of traditional masculinity to discover such bursts of color and variation offers an alternative understanding for both the roles and personal identity of the star. It is also interesting to note that while Hudson chose a non-masculine color scheme for "his" house, he played with quiet strength and gravity a masculine and restrained Texan, which he later transformed into the exaggerated, almost campy masquerade of the Texan Rex Stetson in *Pillow Talk*.

Such intertextual references and in-jokes in Hudson's career are striking, even in comparison to the careers of actors whose star identities rely on similar covert and overt connections among roles. Hudson's roles often play off against his own past roles and against other actors whose effeminate gestures stand as a foil to the overt heterosexuality of the actor's persona. In both films with Doris Day, Hudson's relative restraint contrasts with the fussiness of Tony Randall. Indeed, in Norman Jewison's *Send Me No Flowers* (1964), Hudson's character actually spends the night in bed alongside Randall's Nervous Nelly character. In Howard Hawks's comedy *Man's Favorite Sport?* (1964), Hudson plays a sort of metrosexual author of fishing books who must masquerade uncomfortably as an outdoorsman, even though he's never actually been fishing. While Hudson's pairing with the beautiful Paula Prentiss highlights his sexual appeal, his character's discomfort with the demands of manly outdoor life simultaneously undermines and problematizes his supposed masculinity. In John Sturges's *Ice Station Zebra* (1968), Hudson is at his most understatedly and convincingly masculine, cleverly underplaying scenes with British actor Patrick McGoohan, whose showy, exaggerated gestures appear mannered and effeminate by contrast. Hudson's range in terms of gender and genre is remarkable, especially in light of the common and, I would argue, false wisdom about Hudson's lack of acting skill and depth.

In an effort to get at the effect of public knowledge of an actor's personal life on viewers' perceptions of performance, Mark Rappaport constructed a film tribute entitled *Rock Hudson's Home Movies* (1992). As a testament to the inadequacy of traditional, chronological historical analysis of star figures, this film is narrated by Rappaport, as Hudson, with snippets of films that demonstrate—in his view—a purported gay undertone. In response, Hudson's personal assistant and thirty-year friend, Mark Miller, ridicules the notion that Hudson infused his roles with gayness or that his roles were anything but conventionally masculine, first pointing to Hudson's absolute adherence to the written dialogue and more importantly to his strict compliance with contemporary enactments of masculinity: "As to whether Rock was cast in sexually ambiguous roles, certainly that would have come as news to Rock Hudson himself—and to his audiences back in the 1950's and 60's. Finally, most people would agree that Rock had no gay traits either on-screen or off, a fact that served him well as he drifted through both the gay and straight worlds of the times."[23]

This attention to intention overlooks a salient point that Rappaport makes concerning the later reception of Hudson's films: "Once an issue is raised, it can never be made invisible again, except perhaps for those with a very perverse interest in denial. Rock Hudson is certainly a product of that Zeitgeist."[24] Dana Luciano argues for a somewhat similar approach that allows for "opening up but not effacing history—not, that is, sentimentalizing the possibilities of queer relations to the past," but instead "incorporating the suggestive record of queer attachments not to 'fix,' in turn, the time of the queer but to engage its impulses

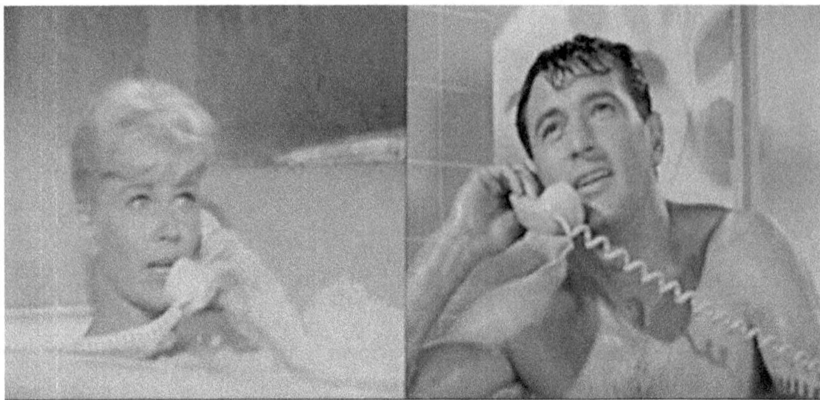

Rock Hudson and Doris Day in *Pillow Talk* (1959). Fans, hanging onto Hudson's Casanova image, had considerable difficulty accepting Hudson when his sexual orientation became common knowledge.

to move toward a future that history has not yet envisioned."[25] This multivalent approach to interpreting performance in light of both past understandings and later insights may seem like an open invitation to anachronistic errors, but it also offers a way to deepen our perception of how viewers receive film texts.

To appreciate this notion, let's take, for example, a portion of Hudson's much analyzed breakout film in the comedy genre, added to the National Film Registry in 2009, *Pillow Talk*, which relies on an elaborate role-playing conceit. Hudson plays Brad Allen, a composer and notorious womanizer who masquerades as the gallant Texan Rex Stetson in a ploy to seduce interior decorator Jan Morrow (Doris Day). She has never met the real Brad, but during a party-line phone discussion Brad suggests to Jan that "Rex" may be one of those men who are "very devoted to their mothers" and "like to collect cooking recipes," to which she replies, "What a vicious thing to say. You are sick!"[26] On the next date, alter-ego Rex displays the supposed homosexual markers of a raised pinky, devotion to his mother, and interest in cooking, all of which prompt Jan to test his masculinity and invite him to make a pass at her.

Several elements add layers to viewers' reading of a neglected element of this scene. First, of course, is the intended irony of masquerade and hidden identities, explored in depth by Steven Cohan, Richard Meyer, and Richard Dyer, among others. Cohan notes that from both a pre- and post-AIDS perspective, such irony-laden scenes offer a "*subversion* of heterosexual masculinity" that is "pointed directly at the authenticity of the star's persona and the masculinity he exemplified in fan discourse," since the "pureboy characteristics chided by Brad for their queer implications were the very elements of Hudson's star persona that the magazines celebrated."[27] A second irony in this scene is not directly connected to sexuality, but it may offer more subtle and subversive connections to the power dynamics inherent in both race and gender. The camera's focus rests on the onlooking gaze of the female African American singer/pianist, who witnesses and silently interprets Brad's plot to deceive Jan. The singer's reaction shots place viewers in her position as the knowing outsider, more sophisticated yet removed from the drama. She overhears the entire plot of deception and seduction, and she closes the scene by singing, "You lied, and you'll be sorry," delivering an accusatory glance at Brad. A look of guilt passes over the actor's face for a moment, and then he grins and winks at her. She, in turn, shakes her head, not persuaded by the character's attempt at charm. Her song lyric foretells the outcome of the narrative and places viewers briefly in the point of view of an African American woman. At yet another layer of ironic distance from the scene, post-AIDS audiences consider other multivalent and contradictory messages in the playboy ploy and in Day's line about how "vicious" it is to accuse someone of homosexuality. The character's masquerade of gayness, in contrast to Hudson's real-life masquerade of heterosexuality, offers an in-joke that may leave astute modern viewers wondering how Hudson fared emotionally as he played this scenario of gay self-loathing. Add to this the biographical background that Hudson's early introduction to the gay social world of Hollywood included going to bars and listening to black entertainers sing, and the entire scene resonates with greater depth and complexity by linking the oppression of racial inequality and gender conformity. In the frequently overlapping intertextuality of Hudson's career and private life, his characters and the actor himself both prove adept at playing and living multiple levels of performance, successfully masking any discomfort he may have felt as he enacted a character or impersonated a deceptive version of himself publicly.

SECOND LIVES

In the sixties, an aging Rock Hudson found his career in decline, and he responded by finally firing Willson as his manager, who had long since become more of a liability than an asset. In the most abrupt change of his career, Hudson took an enormous risk in pursuing the lead role in John Frankenheimer's psychedelic science-fiction film *Seconds*, a film that has not received the same analysis as Hudson's more successful earlier repertoire. The actor was eager for a challenging role that would offer him a chance to work with the famed director, but Frankenheimer did not choose Hudson initially.[28] The popular actor was eventually brought into the project because the studio wanted a well-known star to boost box office success. The project had promise, with James Wong Howe's edgy camera work garnering an Academy Award nomination for cinematography, and Frankenheimer's daring direction bringing out Hudson's acting ability and capitalizing on the actor's own personality and life experience. *Seconds* was doomed to failure, though, primarily because it strayed so far from audience expectations for the debonair, romantic figure Hudson usually projected. The star's casting only created a false impression of the film—a fatal mistake for any project—and it proved simply too bizarre for the rather conservative, older American viewers that Hudson generally attracted. The film was also booed by international audiences at Cannes, who expected melodrama, action, or comedy.

Seconds, based on David Ely's science-fiction novel, fits none of these categories but instead offers a painful mixed- or non-genre portrait of conventional masculinity and social conformity. Frankenheimer's adaptation carries a closely related critique of blacklisting and the entire McCarthy era as well, through the inclusion of previously blacklisted artists for minor yet important roles in the film and on its crew. The aura of conspiracy and suspicion in the plot also mimics the atmosphere of 1950s HUAC hearings. For example, in an echo of McCarthy's pressure tactics, one character grills Hudson's central character, Tony Wilson, to give up names of others who might like second lives, but Wilson refuses.

Connecting this fictional interrogation to McCarthyism was deliberate on Frankenheimer's part, but connecting it to the culture of stalwart silence and loyalty makes for a complicated reading in light of Hudson's personal life and political opinions. On the one hand, Hudson owed his livelihood and survival as a star to people who refused to name names or force gay men to disclose their sexual orientation, thanks to a combination of Hollywood's loyalty to its own and to Henry Willson's almost mafia-style tactics against publishers who threatened to reveal Hudson's sex life. On the other hand, like Willson, Hudson was politically conservative, with one of his proudest moments in life being an invitation to Ronald and Nancy Reagan's White House, after rumors of his AIDS condition had surfaced. FBI head J. Edgar Hoover—whose own sexual orientation is often and fruitlessly questioned—had defended the McCarthy hearings and linked Communism and homosexuality, explaining to reporters that "if you want to be against McCarthy, boys, you've got to be either a Communist or a cocksucker."[29] In the public imagination and in retrospect, the Red scare and the Lavender scare about outing homosexuals created strange bedfellows.

By 1966, Hollywood was well aware of Hudson's sexual orientation, and just as his earlier vehicles demonstrated, his casting in *Seconds* was in many ways a perfect

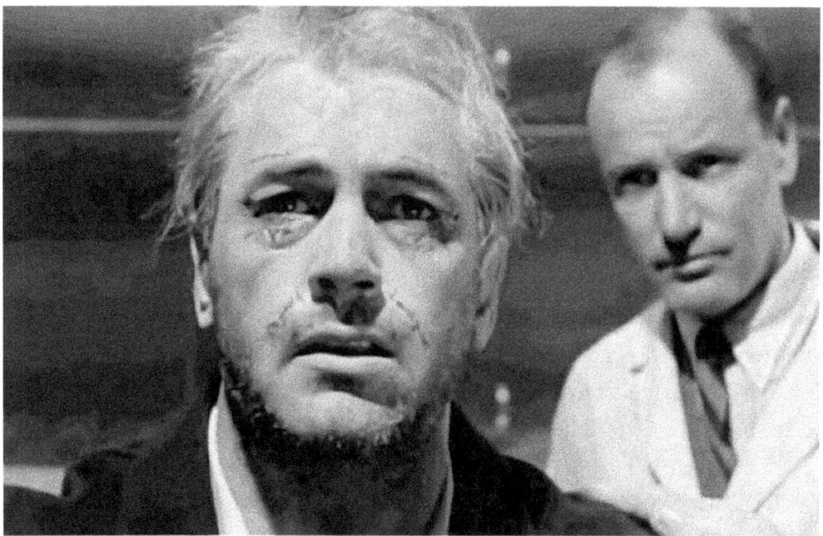

Hudson's performance in the strange sci-fi thriller *Seconds* (1966) disrupted his hitherto carefully manufactured image.

fit for his divided sexual identity. The story opens with Arthur Hamilton, the film's aging central character, searching for meaning in life and looking for a change. In the early scenes pudgy, middle-aged John Randolph plays Hamilton, a man uninterested in sex with his wife and alienated from the routines of his life. He receives a call from an old friend, who convinces him to "die" from his own life and take on an exciting new second life, with help from the mysterious Company. Frankenheimer had to render believable the film's technical gimmick—that the shorter, pudgier body of the older John Randolph could be transformed through advanced plastic surgery to the body of the tall, gorgeous Rock Hudson. This required aging makeup and a sort of reverse engineering, to lessen the magnificence of a body so carefully constructed and beautified over the years on its way to stardom. In the film's post-surgery close-ups, unflattering lighting and a fish-eye lens make Hudson's face look wrinkled, puffy, and swollen, with sutures and graying hair aging him and undermining his good looks. In an effective montage sequence the new "Tony Wilson" in Hudson's body exercises and heals, at least physically. His psychological recovery is not so easily assured.

Like so many of the characters Hudson played in romantic comedies, this man is a bachelor, "alone in the world, absolved of all responsibility except to [his] own interest,"[30] but unlike characters in his previous films, he has no happy or noble redemption in store. Tony Wilson settles in his modern bachelor pad, where

Nora (Salome Jens), a woman he met on the beach, and his curiously solicitous assistant John (Wesley Addy) facilitate adjustment to his new identity. Meanwhile, Wilson tries to drum up some artistic talent, but disgusted by his lack of ability, he crumples up drawing after drawing. One can only imagine Hudson seeking motivation by remembering his own past as a beginning actor, when he was obliged to repeat lines dozens of times before arriving at a successful take.

As is often the case in Hudson's melodramas, a mysterious figure delivers words of wisdom, this time in the form of Nora, who does a tea-leaf reading in which she tells him, "Somewhere in the man there is still a key unturned." This mysterious "key" is never explained, but hearing these lines in light of later revelations about Hudson's orientation, today's viewers are likely to make the association with the actor's homosexuality. Two bacchanalian scenes exhibit potential links between Wilson's uptight character and Hudson's personal identification with the part of a nervous man hiding a secret. One of the few times we see Wilson's character move from repression to release is during a scene shot on location at a wine festival in Santa Barbara, with extras dancing and embracing naked in a huge grape-crushing vat. The progression from polite reluctance to frightened participation to ecstatic indulgence was, according to Frankenheimer's DVD commentary, an authentic reaction rather than a mere performance, which was captured in a single take: "That's not acting from Rock. He just didn't want to get in." The transformation was believable. As Hudson had done with other directors—older men whom he claimed to admire and view as father figures—he made himself "putty" in the director's hands for this scene.

For his part, Frankenheimer clearly knew how to direct the restrained actor, getting him completely drunk again later on, this time in preparation for the big disclosure that all of Wilson's supposed friends are "seconds" too. Like the "key" Nora mentions, the word "seconds" takes on added resonance during this climactic encounter. Although the political message of conformity or modern anomie is an overt theme, a more pervasive subtext of paranoia and hidden identity resides in the biographical context of Hudson's life, expressed through his body language and movements among throngs of male bodies and through framing in this revelatory party scene. Wandering through the crowd, followed by a handheld camera, Hudson talks to a matronly woman (Elisabeth Fraser) who admits she's in a secret organization that changes "sects." He thinks for a moment that she said they change sex, and then she laughingly corrects him. This misperception calls attention to gender in a way that occurs frequently in Hudson's films, written in, no doubt, to make an ironic comment that draws attention to his large maleness. Yet his physical presence often belies his alpha body. In most of his films, far from gesturing largely, swaggering, or taking up too much space in relation to others, Hudson's hesitant gestures neutralize gender. Not only does this quiet restraint have the effect of avoiding the gay cliché of excessive hypermasculinity, but it also appeals to many female viewers, who constitute a significant portion of his fan base. In this scene, Hudson loses some of that restraint and laughs drunkenly as he drapes his large arms over the men, who eventually carry him out and surround him on his bed. His butler explains that they are all "like you—reborns," and that Nora was simply paid by The Company to ease his transition into his new life.

The final meeting with the old friend who introduced him to The Company provides the occasion for another mysterious phrase, when the two talk about how they can "recognize someone and not really recognize him." Like the hidden "key," it points to concealed knowledge, left deliberately vague. When Hudson delivers the lines, "The years I spent trying to get all the things I was told were important. Things, people, meaning, just things. . . . They made the same decisions for me all over again and they were the same things, really," he could be speaking of his early life in Hollywood, when he was told what to do and how to act to become a success. The final scene shows him talking with the head of The Company, sitting by his bed like a father talking to a child, telling him he wished he had found his "dream come true." Unlike the connections in his earlier melodramas and comedies, the similarities between film and personal narratives offered no comfort, none of what Tania Modleski identifies as film's ability to "arouse and contain" viewer anxieties.[31]

The unhappy ending of this film spelled an unhappy audience, and the film failed, at least for a time. That wasn't the end of the story, though. *Seconds* gave Rock Hudson a chance to prove himself as an actor, and although the initial audience response was harsh, the film rode out the critical storm and endured as an example of his best work. Hudson's portrayal of the artist recalls the actor's own desire to become a good actor, and yet he found himself always haunted by the second life and the private life he struggled to hide. Eventually, the film evolved from dismal failure to cult favorite through a combination of extrafilmic factors, not the least of which was Hudson's supposed miscasting as the troubled lead. Just as Hudson's fans didn't expect such a dismal film from their reliable idol, Hudson's detractors didn't expect such a disturbing film and powerful performance from someone they considered a dramatic lightweight. As later post-1985 viewers discovered the film, they read more into it with each new revelation about the actor's private life. In addition, a chance incident with Brian Wilson, composer for the Beach Boys, contributes to the film's underground status. The musician Wilson tells the story of entering a theater under the influence of LSD and walking into a showing of *Seconds*, just in time to hear a flight attendant in the scene speak directly to "Mr. Wilson." Thinking, in his befuddled state, that the film was speaking directly to him, Brian Wilson watched the story of the failed artist, all the while deluded into thinking that Phil Spector had somehow convinced Paramount to engineer a story designed especially for Wilson. He confided later, "The whole thing was there. I mean my whole life. Birth and death and re-birth."[32]

After *Seconds*, Hudson's movie options slowly declined, eventually sending him to television from 1971 to 1977 to play a stylish detective in *McMillan & Wife*, an affable, comic role in which he was paired for a time with perky Susan St. James (before the series was retooled as simply *McMillan*). Shortly before the shocking news that Hudson had AIDS, he appeared visibly unhealthy in seven *Dynasty* episodes and finally, shockingly emaciated, weak, and inarticulate in *Doris Day and Her Friends* on the Christian Broadcast Network. Day claimed to have had no thought of AIDS when she saw his condition, just concern for her longtime friend and the hope that people would remember how funny Hudson was.[33]

IN AND OUT OF THE HETERONORMATIVE WORLD

Looking back on this chain of events, many modern viewers wonder how an actor as famous as Hudson could have concealed his sexual orientation for so long. The fact was, he didn't. The actor's "coming out" actually took place over decades, in an atmosphere that went from carefree frivolity to panic and paranoia. Hollywood's willingness to play along and not mention an open industry secret during the era of the 1950s reflected just how devastating it would have been for the affable star to be revealed as a homosexual, considering the popular association of homosexuality with Communism, not to mention immorality. In addition to being motivated by their sympathetic loyalty, many in the industry had their own skeletons that they didn't want revealed.

Sleazy fan magazines were not so concerned or cooperative, however, and in 1954, *Confidential* seemed to be on the verge of exposing solid proof of Hudson's homosexual activity. In the same year that Hudson emerged as the most popular male star of the year, scandal threatened. Willson's role in suppressing this devastating news was complicated, with competing versions of the facts. When *Confidential* came out with a spread about actor Rory Calhoun's criminal record—rather than the anticipated bombshell about Hudson—many assumed that Willson must have offered this dirt in exchange for *Confidential*'s silence on Hudson's sex life.[34] The exposure of Calhoun's criminal conviction actually ended up increasing his popularity, but news about Hudson coming out in the fifties would have been another story. Petersen explains that "in 1950s America, revealing that America's leading heartthrob was, in fact, gay—it would've not only pulled Hudson's career asunder, but spoken truth to the implicit lies of star production."[35]

Willson's most elaborate solution to this cloud on the horizon seemed to have been his willingness to play matchmaker in a romance and marriage between Hudson and his own secretary, Phyllis Gates, to quash rumors about Hudson's homosexuality. Gates herself offered conflicting explanations for their marriage, maintaining at first that she wasn't aware of his sexual orientation, a claim that was later somewhat undermined by secret taped interviews and scandal sheet reports. She eventually became quite harsh in her criticism of Hudson, maintaining throughout her own lack of awareness of his secret life.[36]

The *Confidential* anti-gay scare was one among many painful incidents, and in 1955 *Life* even published an article with the headline "Fans are urging twenty-nine-year-old to get married—or explain why not."[37] While some accounts of Hudson's personal life describe him as promiscuous and always ready to "score" with gay talent new to the Hollywood scene, Hudson's personal assistant Mark Miller paints a different picture. His stories of Hudson's efforts to avoid places and behaviors that would prompt gay associations are heart-rending. For example, in the 1960s after returning from a boat trip to Catalina with some lesbian friends to his home on Lido Isle, he was greeted by "whistles, cat-calls, and shouts of 'Faggot'" from local residents. After this and repeated anti-gay graffiti incidents, Hudson sold his boat and moved to Beverly Hills. Miller describes how from 1970 to 1985 every interviewer would open by asking if Hudson was gay, to which he would simply reply, "Next question." A troubling but unsubstantiated story was about a fund-raiser for Bobby Kennedy held at Hudson's house. According to Miller, Kennedy asked loudly, "Why are we raising money at this faggot's house?" Miller describes how Hudson told Kennedy, "I'm the faggot who owns this house and I'd like you to leave—now."[38] According to this account, a week later, just a few days before Bobby's assassination, Kennedy's office sent a letter of apology.

The 1985 press release announcing Hudson's AIDS infection prompted sympathetic, supportive responses from all over the entertainment world and the gay community. William M. Hoffman, who authored the AIDS-centered play *As Is* (1985), pointed out the significance of this revelation: "If Rock Hudson can have it, nice people can have it. It's just a disease, not a moral affliction." When Hudson revealed his illness, Joan Rivers was quoted as saying that she couldn't find stars to turn out for an AIDS benefit two years previously: "Rock's admission is a horrendous way to bring AIDS to the attention of the American public, but by doing so, Rock, in his life, has helped millions in the process. What Rock has done takes true courage."[39] Too weak to attend a 1985 Hollywood benefit for AIDS, Hudson sent a telegram: "I am not happy that I am sick. I am not happy that I have AIDS. But if that is helping others, I can at least know that my own misfortune has had some positive worth."[40] Was this a genuine sentiment or another of those concepts Hudson got from playing characters who learned to be selfless and contribute something worthwhile to the world? According to Roger Ebert's interview with Sara Davidson, who had access to Hudson during the final month of his life, his sacrifice and exposure were not intentional:

> "A lot of people said it was so brave of Rock to admit that he had AIDS," Davidson told me. "But actually he wanted it to be hushed up. He thought of AIDS as the plague. It made him feel unclean, and he felt it would destroy the image he had carefully built up over 35 years. If he had collapsed in L.A., he would have been taken to a place like Cedars-Sinai, a hospital used to hushing up the details of movie stars' illnesses. The news would never have leaked out, just as it hasn't in the case of several other AIDS deaths of famous people.
>
> "But he collapsed in Paris, and the officials at the American Hospital were enraged. They didn't accept AIDS cases in the hospital, and they said either he would have to announce it, or they would. When the statement was drafted, Rock's publicist and his secretary read it to him, and all he said was, 'Go ahead, it's been hidden long enough.'"[41]

It could be argued that Hudson's "sincerity" doesn't really matter, given the impact his performance and experience had on the world. His story is one of many that spurs people to resist (as Alexander Doty has requested) people's "continued acquiescence to such cultural paradigms as connotation, *sub*cultures, *sub*cultural studies, *sub*texting, the closet, and other heterocentrist ploys positioning straightness as the norm."[42]

When Rock Hudson died, his body was immediately cremated, offering a lesson that Liberace might have learned from before he died in 1987. Instead of resting in peace, the deceased Liberace was subjected to the humiliating spectacle of having his body exhumed to determine if he had died from AIDS complications.[43] This indignity was one of many inflicted on people around the world who suffered from the "plague" of the AIDS epidemic. No doubt, some homophobic fans reversed their allegiance to Hudson in response to the revelation of his disease and his sexual history. Dyer makes the case concerning treatment of the two men that Hudson was excoriated by the press for his deception, receiving the brunt of public hysteria over the AIDS epidemic, while Liberace was spared, relatively speaking. Far from altering the discourse about homosexuality, the ubiquitous presence of before-and-after pictures serve as testament to Dyer's claim that "beauty and decay is part of a long standing rhetoric of queerness."[44] In counterpoint to this compelling observation, I hold nonetheless that the example of Rock Hudson demonstrates as well just how swiftly and profoundly public opinion can change, when it concerns a beloved figure that people feel they know intimately through the vehicle of stardom. Discovering the naked personal suffering of someone who has fallen from a position of such elegant invulnerability, who seemed so innocently privileged and carefree, gives people a sense that they have witnessed a genuine tragedy, in the Greek sense. And it calls on us, as viewers, to reconsider in a new light those performances—some light-hearted or hilarious, others maudlin or moving, some wooden, and others profoundly subtle, skilled, and close to the bone. Taken together, Hudson's performance in life and in film may emerge as transcendent expressions of courage and seeming nonchalance in the face of a hidden suffering that we all recognize as somehow our own.

NOTES

1. Available at www.youtube.com/watch?v=mZUVP_nsRjw.
2. Boze Hadleigh, *Conversations with My Elders* (New York: St. Martin's Press, 1988), 195.
3. Richard Dyer, "Rock–The Last Guy You'd Have Figured," in *You Tarzan: Masculinity, Movies and Men*, ed. Pat Kirkham and Janet Thumim (New York: St. Martin's Press, 1993), 28.
4. Ibid, 32.
5. Ibid.
6. Robert Hofler, *The Man Who Invented Rock Hudson: The Pretty Boys and Dirty Deals of Henry Willson* (New York: Carroll and Graf, 2005), 188.
7. Director's commentary, *Magnificent Obsession*, directed by Douglas Sirk (1954; Paramount, 2009), DVD.
8. Ibid., 233.
9. Mark Rappaport, "The Sirk-Hudson Connection," January 21, 2009, Criterion Collection, www.criterion.com/current/posts/935-the-sirk-hudson-connection, accessed June 20, 2013.
10. Rebecca Bell-Metereau, "Movies and Our Secret Lives," in *American Cinema of the 1950s: Themes and Variations*, ed. Murray Pomerance (New Brunswick, N.J.: Rutgers University Press, 2005), 89–110.

11. Rock Hudson interview, 1980, available at www.youtube.com/watch?v=enk3x23a030, accessed July 23, 2013.
12. For more recent instances, see Michael Paul Rogin, *Ronald Reagan the Movie: And Other Episodes in Political Demonology* (Berkeley: University of California Press, 1987), 83; and for historical context, see Elizabeth Skerpan-Wheeler, "The First 'Royal': Charles I as Celebrity," *PMLA* 126, no. 4 (October 2011): 912–34.
13. Anne Helen Petersen, "The Rules of the Game: A Century of Hollywood Publicity," *Virginia Quarterly Review* 89 (Winter 2013), www.vqronline.org/articles/rules-game, accessed June 20, 2013.
14. Barbara Klinger, *Melodrama and Meaning: History, Culture, and the Films of Douglas Sirk* (Bloomington: Indiana University Press, 1994), 99.
15. Richard Meyer, "Rock Hudson's Body," in *Inside/Out: Lesbian Theories, Gay Theories*, ed. Diana Fuss (London: Routledge, 2013), 261.
16. Sirk, *Magnificent Obsession* commentary, DVD.
17. Meyer, "Rock Hudson's Body," 262.
18. Tamar Jeffers McDonald, "'Very Little Wrist Movement': Rock Hudson Acts Out Sexual Heterodoxy," *Canadian Journal of Communication* 31 (2006): 843–58, 846.
19. Ibid., 856.
20. Jackie Stacey, "Feminine Fascinations: Forms of Identification in Star-Audience Relations," in *Stardom: Industry of Desire*, ed. Christine Gledhill (London: Routledge, 1991), 152.
21. Ibid.
22. Thomas Elsaesser, "Tales of Sound and Fury: Observations on the Family Melodrama," in *Home Is Where the Heart Is: Studies in Melodrama and the Woman's Film*, ed. Christine Gledhill (London: BFI Books, 1987), 61–62.
23. Ibid., 19.
24. Mark Rappaport, "Notes on *Rock Hudson's Home Movies*," *Film Quarterly* 49, no. 4 (Summer 1996): 16–22, 21, available at www.jstor.org/stable/1213554, accessed July 22, 2013.
25. Dana Luciano, "Coming Around Again: The Queer Momentum of *Far from Heaven*," *GLQ: A Journal of Lesbian and Gay Studies* 13, no. 2–3 (2007): 249–72, 269.
26. *Pillow Talk*, directed by Michael Gordon (1959; Universal Studios, 1987, 2004), DVD.
27. Steven Cohan, *Masked Men: Masculinity and the Movies in the 1950s* (Bloomington: Indiana University Press, 1997), 302.
28. Rebecca Bell-Metereau, "Stealth, Sexuality, and Cult Status in *The Manchurian Candidate* and *Seconds*" in *John Frankenheimer and American Film*, ed. Murray Pomerance and R. Barton Palmer (New Brunswick, N.J.: Rutgers University Press, 2011), 48–61.
29. Hofler, *The Man Who Invented Rock Hudson*, 217.
30. This and subsequent dialogue quotes are taken from *Seconds* (1966), screenplay by Lewis John Carlino, based on the novel by David Ely.
31. Tania Modleski, *Feminism without Women: Culture and Criticism in a Postfeminist Age* (London: Routledge, 1991), 77.
32. Domenic Priore and Becky Ebenkamp, *Look! Listen! Vibrate! Smile!* (New York: Last Gasp, 1995), 266.

33. See www.dorisdaytribute.com/rockhudson.htm. Excerpts appear on www.youtube.com/watch?v=z21shqPRTP8. Her comments about her position as a sort of gay icon can be found in such statements as the following: "In David Butler's 1953 musical Western *Calamity Jane*, a butched-up Doris Day sings the Oscar-winning song 'Secret Love.' Written by Sammy Fain and Paul Francis Webster, the song has become a sort of gay anthem. When asked how she felt about 'having a song that's taken on such meaning for marginalized people,' Day responded: 'I was not aware of that, but that's wonderful.'" Alt Film Guide, www.altfg.com/blog/movie/doris-day-rock-hudson-aids/, accessed April 5, 2014.
34. See Hofler, *The Man Who Invented Rock Hudson*, 248–50; Jerry Oppenheimer and Jack Vitek, *Idol Rock Hudson: The True Story of an American Film Hero* (New York: Villard Books, 1986), 55.
35. Petersen, "Rules of the Game."
36. Larry King, interview with Phyllis Gates, CNN, edition.cnn.com/TRANSCRIPTS/0403/20/lkl.00.html, July 24, 2013.
37. Hofler, *The Man Who Invented Rock Hudson,* xii.
38. Brian Slade, "Rock Hudson's Hollywood," *Harvard Gay and Lesbian Review* (Spring 1996): 18–20, 19.
39. Jeff Yarbrough, "Rock Hudson: On Camera and Off, The Tragic News That He Is the Most Famous Victim of an Infamous Disease, AIDS, Unveils the Hidden Life of a Longtime Hollywood Hero," *People*, August 12, 1985.
40. Joseph Berger, "Rock Hudson, Screen Idol, Dies at 59," *New York Times*, October 3, 1985.
41. Roger Ebert, "Rock Hudson's Secret," *Balder and Dash*, October 22, 2010, www.rogerebert.com/balder-and-dash/rock-hudsons-secret, accessed July 24, 2013.
42. Alexander Doty, *Making Things Perfectly Queer: Interpreting Mass Culture* (Minneapolis: University of Minnesota Press, 1993), 104.
43. "Liberace to Be Tested for AIDS," *Sun Sentinel*, February 7, 1987, articles.sun-sentinel.com/1987-02-07/news/8701080508_1_sabas-rosas-coroner-raymond-carrillo-death-certificate, accessed July 24, 2013.
44. Richard Dyer, *The Culture of Queers* (London: Routledge, 2002), 172.

PART 3
GROWING PAINS

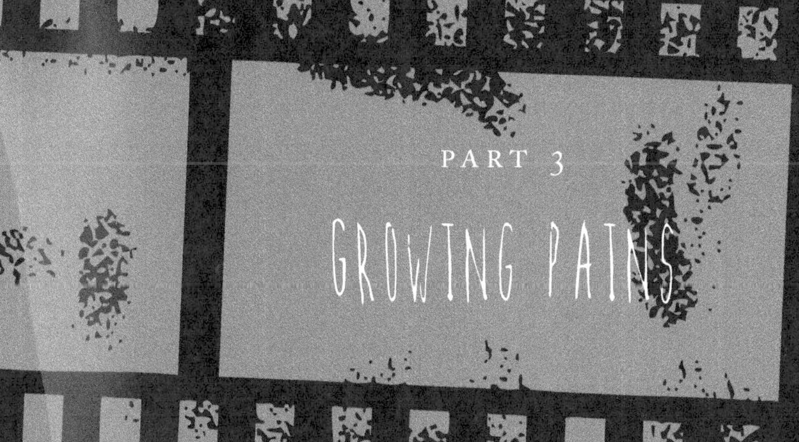

8

MISFITTINGS: *THE MISFITS* AS MARILYN MONROE'S SPIRITUAL AUTOBIOGRAPHY

Peter J. Bailey

> [Monroe] told one relative that she believed there were "people out there" who felt that they had "won" when her marriage to Joe Dimaggio had failed. "'Ah-ha—See? she's not happy at all,' they said about me," Marilyn observed bitterly. "'She's stupid and talentless and she can't keep a husband.' But this [marriage to Arthur Miller] is going to last because I don't want people to have the satisfaction of watching me suffer."
>
> J. Randy Taraborrelli, *The Secret Life of Marilyn Monroe*

WHILE ARTHUR MILLER WAS DRAFTING THE SCREENPLAY OF *THE MISFITS*, Mrs. Miller—Marilyn Monroe—was making *Some Like It Hot* (1959), a Billy Wilder comedy. Monroe's role as perky, breathy-voiced Sugar Kane seemed to her a sour reversion to the sort of sexpot typecasting she had fled Hollywood in 1954 to escape, but upon which her stardom was largely predicated. Undertaking lessons with Actors Studio guru Lee Strasberg was Monroe's strategy for reshaping her film career, but Method techniques proved wildly inappropriate in the context of a comedy as broad as *Some Like It Hot*. Her director and co-stars grew increasingly impatient with her insistence on Strasbergian principles of endless retakes of scenes.[1] Consequently, Monroe's ambivalent desire to reassert her star status while simultaneously becoming a more serious actress alienated her from the cast and crew. Miller attempted to invoke and mediate this emotional and professional tension in his wife in an appreciatory essay, written during this period to accompany a collection of Richard Avedon photographs of Monroe portraying her predecessor Hollywood sirens. He celebrated her projection of Jean Harlow's childlike intensity and erotic maturity while affirming Monroe's identification with "what was naïve [in Harlow], what was genuine lure and sexual truth."[2]

Miller's creation of Roslyn Taber in *The Misfits* (1961) may be seen as his extended attempt to resolve cinematically the conflicts burdening Monroe, acknowledging and celebrating the allure and sexual honesty that underlie Monroe's star quality and draw the three male protagonists to her character in search of redemption. Miller ascribes to Roslyn and to Marilyn as well a remarkably sophisticated sensibility that comprehends the males' needs—until those needs involve defining their masculinity by dominating and destroying animals. Roslyn is reconciled with Gay Langland (Clark Gable) in the movie's much-revised ending, but the disparity between filmic and real-life outcomes in *The Misfits* is effectively epitomized in Miller's admission: "By the start of *The Misfits*, it was no longer possible to deny to myself that, if there was a key to Marilyn's despair, I did not possess it."[3] Ultimately, following a protracted contention between Marilyn/Roslyn as subject/object, both the plot and the making of the movie suggest that the character of Roslyn (as a projection of Monroe) remains a woman created by others' desires, a misfit who desperately but futilely insists on her possession of personal substance and an individual subjectivity all her own. During shooting, the film's producer, Frank E. Taylor, described *The Misfits* as Monroe's "spiritual autobiography": "It's what Marilyn truly is. That's why life is so painful for her, and always will be."[4] My contention in this essay is that Taylor described the movie with uncanny yet little-credited accuracy.

Richard Dyer challenges this textured, nuanced reading of *The Misfits* in "Monroe and Sexuality," a discussion that is crucial to an understanding of the erotics of Marilyn Monroe as a cinematic body—as the tortured incarnation of conflicting notions of human sexuality in the 1950s. Dyer acknowledges that the star may have been a talented comedienne possessing gifts unrelated to concupiscence, but he affirms that his "purpose is to understand the grain [through which she was understood/apprehended by the audience] and there is no question that this is overwhelmingly and relentlessly constructed in terms of sexuality. Monroe = sexuality is a message that ran all the way from what the media made of her in the pin-ups and movies to how her image became a reference point for sexuality in the coinage of everyday speech."[5] Dyer notes that "Monroe's image spoke and articulated the particular ways that sexuality was thought about and felt in the period," to some extent authenticating "those discourses [of the *Playboy* philosophy and female sexuality], but there is a sense in which she begins to act out the drama of the difficulty of embodying them."[6] The growing critical tendency to interpret Monroe as dramatizing that tension has mitigated the negativity with which her films were perceived by many feminists in the years following her death, but for Dyer *The Misfits* wasn't one of those nuanced film performances. "The tendency to treat her as nothing more than her gender reaches its peak with *The Misfits*," he argues, "where, from being a 'girl' in the early films, she now becomes 'the Woman, or perhaps just 'Woman'—Roslyn has no biography, she is just 'a divorcée'; the symbolic structure of the film relates her to nature, the antithesis of culture, career, society, history."[7]

Dyer ascribes a certain texture to the film ("Only *The Misfits* begins to hint at a for-itself female sexuality"), but he then reconsiders, suggesting that the movie casts her "utterly within the discourse of female sexuality as formlessness. The men in the film look on, unable to comprehend her sensuality; grasping a tree she looks out at us/them with a hollow expression of beatitude, straining to express what is already defined as inexpressible."[8] This scene of three drunken males competing for her affections enacts the inexpressibility of the female, and Dyer's characterization conveys the scene's melodramatic excesses in evoking the incomprehensibility of the female sensibility to Gay, Guido, and Perce, *and* to both screenwriter Arthur Miller and director John Huston.

This essay takes issue with Dyer's notion that the practice of treating Monroe as "nothing more than her gender" peaks in *The Misfits*. Such moments certainly exist in the film, but his argument overlooks the historical record of how much of the scripting, directing, and shooting of the film was fraught with contestations dealing with gender. The film's conflicting dramatic vectors embodying male objectification of the female are juxtaposed against Monroe's characterizations of Roslyn granting her intelligence, subjectivity, and compassion, which the film fleetingly projects but cannot sustain consistently enough to affirm conclusively. *The Misfits* constitutes, in my reading, nothing more clearly than the excruciating drama of the "difficulty of embodying American sexual discourses" that was Marilyn Monroe's film career and psychic burden.[9]

Consequently, *The Misfits* resolutely declines to dramatize the victory Monroe wanted her life to delineate: the ascendency of her spirit over the cinematic palpability of her Marilynesque embodiment, even as she failed to effect the real-life reversal of Roslyn's sad assertion, "I never had anybody much." The disjuncture between the exterior that drew humanity ecstatically to her and the pain that dominated her private life could be resolved in the movie only through an imposed sentimental closure thoroughly at odds with the actress's own grimly physical, desperately solitary ending. Close analysis of the adaptation and revision process of *The Misfits* reveals how a film initially intended to mediate the conflicts in Monroe between allure or sexual honesty and serious acting left only Marilyn grasping the painful ramifications of Miller's choices for the character intended to capture her essence.

Monroe's reactions to *The Misfits* are few and widely dispersed throughout the massive biographical material devoted to her, but a summary of Miller's judgments on the production shed some light on the bafflement expressed in another of his dour post-production characterizations of the experience: "I still don't understand it. We got through it. I made a present of this to her, and I left it without her. I didn't even ride home with her on the last day."[10] Examining Monroe's sparse comments on the film and termination of the marriage in conjunction with details of the production's evolution and plot illuminates why Miller's "gift" of a screenplay dramatizing a redeemed Roslyn struck Monroe as so remarkably unredemptive that Miller "came out of it without her."[11] Analyzing connections between the film and its principals' biographies and recollections substantiates Sam Girgus's claim that "in *The Misfits* especially, fictional characters and real lives work off each other. The real interacts with the fictional, providing an extra dimension of meaning to the film."[12] That meaning, I contend, is Monroe's "spiritual autobiography."

Before his death in 2005, Miller had numerous opportunities to offer his views of the personal and perhaps cinematic failure of *The Misfits*. Beginning with journalist James Goode's on-location diary of the film's production, *The Story of The Misfits* (1962), Miller provided in intensely guarded interviews a version of the movie's (and his marriage's) troubled condition. In his 1964 play *After the Fall*, he dramatized a disintegrating marriage modeled on that of his own to Monroe. In his autobiography *Timebends* (1987), Miller wrote forthrightly (and, many Monroe biographers insist, defensively) about the couple's deepening disaffection as the production wore on. In *The Misfits: Story of a Shoot* (2000), Serge Toubiana conducted a final formal interview with Miller that was devoted entirely to the film, and Jeffrey Meyers interviewed Miller at length for his biography of the marriage, *The Genius and the Goddess: Arthur Miller and Marilyn Monroe* (2009), as did Christopher Bigsby for his *Arthur Miller: 1916–1962* (2009).

As these accounts reveal, and as Sarah Churchwell argues, no critical judgment in this cinematic/marital contestation is untainted by whom the commentator "likes,"[13] and consequently, to those unsympathetic toward Miller, dialogue from *After the Fall* epitomizes the playwright's overall attitude toward Monroe. His tendency to view her as a symbol emerges when Quentin, Miller's stand-in, tells Maggie (Monroe's avatar): "But you're a victory, Maggie, you're like a flag to me, a kind of proof that people can win."[14] Quentin later realizes, "You need more love than I thought," sounding like the Miller who believed that *The Misfits* could prove his adoration and redefine Monroe as a serious actress. When he tells her, "But I've got it, and I'll let you see it, and when you do, you're going to astound the world,"[15] Maggie reminds Quentin that "the only reason I went to Ludwig [a musical mogul and apparent stand-in for Lee Strasberg] was so I could make myself an artist you'd be proud of! You're the first one that believed in me!" Quentin responds, "Then what are we arguing about? We want the same thing, you see? Yes, power! To transform somebody, to save!"[16] As Churchwell suggests, by the end of the play Quentin is as much concerned with protecting himself against Maggie's threats of pinning her suicide on him as he is with saving her.[17]

There is, admittedly, a recurrent strain of Quentin's self-protectiveness in Miller's comments: "I knew by this time [the beginning of shooting *The Misfits*] that I had initially expected what she satirized as 'the happy girl that all men loved' and had discovered someone diametrically opposite, a troubled woman whose desperation was deepening no matter where she turned for a way out."[18] Miller *did* tend to emphasize Monroe's instability and his ultimate incapacity to deal effectually with it—but he is arguably more sensitive to the professional sources of her mental conflicts than his detractors have noticed. As he wrote in *Timebends*:

> To have survived, she would have to be either more cynical, or even further from reality than she was. Instead, she was a poet on a street corner trying to recite to a crowd pulling at her clothes. Coming out of the '40s and '50s, she was proof that sexuality and seriousness could not coexist in America's psyche, were hostile, mutually rejecting opposites, in fact. At the end she had had to give way and go back to swimming naked in a pool in order to make a picture.[19]

Few commentators on Monroe have articulated so perfectly her cultural suitability for a role in a film titled *The Misfits*. As Miller observes, Monroe's life was a contested terrain between her desire to become a "serious dramatic actress" and Hollywood and Twentieth Century–Fox's insistence on typecasting her in roles as the sexy ingénue whose erotic appeal to men is a primary source of her other films' humor and profitability.

This conflict between the roles of actor and commercial product began early in her career, as Jeffrey Meyers observes. Even though Monroe posed nude for a calendar to finance auto repairs, she always wanted legitimacy: "Despite her success and financial independence, she felt as conflicted about modeling for girlie magazines as she would, later on, playing dumb parts in third-rate movies," Meyers asserts. "She craved respectability. 'When I was a model,' she said, 'I wanted more than anything in the world for my picture to be in the *Ladies Home Journal*. Instead, I was always on magazines with names like *Peek* and *See* and *Whiz Bang*. Those were the kinds of movies I made, too.'"[20] In evaluating her film career, Monroe never listed roles such as Lorelei Lee in *How to Marry a Millionaire*, "the girl" in *The Seven Year Itch*, or Sugar Kane in *Some Like It Hot* as among her favorites; despite the insistence of Miller and reviewers that she had a "natural gift for comedy," she preferred even her tiny part in Huston's film noir *The Asphalt Jungle* (1950). As early as her casting in *All About Eve* (also 1950), Monroe recognized the pattern of roles Fox was offering her: Miss Caswell differed little from the beauty she had played in *Asphalt Jungle*. "Miss Caswell was a dumb blonde, and though the part was a small one, when Darryl Zanuck viewed the first day's rushes he immediately offered me a contract," Monroe explained. "I was once again back at 20th Century Fox studios. I began to feel—with such great men as John Huston and Joseph H. Mankiewicz offering me roles, and with Darryl Zanuck's confidence in me—I just had to work harder and harder to show others that I really wanted to be considered a serious actress."[21]

As W. J. Weatherby suggests, "She was struggling to break out of the role Hollywood had written for her. Betty Grable hadn't managed it, but Marilyn was determined to succeed. That was what *The Misfits* was about to her: her big chance to convince the world that she was a real actress."[22] As early as 1955, however, she was convinced that typecasting would remain her fate, telling Truman Capote, "Everybody says I can't act. They said the same thing about Elizabeth Taylor. And they were wrong. She was great in *A Place in the Sun*. I'll never get the right part, anything I really want. My looks are against me. They're too specific."[23] *The Misfits*, clearly, was Miller's effort to give her "the right part." He attempted to mitigate the failure of *The Misfits* by observing, "I had written it to make Marilyn feel good. And for her, it resulted in complete collapse. But, at the same time, I am glad it was done, because her dream was to be a serious actress."[24] Given this failure, we need to consider what Monroe thought the "right part" was and wasn't.

That failure has as partial context Monroe's terrible overall ambivalence about acting and stardom. "Even though she had difficulty making *The Misfits,*" Miller told Serge Toubiana, "It had nothing to do with John [Huston] or me. She was scared, she was frightened. She barely could get herself to face the camera."[25] Taraborrelli cites a passage from a notebook she kept during the shooting of *Let's Make Love*: "What am I afraid of?" she wrote. "Why am I so afraid? Do I think I can't act? I know I can act, but I am afraid. I am afraid, and I should not be and I must not be."[26] Her inveterate failure to arrive on sets on schedule was very probably a function of this fear, as was her inability to learn her lines, both of them enacting her terror of being on the set, of being exposed as an actress who cannot act. Ballerina Irina Baronova, who knew Monroe from the London shoot of *The Prince and Showgirl*, said that Monroe had "a quite unconscious but basic resistance to acting. She loves to show herself, loves to be a star, loves all of the success side of it, but to be an actress is something she does not want at all. They were wrong to try to make one of her. Her wit, her adorable charm, her sex appeal, her bewitching personality—are all part of her, not necessarily to be associated with any art or talent."[27] Being regarded as a serious actress appears to have been Monroe's notion of a solution to her paralyzing fears, but her director on *The Misfits* would offer a crushing judgment on that hope after the film was released: "She had no techniques. It was all the truth. It was only Marilyn."[28]

For Monroe, being a "serious actress" wasn't about being the person who won her first contracts and who had emerged out of her body at age thirteen, turning all eyes on Norma Jeane. In her autobiographical narrative *My Story*, Monroe describes the sensation of having grown two heads in junior high: "They were under my sweater."[29] Not many months later, she stripped down to her bikini by removing her slacks and sweater on the beach with a date: "I thought, 'I'm almost naked,' and I closed my eyes and stood still."[30] The "magic friend of sexuality"[31] had transformed her life, although she didn't think of it in sexual terms: "I paid no attention to whistles and whoops. In fact, I didn't hear them. I was full of a strange feeling, as if I were two people. One of them was Norma Jeane from the orphanage who belonged to nobody. The other was someone whose name I didn't know. But I knew where she belonged. She belonged to the ocean and the sky and the whole world."[32] This sense of being two people would follow her throughout her career.

Once such a trope becomes an HBO movie, its capacity to illuminate its referent is probably exhausted. Yet Churchwell's dismissal of the split-protagonist Norma Jeane/Marilyn Monroe construction as a cliché notwithstanding, this dichotomy pervades subsequent attempts to clarify Monroe's career and life, largely because Monroe herself so consistently invoked it. What the trope preserves is a sense of Monroe's continuing gratitude to and identification with Marilyn, despite her comments like this one:

> All my life I've played Marilyn Monroe, Marilyn Monroe, Marilyn Monroe. I've tried to do a little better, and when I do I find myself doing an imitation of myself. I so want to do something different. . . . When I married Miller, one of the fantasies I had in my mind was that I could get out of Marilyn Monroe through him, and here I find myself back doing the same thing, and I just couldn't take it. I had to get out of there. I just couldn't face doing another scene with Marilyn Monroe.[33]

Of course, without Marilyn Monroe, Norma Jeane would have continued to belong nowhere, with no shot at all of becoming a serious actress, or any other kind. In conversation with Weatherby, Monroe sought to dismiss her fame, but when she was asked where she would be without it, her answer was, "On a nude calendar."[34] Still, there were times when she articulated her hatred of the persona who brought her fame: "I'm more than one person and I act differently each time. . . . Most of the time I'm not the person I'd like to be—certainly not a dumb blonde like they say I am: a sex freak with big boobs."[35] No matter how ineffective Miller's therapy-by-screenplay proved, he was certainly prescient in this judgment of his ex-wife's conflicted state: "Physical admiration threatened to devalue her person, yet she became anxious if her appearance were ignored."[36]

If Marilyn was the body, the split-protagonist metaphor assumes, Norma Jeane was the soul, and affirming her possession of a soul (or self, or ego) is an essential component of Monroe's notion of becoming a respected actress. Meyers suggests that "her attempt to become a serious actress is part and parcel of her effort to prove that she wasn't only a photogenic body—to establish that she had inner resources that had little to do with how sexy she was."[37] In *My Story*, Monroe implicitly ascribes the source of this conflict between photogenic body and inner resources to the movies: "In Hollywood, a girl's virtue is always much less important than her hair-do. You're judged by how you look, not by what you are. Hollywood's a place where they pay you a thousand dollars for a kiss, and fifty cents for your soul. I know, because I turned down the first offer often enough and held out for the fifty cents."[38] Perhaps so. Nonetheless, her emphasis on inwardness and an interior life permeates her evocations of the actress she hoped to become. "When anyone asks me for advice on how to become an actress," Monroe told George Barris, "the only advice I feel qualified to give is only through my own experience. So here goes: always be yourself. Retain individuality, listen to the truest part of yourself."[39]

The "truest part" of Monroe proved difficult to locate because, even before the dawning of her fame, she had already been told that, in terms of self, there was nobody home. After marrying Jim Dougherty at age sixteen to avoid an orphanage, Marilyn found the first love of her life in Fred Karger, who initiated her into the fulfillments of erotic attraction: "When he said, 'I love you' to me," she explained, "it was better than all the critics saying I was a great star."[40] Before long, however, Karger was drubbing her with the dichotomy between mind and body: "Your mind isn't developed. Compared to your breasts, it's embryonic. Your mind is inert. . . . You never think about life. You just float through on that pair of water wings you wear."[41] Billy Wilder, her director on *The Seven Year Itch* and *Some Like It Hot*, years later ascribed a similar vacancy to her: "The question is whether Marilyn is a person at all, or one of the greatest Dupont products ever invented. She has breasts like granite, and a brain like Swiss cheese, full of holes."[42] At times, Monroe would accept these perceptions as truths, confessing, "There was no hiding from it—I was terribly dumb. I didn't know anything about painting, music, books, history, geography. I didn't even know anything about sports or politics."[43] Nonetheless, "dumb" is far from admitting that she had no self. Recalling Johnny Hyde, a William Morris vice president who adored her, she asserted that he "not only knew me, he knew Norma Jeane, too. He knew all the pain and all the desperate things in me."[44] Joseph H. Mankiewicz, her director on *All About Eve*, seconded this judgment, though with a disquieting innuendo that her ego was dependent on others: "More than anyone else in her life, I think, [Hyde] provided for her something akin to an honest ego of her own; he respected her. Permitting her, in turn, to acquire a certain amount of self-respect."[45]

If *The Misfits* was going to resuscitate that damaged self-respect and her troubled marriage, Miller's screenplay would, above all else, have to enhance Monroe's self-image by depicting Roslyn as a woman capable of a triumph unrelated to sexually arousing and getting the guy. The role would then have to project a woman whose interior life surpasses male notions of female individuality, a nearly impossible imaginative undertaking for a male playwright in 1959. Consequently, the film's equivocal depiction of Roslyn's role in freeing the mustangs at the movie's close clearly reflects Miller's gradual acquiescence to the notion that Gay—not Roslyn—is the film's central character, a trajectory that director Huston unambiguously endorsed. This evolution of the script of *The Misfits*, and its devastating impact on Monroe, is the story I seek to illuminate.

Miller's memoirs recall Monroe's reluctance to sign on for the role of Roslyn after her initial reading of the script, which has led some commentators to assume that she found Roslyn far too close to herself for comfort: "She craved [Miller's] attention and knew she'd inspired him," Meyers argued, "but [she] objected to playing a role that seemed to analyze and expose her real self. Alternately encouraging and berating him, she was never satisfied with the finished product, and constantly criticized his portrayal of the character as they were filming."[46] Others have contended that her objection was to the credibility of a Roslyn severed from the kind of traumatic childhood Marilyn had experienced. Barbara Leaming adopts this tack: "Marilyn felt betrayed because Arthur seemed unable to acknowledge her past. From the first, the whole point of marriage was to be accepted by such a man. She needed Arthur to love her in spite of all the shameful things she had done. Marilyn saw the script as proof that he had never really accepted her. How could he, when he seemed to refuse to acknowledge who she was in the first place?"[47] To some commentators, Roslyn was too much like Marilyn; to Leaming, she was insufficiently similar. Such contradictory statements typify the assessments of Monroe that the public has received. Her own comment on the issue suggests that Roslyn's likeness to herself *was* a problem, at least for her: "I didn't have enough distance from the character. Arthur wrote me into it, and our marriage was breaking up at that period. Maybe I was playing *me* too much, some ideal me. Maybe I was really playing me, and Arthur was writing how he saw me instead of a character—or how he saw me before we broke up. Roslyn might now be more of a bitch."[48] As we shall see, Miller was intent on including in the film a markedly less ideal Roslyn in the scene that Monroe hated most.

Through the early days of shooting *The Misfits*, however, Monroe put a positive public face on the script, telling Goode, "As far as I'm concerned, I play a girl—a contemporary young woman who is searching, probably yearning, but she doesn't know it and she doesn't know what for. I found more to it as I played it. It's a wonderful part for anyone to do."[49] Guus Luitjers cites a statement from Monroe that represents a much more negative midterm take on the project: "Arthur said it's *his* movie. I don't think he even wants me in it. It's all over. We have to stay with each other because it would be bad for the film if we split up now. I don't know how long I can put up with this. I think that Arthur's been complaining to Huston about everything he thinks is wrong with me, that I'm mental or something. And that's why Huston treats me like an idiot with his 'dear this' and 'dear that.'"[50] At this point in the production, in Monroe's perception, the camps had been formed: Miller, Huston, Frank Taylor, and Eli Wallach against Monroe, Montgomery Clift, and Monroe's drama coach, Paula Strasberg. Monroe never uttered a critical word about Gable, who remained on the sidelines, perhaps waiting to be enlisted on the side that offered the ending that flattered his role the most.[51]

All of Monroe's other comments about playing Roslyn followed the film's completion and Miller's withdrawal from the marriage, and they may therefore reflect the bitterness of divorce more than a neutral evaluation of the role. In *Timebends*, however, Miller recalls: "One afternoon Marilyn, with no evident emotion, almost as if it were just another script, said, 'What they [Roslyn and Gay] should really do is break at the end.' I instantly disagreed, so quickly, in fact, that I knew I was afraid she was right. But the irony was too sharp, the work I had created to reassure her that a woman like herself could find a home in this world had apparently proved the opposite."[52] The optimistic—some viewers thought sentimental—joining of Gay and Roslyn at the close of *The Misfits* was one that he told Weatherby was difficult for him to reach, especially considering his tendency to close his plays on darker intonations: "For a long time now, I've wanted to make something of existence. . . . It's tragic, after all, we all die here—but there's something in between. Gay and Roslyn will die, but they can face it with dignity. They can do right, and not be like the jerks. It may not sound much but it's taken a lot to get me to that point."[53] As Miller told Serge Toubiana, Roslyn was to be the locus of that affirmation as "a woman, as homeless as [the cowboys], but whose intact sense of life's sacredness suggests a meaning for existence."[54] As Norman Mailer argued, perceptions like this one underlie Miller's promise to give Monroe a screenplay and film "that would bestow upon her public identity a soul."[55]

To ascertain Monroe's other feelings during the shoot, we need to consult witnesses, and therein lies a difficulty. Given the contradictory testimony on all sorts of issues from those close to Monroe, one might question publicist Rupert Allen's claim that Monroe was "desperately unhappy at having to read lines written by Miller that were so obviously documenting the real-life Marilyn. . . . She felt isolated, alone, abandoned, worthless, that she had nothing more to offer than this naked, wounded self."[56] Monroe's description of her Method acting practice ("You find out what she's like—the character you're playing, I mean, what she means to you. How you're like her and not like her")[57] provides no evidence that her most recent role represented an exception to the "how you're like her and not like her" inventory. Taylor's characterization of the film as Monroe's "spiritual autobiography" suggests such a close likeness between Roslyn and Monroe that it is difficult to imagine why a woman longing to be a serious actress could object to portraying a "naked, wounded self," especially if these struggles resembled her own.

Many of the convergences between Roslyn and Monroe seem obvious. Roslyn's mother was an inconstant presence throughout her childhood, and Roslyn never completed high school. Perce Howland (Clift) asks her, "How come you got such trust in your eyes? Like you was just born," invoking the quality of naiveté many friends attributed to Monroe, and which she sometimes ascribed to herself. Monroe's tendency toward affective bipolarity is invoked by the comment of the cowboy character, Gay Langland: "I think you're the saddest girl I ever met," and her response, "You're the first man ever to say that. I'm usually told how happy I am."[58] Add to these parallels the fact that Gay has posted on a closet door photographs that are clearly Monroe publicity shots, and the identification is inescapable.

Other links between Monroe's life and the fictional Roslyn are less evident. In her first scene in the movie, Roslyn is having difficulty memorizing the language that her friend, Isabelle Steers (Thelma Ritter), has written for Roslyn's divorce hearing that morning. Monroe was so notorious for not knowing her lines that Billy Wilder offered her one of the most back-handed compliments in film history: "Anyone can remember lines, but it takes a real artist to come on the set [of *Some Like It Hot*] and not know her lines and give the performance she did."[59] Rather than reciting Isabelle's script, Roslyn, sounding like an Actors Studio convert, wants to express precisely what she feels: she's seeking a divorce from Taber "because he just wasn't there. If I'm gonna be alone, I want to be by myself." Miller would have heard this criticism often while he was working on *The Misfits*. During the composition process, he acknowledged being "apprehensive and unspontaneous with Monroe,"[60] and many of her biographers cite versions of her displeasure with Miller's remoteness. The line "because he just wasn't there" fits the description of dialogue offered by Monroe's makeup man, Whitey Snyder: "Honest to God, there were lines in that movie that were right out of her experience with Arthur Miller."[61]

A still more significant trait shared by Monroe and her *Misfits* character is her desperate, protective love for animals. Donald Spoto's biography cites numerous incidents testifying to Monroe's preoccupation with animals: a wounded seagull reduced her to weeping, a stray dog on a country road broke her heart, and she denounced deer hunting as a "killing sport."[62] Miller's 1960 story "Please Don't Kill Anything" draws heavily on Monroe's phobia. Meyers's *The Genius and the Goddess* was the first to note that *The Misfits* screenplay conflates Miller's original short story "The Misfits" (1957) and "Please Don't Kill Anything." The earlier story introduces Gay, Guido, and Perce, the pursuers of Roslyn in the film, though she is purely a backstory presence in the narrative. It makes no attempt to create resemblances between Roslyn and Monroe, an idea that clearly occurred to Miller only later, as he began writing the screenplay in hopes of consoling Monroe after the second miscarriage of their marriage.[63]

In contrast, the unnamed female protagonist of "Please Don't Kill Anything" is obviously modeled on Monroe. The fishermen have cast their catch on the beach, leaving to die the "junk fish" they cannot sell. Sam describes how "he had to open a window at home, once, to let out a moth, which ordinarily he would have swatted, and while part of his heart worshipped her fierce tenderness toward all that lived, another part knew that she must come to understand that she did not die with the moths and the spiders and the fledgling birds, and, now, with these fish."[64] Her request to save the fish is just as emotional: "Just those two. Go on, Sam. They might be alive."[65] Alive they are. Sam returns them to the sea, winning her gratitude, as Miller's narrator explains: "Now she looked up at him like a little girl, with that naked wonder in her face, even as she was smiling in the way of a grown woman, and she said, 'But some of them might live now until they're old.'" When he answers that they would then die, she responds, "'But at least they'll live as long as they can.' And she laughed with the woman part of herself that knew of absurdities."[66] There's no evidence elsewhere in the story, however, that "the woman part of herself that [knows] of absurdities" is operating in her defense of animal life. Sam (via the narrator) is the one who imputes to her humane stance the presence of "absurdities" that she would never acknowledge. To the character (and to Monroe), there's nothing absurd in wanting animals to live "as long as they can."

Miller makes this same conflict in his marriage a central tension between Roslyn and Gay in *The Misfits* screenplay, amplifying it to represent a clash between Gay's male cowboy freedom and Roslyn's badly bruised female sensibilities, thereby ensuring a very different outcome from that of "Please Don't Kill Anything." Depressed by the divorce she has come to Reno to finalize ("I just don't believe in the whole thing [marriage] any more"), and deeply skeptical about human commitments in general, Roslyn suggests, "Maybe you're not supposed to believe what people say, maybe it's unfair to them."[67] Her pessimistic summation of human relations sounds like a version of something Miller heard Monroe say and wants the screenplay to disprove: "Maybe all there really is is what happens next, just the next thing, and you're not supposed to remember anybody's promises."[68]

Up until this point in the narrative, not making promises has worked for Gay, who has lived off the land and the occasional wealthy widow as well. Even more than Guido (Wallach) and Perce (Clift), Gay is temperamentally opposed to suffering any constraints upon his liberty, for, as Isabelle warns Roslyn, "Cowboys are the last real men in the world, and they're about as reliable as jackrabbits." These cowboys' habitual mantra rationalizing mustanging—"it's better'n wages"—loses its punch with the dwindling of horses to capture in the desert and the fact that their haul is turned into dog food. Gay's impulse toward freedom is already compromised by having moved with Roslyn into a house Guido owns. Then, although it betrays his deepest instincts, he's so eager to please that he plants a garden. A rabbit finds the lettuce sprouts, and Gay plans to eliminate the intruder with his shotgun, precipitating Roslyn's first argument with him. "I can't stand to see anything killed," she tells Gay, and when he accuses her of being silly, she replies, "I'm not being silly. You don't respect what I feel." *The Misfits* makes it clear that Miller didn't respect what Monroe felt about animals, and that he placed in Gay's mouth basically the same argument Sam offers to his wife in "Please Don't Kill Anything"—an argument that, Miller seemed to assume, says all that men need to say about the relationship between animals and humanity.

Roslyn and Gay's garden argument is interrupted by the arrival of Guido and Isabelle, but it revives out on the desert the night before the males go mustanging. Guido, wrangling to seduce her away from Gay, tells Roslyn that what she has is more valuable than what Guido has learned in books: "You care. Whatever happens to anybody happens to you. You're really hooked into the whole thing. It's a blessing."[69] This is clearly Miller's sideways encomium to Monroe's sensitivity, but its sincerity is rendered equivocal by having the same speaker, in a subsequent scene, offer to release the captive mustangs in exchange for her leaving Gay for himself. At this point, the narrative moves into the final movement of the film in which, despite Roslyn's apparent salvaging of the mustangs, Gay will ultimately eclipse the other characters in the screenplay's concluding dispersal of sympathies. Roslyn's plea for kindness to animals prevails somewhat indeterminately, only to be trumped by the ethic of "a man's gotta do what a man's gotta do." As Mailer speculates in *Marilyn*, "Perhaps she never recognized how completely *The Misfits* was a narrative about men."[70] However, given her desperate unhappiness with the script—expressed through increasing her barbiturate intake to the point of requiring hospitalization and shutting down the production for a week[71]—she seems to have realized this all too clearly. Donald Wolfe cites Monroe's response to *The Misfits*: "It was to be 'our movie'! But Arthur changed the script. [Roslyn's] not like me at all. She's almost incidental to the story. All he cares about are the men. . . . All Arthur wanted was to use me to regain his prestige! I'll never forgive him—never!"[72]

Before their arrival in the desert, Roslyn has not allowed herself to ask what mustanging entails, and Gay finally has to tell her what pursuing these horses is about. When she finally asks if they kill the horses, he replies, "No, no—we sell 'em to dealers." "*They* kill them," Roslyn responds, understanding. Gay then offers an argument similar to Sam's in "Please Don't Kill Anything": "Honey, nothin' can live unless something dies."[73]

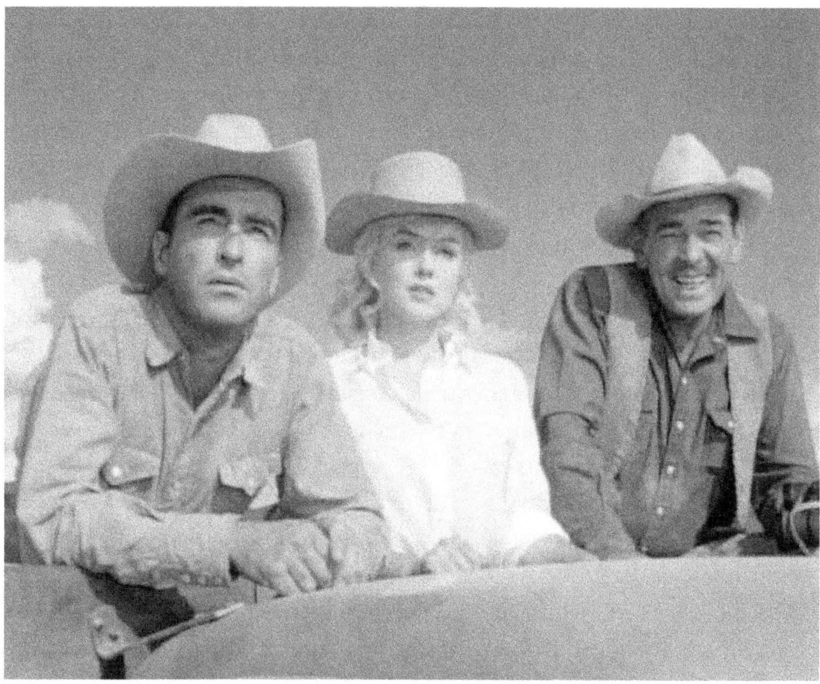

Gay (Clark Gable, right), seeing the mustangs Guido has chased into the canyon: "They're nothin' but misfit horses, honey."

Roslyn begs him, "Oh, *stop*," but he won't because this is the highly gendered lesson that he has to impress upon Roslyn, and which Miller needs his script to impress upon Monroe. Both men rationalize their indifference to the animal deaths they cause or witness by invoking a jungle ethic irrelevant to the immediate circumstance; the inevitability of "nature red in tooth and claw" is in both instances cited to justify completely needless extinctions. "Junk fish" are doomed only if the human beings standing by ignore their sufferings; the fact that animals devour each other doesn't necessitate that mustangs be sacrificed so that Gay Langland can remain a cowboy. Gay explains that these are "chicken feed horses" they're after, mustangs once corralled so that parents could buy them for children to ride. Now, things have changed: children ride motor scooters, and the horses are ground up for dog food. "Honey, I just round 'em up and sell 'em to the dealer," Gay explains. "See, I'm doing the same thing I always did. It's just that they changed it all around. . . . I hunt these horses to keep myself free. I'm a free man. That's why you like me, isn't it?"[74]

The risk for Gay in this scene is apprehending the film's informing parallel: as Gay puts it, "They're nothing but misfit horses, honey." The mustangs are holdovers—misfits—from an earlier world just as the three cowboys are; the disappearance of the mustangs creates a void into which the cowboys, too, disappear. In the original short story, Gay can't resolve the dilemma that confronts him, and, like Roslyn, he finds himself in the same place he has always been. In this distinctly Hemingwayesque moment, Gay is groping toward the realization of change that he haltingly articulates and mourns in an extended monologue.

Gay's stoic admonition about life and death appears in his longest monologue in *The Misfits*, one in which Miller's objectives of appreciating Monroe and attempting to mediate her professional conflict between cinematically projecting sexuality and artistic seriousness emerge most substantively. Having apprised Roslyn of the fate of the mustangs the men plan to capture the following morning, Gay rationalizes the work he's always done by comparing it to her experience with dance:

> We start out doing something, meaning no harm, something that's naturally in us to do. And somewhere down the line it gets changed around into something bad. Like dancin' in a night club. You started out just wanting to dance, didn't you? And little by little it turns out that people ain't interested in how good you dance, they're gawking at you with something altogether different in their minds. And they turn it sour, don't they? I could've looked down my nose at you, too—just a kid showin' herself off in nightclubs for so much a night. But I took my hat off to you. Because I know the difference. . . . This [mustanging] is how I dance, Roslyn. And if they made something else out of it, well . . . I can't run the world any more than you could. I hunt these horses to keep myself free. That's all.[75]

In the short story, Gay hasn't comprehended that what kept the mustanging from being "all that it ought to be" was that "they changed it all around," so that his continuing to do what he always did is now having consequences that he can't explain to Roslyn. In the screenplay, Gay presents himself and Roslyn as victims of forces they can't control, but once he knows the fate of the animals he rounds up, can he with any credibility claim to simply be doing what he had always done? What is his cowboy's freedom worth if it consigns his totem animals to dog food cans?

For her part, Roslyn is mollified by his suggestion that "I took my hat off to you," and the argument he makes for her guiltlessness in spite of others' perceptions is one Monroe offers for herself in *My Story*: "People had a habit of looking at me as if I were some kind of mirror instead of as a person. They

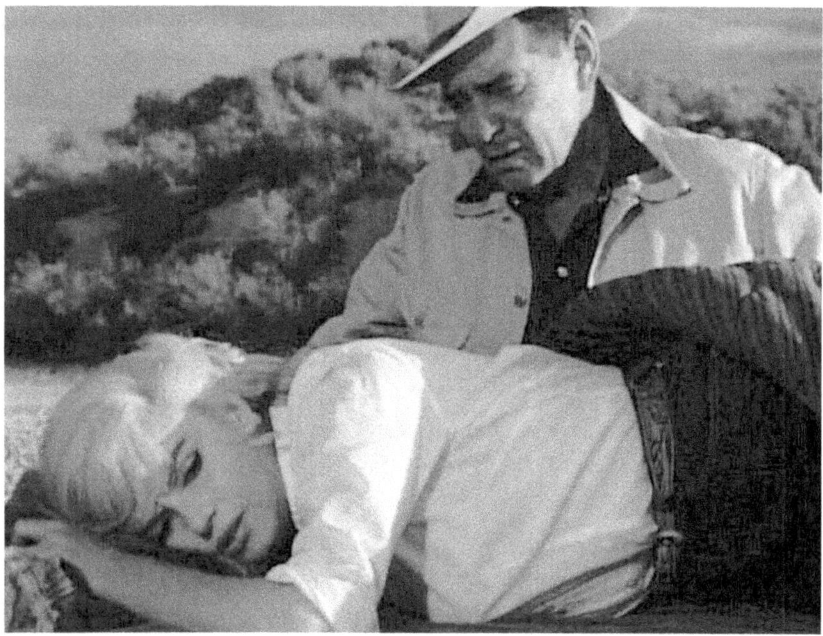

Gay to Roslyn: "Honey, I just round up [mustangs] and sell 'em to the dealer—always have."

didn't see me, they saw their own lewd thoughts. Then they white-masked themselves by calling me the lewd one."[76] Although spectators often do project their desires upon the performer they are viewing, the conflict in Monroe that Miller was seeking to resolve through Gay's monologue couldn't be so readily mediated because of the degree of Monroe's complicity and agency throughout her career in allowing her "dancing" to be turned into "something bad." Gay may think he "knows the difference" between acts well intended and others' scurrilous perceptions or distortions of them, but the actress who was to agree—as Miller suggested—to a nude swimming scene in her next film, *Something's Got to Give*, could find neither solace nor validation in the argument that perceivers alone had "turned it sour." In *The Misfits* itself, some of Monroe's more memorable scenes display her dancing drunkenly around a phallic tree, playing paddle-ball in a Reno bar with all her parts engaged and bouncing, and riding a horse with cinematographer Russell Metty's camera pulling in for a close-up of her jouncing derriere. She hated being depicted in films in a purely sexual way, but her studio, her director, and her screenwriter husband all conspired to make that depiction part of Roslyn's character in *The Misfits*. The conflict over mustanging comes to a head as Roslyn watches in outrage as five horses (one a colt) are lassoed, roped to old truck tires, and finally brought to ground. Horrified, she turns against all three men for their shared ethic of kill-or-be-killed: "Murderers! Liars! You're only happy when you see something die! Why don't you kill yourselves and be happy? You and your God's country! Freedom! I hate you!"[77] Meyers dismisses Roslyn's position throughout *The Misfits* as "simple, or even simpleminded New Age wisdom," and although Miller and Huston wouldn't have recognized his modifier, they would likely have endorsed his overall dismissal. Even though the male protagonists say flattering things about Roslyn throughout movie—she has the "gift for life" and is "hooked into the whole thing"—her female sensibilities and identification with the bodies of animals are not going to prevail in *The Misfits*. Monroe intuited that drift, and we see in this scene, at least, what she intensely disliked about Miller's choices for her character: "I convince them by throwing a fit, not by explaining why it's wrong [to round up the mustangs for dog food]," Monroe fulminated to Lena Pepitone: "I guess they thought I was too dumb to explain anything. So I have a fit, a screaming, crazy fit . . . and to think, Arthur did this to me. He could have written me *anything*, and he came up with *this*. If that's what he thinks of me, well, then, I'm not for him and he's not for me."[78]

This pivotal scene has become one of the cruxes of *The Misfits* debate because it so inextricably interweaves marital, existential, and cinematic issues. Weatherby argues that *After the Fall*'s Maggie, with her incessant demanding and blistering tongue, is the side of Roslyn largely omitted from Miller's screenplay of *The Misfits*, and that this idealization was what made it so difficult for Monroe to portray Roslyn effectively.[79] Earlier in *Conversations*, however, Monroe admits to the demonic side of her character that shocked Miller when she first unleashed it: "I disappointed him when that happened. But I felt he knew and loved all of me. I wasn't sweet all through. He should love the monster, too. But maybe I'm too demanding. Maybe there's no man who could put up with all of me."[80] When Christopher Bigsby interviewed Miller in 1995 about the Monroe/Roslyn likenesses, Miller readily acknowledged the parallels: "Oh, yes, she was just that way. She wasn't acting very much. Off-screen she was a lot like on-screen excepting that she got angry. She wouldn't show that, excepting that I had her do it in the last scene of *The Misfits*, when she was furious at them for capturing the horses. Then she was quite a different person, and she became herself: quite paranoid."[81] Miller's unsympathetic recollection undermines the argument that Miller's portrait of Roslyn idealized Monroe by including only her positive traits.

It seems likely that Monroe despised the "throwing a fit" scene not only because of Roslyn's perfervid explosion but because Metty's cinematography makes her eruption look so tiny and ineffectual: he photographed her from a terrific distance, surrounding her outburst with miles of empty desert. Huston, we assume, had the scene shot as he did to make exactly that point: Roslyn's protests against male power and manly stoicism toward mortality are not what *The Misfits* is about, and from this scene onward, the movie becomes the medium for Gay to achieve what his counterpart in the short story fails to accomplish: a tentative resolution of the dilemma of his own superannuation, and a purely symbolic rebellion against those who "changed mustanging all around." The last twenty minutes of *The Misfits* consist largely of Gay regaining his nobility, for, as Huston says of the film's protagonist, "Gay is the same man he was, but the world has changed. Then he was noble. Now he's ignoble."[82] Roslyn's issues don't stand much chance of being effectively addressed in a film whose director exclaimed on the set, "Gay Langland is a modern hero or about as close to one as I have read about."[83] Gay's heroism displaces that of *The Misfits*' other potential hero, Roslyn, who is thereafter relegated largely to the role of passive appreciator of male initiation and self-restoration.

Evidence remains in the released film that the Roslyn subplot was initially intended to matter more. The subplot is introduced by Isabelle's admonition to Roslyn early in the film: "Dear girl, you have to stop thinking you can change things." In well-intended befuddlement Roslyn replies, "But if there's something you can do . . . I don't know what to do, but, if I did, I'd do it!"[84] She is befuddled in part because change is what she fears most, as she confesses to Gay: "That's what I could never get used to—everything's always changing, isn't it?"[85] Once the four characters are out on the desert, Roslyn devotes herself to the change that will free the horses, even if it means annulling the cowboys' freedom. Perce is the first to suggest that, since there are only five mustangs and the take will be accordingly minimal, they give the herd to Roslyn—in other words, release them. Gay objects to this form of horse trading on the grounds that "I sell to horse dealers only. All they're lookin' to buy is the horse."[86] The "horse" *does* mean more to her than just a physical animal, and she does "change things" by contributing to the cowboys' decision to set free the mustangs and to abandon mustanging for good.[87] Her responsibility for that conversion is eclipsed, however, by the addition of Gay's muscular subduing of the stallion, which is part of the final Miller rewrite that Gable approved, and which is also the clearest evidence of Miller's latest intentions (prodded by Huston) for his screenplay. The cowboys give Roslyn no credit for changing their minds, and if she is gratified to have intervened successfully on the animals' behalf, this is signaled only obliquely by her increased affection for Gay in the final scene. (Given gender attitudes of the period, most contemporary viewers would very likely ascribe her warming up to Gay again as a reward for his singlehandedly dispatching the stallion, an act that has meaning only in terms of his personal self-redemption, since he will immediately release the horse.) Isabelle's admonition for Roslyn not to believe she can change things then sets Roslyn up for prevailing far more significantly than the film's final release dramatizes. The ending gravitates clearly toward conferring upon Gay the status of late-emerging protagonist and hero of *The Misfits*. His triumph, however, has its ambiguities.

Montgomery Clift noticed the shift and believed he knew what it meant, revealing in his analysis the permeability between stars and their roles. Clift was convinced that Roslyn should go off with Perce, but Miller was, in Clift's view, too involved in wish fulfillment, wanting to see Gay end up with her. "He identified with the character played by Gable," Clift told Weatherby: "[Miller and Monroe's] marriage is over, and he might as well face it. . . . No, Arthur's got it wrong. Maybe that's what's wrong with his relationship to her. Maybe he was too paternal. I know she respected him too much, looked up to him. All idols fall eventually. Poor Marilyn, she can't keep anyone for long."[88] Years later, in his interview with Bigsby, Miller reaffirmed his vote for Gay's prevailing: "[Huston] sensed that I was after something that was important to him, too. The disintegration in life of commitment—of people to people, of people to an ideal. All that was left to us was the moment-to-moment reality. . . . He could have been Gay Langland."[89] The film quietly ignores Roslyn's commitment to an ideal of coexistence with animals, as well as her articulation of Miller's cultural critique that there may be nothing more than "what happens next."

Monroe did leave behind one other comment suggesting that she fully understood this overshadowing of Roslyn's character as the film moved toward completion. She comments that *The Misfits* was "their [Miller's and Huston's] movie": "It's really about the cowboys and the horses, they don't need anything else. As for me, they don't need me at all, not as an actress. Only for the money. To be able to put my name on the film. To seduce people to come and spend their money, to see another sex film about a dumb blonde."[90] Her reservations about what she perceived as Huston's late alterations in the script point in the same direction: "About my last picture, *The Misfits*, some people like it, but not me," she told George Barris. "I was disappointed. The director, John Huston, he sort of fancied himself a writer, and he changed it from the original intention of Arthur Miller. Now, this director also did *The Asphalt Jungle*, but he didn't fool around with the script. I personally preferred the script be left as the writer did it. Mr. Miller at his best is a great writer."[91] No other participants in the production recall Huston revising the screenplay during shooting, but there is substantial evidence that Miller was constantly engaged in revision into the final week. The fact that Monroe attributed script changes to Huston may reflect her apprehension that the film had indeed progressively become a celebration of Huston's conception of "a modern hero"—one who was not female.

In *Timebends*, Miller tracks the film's and his marriage's trajectories, both of which were running downhill: "I had sensed something withdrawn in her, not merely in the character she was playing, but I insisted that it was only her insecurity showing: surely we still had a future, and the work on this film would somehow make it happen. It was far from accidental that by the end of the film Roslyn does find it possible to believe in a man and in her own survival."[92] It is also conceivable that Roslyn's "believing in a man" was more at the top of Miller's agenda for Monroe than it was Monroe's agenda for her protagonist. A few pages on in *Timebends*, Miller suggests, "I kept trying to rewrite the last few minutes of the film, which had never been quite right. Aware of the hopefulness with which I had conceived the story and my uncertainty about the future now, I still could not concede that the ending had to be what I considered nihilistic, people simply walking away from one another."[93] Monroe sympathizers have argued that Miller undertook these revisions to bedevil his wife's dialogue-memorizing challenges and as retribution for betrayals during the production, such as her moving out of their hotel room to stay with Paula Strasberg. The fact that Gable, who had script approval, refused to agree to more changes in his role in the last days of shooting indicates that it was Gay's role, rather than Roslyn's, that was being revised. Gable withdrew his prohibition after reading the last revision: "I didn't like the original ending of the screenplay [in which the stallion defeats Gay and leaves him on the lake bed, arousing Roslyn's compassion]," Gable explained, "but I didn't know the solution. I think Arthur's new ending is the answer."[94]

The "answer" is that Perce, ever the reluctant mustanger, releases the animals, and Gay takes it upon himself to recapture one of them. He singlehandedly subdues the stallion, then cuts him loose, and when Guido asks why he overcame the stallion only to release him, Gay responds with the bravado of a resurrected cowboy: "Don't like nobody makin' up my mind for me, that's all."[95] If a horse is to be released, Gay must release it—not Perce, nor Roslyn's emotional, ethical arguments. Gay then reprises his "they" argument, with a significant reversal at the end: "Damn it, they changed it all around, smeared it all over with blood. It's like ropin' a dream now. I've just gotta find another way to be alive—if there is one."

Were Roslyn given the chance to assess Gay's reversal and recognition, she might notice that he is renouncing mustanging not out of concern for the animals, but because it was "like ropin' a dream now." Would she understand, any more clearly than the screenplay seems to, that Gay is nonetheless responsible for his choices even if some distant *they* have "changed it all around"? Does he ever really understand that predicating his freedom on the horses' loss of freedom and ultimate destruction, as Roslyn forthrightly assures him, simply "isn't right"? Roslyn's reactions to all these issues—and the question of whether Gay's subduing of the stallion has an effect on anything more significant than bolstering his aging, battered ego—are summarily dispensed with by the film. The release of the mustangs apparently mollifies Roslyn, and, back in Gay's truck with him, she shifts from leaving to staying: "If . . . if we weren't afraid! Gay? And there could be a child. And we could make it brave. One person in the world who could be brave from the beginning! I was scared to when you asked me last night [about having children], but I'm not so much now. Are you?"[96]

Roslyn's change of heart is sparked, clearly, by her vision—beautifully framed by Metty—of the mare and her colt running free. Resolving the Roslyn plot by having her express a desire to bear children would have seemed an acceptably sentimental culmination for an audience in 1961, and Miller clearly viewed the film's closing promise of a future for Gay and Roslyn optimistically. In this instance, Roslyn's projected resolution is much happier than Monroe's, since the surgery she had in 1959 to help her bear children resulted in the diagnosis that she would never be able to conceive.[97] By the end of shooting *The Misfits*, of course, neither Monroe nor Miller was interested in jointly producing a child.

Miller's novelization description of Gay and Roslyn in his truck cab ("The love between them is viable, holding them a little above the earth")[98] reflects the intensity of Miller's desire to "make something of existence" through an ending of romantic reconciliation. Accordingly, the closing dialogue of *The Misfits* has been widely criticized as sentimental—particularly so, given the real-life marital split that followed closely upon the film's completion. As Gay drives Roslyn out of the desert in his truck and she asks how he finds his way home in the dark, he answers, "Just head for that big star straight on. The highway's under it; take us straight home."[99] Except that, having feuded with Guido over Gay's refusal to continue mustanging, Gay has probably voided his lease at Guido's house, leaving him and Roslyn with no home to go to.

Miller had begun the scripting process for *The Misfits* with the assumption that "there was a greatness of spirit in [Monroe], even a crazy kind of nobility that the right role might release, and if that happened she might step outside of herself and see her own worth."[100] One of his closing comments on the movie suggests the radical change that had taken place in the course of the film's production: "By now Clark

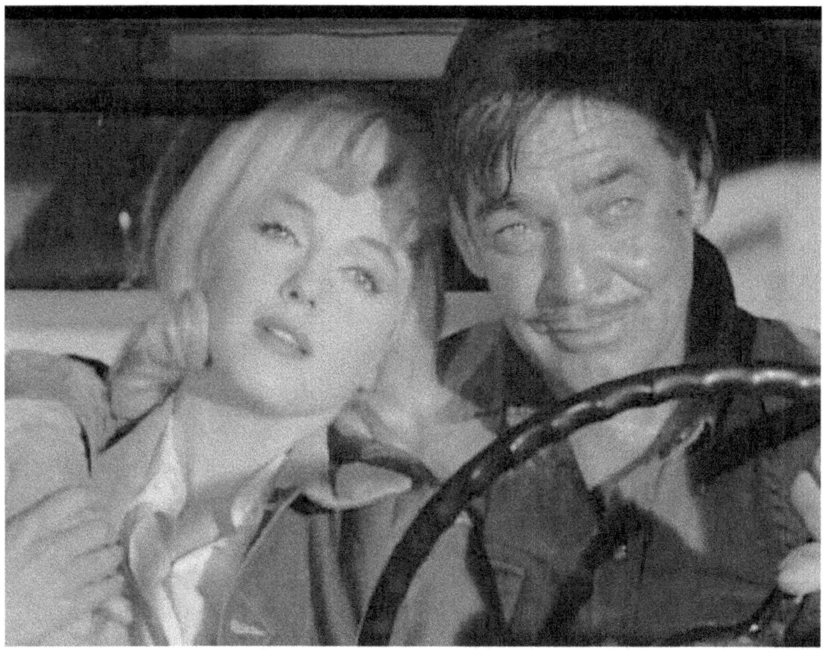

Roslyn: "How do you find your way home in the dark?"

Gable and Gay Langland are one and the same guy. I don't know where one leaves off and the other begins. Clark is a hero in the mythical sense of the word as well as being real. All of the pieces became one strand of emotion. Clark, the picture, have a majesty about them that is deeply moving to me. I felt proud that we could create it."[101] In 2001, Eli Wallach (Guido) offered his own summary pronouncement on *The Misfits*, emphasizing separation and dissolution: "Something happened in the relationship [between Monroe and Miller] that was tearing it apart," he recalled. "She was conflicted between her real life and the acted life. Arthur had written her a valentine, a love piece. Each male in the movie spoke of how glamorous she was, how wonderful, how beautiful, how sensitive. And each one was going to resurrect and save that woman. That made her more unhappy."[102] Forty years after the film's completion, Wallach, no less culpable of conflating Monroe's "real life and acted life" than he accuses her of being, unintentionally summarizes many of the reasons that *The Misfits* was such a demoralizing experience for her.

The "valentine, a love piece" Miller wrote for Monroe romanticized her without granting her character any agency beyond her capacity to attract males sexually. He also could not allow Monroe, as an actor, to affect the plot's evolution. Males in the cast flattered her for her glamor, beauty, and wonderfulness (as does Metty's cinematography), but the screenplay values her sensitivity not at all, revealing it to have only minimal effect on the narrative's resolution. Each character "was going to save and resurrect that woman"—except that throughout most of the film, the males are the ones most needful of salvation and resurrection, to which task Roslyn devotes much of her energy.

The fact that all of this had the effect of making Monroe unhappier seemed to Wallach one of those unintelligible mysteries of woman. Thus the film that Miller intended to allow Monroe to find "her own worth" turned out, in her mind, to be just another vehicle exploiting her in order to seduce people to come and spend their money, to see another sex film about a "dumb blonde" or a "sex freak." Like Roslyn, who comments shortly after the divorce hearing early in *The Misfits*, "The trouble is I'm always back where I started," Monroe would find herself reciting the line, "I never had anybody much. Here I . . . am,"[103] invoking the sad story of her irremediably split identity, dramatized onscreen by *The Misfits* much as she had experienced it so painfully in her life.

NOTES

1. J. Randy Taraborrelli, *The Secret Life of Marilyn Monroe* (New York: Grand Central Publishing, 2010), 308.
2. Arthur Miller, "My Wife Marilyn: An Affectionate Tribute to Her Feat," *Life*, December 22, 1958.
3. Arthur Miller, *Timebends: A Life* (New York: Grove Press, 1987), 466.
4. James Goode, *The Story of the Misfits* (New York: Bobbs-Merrill, 1963), 257.
5. Richard Dyer, *Heavenly Bodies: Film Stars and Society*, 2nd ed. (London: Routledge, 2004), 18.
6. Ibid., 25.
7. Ibid., 19.
8. Ibid., 56.
9. Sabrina Barton's excellent essay on *How to Marry a Millionaire* and *Gentlemen Prefer Blondes* admonishes viewers/critics: "If we, as film viewers, habitually reduce Monroe to a fetishized object, then we fail to see the forms of power she yields. In particular, we overlook her ability to control or elude the male agendas of the male characters who (they think) have her snared for their own desires." Sabrina Barton, "Face Value," in *All the Available Light: A Marilyn Monroe Reader*, ed. Yona Zeldis McDonough (New York: Touchstone Books, 2002), 129–30. Her argument is that in those films, the Monroe character triumphs through her conveyance of "play and the playfulness of surfaces," and that critics err in seeking to penetrate the surface of Monroe's performances in pursuit of some fixed self underlying them. Although this essay is guilty as charged, it nonetheless attempts to document the "forms of power [Roslyn/Marilyn] yields" until the "male agendas" of Miller and Huston snare her for the purposes of advancing their own desires in making *The Misfits*.
10. Goode, *The Story of the Misfits*, 300.

11. Jeffrey Meyers, *The Genius and the Goddess: Arthur Miller and Marilyn Monroe* (Urbana: University of Illinois Press, 2009), 226.
12. Sam B. Girgus, *Levinas and the Cinema of Redemption: Time, Ethics, and the Feminine* (New York: Columbia University Press, 2010), 95.
13. Sara Bartlett Churchwell, *The Many Lives of Marilyn Monroe* (New York: Picador, 2004), 113.
14. Arthur Miller, *After the Fall* (New York: Penguin Books, 1964), 88.
15. Ibid., 93–94.
16. Ibid., 95. In *Timebends*, Miller ascribed to himself and Monroe early in their relationship similar role expectations: "I had joyously accepted the role she had long been fashioning for someone who would save her, and so far I had not made it happen; just as she had seemed all-forgiving and the sensuous beloved that a self-denying life had been preparing me for long before she arrived" (460).
17. Churchwell, *The Many Lives of Marilyn Monroe*, 111.
18. Miller, *Timebends*, 466.
19. Ibid., 532.
20. Meyers, *The Genius and the Goddess*, 27.
21. George Barris, *Marilyn: Her Life in Her Own Words* (New York: Citadel Press, 2003), 98.
22. W. J. Weatherby, *Conversations with Marilyn* (New York: Paragon House, 1992), 67.
23. Truman Capote, "A Beautiful Child," in *Portraits and Observations: The Essays of Truman Capote* (New York: Random House, 2007), 474.
24. Meyers, *The Genius and the Goddess*, 226.
25. Arthur Miller and Serge Toubiana, *The Misfits: Story of a Shoot* (London: Phaidon, 2000), 44.
26. Taraborrelli, *The Secret Life of Marilyn Monroe*, 322.
27. Sir Laurence Olivier, "The Prince and the Showgirl," in *All the Available Light: A Marilyn Monroe Reader*, ed. Yona Zeldis McDonogh (New York: Touchstone Books, 2002), 159.
28. John Huston, quoted in Ty Burr, *Gods Like Us: On Movie Stardom and Modern Fame* (New York: Pantheon Books, 2012), 176.
29. Marilyn Monroe with Ben Hecht, *My Story* (Lanham, Md.: Taylor Trade Publishing, 2007), 22.
30. Ibid., 24.
31. Ibid., 23.
32. Ibid., 25.
33. Meyers, *The Genius and the Goddess*, 105.
34. Weatherby, *Conversations*, 153.
35. Meyers, *The Genius and the Goddess*, 237.
36. Miller, *Timebends*, 489.
37. Meyers, *The Genius and the Goddess*, 112.
38. Monroe, *My Story*, 53.
39. Ibid., 137.
40. Ibid., 93.
41. Ibid., 95.
42. Meyers, *The Genius and the Goddess*, 75.

43. Monroe, *My Story*, 138–39.
44. Meyers, *The Genius and the Goddess*, 33–34.
45. Ibid., 34.
46. Ibid., 212.
47. Barbara Leaming, *Marilyn Monroe* (New York: Three Rivers Press, 1998), 367.
48. Weatherby, *Conversations*, 174.
49. Goode, *The Story of the Misfits*, 199.
50. Guus Luitjers, *Marilyn: The Never Ending Dream* (New York: Grosset and Dunlap, 1974), 18.
51. In *Legend: The Life and Death of Marilyn Monroe*, Fred Lawrence Guiles quotes Monroe's masseur, Ralph Roberts, to the effect that Miller, Huston, and Wallach conspired late in the shooting to change the script so that Gay Langland became an "alcoholic bum," Roslyn was "not only a divorcee, but a prostitute," and Wallach's character, Guido, became the film's hero (390). Only those who have nothing but contempt for Miller, Huston, and Wallach as artists could possibly accept such a story or believe that Fox executives would endorse this radical reshuffling of star personae, which contradicts nearly everything that the first two-thirds of the film has established.
52. Miller, *Timebends*, 474.
53. Weatherby, *Conversations*, 49.
54. Miller and Toubiana, *The Misfits: Story of a Shoot*, 54.
55. Norman Mailer, *Marilyn* (New York: Grosset and Dunlap, 1974), 203.
56. Meyers, *The Genius and the Goddess*, 223.
57. Weatherby, *Conversations*, 59.
58. Arthur Miller, *The Misfits* (London: Methuen, 2002), 33. I usually cite Miller's screenplay/novelization of *The Misfits* (1961) in quoting from the film, since readers can locate dialogue more easily there than in the film. The most significant variations between film and novel are in the amplifications via narrative rendering; substantial dialogue variances are signaled in these notes.
59. Meyers, *The Genius and the Goddess*, 197.
60. Miller, *Timebends*, 460.
61. Taraborrelli, *The Secret Life of Marilyn Monroe*, 331.
62. Donald Spoto, *Marilyn Monroe: The Biography* (New York: Harper Paperbacks, 1993), 483.
63. Christopher Bigsby, *Arthur Miller: 1915–1962* (Cambridge, Mass.: Harvard University Press, 2009), 603.
64. Arthur Miller, "Please Don't Kill Anything," in *I Don't Need You Any More* (New York: Bantam Books, 1968), 59.
65. Ibid., 59.
66. Ibid., 60.
67. Arthur Miller, *The Misfits* (London: Methuen, 2002), 21.
68. Ibid., 80.
69. Ibid., 91.
70. Mailer, *Marilyn*, 204.
71. Leaming cites Metty as indicating that Monroe's eyes wouldn't focus and therefore she could not be photographed—thus the shutting down of the production (*Marilyn*

Monroe, 370). Spoto contends that Monroe's drug use was a pretext for ceasing production that was actually provoked by production cost overruns and Huston's massive gambling debts (*Marilyn Monroe: The Biography*, 545–46).

72. Donald H. Wolfe, *The Assassination of Marilyn Monroe* (New York: Warner Books, 1999), 438. Wolfe provides no source for this quotation.
73. Miller, *The Misfits*, 44.
74. Ibid., 94.
75. Ibid., 95.
76. Monroe, *My Story,* 183.
77. Miller, *The Misfits,* 120.
78. Lena Pepitone and William Stadiem, *Marilyn Monroe Confidential* (New York: Pocket Books, 1979), 150.
79. Weatherby, *Conversations*, 220.
80. Ibid., 187.
81. Bigsby, *Arthur Miller,* 628.
82. Goode, *The Story of the Misfits*, 45.
83. Ibid.
84. Miller, *The Misfits*, 28.
85. Ibid., 42.
86. Ibid., 115.
87. Miller's *Misfits* includes Roslyn's commentary on the mustangs' freeing: "But you know something?" she asks Gay. "For a minute, when those horses galloped away, it was almost like I gave them back their life. And all of a sudden, I got a feeling—it's crazy!—I suddenly thought, 'He must love me, or how would I dare do this?'" (133). This passage clearly elides Roslyn's triumph in freeing the horses with that triumph's more gendered, conventional meaning: "He must love me."
88. Weatherby, *Conversations*, 75–76.
89. Arthur Miller, "Making *The Misfits*," directed by Gail Levin, on *The Misfits*, directed by John Huston (1961; Image Entertainment, 2001), DVD.
90. Luitjers, *Marilyn,* 18.
91. Barris, *Marilyn*, 126.
92. Miller, *Timebends*, 464.
93. Ibid., 473.
94. Meyers, *The Genius and the Goddess*, 233.
95. Miller, *The Misfits*, 131.
96. Ibid., 134.
97. Taraborrelli, *The Secret Life*, 312.
98. Miller, *The Misfits*, 134.
99. Ibid.
100. Miller, *Timebends*, 459.
101. Ibid., 331.
102. Eli Wallach, quoted in "Making *The Misfits*."
103. Miller, *The Misfits,* 15.

9

HOLLYWOOD'S "PROPER STRANGER": NATALIE WOOD'S KNOWING INNOCENCE AND UNCERTAIN EXPERIENCE

Cynthia Lucia

IF FASCINATION WITH HER BEAUTIFUL FACE AND DEEP BROWN EYES dominated fanzine and popular press accounts of Natalie Wood during her years as a child actor and later as an adult star, it was not until her untimely death by drowning in 1981 that the star's body sparked vaguely erotic and persistent interest in the press and among the public and authorities. In many ways allegorizing the tension between presence (on the imaginary space of the screen) and absence (in the real space of the theater) central to the often-elusive dynamic of desire underpinning screen stardom, the fascination with Wood's death expresses forms of unrequited desire for knowledge, which the star's body potentially provides but continues to deny. Neither the initial investigation nor the one thirty years later in 2011 and 2012—which amended the death certificate to include "other undetermined factors" in addition to "drowning" as the cause of death and to replace "accidental" with "undetermined"—clarifies the manner of death.[1] Competing narratives concerning the circumstances of Wood's death disturbingly fracture the melodramatic tendencies stardom itself embodies and articulates—tendencies that Christine Gledhill describes as aimed at creating moral legibility by enacting narratives in which "deliberate deceptions" and "hidden secrets" are uncovered and "true identities" revealed.[2] The multiple narratives surrounding Natalie Wood's death compete not only in their real-world referents, but also with and against Wood's roles and her star persona—the part-real, part-fabricated actress and woman that studio publicity departments honed and mainstream media distributed for public consumption.

The illegibility of Wood's death—on a Thanksgiving-weekend yacht excursion—is heightened by the presence of two additional stars: her husband, former matinee idol and then television personality Robert Wagner, who owned the yacht (called *Splendour*, in honor of *Splendor in the Grass*, arguably Wood's most iconic role as a film actress), and actor Christopher Walken, co-starring with Wood in *Brainstorm*, a movie on which they were working at the time. Also present, if only metaphorically, was Natalie's consummate stage mother, Maria, who, by all accounts, lived vicariously (and perhaps parasitically) through her daughter. Maria not only aggressively engineered her four-year-old daughter's entry into movies, but she also infused the child with a catalogue of anxieties and fears, chief among them a fear of drowning in dark water—the fate a gypsy fortuneteller reportedly predicted for the mother that hauntingly would end not her own life but that of her daughter.[3]

The mother, the husband, the co-star, and Hollywood itself all placed demands on the child, the woman, the actress, and the star—sometimes in conflicting directions—with which Wood at times complied and against which she at other times rebelled. Her best film performances were in roles she pursued most aggressively, perhaps because they spoke powerfully to her in some personal way: those for which she earned Academy Award nominations, as supporting actress in *Rebel Without a Cause* (1955) and as actress in a leading role in *Splendor in the Grass* (1961) and *Love with the Proper Stranger* (1963); and those in films that earned lesser critical acclaim, in spite of her moving performances, including *Gypsy* (1962), *Inside Daisy Clover* (1965), and *This Property Is Condemned* (1966). All these roles involve her character's attempt to assert independence, whether from overprotective parents and family members or from demands of the entertainment industry—the two defining poles in her real life. Truly a child of the Hollywood studio system, Wood was the last of the studio stars to have been raised and nurtured within the industry and to have successfully emerged into adult stardom at the very moment when the system that supported her was disintegrating. As I have argued elsewhere,[4] Natalie Wood—like the system itself at the time—often was perceived and represented as a figure in transition—whether from child actor to adult star, or from Hollywood movie star to serious film actress in the burgeoning New Hollywood, now embracing a heightened realism and Method-trained actors to embody it. Both transitions provided challenges that Wood embraced and about which she also, at times, expressed conflicting feelings, even reportedly on the evening of her death, when she, Walken, and Wagner argued about varying degrees of commitment to career.[5]

THE MAKING AND SHAPING OF NATALIE WOOD

Natalie Wood's movie career began with a non-speaking role in Irving Pichel's *Happy Land* (1943), which was shot in her hometown of Santa Rosa. Born in San Francisco in 1938 to Russian parents as Natalia Nikolaevna Zakharenko, a family name her father changed to "Gurdin" for better placement on Depression job lists, Wood remained fluent in Russian throughout her life.[6] Her father ("Fahd"), a carpenter plagued by alcoholism, eventually was employed in studio set construction after his daughter and his wife became fixtures in the system. Wood's mother, Maria ("Mud"), claimed to be a former amateur ballet dancer and/or actress in her native Russia and devoted herself, in America, to promoting Natalie's career (her older daughter Olga married and raised a family, while her younger daughter Lana also became the focus of Maria's efforts, though at an older age than Natalia had been and with only modest success). Her middle daughter's career was of such intense and immediate importance to the mother that she moved her family from Santa Rosa to Hollywood in 1944—despite their having almost no money—hoping to persuade Pichel to again cast Natalia, who preferred to be called Natasha. Studio press releases typically state that Pichel "sent for" Natasha, but biographer Suzanne Finstad tells a different story, culled from interviews with family members and close family friends at the time. Whatever the case, from the time he had met Natasha when directing *Happy Land*, Pichel had taken a strong interest in the little girl—not so much to make her a star, as studio publicity claims, but to protect her from the deforming effects of life as a child actor that he witnessed her mother so aggressively pursuing. Pichel, in fact, had offered to adopt Natasha, a serious offer that the family took lightly, as most would.[7] Finstad claims that Natasha "felt an oppressive burden, at five, to be a success in Hollywood, thinking she was responsible for the family's upheaval."[8] Maria found that her persistence did pay off, for at the age of seven Natasha Gurdin was christened yet again, this time as Natalie Wood,

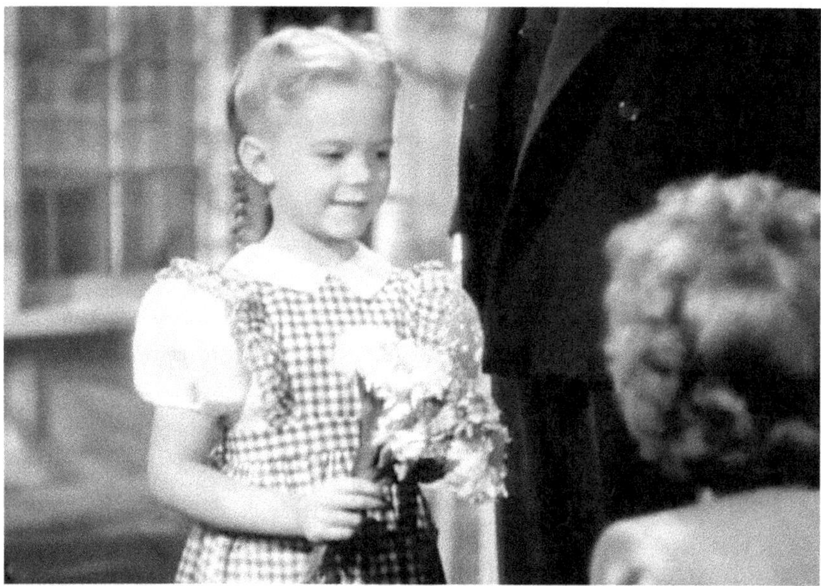

Natalie Wood at age seven in her first speaking role, in Irving Pichel's *Tomorrow Is Forever* (1946).

by producers at International Pictures, where she played her first speaking role as an Austrian refugee—required to speak German and English with a proper German accent—in Pichel's *Tomorrow Is Forever* (1946), alongside Orson Welles and Claudette Colbert. Her childhood career took hold with her performance, at age nine, as the precocious Susan who resists belief in Santa Claus in the box office hit *Miracle on 34th Street* (1947). After that film Natalie worked steadily, making several movies a year, until offers slowed a bit during her early adolescence. But even then she appeared in television roles, more often in pigtails and frilly dresses than in costumes appropriate to her age.

Despite director Nicholas Ray's initial reluctance to cast her in *Rebel Without a Cause* when she was seventeen, citing his concern that her childhood image would be difficult to erase in the public mind—rather ironic, given that, more than twenty years her senior, he was having an affair with the teenager at the time[9]—the film earned Wood her first Oscar nomination and a seven-year contract with Warner Bros. The film also initiated the shaping of a teen star that would persist, in many ways, throughout her adult life. A 1957 issue of *Look* called Wood a "Teenage Tiger," citing her as a "favorite rebel of many teen-agers," while at the same time explaining that she was ambitious and hard-working and continued to live with her parents. Although drawing from her "rebel" image in the film, the article implies that she is a "safe" rebel, politically non-activist, sexually inactive, and, as a result, clearly non-threatening. Often allegorizing the Freudian family drama in which fathers, other male relatives, or controlling mothers must relinquish claims on their daughter's sexual innocence, many of Wood's films reflexively play out, for viewers, the process of witnessing the child star's maturation onscreen, thus actively transferring the erotic tensions underlying family. Among these narratives are *The Searchers* and *A Cry in the Night* (both 1956 films that cast Wood as a kidnapping victim, though in very different settings), *Bombers B-52* (1957), *Marjorie Morningstar* (1958), *Cash McCall* (1960), *Splendor in the Grass,* and *West Side Story* (both 1961 films in which, at age twenty-three, the actress plays teenagers whose sexual innocence—and fulfillment—are at stake).

Attention to Wood's body and to her maturation in these films is animated by larger anxieties surrounding the sexualized female body, at a time, in the 1950s and early 1960s, when repression of female sexual desire remained a dominant cultural and cinematic trope in good girl/bad girl binaries, largely rooted in earlier postwar efforts to return to the "normalcy" of the traditional family with men as sole breadwinners and women as homemakers and caretakers of the children. This trope is reinforced, though never resolved or contained, of course, by film noir narratives bifurcating the female into the domestic nurturer or the sexualized femme fatale, a subject to which so much significant feminist film theory has been devoted. Elaine Tyler May, following those examples, and extending her discussion to later 1950s representations, observes that the sexualized female became less threatening but only if her sexuality was properly channeled: "Sexy women who became devoted sweethearts and wives would contribute to the goodness of life," and "those who used their sexuality for power or greed would destroy men, families, and even society."[10]

Upon Natalie Wood's emergence into adult stardom, her image required careful construction for audiences invested in her childhood innocence who thus imagined her to embody the ideal "devoted sweetheart." At the same time, it was necessary to acknowledge her sexualized womanhood, even if in muted terms, and sometimes with the aid of costuming that supplied curvaceous enhancements. Studio-orchestrated romances further balanced her aura of innocence with hints of sexual experience, the most seemingly marketable of which was her pairing with the wildly popular teen idol Tab Hunter, as both co-star and "real-life" romantic interest. Wood and Hunter frequently were "spotted" out on the town—by studio publicity cameras, always conveniently present. Warner Bros. had hoped that the Hunter-Wood pairing would take hold with teen audiences, but the chemistry didn't work, in part because of Hunter's obvious limitations as an actor. The pairing in many ways stalled Wood's career, as evident in *The Girl He Left Behind* (1956), in which Wood's "good" but implicitly willing Susan quite literally is left behind, as she waits devotedly for her boyfriend to return from the military—and to grow up. The audience also must wait patiently to catch a glimpse of Wood, with the narrative trained mostly on Hunter's exploits.

Those press and studio publicity accounts that did give attention to Wood's body when she emerged into adult stardom always represented her as diminutive, pixie-ish, and petite—rarely if ever in eroticized terms. A 1963 *Look* article describes the twenty-five-year-old Wood as somehow still growing up—as an uncommonly beautiful woman, but one whom, like a child, "men hold tenderly, not passionately."[11] A year earlier *Newsweek* describes her as "tiny, young, and . . . vulnerable," ironically at the very time when she was rehearsing her role as the well-known burlesque performer in *Gypsy*.[12] For audiences who had seen Natalie Wood grow up onscreen, the star represented something of a paradox: The child remained a presence in the woman whose sexuality and personality always hinted at vulnerability and, perhaps, an inscrutable sadness—whether behind her dark eyes or in the occasional crack in her laughter, suggesting something less joyful beneath.

With popularization of the Method and the demise of the studio system came a new dichotomy separating stars from serious actors in critical and popular perception, a division Wood hoped to bridge, admitting that she enjoyed stardom,[13] but also expressing commitment to her craft—as evident in a 1957 *Life* article entitled "Strange Doings of Actress at Practice," in which she and actors Dennis Hopper and Nick Adams are shown honing their craft both in private and on the streets, where they observe everyday people and everyday life.[14] Given her work with Ray in *Rebel*, with Elia Kazan (a founding member of Actor's Studio) in *Splendor*, and in Robert Mulligan's *Love with the Proper Stranger*, Wood appeared perfectly poised to make the transition into a New Hollywood career.

As in *Splendor*, *Love with the Proper Stranger* not only registers a shift through its heightened realism of style and subject matter, very much in tune with the emerging New Hollywood, but it also registers a cultural shift in acknowledging the damaging effects of sexual repression and overprotective families. Each film, in a different way, acknowledges a woman's sexual needs and desires while admittedly bracketed within her more conventional longing for love and marriage. In *Proper Stranger* Wood's character announces her sexual independence through a one-night stand that results in pregnancy, a circumstance the film remarkably refuses to castigate. And, while it still upholds conventional good girl/bad girl divisions concerning female sexuality, *Splendor* exposes mores of the late 1950s and early 1960s as repressive and destructive, albeit in a story set in the explosive year of 1929, the setting itself interestingly anticipating changes to come in the 1960s. The subtle cultural transitions that would eventually lead to a sexual revolution, at the same time that a declining Hollywood would try to keep pace, were conditions that found conflicted expression through the body and roles of Natalie Wood, in a far more persistent and pronounced way than in the case of any other female star of the period. Her status as the last child of the system infused an inherently rich, if not always consciously adopted, reflexivity.

Love with the Proper Stranger, a much-neglected film in her career though one that is quite consciously reflexive in its casting of Wood and shaping of her character, serves as a fascinating case study of the star and her paradoxically sexualized yet vulnerably innocent body—whether through visual echoes with several of Wood's earlier films, most notably *Splendor*, its narrative and visual treatment of Wood's character, or its clear alignment with what would come to be considered New Hollywood aesthetics, defined by location shooting, hand-held camera work, deep-focus shot composition, and black-and-white cinematography.

LOVE WITH THE PROPER STRANGER: NATALIE WOOD AS EXPERIENCED INNOCENT

Regarded by film historian Paul Monaco as a hopeful product of the New Hollywood about to emerge from the ashes of the demolished studios, *Love with the Proper Stranger* also positioned Natalie Wood, now as a woman, who potentially could effect a second transition, this time from the old studio style of stardom to the hip, new, Method-inflected status as a serious actress. Monaco claims, however, that Wood's promise in *Proper Stranger* was undermined by the box office failure of *This Property Is Condemned* (1966)[15]—a conclusion that most certainly is arguable. In that film, loosely based on a Tennessee Williams play, her performance is touching as a woman whose mother, in effect, places her as a commodity on the sexual marketplace in their remote Mississippi town—not unlike *Gypsy* and *Inside Daisy Clover*, which construct Wood's character as a commodity on the entertainment market. All three films, as noted, directly or indirectly echo the roles that first her mother and then the studios would come to play in Wood's own life. Two other notable film roles that hinged on a nuanced interplay of sexual innocence and experience—even when Wood was approaching and over thirty—were *Sex and the Single Girl* (1964), with its "does she or doesn't she narrative," oddly centered on Wood's (academically) experienced sexologist, and her last big hit, *Bob & Carol & Ted & Alice* (1969), with its ensemble cast treating adult sexual ennui and experimentation in the explicit (for its time) and hilarious terms made possible only by the Production Code's final demise.

Arguably Wood's most accomplished screen performance, *Love with the Proper Stranger*, six years earlier, also treats sexuality frankly through Wood's comic yet tender Oscar-nominated role as a pregnant single woman forced to choose among an illegal backroom abortion, a loveless marriage, or single motherhood. *Proper Stranger* represents the convergence of major tropes and themes that came to define Wood, her body and persona, from her teens forward, reimagined here in a humor-inflected narrative. Even though an adult, her character is plagued by an overprotective family. As in her earlier films, *Proper Stranger* reflexively provides the audience a stake in Wood's mature, sexualized body, through costuming and settings recalling her earlier work, while simultaneously repositioning her on the cusp of the New Hollywood.

Whether intentionally reflexive or not, for instance, the fact that Wood as Angie Rossini finds herself back at Macy's department store, the location where she established herself as a child actor in *Miracle on 34th Street*, likely was not lost on viewers—even those as young as sixteen who would have seen her in *Miracle* at age ten. Her precocious nine-year-old in *Miracle* resides palpably within the twentyish, knocked-up pet department salesgirl of *Proper Stranger*. Although independent in spirit, the Italian Catholic Angie still lives (unhappily) with her family in a noisy, cluttered, chaotic apartment, and responds with exasperated affection when her older brother Dominick (Herschel Bernardi) insists on pulling up to Macy's in his fruit truck to drive her home from work. Their Italian-born mother bemoans the new values of America in a manner that unmistakably recalls the song of that title in Wood's 1961 film *West Side Story*, in which her Puerto Rican–born Maria also struggles for independence in love against strong ethnic divisions. Dominick assures his mother he has only to take Angie out for lunch to quell her desire for her own apartment, a yearning for autonomy unheard of in the family's old-world tradition. Although played for humor when family tradition clashes with Angie's more modern Manhattan sensibility, the film never condescends, clearly aware of an audience also in transition.

Angie's one-night stand at a hotel resort—a moment only briefly referenced and never shown in the film—is with Rocky Papasano (Steve McQueen), a horn player looking for work at the local union hall, where Angie also is looking for him as the film opens. Hand-held camera work, along with black-and-white cinematography, establishes the film's realist aesthetic, as hungry musicians gradually populate what is at first an eerily deserted, cavernous space. Here it becomes clear that Rocky can maneuver his way into a job as cleverly as he can into a woman's apartment. When Angie finally finds him in the now overstuffed space in order to deliver her news, he doesn't quite remember her. Although she has no illusions, she is taken aback by this lapse, and when he later seeks her out at Macy's to announce that he will help pay for an abortion, she accepts but with some unease. Wood and McQueen carefully balance their characters' awkward, self-conscious regret, mingled with mild yet growing curiosity when confronting each other on such intimate terms as strangers. When they meet one Sunday afternoon on a cold, deserted meat district corner and find they are fifty dollars short for the procedure scheduled to take place in forty-five minutes, Rocky takes her along to find his only source of extra money—his parents, whom he hasn't seen for some time but knows predictably where they will be on a Sunday afternoon, warm or cold, rain or shine. At this asphalt playground, adjacent to a highway, Angie discovers that their backgrounds are similarly traditional and that both she and Rocky have refashioned themselves for escape. Rocky's family assumes Angie is his girlfriend, and key moments, shot tellingly through her point of view, lead her to understand Rocky's own sense of embarrassed failure when first his father and then his mother surreptitiously press cash into his hand, without his ever asking. Angie also sees his wistful discomfort in talking with a former girlfriend, as her husband introduces Rocky to their kids. Angie's point of view dominates as she learns more about the man with whom she's slept but doesn't yet know—in reversal of the well-worn pattern tending almost always toward male vision and perception, as Laura Mulvey has famously argued.[16] In this sequence as elsewhere, the film privileges Angie's point of view above others, although director Robert Mulligan and cinematographer Milton R. Krasner largely prefer richly layered, deep-focus framing.

Mulligan and Krasner adopt this long-take, deep-focus shooting often throughout the film and to especially strong effect in a set piece when, after obtaining the extra money, Angie and Rocky need to kill some time before the scheduled abortion. They end up in his family's furniture upholstery shop, with a half-finished couch on display, suspended in the process of creation during this Sunday, much as Angie and Rocky are suspended in the process of self-definition in their adult lives, uncertain how to achieve fulfillment or where it may lead. Both do, however, have some idea of what they don't want, but even in that they seem to waver. Although not part of the family business, Rocky "used to sneak up here nights with girls," he tells Angie, offering her wine from the cupboard where it's hidden. Angie and Rocky talk in uncertain terms about their one night together. When she confesses that it was a "stupid experiment," and all she felt was "scared and disgusted," despite the build-up in books and movies, he seems insulted—and she challenges him on this, well aware that their encounter was one of many such nights in his life. He recalls his former girlfriend at the playground: "She's two years younger than me, can you believe that?" he asks, implying that marriage,

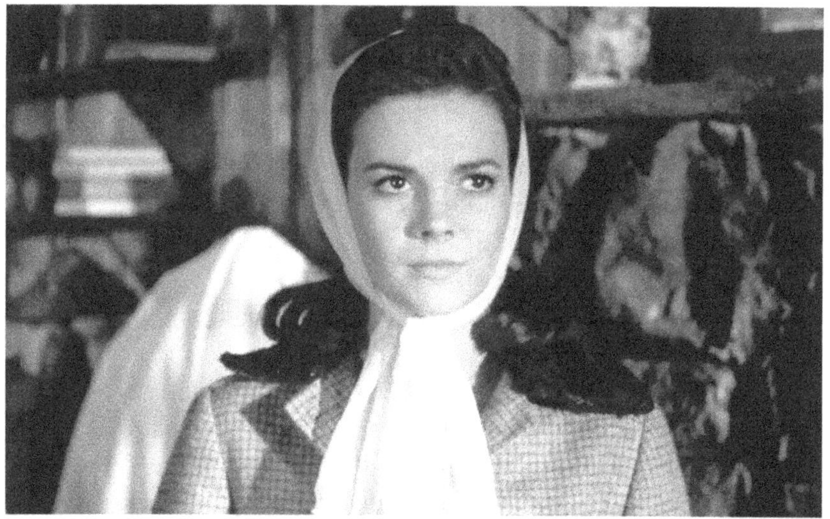

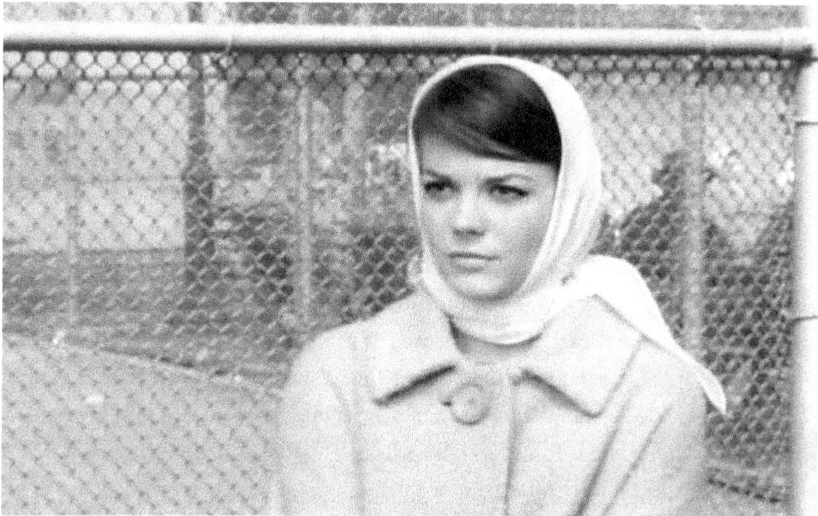

Top: As Deanie in Elia Kazan's *Splendor in the Grass* (1961), Wood's white headscarf signals her sexual innocence. *Bottom:* On the day of her planned abortion, Angie, in Robert Mulligan's *Love with the Proper Stranger* (1963), wears a white headscarf, recalling Wood in *Splendor in the Grass* and conveying a knowing innocence and uncertain experience.

children, and convention drain youth, vigor, and aspiration. "I hate to come back here," he concludes bitterly. She reflects that the "half a dozen kids who couldn't live without each other" in her high school and got married now are "either . . . divorced or miserable." When he likens a married man to a prisoner, however, she resists this notion, saying that the lonely people she observes on the subway seem to look at the world through deadened, "glassy eyes," and that isolation isn't such a good thing. Depth of focus in this scene conveys their complex choreography of tentative approach and embarrassed avoidance.

Wearing a white headscarf on this day of the scheduled abortion, Angie exudes an innocence, insight, and vulnerability that gather reflexive resonance for careful viewers familiar with Wood's earlier performance in *Splendor in the Grass*. As Deanie in that film, she is a high school senior deeply in love with her boyfriend, Bud (Warren Beatty), both in the throes of overwhelming sexual desire—and frustration—for both are inculcated by the attitude of the day, making it clear that good girls don't and bad girls do. While *Splendor* presents a serious critique of the "sexual containment ideology" of the period, as Elaine Tyler May describes it,[17] it does reinforce the good/bad dichotomy through Bud's sister Ginny (Barbara Loden), who had "one of those awful operations," as Deanie's puritanical mother (Audrey Christie) explains. Although sympathetic, Ginny is something of a cautionary figure against whom Deanie is defined, no more apparent than through costuming, with Wood wearing a white headscarf, as in *Proper Stranger*, in a scene with the two women and their beau.

Angie in *Proper Stranger* is, in effect, an amalgam of Deanie and Ginny in *Splendor*—a nice girl who "does" and is about to have "one of those awful operations." In *Proper Stranger* Wood embodies knowing innocence and uncertain experience, vulnerability and independence of spirit, qualities aimed not so much at tempering viewer responses to Angie but rather at suggesting that these qualities are not oppositional. At the same time, the film makes the abortion scene no less awful than imagined in *Splendor*, yet does so not to castigate Angie for seeking it out but rather to rebuke a society that forces her and countless other women into deserted streets and abandoned apartment buildings to obtain it. Deep focus composition, after she is forced to hurriedly undress, speaks to their growing bond as Rocky breaks in and embraces her in the midst of these appalling conditions. Neither she nor he can go through with it—not for moral reasons involving the fetus or sentimentalized notions of motherhood or fatherhood, but rather because it is just too "awful" an experience, under these conditions, for any woman.

The implicitly promiscuous figure in *Proper Stranger* (in addition to Rocky, who is explicitly so) is the stripper Barbie (Edie Adams), with whom Rocky lives. Although somewhat stereotyped through dialect as a rough-and-tumble working girl, Barbie is never positioned as morally "bad," whether in terms of her profession or her liaison with Rocky. Against type, Barbie lives a fairly stable domestic life with a decent apartment and three dogs. These canine characters introduce Barbie as they huddle against her bare legs waiting for their breakfast in a funny send-up of the usual visual cliché. Yet the film does make a distinction—Angie is a woman from a working-class background who sometimes drops the "g" in words that end in it, but in her aspirations, dress, and self-presentation she is coded as significantly more refined than Barbie. At the same time, both are women with lives and ambitions that stand apart from traditional values. Rocky obviously uses Barbie, more for her apartment than for sex, it would seem, while his deepening concern and affection for Angie far outstrip his feelings for Barbie. Barbie's name, of course, at a time when the doll was so popular among young girls, is both a send-up and mild commentary on the contradictory demands placed on women as objects of pleasure, whether for male or childhood female fantasy. This Barbie, however, is no fool, for when Rocky asks "for a friend" if she knows of any "doctors," she sends him packing.

In a humorous yet poignant convergence of characters and values, Barbie returns home one morning to find Angie there—the only place Rocky could take her, with his key still in hand, after her traumatic near-abortion. Shortly after, Rocky appears with a black eye, escorted by Angie's brother Dominick, who had been following the two ever since their meeting in the playground with Rocky's family. With everyone now aware that she is pregnant, Angie feels liberated. When Dominick says of Rocky, "He came like a man and he's willing to marry you," Angie refuses. Rocky's admission that he's as much "to blame" as she is disturbingly recalls his earlier confession that marriage is like a prison sentence. "I don't want to be a warden all my life," Angie proclaims, nor does she want to live in a "household full of unhappy people," which is what marriage and children in this circumstance would mean.

Unwilling to live with a man who feels imprisoned by the arrangement, Angie, at the same time, seems willing to imprison herself by considering marriage to Anthony Columbo (Tom Bosley), a family friend who has always wanted to marry her. Angie extends polite courtesy to Anthony but nothing more, despite her family's relentless pressure. The two Columbo scenes in the film are played for humor—his unassuming earnestness against her well-mannered avoidance; her slender, dark beauty against his short, stocky frame. Comical as they are, the scenes nevertheless register conflicting demands centered on Wood's character, through body and performance. In the first Columbo scene, Angie is about to take a bath in a desperate attempt to secure privacy in the cramped apartment. Dominick unceremoniously enters the bathroom, entreating her to come out and greet Columbo who has come calling. "It's my own fault," Angie reasons with herself. "I'm a big girl. I make my own money. Who says I have to live here if I don't want to live here?" She does, however, comply in the awkward, funny scene to follow. In the second Columbo scene, Angie is "experimenting" again, this time with the possibility of marriage to a man for whom she feels mild friendship but little attraction. She is having dinner with Columbo's mother and two sisters as his intended. Columbo knows that Angie is pregnant and is happy to marry her but would like his family to think the child is his. The dinner scene is a comedy of spills, trips, and contradictions on the part of a nervous Angie, who is trying very hard to please one very conventional and one very liberated, politically astute sister, as well as their imposing, sharp-eyed mother, who has the final word: "She's not a bad-looking girl, but she's so clumsy." This is the last we see of Columbo. Both scenes establish Angie's good-girlness through both conservative costuming—in the first scene she wears slacks and a sweater and in the second scene a skirt and sweater—and her desire to please, if reluctantly at first. While willing to please and to compromise, she never deceives Columbo, thus never verging into femme fatale territory, and always paradoxically capturing a knowing innocence within uncertain experience.

Upon finally moving into her own apartment, Angie's transition toward genuine independence is underway, as she implicitly considers life as a single mother. When she invites Rocky for dinner, the approach/avoidance choreography of the more wistful upholstery shop scene here is leavened with humor as it becomes clear that each is very much attracted to and feels a growing affection for the other, while attempting to resist those feelings. Mingled in also is a complicating, if tentative, sense of possession each seems to claim over the other. Perfect comic timing characterizes their performances as Wood and McQueen negotiate their movements in the pleasant but somewhat constricted space of Angie's apartment. As she prepares dinner before Rocky arrives, Angie, now costumed in a low-cut, black evening dress, is nervously checking the stove when she suddenly is shocked upon looking into a mirror to discover the cleavage her dress displays. Fidgeting with the neckline, then adding a string of pearls, she can't quite seem to get it right. With reflexive tongue-in-cheek resonance, the moment replays the transition narrative central to almost all of Natalie Wood's teen and early-adult film roles and publicity, constructing her as the embodiment of sexualized innocence. Rocky's line when he enters makes this explicit: "You look so . . . you look like a woman."

Expressing a mild sense of entitlement, Rocky takes a taste of what's cooking and stretches out on the couch, admiring the apartment. As they kiss, at first tentatively and then passionately, Angie resists. When he reminds her that they've done far more in the past, she responds with a line typically reserved for male characters: "Don't you understand? I didn't know you then. I care about you

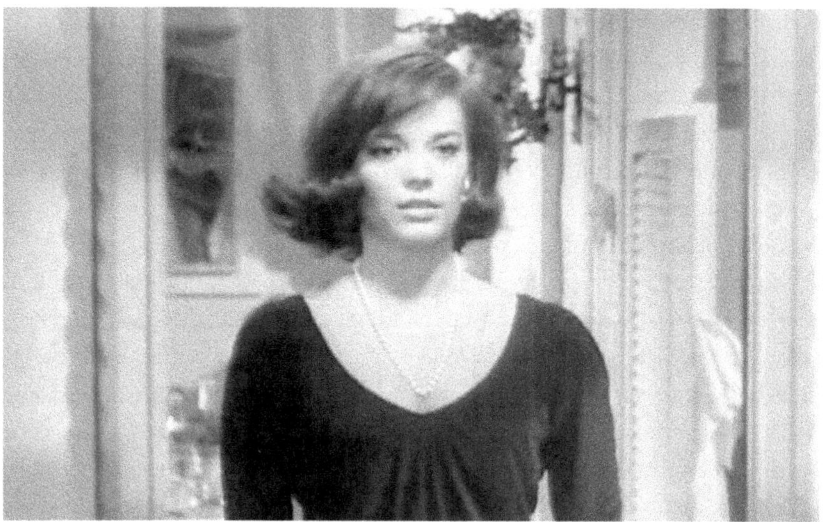

Natalie Wood, as Angie in *Love with the Proper Stranger* (1963), now looks "like a woman," while comically trying to hide her plunging neckline with a string of pearls, thus intimating the vulnerable girl beneath.

now"—words that unapologetically express the liberation she may have experienced in anonymous sex. The evening rapidly devolves, with Angie barely serving dinner before kicking Rocky out and dissolving into tears—her expression of liberation now tempered by the more conventional yet very human desire for emotional connection.

The film's title, of course, suggests a confluence of two seemingly incongruous states—of love, with the emotional intimacy it implies, in the arms of a complete, if "proper" stranger. It also indirectly captures something of the perpetual innocence that resides within the embodied experience of its female star. In Elmer Bernstein's title song, playing diegetically on the radio when Rocky and Angie pass time in the deserted upholstery shop, singer Jack Jones croons: "I could fall in love with the proper stranger, if I heard the bells and the banjos play." The lyrics reinforce a love-at-first-sight ideal, with the implication of a happily-ever-after existence—something Rocky and Angie in their conversation dispute, even if tempered by Angie's point about the "glassy-eyed," emotionally deadened look of people who live alone. When Angie emerges from Macy's in the film's final scene just after the comic, if unhappy, dinner scene, she is distracted by the sounds of a street musician to discover Rocky playing bells and a banjo and carrying a sign that reads: "Better Wed than Dead." Although their final embrace is consistent with the conventional Hollywood ending, bells and banjo are hardly the conventional instruments of romance, and the words on the sign could be read as an expression of resignation and compromise rather than loving commitment. Likewise, as the two embrace on the crowded corner, the hyperrealism of the hand-held camera and chaotic throng of passersby—both anticipating and shaping New Hollywood aesthetics—imply that the two will face challenges, that this is not a liaison of champagne, violins, and roses but rather of challenging, though negotiable, realities.

Love with the Proper Stranger thus mediates transitions that the culture itself was experiencing at the time and does so, significantly and reflexively, through the casting of Natalie Wood as a figure whose film persona serves to allegorize this very transition. Through its visual design and its often comically cluttered sound design, most notably in the apartment Angie shares with her family—and also, once again, through Wood as Angie—the film allegorizes the transition Hollywood also was undergoing toward independence from studio contracts and control and toward a new realism extending also to content—in this case with a political dimension involving the woman, her body, and a "powerful plea," as one reviewer described it at the time, to legalize abortion.[18] The subject of the film is, indeed, the woman's sexualized, eroticized body, yet in keeping with Wood's onscreen and public persona, the film refrains from eroticizing her body in visually explicit terms—the plunging neckline moment played for laughs rather than eroticism. She instead is girlishly sexy—a woman whom men would embrace tenderly rather than passionately, to recall the *Look* article published in the year of the film's release. In reviewing *Proper Stranger*, Stanley Kauffmann tellingly mentions, first, Wood's "beautiful dark eyes," before acknowledging her "gift for comedy."[19] Wood's face always trumped her body (and perhaps her talent), the "silent soliloquy" of the close-up, as Béla Belázs aptly phrased it,[20] always activating the presence/absence dynamic of cinematic desire—the longing for more—so aptly argued by Christian Metz and many who followed.[21] In his essay on "the erotics of the postmodern condition" Mike Goode, following Gilles Deleuze and Felix Guattari, describes the face as "the surface that most immediately identifies the body" with its features providing "bodies with organized, signifying, subjective presences," therefore having "the ability to 'present' a body." The absence of a face "dissolves all traces of the body's presence as a site of desire," thus "mark[ing] the face as the very cusp of presence."[22] The eyes and the face of Natalie Wood promised the "more" of experienced innocence she embodied, casting her as the "proper stranger" around whom fantasies of a certain sort might be given play.

SEIZING THE STAR IN LIFE AND IN DEATH

At age forty-three, her death, then, came as a shock—at the time, in 1981, well before the pervasive presence of electronic media with its news of stars and celebrities, their extraordinary exploits and their tragic ends, filling the infinite ether. The renewed interest in her life, her stardom, and her death, triggered by the Los Angeles sheriff's reopening of the case in 2011, itself allegorizes the paradoxical knowing innocence and uncertain experience Wood embodied, further expressing something akin to the "erotics of suspended subjectivity" that Goode defines, following Georges Bataille and Julia Kristeva, as the "pleasures of indeterminacy" arising "in the act of crossing subjectivity's limits."[23]

Whether further expressive of the postmodern tendency to "blur the lines between history and fiction, life and art," as Goode argues,[24] or a version of "Hollywood's dark tourism," the phenomenon drawing fans to famous gravesites that Linda Levitt explores,[25] the fascination with Natalie Wood's death also has much to do with Christine Gledhill's argument that "stars function as signs in a rhetorical system that works as melodrama," ultimately, therefore, requiring moral legibility.[26] In resisting such legibility, Wood's stardom and death place this notion strikingly into relief. Stardom-as-melodrama implies and uncovers a drive beyond simple knowledge of the on- and offscreen persona, to arrive instead at "seizure," a mode Goode explores in his discussion of Julian Barnes's 1984 novel, *Flaubert's Parrot*. The novel's protagonist acts in some ways as a movie star fan in his obsessive study of Flaubert, rooted indirectly in erotic aims, for his "wife's infidelities and subsequent death rendered the plot of his marriage an all-too-faithful reenactment of *Madame Bovary*"[27]—the dynamics of identification, as in cinema, therefore at play. Identification with Wood, as noted, always was tied up with transition, uncertainty, indeterminacy—all humanly "accessible" qualities, rendering her stardom and star persona compellingly allegorical, as evident in *Proper Stranger*.

Even when in her early forties at the time of her death, Wood appeared to be searching, exuding the indeterminacy of "suspended subjectivity," in an admittedly simplified application of this idea—someone not quite anchored within herself, despite her success in film and her status as a star. Actor Christopher Plummer, who appeared with Wood in *Inside Daisy Clover*, felt that "she underrated herself," recalling her having once said to him, "I'm just a trustworthy pro. I wish I could be more than that."[28] Her words capture Wood's ingenuous quality of self-knowledge much remarked upon by those who knew her. They also convey her confidence in doing the "job" well, mingled with misgivings about its larger power, significance, and artistry. Perhaps this sense of being (merely) a "trustworthy pro," of doing successfully what she was told to do, was rooted in her relationship with her mother, who placed on her daughter's shoulders the burden of success—not so much for the child's fulfillment but rather for the family's sustenance (despite strict rules about income apportionment of child actors by their parents). Her perception was likely also rooted in her relationship with the studios that trained, educated, groomed, and made use of her. In both instances the relationships appeared symbiotic, but the child was so young when she started that her very sense of what she wanted in and from her movie career most probably was shaped by her mother's and the studios' wishes and heightened by the child's desire to please and gain approval. These qualities, offset by willful intelligence, express themselves in her screen roles, as they do in *Proper Stranger*.

While caution is always advisable when drawing too literal a parallel between screen roles and the actor who plays them, it seems fair enough to claim that roles involving mother-daughter dynamics and the struggle for sexual freedom against repressive family and social mores attracted and deeply interested Natalie Wood. She actively campaigned for roles in *Splendor in the Grass*, *Gypsy*, and *Inside Daisy Clover*, turned down a role in *Charade* to play Angie in *Proper Stranger*, and worked a second time with *Proper Stranger* director Robert Mulligan on *This Property Is Condemned.* In *Splendor in the Grass*, *Gypsy*, and *This Property Is Condemned* she plays a daughter dominated by her mother: a repressive, an obsessive, and a consciously cruel and envious mother, respectively. In discussing her role in *Splendor*, Wood admitted the personal impact, while her words also anticipated the struggles her characters in the later films would experience:

> *Splendor* had been a very emotional experience. . . . I felt that in order to play some of those scenes I would have to open doors and relive a lot of feelings that I had put the lid on. . . . It did open up a lot of wounds and led to the marriage breaking up [her first of two marriages to Robert Wagner]. Then I knew I had to get to a doctor. My parents wanted me to go back to them, but I felt strongly that. . . . I needed to get, in today's words, "my head together.". . . I knew I needed to be independent.[29]

For different reasons, though similarly rooted in emotional vulnerability, she embraced the role of Angie in *Proper Stranger*, at a time when she was experiencing the painful breakdown and final break-up of her relationship with Warren Beatty, with whom she co-starred in *Splendor* and had been living for several years after her first marriage to Wagner ended. Of Angie, she said to her sister Lana that it was her "least neurotic role." She later claimed it was "the most rewarding experience" she had as an actor, at a time when her own life was "quite meager"—"the picture was 'it,'" she admitted.[30]

The emotional pressure placed on Natalie Wood as a child when she was directed to cry on cue is well documented in biographies and other sources.[31] In anticipation of Method training, it would seem, her mother Maria and older sister Olga would talk to the child, entreating her to relive the few traumatic events of her early life—most notably the death of her dog crushed under the wheels of a car—letting the director know when she was "ready" for the scene. This possibly is one indelible imprint of the child upon the woman, for as an adult Wood admitted that whenever given a role she "always counted the crying scenes" as a "barometer of how difficult the part would be" for her to play.[32] Perhaps the persistence of childlike vulnerability within the woman also can be traced to Maria's attempt to keep her daughter young beyond her years in order to ensure her continued work in the movies during her "awkward" adolescence. Maria's ambition, indeed, found expression on and through her daughter's body, not only in the pigtails and ruffles that made her appear a little girl, but also in other, more directly damaging ways. One particularly telling incident, when Natalie was ten years old, occurred on the set of *The Green Promise* (1949), where she suffered a broken wrist in an accident during shooting. Fearful that the studio (RKO) would replace her daughter or that other repercussions would result, Maria neither reported the injury nor had it tended to. Wood was forever after conscious of her misshapen left wrist that had healed improperly. She wore a cuff bracelet to cover the wrist in her films and public appearances, one accessory (along with what many critics observed as her excessive makeup) that she used in creating what she later would call "the badge"—the public, performative "Natalie Wood."[33]

Far more seriously as a teenager, around the time when she had completed *Rebel Without a Cause*, she was brutally raped and beaten by a prominent producer-director-star who summoned her to his hotel room purportedly to read for a part. Wood never reported the rape to police nor divulged the name of the assailant for fear that it would ruin her career—a legitimate if unfortunate fear at that time and place, regrettably reinforced by her mother who, according to biographer Finstad, in quoting a close friend of Natalie's at the time, "'thought it was great' that Natalie spent an evening with 'Mr. Show Biz.'"[34] Remarkably, in 2012, this incident resurfaced on an Internet site that identified the prominent man in question, in a posting reportedly written by actor Robert Downey Jr., a friend of Wood's eldest daughter, Natasha, who allegedly revealed this information.[35] The words Wood had spoken to Christopher Plummer conveying uncertainty about the value of her work take on deeper resonance in the context of "professionalism" as she was taught to accept it—the sacrifices and the overtly physical and emotional pain she understood it to entail.

That the body of the actress took center stage thirty years after her death with the reopening of the investigation speaks—beyond its legal implications—to the postmodern blurring of history and fiction that Goode examines when quoting *Flaubert's Parrot*: "We can study files for decades, but every so often we are tempted to throw up our hands and declare that history is merely another literary genre: the past is autobiographical fiction pretending to be parliamentary report."[36] The autopsy diagrams pointing to bruises, along with the original and revised coroners' narratives, in their very indeterminacy, stand as unwitting metaphors for the actress herself, in that the very vulnerability Wood projected as both child and adult star, and the sense of her existing in an indeterminate state of transition, now became literalized. The lingering questions that are both central to and extend beyond the evening of the incident are multiple: Upon retiring for the evening during a contentious, alcohol-infused discussion between Wagner and Walken, did Wood slip on a swim-step and then fall into the chilly Catalina waters as she attempted to secure a loose dinghy that often would bang against the stateroom wall, making sleep impossible?[37] After Walken later retired, did Wood and Wagner argue in that same stateroom, or did Wagner never enter that room until checking on and discovering his wife missing? Had certain bruises on her body been incurred before she entered the water and struggled, trying to hoist herself up into the untethered dinghy to which she clung?

New evidence prompted the reopening of the case not once but twice, with the November 2011 investigation closed in January 2012, only to be reopened again later that year. Among that evidence is information outlined in a book telling the story of *Splendour* skipper Dennis Davern, the fourth person onboard the night of Wood's death, who reports an argument between the couple,[38] as well as information supplied by numerous other witnesses, chief among them a woman on a nearby yacht who, having heard unanswered screams for help on that dark night, contacted authorities in 1981 but was never questioned.[39] The 1981 investigation itself is rife with ambiguities, including the abrupt demotion of chief medical examiner Thomas Noguchi, who was pressured—reportedly by the Wagners' close friend, Frank Sinatra—to desist his aggressive investigation and proposed "psychological autopsy" that would have probed into possible reasons for Wood's having left the yacht that night.[40] Amended on June 15, 2012, the coroner's report states that the source of several bruises remains inconclusive, consequently adding "other undetermined factors" to "drowning" as the cause of death, as noted. The case has remained open through the time of this writing, in mid-2015.[41]

Although indirectly implicated, Wagner has never been considered a legal suspect. By all accounts, the Wagners had a good marriage fraught with no more than the usual disagreements that occur in any long-term relationship. Theirs was a storybook romance, at least by all press accounts, when they first married. As widely recounted, at eleven, Wood spotted Wagner, eight years her senior, on a studio lot and proclaimed to her mother that she would marry that man—which she did at age nineteen in 1957. The marriage ended in 1962, reportedly the result of career pressures (hers was booming; his was in the doldrums) and possibly of Wagner's alleged bisexuality.[42] They remarried in 1972, after each had had a child in a former marriage. The couple were shown as deeply devoted in press accounts throughout their nearly ten-year second marriage, with biographies providing a bit more detail on nagging but negotiable tensions, mostly centered on career conflicts and schedules. At the point of Wood's death, the tables had turned—Wagner had a highly successful television series, *Hart to Hart*, as Wood was struggling to find interesting film roles.

Whether excessive alcohol consumption and the argument onboard concerning acting and career commitment resulted in Wagner's actively harming his wife or failing to come to her aid upon her accidentally slipping into the unsettled waters, or whether he was completely unaware of her having slipped until discovering her missing, are additional questions that remain unanswered. If, indeed, he had anything other than a passive role—perhaps fatally passive by some accounts that trace a lapse of several hours between his discovery of Wood's disappearance and his reporting it to coastal authorities[43]—he has never divulged, although he presented his version of events in a 2008 memoir. Older than Wood, Wagner was firmly rooted in the "Old Hollywood" tradition of stardom,[44] while Wood felt dedicated to bridging the divide between the Old Hollywood in which she was raised and the New Hollywood into which she emerged as an adult actress. With his riveting performance in Michael Cimino's *The Deer Hunter* (1979), Walken represented a second phase of the New Hollywood (as did actors like Robert De Niro, Meryl Streep, and Al Pacino)—a Hollywood that Wood was now attempting to (re)enter, after having taken several years off to concentrate on her marriage and her two daughters—"she was looking for a way to bust out," said a friend to Wood biographer and *Inside Daisy Clover* novelist/screenwriter Gavin Lambert.[45] Despite her stardom and her truly accomplished work in the New Hollywood mode of *Proper Stranger*, she found herself with roles in films like *Peeper* (1976), *Meteor* (1979), and *Brainstorm* (her last film, released in 1983) that were far less than fulfilling. Her desire to be more than a "trustworthy pro" may have fueled the discussion on the night of her death, as her work with Walken most certainly did.[46] Wagner claims that Walken "began talking about his 'total pursuit of a career' and that Natalie should live like that too. . . . He also said it was obvious that I didn't share his point of view, which was an understatement."[47] As in the incident with her mother's refusing to tend to her daughter's broken wrist, it would seem that conflicting feelings centered on her professional life and aspirations ultimately and fatally took a toll on her body—whether indirectly, by accident, or by force.

Upon her death, Natalie Wood, the star, also became "a case," a further mystery to be solved, adding new layers of uncertainty and indeterminacy to the person she was and the acting roles she took on. The interplay of presence and absence that fuels cinematic desire is compounded, in the instance of Natalie Wood, by what Goode refers to in *Flaubert's Parrot* as an "erotic oscillation" arising from attempts and failures to understand the past.[48] In becoming a "case" for authorities and the public, Wood, as in her screen roles, "constitutes a frustrating object of desire, a mystery that promises and yet withholds understanding's pleasures."[49] The body and being of Natalie Wood, on which the husband, mother, studios, and several co-stars had variously laid claims, like Angie in *Proper Stranger*, appeared to comply with while simultaneously resisting "seizures" of and by others. Goode employs the term "seizure" to denote not only "control of an object by an actor" but also "a temporary loss of control over mind and body."[50] The impulse toward "seizure" becomes a parallel aim, then, uniting audience and star, the latter forcibly residing concurrently within and outside of herself, in a state of "suspended subjectivity" as a persona manufactured for consumption. The star, as Gledhill argues, "in condensing select social values becomes him or herself a theatre of the enactment of conflicting forces much in the manner of melodramatic persona"[51]—or, we might also say in the manner of a "case," in which "excess is produced by the insistence on an identity, a personal monopathy"[52] that only partially can cohere and often is entirely withheld. In discussing the Hollywood period Wood was attempting to bridge, as shaped by Method acting and realist aesthetics signifying authenticity, Gledhill might just as well be describing Wood herself and the screen roles she played: "The rationalizations of the rising social and psychological therapies which popularized notions of delinquency, maternal deprivation, and social inadequacy provide the melodramatic imagination with a new articulation of the moral occult, recasting the terms of the struggle: it is now the existence of an individual self that is at stake."[53] In her Hollywood and attempted New Hollywood career—and in her death—Natalie Wood allegorized her time and place in the culture, as well as the times and transitions of the industry in which she worked. The confluence of indeterminacy, suspended subjectivity, and uncertain experience Wood embodied continue to position her as Hollywood's proper stranger—one who belongs yet is alien, a woman whose life and death elicit to inspire in their very illegibility.

NOTES

1. For the complete 1981 and amended 2012 coroner's report, see Andrew Blankstein and Richard Winton, "Natalie Wood: New Coroner's Report," *Los Angeles Times*, January 14, 2013, documents.latimes.com/coroners-report-death-natalie-wood.
2. Christine Gledhill, "Signs of Melodrama," in *Stardom: Industry of Desire*, ed. Gledhill (New York: Routledge, 1991), 211.
3. Suzanne Finstad, *Natasha: The Biography of Natalie Wood* (New York: Three Rivers Press, 2001), 20.
4. See Cynthia Lucia, introduction to *The Wiley-Blackwell History of American Film, Volume III: 1946 to 1965* (Malden, Mass.: Wiley-Blackwell, 2012).
5. Robert J. Wagner, with Scott Eyman, *Pieces of My Heart: A Life* (New York: Harper Entertainment, 2008), 255.
6. Finstad, *Natasha: The Biography of Natalie Wood*, 18.
7. Ibid., 29; Lana Wood, *Natalie: A Memoir by Her Sister Lana Wood* (New York: G. P. Putnam's Sons, 1984), 8.
8. Finstad, *Natasha: The Biography of Natalie Wood*, 33.
9. Ibid., 165–79.
10. Elaine Tyler May, *Homeward Bound: American Families in the Cold War Era* (New York: Basic Books, 1988), 63.
11. "Natalie Wood: Child of Change," *Look* 27, no. 16 (1963): 94.
12. "Movie Star into Actress," *Newsweek*, February 26, 1962, 54.
13. Finstad, *Natasha*, 206.
14. See "Strange Doings of Actress at Practice," *Life*, January 28, 1957, 96–100.
15. Paul Monaco, *History of the American Cinema, Volume 8: The Sixties: 1960–1969* (Berkeley: University of California Press, 2001), 130.
16. See Laura Mulvey, "Visual Pleasure and Narrative Cinema," *Screen* 16, no. 3 (1975): 6–18.
17. May, *Homeward Bound*, 116.
18. R. M. Hodgens, "Love with the Proper Stranger," *Film Quarterly* 17, no. 3 (1964): 62.
19. Stanley Kauffmann, "Sin Days in New York," *New Republic*, February 8, 1964, 25.
20. Béla Belázs, "The Face of Man," in *Film Theory and Criticism: Introductory Readings*, ed. Leo Braudy (Oxford: Oxford University Press, 1979), 293.
21. See Christian Metz, *The Imaginary Signifier: Psychoanalysis and the Cinema*, trans. Celia Britton et al. (Bloomington: Indiana University Press, 1982).
22. Mike Goode, "Knowing Seizures: Julian Barnes, Jean-Paul Sartre, and the Erotics of the Postmodern Condition," *Textual Practice* 19, no. 1 (2005): 156.
23. Ibid., 154.
24. Ibid., 151.
25. See Linda Levitt, "Death on Display: Reifying Stardom through Hollywood's Dark Tourism," *Velvet Light Trap*, no. 65 (2010): 91–94.
26. Gledhill, "Signs of Melodrama," 207, 211.

27. Goode, "Knowing Seizures," 151.
28. Richard Porton, "Acting in the Grand Manner: An Interview with Christopher Plummer," *Cineaste* 34, no. 4 (2009): 15–16.
29. Dick Moore, *Twinkle, Twinkle, Little Star (But Don't Have Sex or Take the Car)* (New York: Harper and Row, 1984), 228.
30. Finstad, *Natasha*, 285–86.
31. See ibid.; Gavin Lambert, *Natalie Wood: A Life* (New York: Back Stage Books, 2005); Lana Wood, *Natalie*; Moore, *Twinkle, Twinkle, Little Star.*
32. Finstad, *Natasha*, 37–38.
33. Ibid., 78, 151.
34. Ibid., 172–73.
35. While impossible to verify either the identity of the author or the legitimacy of the information posted, the fact is that Natalie Wood—her life, her bodily traumas, and her death—remains a subject of concern. See Ryan Tate, "Did Robert Downey Jr. Really Just Accuse Kirk Douglass of a Brutal Rape?" *Gawker*, March 15, 2012, gawker.com/5893793/did-robert-downey-jr-really-just-accuse-kirk-douglas-of-a-brutal-rape, accessed June 20, 2013.
36. Goode, "Knowing Seizures," 151.
37. See Finstad, *Natasha*, 343–440; Lambert, *Natalie Wood*, 308–28; Marti Rulli and Dennis Davern, *Goodbye Natalie, Goodbye Splendour* (Beverley Hills, Calif.: Medallion Publishers, 2009), 295–331; Wagner, *Pieces of My Heart* (New York, HarperCollins, 2008), 254–69; Lana Wood, *Natalie*, 196–214.
38. See Rulli and Davern, *Goodbye Natalie, Goodbye Splendour.*
39. Finstad, *Natasha*, 441–42; see also *Los Angeles Times*, "Natalie Wood Investigation Prompted by Boat Captain's Comments," November 17, 2011, latimesblogs.latimes.com/lanow/2011/11/natalie-wood-investigation-prompted-by-boat-captain-comments.html, accessed March 7, 2015.
40. Finstad, *Natasha*, 434–36.
41. For a comprehensive overview of publications outlining details of the investigation, see Cynthia Lucia, "Natalie Wood," Oxford Bibliographies, www.oxfordbibliographies.com/obo/page/cinema-and-media-studies.
42. Finstad, *Natasha*, 272.
43. Ibid., 440–41; see also Rulli and Davern, *Goodbye Natalie, Goodbye Splendour.*
44. Lambert, *Natalie Wood*, 159; Wagner, *Pieces of My Heart*, 112.
45. Lambert, *Natalie Wood*, 204.
46. Ibid.
47. Wagner, *Pieces of My Heart*, 255.
48. Goode, "Knowing Seizures," 154.
49. Ibid., 153.
50. Ibid.
51. Gledhill, "Signs of Melodrama," 226.
52. Ibid.
53. Ibid., 225.

10

It's the Years *and* the Mileage: Harrison Ford Grows Old Onscreen

Virginia Luzón-Aguado

A FEW YEARS AGO I CAME ACROSS AN ANTI-SMOKING CAMPAIGN FEATURing an actor, now campaigning against smoking, who had played the Marlboro man in the past and later developed lung cancer. The power of the succinct slogan employed in the campaign, "Bob, I've got cancer," resided in the way it deconstructed the myth of the indestructible all-American cowboy, one of the most enduring tropes in popular culture. It did so precisely by drawing on the same classic western iconography that dominated Marlboro advertisements and classical Hollywood westerns. The later phase of Harrison Ford's career, which roughly coincides with the beginning of the new century, has evolved in a similar fashion. Since turning sixty, the ever-popular star has been trying to stay afloat in Hollywood by poking fun at himself and subverting the very same elements that brought him fame over previous decades. In order to accomplish this transformation, Ford recognizes and foregrounds his aging process. Yet this strategy, which has worked wonders for Clint Eastwood, has proven generally unsuccessful for Ford. To account for this failure, I first chart the development of Ford's cinematic persona in order to better account for its current redefinition. Next, I focus on the artistic difficulties he has experienced during this transitional period as a result of his desire to stretch the limits of his image while integrating the unavoidable and often painful aging process into his public persona.

In his late fifties, Ford received two of the most prestigious honorary awards in Hollywood, the AFI Life Achievement Award (2000) and the Cecil B. DeMille Award (2002). Both are bestowed on artists whose contributions to film and culture have been outstanding. Naturally, the recipients are usually "of a certain age," and while neither honor entails a valediction (after all, many Hollywood artists never formally retire), they constitute a public celebration of a remarkably long, successful life in motion pictures. Indeed, a cursory look at recipients reveals that, with some exceptions, they were fast approaching or past the average retirement age. Still, the awards are not meant to be celebrations of major Hollywood has-beens. As the AFI strives to make clear, its award is intended to honor "individuals with active careers and work of significance *yet to be accomplished*."[1] Diminishing opportunities for actors "of a certain age" have made it crucial for film stars of the older generation, whether male or female, to excel at choosing projects that allow them to carefully reconcile their well-established trademarks with the aging process. This constant refashioning allows successful stars to stay professionally active and maintain their fragile status within youth-obsessed Hollywood.

Though Ford has done work in all Hollywood genres, except for the musical, he has mostly been associated with the action/adventure formula. Nevertheless, unlike other actors of his generation, Ford has never come across as a stereotypical action hero in the sense that his brains have always been more prominent than his brawn. Also, insofar as his image can also be said to encapsulate such notions as "everymanness" and vulnerability, he has always stood out as a unique breed of action hero, thereby subverting stereotypical notions of heroic masculinity within the action genre. Still, far from generating inconsistencies and dissonances, Ford's very special brand of heroism has been well received over the years. It is precisely his atypicality within the action formula that has allowed him to produce work in other genres, where his unique heroic image has been used to varying degrees of effectiveness.

Ford's iconic image started forging itself in the 1970s through the popular Han Solo character in the swashbuckling sci-fi *Star Wars* saga (1977, 1980, 1983). However, his small part in *American Graffiti* (dir. George Lucas, 1973) also introduced nuances, such as a certain lack of maturity, egotism, and a mild form of arrogance, which continued developing to more or less comic effect in the *Star War* films and other roles during the late 1970s and early 1980s. Ford's offscreen reputation as a rowdy twenty-something with an attitude contributed significantly to the establishment of such elements in his early star persona.[2] (During the shooting of *American Graffiti*, he and co-star Paul le Mat reputedly threw Richard Dreyfuss into the swimming pool from a balcony on the second floor, leading to a head injury.) This reputation was reinforced through his early roles in *The Frisco Kid* (1979), *Hanover Street* (1979), and *Force Ten from Navarone* (1979), though these parts also managed to imbue the actor's image with a certain patriotic symbolism, in the sense that his characters often came face to face with men of other nationalities, who, on the whole, compared unfavorably to Ford's characters. The star then came to symbolize the American way, especially in terms of his representation of successful masculinity. This devil-may-care attitude is a significant element of his acting persona that further established itself during the next two decades. Ford's well-publicized rags-to-riches story also featured prominently in the construction of his early star image. Despite the initial economic difficulties that led him to pursue a carpentry career outside Hollywood, he never gave up on his ambition to become an actor. Still, the success he enjoyed in his parallel career led him to reject acting opportunities that did not match his professional aspirations.

In 1963, Ford left Ripon College in Wisconsin without an official degree and married shortly after, at the age of twenty-one. In order to make a living, he decided to devote himself to his hobby, acting, and became a successful first performer in a summer stock company working in Wisconsin and, later on, in various theaters along the Californian coast. It was from there that Ford made the jump to Hollywood, where he managed to enter the Columbia "New Talent" program. His beginnings, however, were not easy, not least because he despised the politics and factory-like workings of what Basinger has called "the star machine," the mechanical process involving "the discovery, the screen test, the makeover, the publicity, the casting to type" of stars in the classical period.[3] As one of the last contract players in the history of Hollywood, Ford loathed the inflexible studio system and developed a reputation for being temperamental and difficult at work. Still, at the age of twenty-four he achieved his first, uncredited film role as a bellboy in *Dead Heat on a Merry Go Round*, a 1966 Columbia film starring James Coburn. Yet after watching his short performance, studio vice president Jerry Tokovsky decided to sack him, explaining that "the first time Tony Curtis ever appeared in a movie he delivered a bag of groceries. . . . You took one look at that person and you knew that was a star. You ain't got it, kid."[4] Contrary to this prediction, Ford went on to become the "It Boy" a few years later.

When the actor got a second chance at Universal in 1967, he was offered unimportant occasional roles in TV series such as *The Virginian* and *Ironside*, and then appeared in the made-for-television film *Journey to Shiloh* (1968), but none of these efforts did much to advance his career. By then, the actor had become a father for the first time and needed a better wage. At this time he decided to take up carpentry, which is how he became "the second most well-known carpenter in history."[5] The actor eventually chose to give up his successful eight-year career as a "carpenter to the stars," but this episode in his life, which he recurrently refers to in interviews, had a strong impact on both his acting career and overall public image: "I conduct my profession the way I make furniture. There's no tricks, no magic, no mysteries. There's nothing but work, willpower, technique and lots and lots of patience."[6] Ford's patience and perseverance eventually had the desired effect, and the actor came to stand for the values encapsulated in the hard-work ethic and, more generally speaking, the American dream of opportunity and advancement for all those striving hard to achieve their professional and personal goals. The films *Working Girl* (1988) and, more recently, *Crossing Over* (2009) exemplify this pattern. While doing some carpentry work at Francis Ford Coppola's studio, where George Lucas was auditioning actors for *Star Wars*, Ford was asked to help out by reading the Han Solo part opposite hundreds of candidates for other roles. Since Lucas had already declared that he was not even considering any of the actors from *American Graffiti*, Ford read the part with certain displeasure. His grumpiness, however, inadvertently proved that he had exactly what it took to embody the cynical role of Han Solo.

In the 1980s, the role of Indiana Jones catapulted Ford to superstardom and reinforced his all-American persona. Apart from representing ideals of individualism, imperialism, and patriotism, the character introduced the important notion of the frontier in the construction of Ford's star image and his particular brand of successful masculinity. Such purely generic associations were supported by Ford's offscreen reputation as a "new wester"[7] living on the Wyoming frontier. On the other hand, despite Indy's romantic involvement with various females, the film's child-friendly inclination led to the conscious displacement of sexuality in the construction of the role. Such a displacement, with minor exceptions, would become an essential element in Ford's trademark crossover, wholesome persona, which—together with Indiana Jones's vulnerability and comic use of violence—established the foundations for his unique contribution to the action/adventure formula and its concomitant articulation of contemporary masculinity.

The character is certainly brave but not invincible; he punches but he gets punched just as often and, crucially, he does not hesitate to run away from his

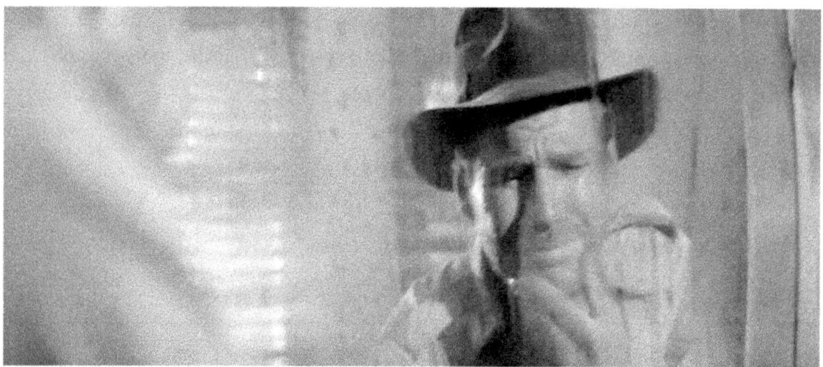

"It's not the years, it's the mileage": physical and psychological vulnerability are essential components of Indiana Jones's brand of Everyman heroism, as shown in *Raiders of the Lost Ark* (1981).

adversaries if necessary. Witness Indy's fight against the temple guardians in *Indiana Jones and the Temple of Doom* (1984) in a scene that, in the context of the film, creates humor rather than confusion and distress, because of the hero's Everyman qualities. In this respect, Ford's character has more in common with the classical swashbuckling hero or even the unlikely heroism embodied by another contemporary average guy of the movies, Jackie Chan,[8] than with the invincible hard bodies that Susan Jeffords[9] or Yvonne Tasker[10] discuss. On the other hand, Jones's characterization is intensely melodramatic, for his suffering, whether physical or psychological, is never hidden from view. Rambo and other Reagan heroes may be admired for their oversized muscles and larger-than-life capacity to endure pain, but Indiana Jones manages to persuade the spectator that heroes can also be normal guys who need to improvise an action plan[11] and, most importantly, who suffer severe pain after a chase or a fight. As Ford states, "It was always as much fun for the audience to see me get beat up as it was to see me beat somebody up. That's kind of unique. Part of the appeal of Indiana Jones is that he was always in over his head. He always hurt."[12]

Jones incorporates the elements of imperfection, vulnerability, and heroism like no other contemporary Hollywood action hero. His barely concealed fear of snakes sits alongside his tenacity and courage, twin personality traits that have inevitably become incorporated into Ford's Everyman public persona, and that critics emphasize over and over again. For instance, conflating the man and the roles, Lazar describes the star's appeal and characteristic trademark as follows: "Unique among action heroes, Harrison Ford brings to the screen believable, flesh-and-blood men, flaws and all. Invariably sympathetic and relatable, Ford relies on his intelligence and wit, rather than on manufactured superpowers, to defeat his foes. Whether he's playing a doctor, lawyer, archaeologist, CIA agent or even the president of the United States, *all of Ford's characters share his humanity, warmth and most significantly, his vulnerability.*"[13]

This vulnerability is key to understanding the star's subsequent successful roles during the 1980s, from Rick Deckard in *Blade Runner* (1982) to John Book in *Witness* (1985), Dr. Richard Walker in *Frantic* (1988), or Jack Ryan in *Patriot Games* (1992) and *Clear and Present Danger* (1994). Many of these melodramatic action films also emphasize the intense suffering Ford's characters endured as a result of dramatic disruptions to their personal lives, frequently involving the family. Still, these characters finally overcome victimization by regenerating their beleaguered sense of masculinity through violence.

Blade runner Rick Deckard was in fact the first in a number of important roles that attempted to stretch the image of the star a bit further by adding complexity and introducing dark undertones that mirrored the contemporary crisis of masculinity. While these novel aspects made the actor an apt casting choice for directors such as Ridley Scott, Peter Weir, and Roman Polanski, they were not well received by mass audiences. Ford's failures (at least in terms of box office and immediate critical reception) in *Blade Runner*,[14] *The Mosquito Coast* (1986), and *Frantic* during the 1980s exemplify the power of audiences to discourage stretching the limits of established star identities.[15]

Because of his desire to change register and expand his acting range, Ford became interested in the complex role of Deckard in Scott's cult film *Blade Runner.* It seems that what drew the British director to Ford were the more low-key, somewhat sinister characters he had played in such films as *The Conversation* (1974) and *Apocalypse Now* (1979), as well as the ambivalent, sensitive potential contained in some of his earlier pieces.[16] More specifically, what made Ford a good casting choice in Scott's opinion was the aura of detachment that characterized such earlier parts as Barnsby in *Force Ten from Navarone* or the hidden gem, Martin Stett, in *The Conversation.*[17] Although Ford was keen to change register and play a more demanding character in the classical mold of a noirish antihero, he insisted (against Scott's alleged wishes) that the film should provide a glimmer of hope. Ford wanted Deckard to be a human and humane character with whom audiences could establish an emotional connection in the midst of bleakness and despair, thereby retaining traces of his earlier, more likeable characters and reinforcing the more popular side of his public persona. Praising Ford's generally underrated performance skills, Nick Lacey declares, "Ford helps the audience sympathize with Deckard's plight. He brings a vulnerability to the role that would have been beyond Stallone or Schwarzenegger."[18] Still, Ford's intense disagreement with Scott's dystopian vision, along with the studio's last-minute decision to add Deckard's voiceover narration, made *Blade Runner* one of the actor's least favorite films, despite its eventual cult status.

Witness successfully exploited Ford's developing image, as it drew on his associations with the frontier, individualism, heroism, and vulnerability, while also highlighting the character's sense of morality, a characteristic that Deckard had already displayed. The film's sentimental undercurrents also reveal the star's increasing inclination toward the melodramatic mode in his choice of characters. In Ford's subsequent output, melodrama is present at several levels, in both structural and thematic terms, since conventional Manichean conflicts and resolutions, together with the suffering hero's victimization, often combine with familial concerns. Although *Witness* could be considered to have been an important precursor, *Frantic* inaugurated an enduring trend in Ford's career in which the defense of the family became the backdrop against which narrative conflict unfolds. Ford's rebranding in the broad media as a successful "new man" and a reformed "new father" certainly made an impact on his screen characterization, and vice versa. During the 1980s, his roles had already displayed a different sensibility as far as the portrayal of masculinity was concerned, while still conforming to hegemonic notions of gender. On the whole, his most popular characters display the usual attributes that characterize conventional heroics in mainstream Hollywood, but they also exhibit a large measure of emotional sensitivity and physical vulnerability, which helped Ford stand out in the overcrowded world of Hollywood stardom. His second marriage and second chance at fatherhood subsequently turned him into a popular role model for contemporary men,[19] and possibly fathers in particular, in the more "caring" 1990s.[20] This new tenderness, which is also noticeably present in the Jack Ryan films and in *Regarding Henry* (1991), reflected contemporary social and political discourses regarding gender and the family that had a great impact on politics and the broad media.

However, Ford's increasing construction as the *über*-father for the 1990s was not without contradictions. Indeed, a certain degree of ambivalence toward the family could be observed in many of these narratives. This ambivalent attitude was clearly evident in Ford's darker roles, including Allie Fox in *The Mosquito Coast*, Dr. Richard Walker in *Frantic*, and Rusty Sabich in *Presumed Innocent* (1990), or even Henry Turner in *Regarding Henry*, films that may be interpreted against this background. However, this undercurrent was also more or less discernible in the rest of his output, which reflects the difficulties involved in reconciling and balancing family life and the typical individualistic drives of Hollywood heroes. Such contradictions were usually resolved, or at least partially hidden from view, by placing a stronger emphasis on the narrative development of Ford's part over and above the other characters in the story, which inevitably confirms Hollywood's strong reliance on the economy of stardom. While this type of investment paid off in the archetypal Harrison Ford vehicle *Air Force One* (1997), it proved to be a problem, though for different reasons, in *The Devil's Own* (1997) and, in particular, *Random Hearts* (1999).

Ford's last film of the decade was in fact one of his most notorious failures. While *Six Days, Seven Nights* (1998) had more or less successfully subverted the star's image with attempts at a comedic role, *Random Hearts* failed to achieve the same feat. It focused far too obsessively on Ford's character's male crisis in middle age. Nevertheless, the notion of the crisis of masculinity and the suffering it inevitably brings about have featured in Ford's work more than is generally acknowledged and surfaced in one way or another in many of his films belonging to different genres, including science fiction (*Blade Runner*), the adventure film (*The Mosquito Coast*), the romantic comedy (*Working Girl*; *Sabrina* [1995]; *Six Days, Seven Nights*), the neo-noir and courtroom thriller (*Frantic*; *Presumed Innocent*), and the male melodrama (*Regarding Henry*; *Random Hearts*). Resolution of the crisis (or, less often, lack thereof) in these films was generally dictated by generic parameters, though the more positive elements in Ford's persona could also be said to have played a prominent part in the achievement of a more or less happy resolution. However, unlike past positive responses to Ford's melodramatic vulnerability, viewers and critics were disturbed by the characters' instability and obsessive jealousy in these later films.

Still, the notion of masculine crisis continued to play a prominent part in Ford's output during the 2000s, an interesting decade in his career in more aspects than one. According to Basinger, in recent times, Ford's persona has become "more urban, more complex. [He has been] playing confused husbands, burdened leaders and beleaguered institutional employees."[21] Indeed, the past decade was characterized by a more complex, self-conscious treatment of his heroic image and a closer focus on the unavoidable effects that aging has had on his persona, a concern already prominent in *Six Days, Seven Nights* and *Random Hearts*. While not explicitly acknowledged as such, this downbeat characterization had started to have an impact on Ford's offscreen image, especially after he started divorce proceedings from his second wife, scriptwriter Melissa Mathison, in 2000. When the actor turned sixty, he expressed his desire to make some fundamental changes in his life and career, despite potentially negative consequences for his public image, in an article aptly entitled "Life Begins at Sixty":

> I am not the first man who want[s] to make changes in his life at sixty, and I won't be the last. It is just that others can do it with anonymity. . . . I have always had the ability to . . . become other people through my acting. I took a good look at myself and decided that I wanted something different. That's not such a bad thing, is it? But, because of my past, I think it took a lot of people by surprise. They wondered what was happening to me. I was very much aware of what was happening. I'm living the way I want to live.[22]

In this rather eloquent manner, Ford was declaring his wish for professional and personal transformation. In professional terms, he had already started to make choices that involved an important revision of his image, favoring roles that either incorporated complex, dark undertones or dealt with his persona from a self-consciously comic perspective. In personal terms, Ford, who had come to incarnate the new man/father ethos of the 1990s to perfection, seemed to be very much enjoying his new bachelor status.

Much was then made of Ford's purported mid-life crisis during the first half of the 2000s, which was supported by an infamous drunken spree in Mexico, an equally infamous earring, and the fact that he started dating much younger women, including his current wife, actor Calista Flockhart. This prompted Caracalla to lament that "it took him thirty-five years to become famous and fifty-eight to destroy the image. Fortunately Calista Flockhart . . . was waiting in the wings. . . . The actor [is] once again a settled man and Hollywood [can] breathe a sigh of relief."[23]

At the same time, Ford's production during the past decade, with the exceptions of *What Lies Beneath* (2000) and the fourth installment in the Indiana Jones saga, proved unsuccessful in economic and critical terms, which signal a lack of ability to choose parts that provide a good enough "fit" (to use Dyer's terminology)[24] with his well-established, albeit inevitably evolving and aging, image. These circumstances no doubt had a direct impact on Ford's standing within the industry. In fact, publicity posters for his more recent films generally foreground his co-stars and only rarely picture Ford on his own.

Despite having been poorly received on the whole, Ford's production during the first decade of the twenty-first century was consistent in the sense that his roles can be viewed as self-conscious, though not always successful, attempts to rework his image. *What Lies Beneath*, one of Ford's few runaway successes in the 2000s, successfully exploited Ford's largely unexplored dark side with more than acceptable results. Moreover, insofar as his character's flaws stem from his desire for constant adulation in middle age and his inability to match his father's achievements, the part constituted a significant further incursion into the painful crisis of masculinity.

Interestingly, Ford's image did not feature on the main publicity poster for *What Lies Beneath*. Director Robert Zemeckis decided not to include images of the film's stars, perhaps because audiences would not identify Ford or Michelle Pfeiffer with the horror film. This was Ford's first foray into the genre and the risk paid off. In the film, he plays a secondary role compared to Pfeiffer's, and he could be considered miscast in the role of murderer. However, the film was a box office success, which reflects that Ford's complex image, and its darker aspects in particular, could be mobilized to great effect. Admittedly, it was easier for Ford to play against type in a secondary role because the audience followed Pfeiffer's character more closely and had less time to ponder on Ford's villain, whose less prominent standing meant that the associations he usually brings to a role did not interfere with the film's suspense or narrative development. Ford was happy with the final result and the fact that his casting managed to confuse audience expectations, this time with the desired effect: "I care a lot about the audience. . . . I'm not so concerned about the people you might call fans. I'm concerned about them as moviegoers; I'm not concerned with their expectations about me. It has been my business, my professional goal, to upset their expectations from time to time. I've tried to do this since the very beginning of the viable phase of my career."[25]

This is an apt summary of what Jeanine Basinger considers the principal characteristic of today's "neo-star." She claims that, unlike the movie stars in the classical period, contemporary stars can create their own trademarks and then successfully break with them in order to prove their acting abilities. As she puts it, "An ability to be both actor and star in a way the public will allow—and pay to see—is the mark of the neo-star."[26] While Basinger sees Ford as one of the most important neo-stars of the older generation, it seems that Ford's ability to be both actor and star in a way the public will allow, *and pay to see*, is perhaps debatable, as critical assessment of the most recent phase in his career suggests.

What Lies Beneath was generally described as a mature film, a reference to both the two stars' respective ages but also to the narrative, which is closer to classic Hitchcock (with many references to his films in evidence) than to a contemporary horror film. The film hinges on the crumbling marriage of Norman Spencer (Ford) and, significantly, his own personal crisis. Claire Spencer

(Pfeiffer) gave up her musical ambitions to become a "proper wife" to her second, apparently loving husband. Still, not all is bliss in their marriage and it appears that Norman's narcissistic desire for admiration and adulation in late middle age has led him to initiate an affair with a student (Amber Valletta). Norman, the plot makes clear, is a proud, academically successful man with a deep inferiority complex. As it happens, even though he is a workaholic in the academic world, he cannot replicate his father's legendary successes in the field of genetics. When his young lover threatens to make their extra-marital relationship public, he fears his professional reputation will be ruined, and thus he finally murders her.

What Lies Beneath is ultimately an interesting film in that it manages to mobilize "what lies beneath" Ford's complex persona in a rather successful manner. The negative aspects that were only intermittently visible during the previous decades were in this case exploited fully, suggesting the tortured dark side of his persona, when correctly handled, could be as magnetic as the successful, heroic aspects of his star image.

With this film's release, journalists increasingly insisted on the possibility of Ford, Spielberg, and Lucas producing a new Indiana Jones film. While keen on the idea, the star acknowledged that it would be fundamental to make reference to Indiana Jones's, or his own, aging and the impact it would have on the character. As he noted in an IMDb interview in 2000, "Adding some flaws and layers is what is going to make Indy even more interesting. We can address issues like whether his virtues are based on his youth or on other aspects of human nature like his wisdom, his toughness, his resourcefulness, his integrity."[27] This comment reveals that Ford was ready to start making his age—and the character's—a narrative concern, although he still considered himself fit enough to return to type in the action adventure formula. As he jokingly reflected, "No one wants to see a hero have to pick up a cane to hit someone, but I'm still quite fit enough to fake it. It's all smoke and mirrors anyway."[28]

While Ford used this image to allude to the visual spectacle the action genre thrives on, it could also be said to apply to the nature of stardom, or the "industry of desire."[29] Ford only reluctantly refers to himself as a star or an icon, preferring to describe himself as a public servant or assistant storyteller. This modesty reflects his desire to please the audience and, at the same time, to project an aura of intimacy, rather than the aloof sophistication that characterizes Hollywood stardom. Ford believes his success derives from the audience's sense of closeness and trust in the characters he plays, a bond that explains why he wants to establish associations between himself and the characters he is famous for playing. He insists that viewers can find out more about his true self through his characters than by reading interviews, where his customary evasiveness becomes evident. However, when it comes to those features that might make Ford a more glamorous star, or a legendary Hollywood icon, the self-deprecating star is always ready to reveal the gap between reality and fantasy, or the "smoke and mirrors" that Hollywood stardom is predicated upon: "Maybe Indiana Jones is a sexy guy, but not me. I'm an average looking man whose sexiness is a wonderful illusion that's created by the movies I'm in."[30] Ford's desire to stretch out the limits of his image by not hiding the effects of his own aging process therefore constitutes a clear attempt to retain the apparent ordinariness and normality that have made him such a popular star over the decades.

Before reprising his iconic role in the fourth Indiana Jones film, Ford continued to enjoy the possibility of experimenting with his popular heroic image. His personal investment in the big-budget *K-19: The Widowmaker* (2002) was such that, for the first time in his career, he would be an executive producer, able to influence every final decision regarding the film's development. For the first time, too, he commanded a fee of $25 million, plus 20 percent of the film's profits, which never materialized because *K-19* became a major economic disappointment. Indeed, Ford's performance and part, while ultimately heroic, were far too somber for mass audience consumption. At a time when the United States was preparing itself for war against Iraq in the aftermath of the September 11 attacks, Ford's "defection" to the Russian enemy in a film that strove to redefine the notion of heroism was certainly not well received by the public.

The film was directed by "genre-bender" Kathryn Bigelow.[31] Although some critics claimed that Bigelow's auteurist concerns were absent from *K-19*, on the evidence provided by Ford's problematic casting as USSR submarine Captain Alexei Vostrikov, Bigelow's penchant for genre manipulation was still very much present in *K-19*. Along these lines, her desire to turn the war film on its head by explicitly turning the Soviets into heroes was also evidence of her innovative tendencies. Indeed, in such warmongering times it was a bold move on her part to make a film about the archetypal U.S. enemy's unknown heroic deeds during the Cold War. In fact, the film's stakeholders were adamant that the fundamental "Sovietness" of the story should be stressed. Ford insisted that the cast should adopt subtle Russian accents, lest the spectator forget that the crew is Russian, a decision that was not welcomed by reviewers in general, let alone the audience.

On the other hand, the film, which was based on true historical events, sent a very powerful anti-nuclear and anti-war message, which was in tune with both the director's ideology and the political and ecological concerns of the film's main star, whose environmental work in order to, literally, save the world was becoming increasingly active. Still, a critical film with "no hint of American jingoism [and] no bad guys in it,"[32] in Ford's words, seemed to be out of tune with the nationalistic fervor that was sweeping the country. Thus, perhaps because it was out of step with the warmongering times and because it challenged the audience's typical understanding of Cold War propaganda and the nature of bravery and heroism, the film was a disappointment at the box office. Not only was the audience not seduced by the film's bold political proposition—the fact that, according to Bigelow, "we are the same, that geopolitical borders aren't real"[33]—but the director's genre-bending and innovative take on heroism clearly extended to Ford's bona fide persona with disastrous consequences.

Indeed, Ford's is a rather unsympathetic character, and the features that had until then constituted an integral part of his popular persona belong instead to Liam Neeson's character, Captain Mikhail Polenin. The film thus pitches two styles of masculinity against each other, initially portraying Vostrikov as the stern, older "bad father" and Polenin as the caring, younger "good father." However, the narrative eventually reveals Vostrikov's hardline, traditional command style as necessary and effective in the extreme dramatic circumstances the crew is placed in. It is thanks to Vostrikov's capacity to make difficult decisions that the threat of nuclear war is averted, despite the death toll involved. While ultimately heroic, therefore, Ford's hardhearted character did not find a sympathetic audience. Zemeckis managed to subvert Ford's image to great effect, but Bigelow's extreme form of star persona-bending alienated the audience instead.

K-19's box office disappointment did not deter Ford, who remained keen to stretch the audience's understanding of his persona, this time in the comic buddy cop film *Hollywood Homicide* (2003). The actor, who at the time declared himself to be a firm admirer of the slapstick comedy *Dumb and Dumber* (1994),[34] was interested in testing his comic abilities outside the more familiar territory of the romantic comedy. The fact that Josh Hartnett, a popular teenage idol at the time, had agreed to star as rookie J. C. Calden made the project more attractive, since Ford, who was keen to recuperate his box office clout, thought that Hartnett's presence would draw the crucial teenage segment of the audience to the cinemas in the summer of 2003. As he bluntly put it, "One of the things that appealed to me about this kind of summer caper movie was the business sense that the whole thing made."[35] However, the film was another economic failure in Ford's career. While the plot was criticized for being excessively formulaic and devoid of truly effective comic moments, Ford's performance was attacked for lacking enthusiasm and genuine comic spirit. Lael Loewenstein, one of Ford's harshest critics, reported that the film failed because Ford, "unlike Jack Nicholson," had given up his ambition to be "an actor" and was content with simply being "a star doing variations on a theme."[36] In other words, Ford was criticized for adhering to (his own) formula or trademark as a "professional" actor and not taking enough risks as a "performer," in the sense proposed by Christine Geraghty,[37] even though it was due to his desire to diversify and, to a certain extent, play against the audience's expectations that he had accepted the role of Joe Gavilan in *Hollywood Homicide*.

While it is true that the film and Ford's part are forgettable, neo-star Ford's desire to push the envelope by incorporating the painful humiliations of aging should also be acknowledged. Sergeant Gavilan is a veteran police officer, though lately ineffectual and forced to rely on the powers of his psychic girlfriend (Lena Olin) in order to solve his latest case. In addition, he is a thrice-divorced man who relies on his second income as a realtor to pay alimony to his ex-wives (paralleling Ford's expensive divorces and real-life difficulties, to a large extent). Gavilan is being investigated by the Internal Affairs Department for "commingling of funds," a lapse that undermines the virtue and honesty audiences expected from a typical Ford character. Significantly, his failures are also partly attributed to his age throughout the film, though, in most respects, he still compares favorably to the much younger, under-prepared, and under-motivated Calden. Indeed, Gavilan's retirement from the frontline of duty is never considered a possibility.

While *Hollywood Homicide* is a buddy film, the homosocial or homoerotic subtext that had by then become commonplace in the genre is notably absent. The characters' antagonism apparently also reflected the actors' lack of offscreen rapport. As Ford explained, "These two characters are not buddies. They're guys who work together, who don't understand each other at all. I thought that pretty much was reflected in our relationship, and I didn't try to disturb it."[38] Moreover, the heterosexuality of both characters is continually stressed throughout the narrative, especially that of Calden/Hartnett, who, true to type, is an irresistible sexual magnet. Gavilan, for his part, is also portrayed as seductive and sexually active, which was a rather novel aspect in a Harrison Ford role. Still, the character's sexualization becomes the butt of the film's only truly comic joke. Referring to his sexual ability in old age (Ford was sixty-one), Gavilan confesses to his lover: "If I take my ginkgo, I can still remember where I put the Viagra," a line which, as one reviewer commented, "could kill a lesser man."[39] This no doubt signals Ford's continuing self-awareness as an aging star in the competitive Hollywood marketplace and his willingness to start reconfiguring his rapidly deteriorating heroic manly-man trademark.

However, viewers' ultimately negative reception led Ford to revert to type as a virtuous heroic father in the formulaic family-in-peril vehicle *Firewall* (2006), with the hope that spectators would be drawn to the cinemas en masse and allow the star to retain his box office clout. Ford also felt comfortable with the part since family, despite his two divorces, together with "flying, conservation and human rights," continued to be Ford's most enduring interests.[40] While *Firewall* performed a little better than his previous two films in economic terms, it did little to redeem his damaged box office reputation, possibly because the character and the actor's age were not considered to be an important enough issue to deal with directly.

The plot revisits familiar action territory for Ford and was aptly described as "*Patriot Games* with a laptop."[41] The film's investment in new technologies is indeed notable and constitutes a good attempt at updating the Ford brand for the Internet generation. However, the "home invasion" trope, though appealing to the star, did not resonate with public concerns in 2006. While family values had become a key dramatic focus in Hollywood during the 1990s, it was not what cinema audiences in the more cynical, less sentimental 2000s seemed to want. On the other hand, most reviews mentioned Ford's advanced age and unwillingness to take artistic risks. One critic described Ford as "desperate";[42] others criticized him for "running on autopilot"[43] and for repeating himself to exhaustion: "Ford, in late middle age, seems bored stiff playing taciturn Harrison Ford–type heroes, with their suits and their gravitas, their honor and their tired old sprees of derring-do."[44] However, the star, who in the past stated that he had no time for more artistic projects, had no qualms about confessing his preference for more commercial, formulaic, or less artistically driven projects since "entertainment for entertainment's sake [had] been paying [his] bills for a long time."[45]

Ford was also criticized and ridiculed for accepting a physical role for which he was considered far too old. One critic joked about the possibility of mistaking Ford's uneasy walk after the film's final showdown for "signs of osteoarthritis."[46] It is evident that by the time *Firewall* was released, age had become a complicated matter that was difficult to accommodate in the evolution of Ford's star persona.

The overall negative reception of the film revealed that Ford's aging body no longer fit the action formula. While the actor denied being worried about the scarcity of interesting projects available to him, he reflected on Hollywood's ageist culture,[47] conceding that he would retire only when he felt he had ceased to be useful to the industry.[48] More than ten years after this statement and despite the past decade's many disappointments, Ford continued to work with varying degrees of success, having participated in no fewer than five films in 2013 and 2014, namely *42*, *Paranoia*, *Ender's Game*, *Anchorman 2*, and *The Expendables 3*.

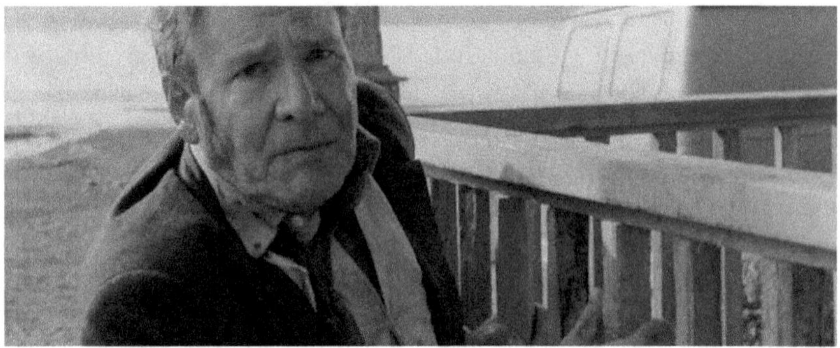

Jack Stanfield can barely stand at the end of the predictable *Firewall* (2006), highlighting both the character's and the actor's age and fragility.

Clearly, as Indiana Jones used to say, "It's not the years, it's the mileage," a maxim that Ford frequently applies to his long career.

Eventually, the most awaited cinematic comeback in years materialized in 2008 with the release of *Indiana Jones and the Kingdom of the Crystal Skull*, almost twenty years after *Indiana Jones and the Last Crusade* (1989). This time, age was a central concern of the narrative and Ford refused to dye his hair in order to make the character look younger. To the star, age was just one more "physical challenge" that the character had to go through.[49] However, in order to maximize the film's economic potential and relieve Ford/Jones of some responsibility over the story, the younger generation was also integrated in the new installment, thanks to the introduction of Indy and Marion Ravenwood's (Karen Allen) love child, Mutt (Shia LaBeouf), who calls Indy "Gramps" and whose role is prominent in many of the action pieces. To critics and filmmakers, acknowledging Indy's aging process was essential, mostly because the star and this iconic character in particular have perhaps become indissoluble, unlike, say, Tarzan, Batman, James Bond, or, interestingly, Jack Ryan, all mythical ageless heroes embodied by different actors at various points in the history of Hollywood. Ford also conceded that he felt there was a perfect fit between his own identity and that of the character that made him an icon, "because the minute I put the costume on, I recognize the tone that we need and I feel confident and clear about the character."[50]

Philippa Gates has theorized the relatively successful comeback of certain popular action heroes of the 1980s, such as Indiana Jones, John McClane, or Rocky Balboa.[51] She concludes that by acknowledging age, failure, and vulnerability and by renouncing individualism and embracing family values and team spirit, these heroes have successfully adapted to the times, clearly following in the footsteps of the *über*-hero in old age, Clint Eastwood.[52] Despite these heroes being noticeably older, they are still fit enough and able to perform many of the prerequisite action stunts. In Gates's view, they represent a further example of Hollywood's continuing ability to generate myths, especially as far as the representation of heroic masculinity (in old age) is concerned, for these characters are paradoxically able to show their age; at the same time, however, she concludes that "these stars and their heroes are once again popular, because they are *not* acting their age."[53] Indeed, most reviews remarked on "the sinewy sixty-five-year-old star"[54] still being in good shape and looking like he did when he was "fifty-five or forty-six."[55] Finally, I would suggest that the fact that the plot reunited Indiana and Marion at last did not simply constitute a clear homage to fans who had been longing for this reunion for almost thirty years. By pairing the hero with what could be described as a "real," average-looking woman of his own generation, the plot manages to handle the age issue in a more realistic manner and contributes to both characters' likeability for members of the older generation in the audience.[56] After all, despite certain moments of exaggerated, comic book–like ability, such as when Jones crosses the Atlantic holding onto a submarine in *Raiders of the Lost Ark* (1981), Jones/Ford generally personifies a believable, rather than superhuman, kind of hero. Spielberg once expressed delight that the actor "knew how to suffer, be afraid, cry [and thereby give] the audience permission to be Indiana Jones, too."[57] To Spielberg's appreciation, one might now add that he also knows how to age.

Still, the late film critic Roger Ebert remarked that Ford has one of those typical "Robert Mitchum faces that does not age."[58] Ford's enduring associations with the male stars of the classical period continued to feature prominently in the film's reviews and promotional features. Co-star Karen Allen thought of him as

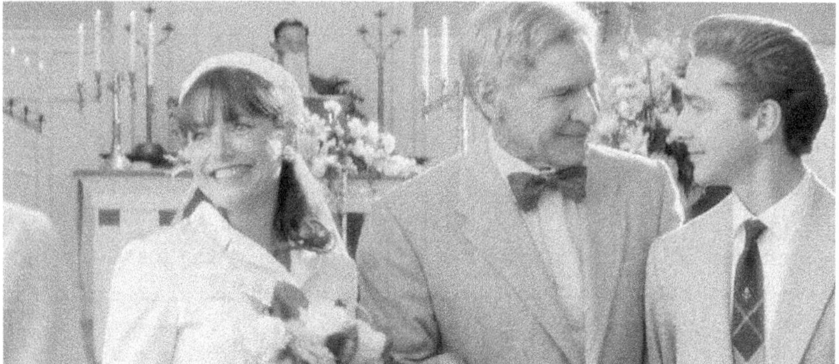

Marion (Karen Allen) and a noticeably older Indiana Jones are married at last in *Indiana Jones and the Kingdom of the Crystal Skull* (2008).

Jimmy Stewart,[59] while producer George Lucas likened him to Bogart and Gable and concluded that Ford was "a movie star because he is a character actor."[60] What Allen and Lucas were actually referring to was Ford's status as a "professional actor,"[61] or his ability, like the stars of the studio era, to personify a certain set of enduring yet evolving attributes that developed after the release of *Raiders of the Lost Ark* and have remained until more recent times, as *Crystal Skull*'s ability to draw the audience to the cinemas demonstrated. The fact that the shooting of a fifth installment in the saga has been announced further corroborates this point.

The film was a great financial success and the second most watched film in 2008.[62] After a string of cinematic failures, Ford finally achieved success thanks to his rather self-conscious reprising of the second most popular hero in Hollywood history, after only Gregory Peck's Atticus Finch.[63] Much of the money that Ford earned from this film was to be donated to his pet cause, environmental protection. A firm believer in social responsibility, the star became involved in this and other issues, manifested in the small-budget, politically aware ensemble film *Crossing Over*. Although completed in 2007, the film was not released commercially until 2009 and not shown in countries such as Spain until 2011, after rather poor previews. It was reported that Ford accepted the role because he regretted not accepting lead roles in *Traffic* (2000) and *Syriana* (2005), which he considered to be far too somber and ambiguous for him to play. He rarely expresses his political opinions in public, but he made an exception in this particular case. When asked in an interview in 2008 whose job he would like to have for a day, he responded, "I'd like to be George W. Bush, and boy, I'd get a lot done. You'd remember me for a long, long time."[64]

For the first time in decades, Ford chose not to become involved in a film's production. He played LA-based immigration officer Max Brogan, who tracks illegal aliens and returns them to their countries of origin. In this sense, the character was reminiscent of Rick Deckard's replicant chasing and eventual moral reawakening. *Crossing Over* was a commercial and critical disappointment that was often unfavorably compared to *Crash* (2004) and *Babel* (2006) for being overly contrived in its depiction of melodramatic coincidences. Ford's performance in the film, however, was in the critics' opinion the only redeemable feature in the film. While the plot was regularly described as predictable, one critic summarized Ford's critical input as follows: "His role is more that of a witness than a participant, but he lends integrity and truth to his role as a compassionate INS officer. Indeed there's more genuine conviction in Ford's face, more complexity, honesty and ability to incite compassion, than everything else in *Crossing Over* combined."[65]

It is easy to identify Ford's enduring trademark star persona in this assessment in a film whose plot was described as almost laughably implausible. To these, one could add Max Brogan's compassionate belief in democratic opportunities in the land of the free. While Ford's perfect fit with the part could easily add to the plot's alleged predictability, his solid performance and willingness to play just one more character in this failed art-house project received critics' approval.

Ford's next project, *Extraordinary Measures* (2010), for which he also served as executive producer, was another box office dud. Ford played Robert Stonehill, a maverick university researcher who helps John Crowley (Brendan Fraser), the father of two children with a rare disease, to find a cure for them. Most reviews criticized the film for having little ambition and resembling a TV movie in its melodramatic treatment of the Crowley family's predicament. Ford and Fraser's respective star performances were not considered powerful enough to attract attention. Ford's part as the gruff, taciturn scientist in particular was also considered to evince little artistic ambition. As one critic put it, "This role was made for Harrison Ford . . . , who seems to have made it his mission to play this character while moving as few facial muscles as possible. He has two expressions, the scowl and the reluctant half-smile. If nothing else, the performance is a marvel of economy."[66]

What is interesting about the part, however, is the fact that, at almost seventy, Ford seemed bent on reprising some elements of his earliest 1970s star persona, that of the maverick, self-centered, twice-divorced hero with no strings attached and no social skills—but ultimately a very persevering professional with a conscience who is able to relent and compromise for a good cause—yet again reflecting his desire for artistic renewal in old age. In addition, the star was certainly not afraid to let his reputed surliness emerge through this role, or in his cameo part in *Brüno* (2009), for that matter, which was dramatically modified to fit his public persona (the original scientist was a Taiwanese researcher, after all). The film also was familiar territory for Ford, as it criticized the internal workings of pharmaceutical companies (interested in making money by selling drugs rather than curing people), a trope that had already figured in Ford's successful turn in *The Fugitive* (1993) almost two decades earlier and that clearly continued to resonate with the public.

Ford followed up with *Morning Glory* (2010), dealing with the transformation of TV newscasts, though this time the approach was uncritical since the film favored light "infotainment" over and above hard news or critical investigative journalism. This comedy was comparatively better received than *Extraordinary Measures*, but that was mainly thanks to Rachel McAdams's energizing star performance as a beleaguered TV producer rather than Ford's own, which was generally described as slow or flat. However, such a performance was considered to be in tune with both Ford's subdued performance style over the years and the character's own standing within the narrative.

In this film, Ford plays Mike Pomeroy, a formerly popular investigative journalist, now in professional decline, who is forced to present a lightweight morning news program because of a loophole in his contract. Naturally, Pomeroy accepts the offer reluctantly and creates all sorts of problems for the program's producer, including demanding diva-like perks such as a daily basket of fresh tropical fruit, which goes against the star's actual on-set reputation. Former co-star Melanie Griffith once described Ford as "not the kind of guy who before a take has a mirror in front of his face to see if he looks good [but] the kind of guy who'd be helping the dolly grip move the dolly,"[67] which is consistent with his characterization in this film, yet another indication of Ford's continuing willingness to take a humorous approach on his enduring, though fading, stardom. At the same time, the cantankerous journalist seems to be an apt continuation of Ford's earlier role as Professor Stonehill in *Extraordinary Measures*. Most interestingly, however, Pomeroy's comic diva-like reluctance to adapt to new trends in TV news programs could also be understood as a self-conscious reflection of Ford's own standing within Hollywood today. As one reviewer put it, "Forget that Mike doesn't want to be on the show; Ford looks like he barely wants to be in *the movie*. And that's why he's easily the best thing in it."[68] This may appear to be contradictory, but it exposes Ford's role in both the film and in contemporary Hollywood quite adequately. Though over the years Ford has plainly stressed his interest in devoting his professional efforts to the generation of entertainment, a trend that the high-concept *Cowboys and Aliens* (2011) confirmed, one cannot help but wonder whether the many failures that he has accumulated in the twenty-first century as a result of his desire to experiment and add complexity to his aging persona (excepting *Crystal Skull*, the epitome of Hollywood entertainment) have not forced him to sell his soul to the Hollywood devil in an attempt to bolster his deteriorating standing.

It is therefore difficult to make predictions as to whether Ford will continue along the same revisionist artistic track. Given the failures he has had to face up to, it might be more logical to assume that he will change strategy and exploit, though not undermine, the very same features that made him an icon. Critical response indicates that this should be done without hiding from the age issue. Ford's appearance on the cover of the American Association of Retired People's magazine in 2011 clearly suggests a change of tactics. Still, given Ford's age (he turned seventy-two in 2014) and Hollywood's ageist culture, he will lose his leading man status and become an honorable supporting figure or a character actor, harking back to a bygone cinematic era. Maybe, in the autumn of his career, the time has come for Ford to become what Alec Guinness/Obi-Wan Kenobi meant for the first Star Wars generation. It has now been confirmed that Han Solo will come back to life at the end of 2015, and although there is still very little information regarding this comeback, judging from the film's teaser trailer it seems that the new generation will be given more scope within the narrative. However, the film's epic motto, *The Force Awakens,* suggests that "the Force" will still be with the iconic original characters, whose significant star presence in the film (unlike Guinness's back in 1977) virtually guarantees success.

Ford's recurrent associations with the stars of the classical period, regarding both his performance style and public persona, still feature prominently in publicity materials and film reviews. Jon Favreau, the director of *Cowboys and Aliens*, thought he was perfect for the part of cantankerous rancher Colonel Woodrow Dolarhyde and compared him to the older John Wayne in movies like *The Searchers* and *True Grit*.[69] The actor fosters such associations and often refers to himself as unfashionable or "unhip," as those "old shoes" that you like to wear over and over again because "they never go out of fashion."[70] This is perhaps the main reason his film career has lasted so long and why, one may assume, we might yet see Ford die with his boots on.

NOTES

The research for this essay has been funded by the Spanish Ministry of Education and Culture (project reference number FFI2010-15263).

1. "The AFI Life Achievement Awards," American Film Institute, www.afi.com/laa/default.aspx, accessed November 21, 2013 (emphasis added).
2. All biographical references in this section have been sourced from Ford's unofficial biographers: Robert Sellers, *Harrison Ford: A Biography* (London: Warner Books, 1993); Garry Jenkins, *Harrison Ford: Imperfect Hero* (New York: Pocket Books, 1998); and Brad Duke, *Harrison Ford: The Films* (Jefferson, N.C.: McFarland, 2005).
3. Jeanine Basinger, *The Star Machine* (New York: Vintage Books, 2009), 523.
4. Sellers, *Harrison Ford*, 27.
5. Ian Nathan, "The New Ford Solo," *Empire,* November 2002, 116.
6. Laurence Caracalla, *Harrison Ford* (San Francisco: Fitway Publishing, 2007), 8.
7. Michael L. Johnson, *New Westers: The West in Contemporary American Culture* (Lawrence: University Press of Kansas, 1996).
8. While Jackie Chan is certainly an extraordinary, tremendously popular martial arts expert, he has over the years cultivated a comic "average guy" persona, willing to run away from, rather than confront, his adversaries should the situation require him to do so. It is in this sense that a link could be established between the Indiana Jones

character and the Jackie Chan film persona. For more on Chan's persona, see Mark Gallagher, *Action Figures: Men, Action Films, and Contemporary Adventure Narratives* (New York: Palgrave Macmillan, 2006).

9. Susan Jeffords, *Hard Bodies: Hollywood Masculinity in the Reagan Era* (New Brunswick, N.J.: Rutgers University Press, 1994).
10. Yvonne Tasker, *Spectacular Bodies: Gender, Genre and the Action Cinema* (New York: Routledge, 1993).
11. Here is a classic example: in *Raiders of the Lost Ark*, after Belloq and his Nazi bosses manage to steal the Ark of the Covenant and load it on a truck bound for Cairo, Sallah (John Rhys-Davies) asks Indy what he plans to do; Indy answers, "I don't know. I'm making this up as we go along." This moment leads to one of the most spectacular stunts in Hollywood history: the truck chase, after which Indiana Jones manages to recover the Ark, only to lose it once again.
12. Michael Fleming, "Harrison Ford: The Playboy Interview," *Playboy*, July 2000 (accessed July 7, 2003), playboy.co.za/playboy-interview-harrison-ford, accessed March 7, 2015.
13. Rochelle L. Lazar, "The Achievement of Harrison Ford," American Film Institute, www.afi.com/tvevents/laa/laa00.aspx, accessed May 2, 2007 (emphasis added).
14. Even though the subsequent versions of the film have never been successful, economically speaking, Marcus A. Doel and David B. Clarke have perceptively pointed out that *Blade Runner* "has . . . achieved the oxymoronic status of a canonical postmodern cultural artefact." Marcus A. Doel and David B. Clarke, "From Ramble City to the Screening of the Eye: Blade Runner, Death and Symbolic Exchange" in *The Cinematic City*, ed. David Clarke (London: Routledge, 1997), 141.
15. Michael Allen, *Contemporary U.S. Cinema* (Harlow: Pearson, 2003), 128.
16. Phil Edwards and Alan McKenzie, "Interview with Ridley Scott," *Starburst*, no. 50 (1982): 29; Duke, *Harrison Ford*, 89.
17. Jenkins, *Harrison Ford*, 126. Jenkins considers this part to be the "most striking cameo" in Ford's career, while Ian Freer laments "if only he'd take such chances these days." Ian Freer, "The Top Ten Harrison Ford Performances," *Empire*, April 2006, 137.
18. Nick Lacey, *Blade Runner* (London: York Press, 2000), 11.
19. Harrison Ford has frequently been featured on the covers of such non-cinema magazines as *GQ*, *Esquire*, and *Men's Journal*, which evinces his popularity among men. The cover story in the September 1999 issue of *Men's Journal*, for instance, featured Ford and was entitled "The Great Life."
20. Susan Jeffords, "The Big Switch: Hollywood Masculinity in the Nineties," in *Film Theory Goes to the Movies*, ed. Jim Collins et al. (New York: Routledge, 1993); Jeffords, *Hard Bodies*.
21. Basinger, *The Star Machine*, 539.
22. Sarah Cassidy, "Life Begins at Sixty, Says Harrison Ford," *Independent*, July 25, 2005, findarticles.com/p/articles/mi_qn4158/print, accessed June 4, 2007.
23. Caracalla, *Harrison Ford*, 98.
24. Richard Dyer, *Stars*, new ed. (London: BFI Publishing, 2004), 126–31.
25. Joe Mauceri, "What Lies Beneath: A Shivers Interview," *Shivers*, no. 82 (2000): 31.
26. Basinger, *The Star Machine*, 537–38.

27. "A Breed Apart," Internet Movie Database, www.imdb.com/NewsFeatures/hford, accessed April 25, 2011.
28. Duke, *Harrison Ford*, 261.
29. Christine Gledhill, ed., *Stardom: Industry of Desire* (New York: Routledge, 1991).
30. "A Breed Apart."
31. Deborah Jermyn and Sean Redmond, eds., *The Cinema of Kathryn Bigelow: Hollywood Transgressor* (New York: Wallflower Press, 2003); Philip Kemp, "Close-Up: Genre Bender," *Sight and Sound* 13, no. 7 (2003): 66.
32. Dotson Rader, "Dark Star. Harrison Ford: Hollywood's Melancholic Hero," *Sunday Times Magazine*, August 11, 2002.
33. Dan Chavkin, "Action Figure," *Premiere* 15, no.2 (2002): 88.
34. Duke, *Harrison Ford,* 268.
35. Lael Loewenstein, "The Buddy Factor," *New York Daily News,* June 8, 2003.
36. Ibid.
37. Christine Geraghty, "Re-examining Stardom: Questions of Texts, Bodies and Performances," in *Reinventing Film Studies*, ed. Christine Gledhill and Linda Williams (London: Arnold, 2000), 183–202.
38. Hugh Hart, "Ford Lightens Up (a Little)," *Boston Globe Online*, June 8, 2003, www.highbeam.com/doc/1P2-7777707.html, accessed March 7, 2015.
39. Cindy Pearlman, "Ford Stays Focused despite Hollywood 'Hardships,'" *Chicago Sun-Times*, June 8, 2003.
40. Debra L. Wallace, "Harrison Ford: el último gran héroe," *Cinemanía*, no. 138 (March 2007): 86.
41. Neal Smith, review of *Firewall, BBC Online*, March 2006, www.bbc.co.uk/films/2006/03/17/firewall_2006_review.shtml, accessed April 27, 2007.
42. Ibid.
43. John Migliore, review of *Firewall, Premiere,* February 2006, www.premiere.com/moviereviews/2478/firewall.html, accessed April 24, 2007.
44. Lisa Schwarzbaum, review of *Firewall, Entertainment Weekly*, July 2006, www.ew.com/ew/article/0,,1157675,00.html, accessed April 24, 2007.
45. Rebecca Keegan, "Harrison Ford," *Time*, February 13, 2006, 99.
46. Michael Atkinson, "Fire Bomb," *Village Voice*, January 31, 2006, www.villagevoice.com/2006-01-31/film/fire-bomb, accessed April 24, 2007.
47. See Anne E. Lincoln and Michael Patrick Allen, "Double Jeopardy in Hollywood: Age and Gender in the Careers of Film Actors, 1926–1999," *Sociological Forum* 19, no.4 (December 2004): 616; and Chris Holmlund, "Celebrity, Ageing and Jackie Chan: Middle-aged Asian in Transnational Action," *Celebrity Studies* 1, no. 1 (2010): 100. Although older male actors are also victims of occupational ageism, Lincoln and Allen's research demonstrates that the "double jeopardy" effect, or the combined discriminatory effect brought about by gender and age, is felt much more strongly among female actors. Among other findings, they report that the term "older" is generally employed to refer to women over thirty but men over forty. It also appears to be the case that women actors are nominated for and win Oscars at a significantly younger age than their male counterparts. Finally, male actors such as Ford continue to be cast as leads in

their sixties, but it is rarer for a woman over forty to be cast as a film protagonist (628). Holmlund quotes similar data issued by the U.S. Screen Actors Guild in 2009.

48. Nathan, "The New Ford Solo," 116.
49. Anthony Breznican, "Harrison Ford: A Portrait," *USA Today,* April 16, 2008, usatoday30.usatoday.com/life/movies/news/2008-04-16-harrison-ford_N.htm, accessed April 29, 2011.
50. Jim Windolf, "Keys to the Kingdom," *Vanity Fair*, February 2008, www.vanityfair.com/news/2008/02/indy_update200802, accessed April 24, 2011.
51. Philippa Gates, "Acting His Age? The Resurrection of the 80s Action Heroes and Their Acting Stars," *Quarterly Review of Film and Video*, no. 27 (2010): 276–89.
52. See Chris Holmlund, *Impossible Bodies: Femininity and Masculinity at the Movies* (New York: Routledge, 2002); and Neal King, "Old Cops: Occupational Aging in a Film Genre," in *Staging Age: The Performance of Age in Theatre, Dance, and Film*, ed. Valerie Barnes Lipscomb et al. (New York: Palgrave Macmillan, 2010).
53. Gates, "Acting His Age?" 288 (emphasis in the original). Neal King has similarly argued that Hollywood's older action heroes' capacity to act young and attract extremely beautiful women half their age does not necessarily reflect the reality of the older generation but rather the filmmakers' industrial concerns and Hollywood's deeply ingrained ageist culture ("Old Cops," 60, 73).
54. Geoff Boucher, "Harrison Ford Returns as Indiana Jones," *Los Angeles Times*, May 4, 2008, www.latimes.com/entertainment/la-ca-indy4-2008may04-story.html, accessed April 29, 2011.
55. Roger Ebert, review of *Indiana Jones and the Kingdom of the Crystal Skull*, *Chicago Sun-Times*, May 18, 2008, rogerebert.suntimes.com/apps/pbcs.dll/article?AID=/20080518/REVIEWS/969461084/1023, accessed April 29, 2011.
56. Admittedly, Ford's real-life relationship with Calista Flockhart, who is more than twenty years his junior, would easily contradict this argument.
57. Caracalla, *Harrison Ford*, 46.
58. Ebert, review of *Crystal Skull*.
59. Allison Glock, "Blade Runner," *Telegraph Magazine*, May 10, 2008, 50.
60. Windolf, "Keys to the Kingdom."
61. Geraghty, "Re-examining Stardom."
62. According to Internet Movie Database and Box Office Mojo, the film's international box office takings amounted to $786.6 million (its budget was estimated at $185 million), only surpassed by *The Dark Knight*'s impressive topping of $1 billion. "2008 Yearly Box Office Results," *Box Office Mojo*, boxofficemojo.com/yearly/chart/?view2=worldwide&yr=2008, accessed June 20, 2013; and "Indiana Jones and the Kingdom of the Crystal Skull (2008)," Internet Movie Database, www.imdb.com/title/tt0367882/business?ref_=tt_ql_dt_4, accessed June 20, 2013.
63. In 2005, the American Film Institute voted Indiana Jones the second most popular hero in the history of U.S. film, topped only by Atticus Finch from *To Kill a Mockingbird* (1962). James Bond in *Dr. No* (1962) was voted third, while Han Solo finished a distant fourteenth. "AFI's 100 Years … 100 Heroes & Villains," American Film Institute, www.afi.com/100years/handv.aspx, accessed July 2, 2013.

64. David Hochman, "Harrison Ford Interview: Ford in Focus," *Readers' Digest*, May 2008, accessed April 29, 2011, www.rd.com/celebrities/movie-celebs/harrison-ford-interview-may2008/article55736.html.
65. Mick LaSalle, review of *Crossing Over*, *San Francisco Chronicle*, March 13, 2009, www.sfgate.com/cgi-bin/article.cgi?f=/c/a/2009/03/13/DDoC16DE15.DTL, accessed May 3, 2011.
66. Stephanie Zacharek, review of *Extraordinary Measures*, *Salon,* June 2010, www.salon.com/topic/extraordinary_measures, accessed May 13, 2011.
67. Jill Smolowe, "Harrison Ford," *People* 51, no. 10 (March 1999): 155.
68. Owen Gleiberman, review of *Morning Glory*, *Entertainment Weekly*, November 12, 2010, www.ew.com/ew/article/0,,20440727,00.html, accessed May 5, 2011 (emphasis in the original).
69. Nancy Griffin, "Harrison Ford: Hollywood Hero," *AARP The Magazine Online*, July-August 2011, www.aarp.org/entertainment/movies-for-grownups/info-05-2011/harrison-ford-interview-full-throttle.html, accessed March 27, 2013.
70. Tony Horkins, "In Conversation with Harrison Ford," *Empire,* April 2006, 133.

PART 4

DAMAGE CONTROL

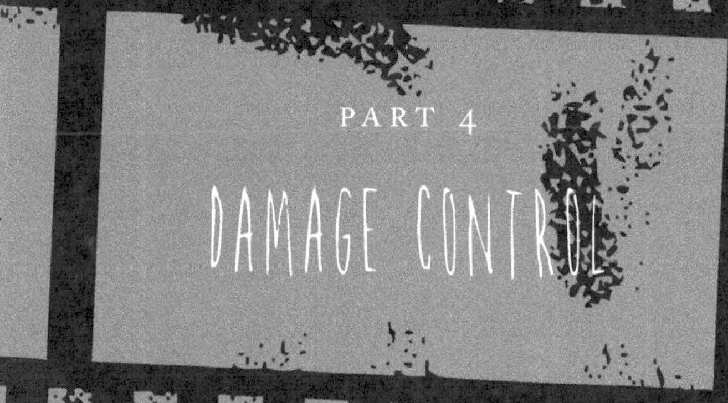

11

BLOOD, FRECKLES, AND TEARS: SISSY SPACEK'S SURFACE SUBVERSIONS AND NEW HOLLYWOOD'S ABJECT FEMINISM

Alison Hoffman-Han

IN HER 2002 APPEARANCE ON *INSIDE THE ACTOR'S STUDIO*, SISSY SPACEK was asked by the show's perpetually serious and fawning host, James Lipton, what was going through her mind as she accepted the Academy Award for Best Actress in 1980 for her role as Loretta Lynn in *Coal Miner's Daughter*. With barely a pause, Spacek replied, "I was waiting for the bucket of blood to drop." Referencing the famous "money shot" that sealed her fame in Brian De Palma's *Carrie* (1976), Spacek certainly lightened the mood of the interview and got a good laugh from the audience. However, just after the laughter subsided, the remark made for an uncomfortable moment, one that provides a brief glimpse into Spacek's self-consciousness regarding her talent, looks, and status as a recognized, award-worthy movie star. A bit later in the interview, during the Q&A session with Lipton's acting students, Spacek continued down this path, remarking on how she built her career on a foundation of "ugly duckling" roles often requiring nudity and, as she put it, the bodily "humiliation and exploitation" of her characters. Rather than delving into the visual and cultural politics of these roles—of why, in her early career, Spacek felt limited to playing such parts, and the industrial contexts that produced and maintained such limitations for young actresses—Lipton instead made a crack that Spacek, throughout the 1970s, "just couldn't seem to keep her shirt on."

For the most part, Lipton had a point: Spacek did—in the spirit of the seventies—"let it all hang out" onscreen, so much so that her nude scenes in films such as *Prime Cut* (1972), *Welcome to LA* (1976), and *Carrie* have been archived on various soft-core porn websites such as *Mr.Skin.com*. Nonetheless, I think Lipton's crack requires some tweaking. It was not necessarily Spacek who "couldn't keep her shirt on," but rather the overwhelmingly male screenwriters, production designers, and directors responsible for constructing her individual characters who usually imagined Spacek as shirtless and, as such, demanded her nude representation. In a different interview, Spacek reminisced about her many topless roles, acknowledging and commenting upon the "humiliation and exploitation" she experienced during the first stages of her career in the 1970s: "They exploited me, but I exploited them. They filled a space in their picture and I used them as a stepping-stone in my career."[1] Here "they" refers to the directors with whom she worked in her early career, and the boys club of New Hollywood in general.

Understood as a renaissance taking place in mainstream American cinema between the mid-sixties and mid-seventies (i.e., from *Bonnie and Clyde* [1967] to *Star Wars* [1977]), the New Hollywood emerged from a confluence of regulatory, industrial, artistic, and cultural forces. The dissolution of the Production Code and the introduction of the ratings system allowed for a relaxation of censorship during that ten-year window, and the New Hollywood auteurs (Coppola, Scorsese, Bogdanovich, Spielberg, Lucas, Penn, De Palma, etc.) were provided opportunities to create taboo-breaking films in touch with a countercultural ethos upon the crumbling foundations of the studio system. In terms of their form and content, these films linked "classical Hollywood genre filmmaking with the stylistic innovations of European art cinema"[2]—a "countercultural-conservative ideological schema" exhibiting an astonishing amount of ideological and representational contradictions.[3] In his essay on New Hollywood, Thomas Elsaesser sketches out these contradictions and ties them to gender, characterizing this period as one of "male obsession . . . in which one detects, in often distorted form, the changing role of women and the rise of feminism."[4] Similarly, Peter Krämer, in his book *The New Hollywood: From Bonnie and Clyde to Star Wars*, argues that the "breakaway hits from 1967 to 1976 tended to be narrowly focused on male protagonists, marginalising women in the process."[5] In a similar vein, he asserts that films "that attracted the largest audience mirrored increasingly liberal attitudes towards sex, race and ethnicity as well as a widespread fascination with, and anxieties about, violence, while inverting the growing egalitarian attitudes about gender."[6] As Krämer and Elsaesser hint, but never plainly state, one of New Hollywood's primary modes of visualizing such violence onscreen was through the brutalization and abject exposure of women's bodies.

Molly Haskell, in her famous feminist take on Hollywood history, *From Reverence to Rape: The Treatment of Women in the Movies*, describes how New Hollywood cinema, "with its successive revelations, progressed like a stripper, though awkwardly—like a novice in a hurry to get off the stage."[7] I argue that these particular early roles of Spacek's represent what Celine Parreñas-Shimizu terms the "binds of representation" and "enforced embodiments."[8] The actor's body, as it is raced, gendered, and aged in films that image the human body through realist aesthetics, functions as an interface where their tangible flesh—along with their gestures, expressions, and comportment—collides with the prescribed, culturally constructed, and historically resonant meanings of that flesh. As a white, young, not conventionally beautiful actress of her generation—one with a skinny body, B-cup breasts, some professional Method training under her belt, and not much else—Spacek had little choice in how she made her screen debut. The masculinist bent of New Hollywood cinema, what Elsaesser cites as the "macho flavour" of its films and industrial community,[9] generally allowed for the "realness" of female subjectivity to be expressed only through the proof of women's exposed bodies, figured exploitatively and often abjectly onscreen. Ironically, for Spacek to build her career as a screen actress who is taken seriously, she had to begin by repeatedly playing a girl who literally bares it all through crude, often bloody, and tearful bodily displays.

However, after her performance in *Coal Miner's Daughter*, Spacek's star text shifted; temporarily, throughout the 1980s, she was pitched as the "all-American country girl" by Hollywood's publicity narratives and various popular and academic star studies.[10] Indeed, Spacek has negotiated her forty-year acting career by simultaneously embracing and subverting this limited, gendered, and ageist designation. While she has performed the "country girl" role many times over both onscreen and off, her star body has just as frequently, and perhaps more iconically, been the site of (and *a sight of*) abjection, exploitation, and monstrous femininity in horror films (*Carrie*, *The Ring 2* [2005], *An American Haunting* [2005]), crime dramas (*Prime Cut*, *Katherine* [1975], *Missing* [1982],

In the Bedroom [2001]), art cinema (*Badlands* [1973], *3 Women* [1977], *Welcome to LA*), and women-centered melodramas (*Ginger in the Morning* [1974], *Coal Miner's Daughter, Marie* [1985], *'night Mother* [1986], *Crimes of the Heart* [1986], *The Long Walk Home* [1990], *If These Walls Could Talk* [1996], *Nine Lives* [2005], *North Country* [2005], *The Help* [2011]). Such roles are not limited to her seventies-era filmography: repeatedly, Spacek returns to and refashions her star body's roots in abjection and female masochism. Spacek comments on this in her recent memoir, *My Extraordinary Ordinary Life* (2012). Through the codes of autobiography, Spacek performs a reading of her own stardom, attempting to manage her celebrity persona by claiming that in choosing her roles strategically since the beginning of her movie career, she sought to "steer away from" and "minimize [her] country girl image."[11]

Considering the totality of Spacek's roles, I propose that her work from the 1970s set the template for her career, keeping her, through her own admission, perpetually waiting for that bucket of blood to drop. A phenomenological, feminist analysis of Spacek's seventies-era star body unmasks the ontology of Spacek's most iconic bodily surfaces—the blood, freckles, tears, and countercultural fashions that often style and/or expose her flesh—as they are imaged in her early films. Tracing this process sheds light on how second wave feminism, along with the irrational sociopolitical fears it produced, remarkably *and superficially*, became the subtext of Spacek's star text.

To be sure, Spacek's face, quite literally, served as the synecdoche for New Hollywood's cadre of actresses at mid-decade: in a photo composed and lit to highlight her freckles, green eyes, and small, doll-like features, Spacek graced the cover of the February 1977 issue of *Newsweek* with a headline reading "The New Actresses."[12] While an interview with Spacek takes up only one-third of this feature article, entitled "Year of the Actress," the remainder reads as a sublimated feminist critique of the "stark reality of . . . the fallen estate of women in Hollywood" where "seventy-three percent of featured and supporting roles go to men."[13] Yet tellingly, Spacek is described in the article as "American-freckled, with hair the color of sunlit wheat, and a 5-foot-2.5 inch frame resembling that of a full-breasted tomboy."[14] The article emphasizes her bodily features and mobilizes her onscreen image and early star biography to "exemplify the problems—and promise—of the young Hollywood actress" in the 1970s.[15]

Just like many actresses of her generation who emerged during the New Hollywood era, Spacek's offscreen feminism could only manifest itself onscreen tangentially, and in rather curious, corporeal ways. Film historian Peter Lev, in his book *American Films of the Seventies: Conflicting Visions*, alludes to this when he argues that Hollywood resisted an explicit representation of feminism "more than it resisted the youth culture or the antiwar movement or the Black Pride movement."[16] When it comes to visualizing second wave politics in New Hollywood cinema, Lev notes that any direct representations of the women's movement were "gradual, incremental."[17] Adding to Lev's descriptors, I would include the word "oblique." In this regard, I perceive Spacek's countercultural feminine body, in its many abject, filmic, and televisual renderings, as encoding "New" and contemporary Hollywood's animosity toward, precarious ties to, and opaque manifestations of feminism.

The term "abject" applies in both the pedestrian sense—simply defined as debased, lacking bodily integrity, or degraded—and in the more theoretical sense stemming from Julia Kristeva's book *Powers of Horror*, in which she situates the abject as the rejection of what both is and is not the body.[18] She argues that because the "body's boundaries are both necessary and dangerous to the self-constituting subject," one must deny its internal chaos (blood, feces, vomit, etc.) to become a clean, ordered, social being.[19] Simultaneously though, the abject "hovers at the margins of life, never fully abolished. . . . Abjected matter is the remnant, then, of our chaotic, uncontrollable bodies and world, always threatening to erupt and disrupt the social order."[20] Such "uncontrollable" bodies on film (those that cannot "contain themselves"), then, become a safe, distanced way to experience abjection. The "waste" of these bodies is literally contained by the cinematic frame, yet psychically and physically—or "cinesthetically," as Vivian Sobchack suggests[21]—it maintains an ability to disrupt the coordinates of our sense of order while also allegorizing the fears and/or fantasies of the cultural and industrial contexts from which it emerged.

Appropriately enough, for an actress whose work makes visible the "waste" of abjection, Spacek's first small part in a film was as an extra in Andy Warhol and Paul Morrissey's *Trash* (1970). However, her moment on camera never made it into the final version of the film; Spacek's image became part of the trash of *Trash*, as it were. Practically a conceptual art piece in abjection, Spacek's discarded image in *Trash* eventually led her to other film roles in the seventies that could actually be seen onscreen. Each of these films, all exercises in abjection, image Spacek's body as "excessive" in some way: her body is "too much," continually erupting in emotional and physical displays involving blood, tears, and/or bared flesh.

In working through this argument, it is useful to sketch out, and then closely investigate, the three different categories of Spacek's seventies-era onscreen embodiments, along with their "excessive trait(s)" and relation to feminism.

CATEGORY	EXCESSIVE TRAIT(S)	FILMS	RELATION TO FEMINISM
Exploited Body	Flesh	*Prime Cut, Welcome to LA*	Antagonistic, Dismissive
Destructive Body	Blood	*Carrie, Badlands, Katherine*	Partially Aligned, Paranoid, Evocative
Transformative Body	Tears, Styling, Costumes	*Ginger in the Morning, 3 Women, Coal Miner's Daughter*	Conservatively Aligned, Superficial

In these films, Spacek's most prominent "natural" bodily features, which in American cinema, historically and culturally, signify girlish innocence—big eyes, upturned nose, red hair, the many freckles marking her white skin, petite bone structure, and thinness—work against the monstrous, "unnatural" and performative elements "put on" her body through the processes of film production (fake blood, tears, costumes, character design, acting techniques). The actress's natural features instantiate "rawness" and "girlishness," but when they are covered in blood or tears, and are given life through the fierce intensity and/or hyper-passivity of her acting, Spacek's onscreen embodiments epitomize a kind of uniquely feminine rage and/or victimization that speaks both with and against its offscreen correlative, second wave feminism. Throughout her character embodiments in the seventies, this victimization and rage emerge from patriarchal constraints that limit the full, complex expression of her feminine body and its desire for agency and coherence. Her characters' bodies trace the defining contours of abjection in that they get caught up in a double-bind of expression, enunciating feelings of both narcissism and self-loathing simultaneously. Kristeva's formula for abjection describes this double-bind: "I abject *myself* within the same motion through which 'I' claim to establish *myself*."[22] Kristeva writes that "the abject simultaneously beseeches and pulverizes the subject" and that "all abjection is in fact recognition of the *want* on which any being . . . or desire is founded."[23] I find that Kristeva's formulation uncannily resonates with Spacek's seventies-era onscreen embodiments and their contradictory comportments—at once subjects of powerful, painful want *and passivity*. Using this formulation to think through New Hollywood's contradictory representations of gendered power and desire, Kristeva's words prove resonant in capturing how Spacek's characters enunciate their want for recognition and validation by "acting out" a decidedly feminine mode of bodily abjection.

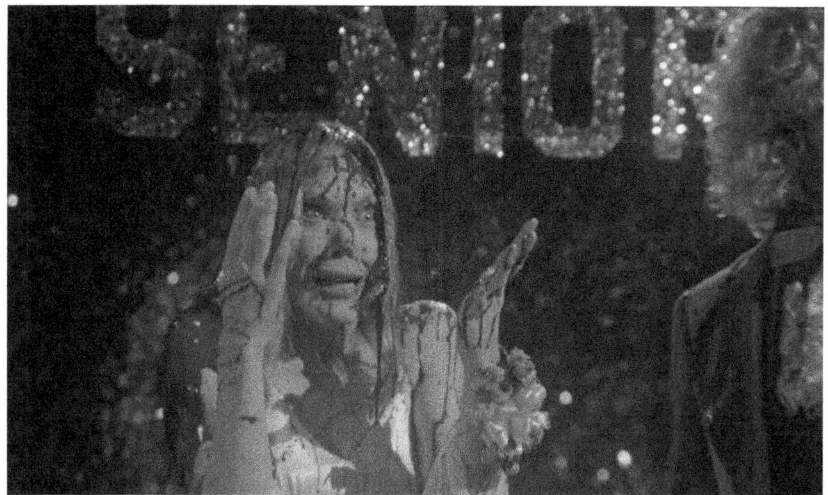

Spacek in *Carrie* (1976), her most iconic role.

THE EXPLOITED BODY

In Spacek's onscreen debut, *Prime Cut*, and another of her early films, *Welcome to LA*, this bodily abjection is figured through her character's posture of submission and subservience to a patriarchal figure. Of course, such a posture is underscored by her constantly nude physical form. In *Prime Cut*, a much older man, Nick (Lee Marvin), saves her drugged out and always naked character, Poppy, from a white slavery ring, but then continues to exploit her body for both erotic thrills and personal revenge against her "master" and pimp (Gene Hackman). In director Alan Rudolph's *Welcome to LA*, Spacek plays Linda, a sweet but clueless hippie who works as a maid—one who is so "free" and flighty that she often performs her domestic work topless. She also prostitutes herself with one of her employers, Jack (John Considine), who eventually rapes her. In this category, Spacek's characters read as miserably flat in their perpetual exposure and violent exploitation—ciphers used for erotic spectacle and to frame either the potency or perversity of the male characters surrounding her. Importantly, with both films, Spacek's wide-eyed characters' emotional registers are limited to expressions of innocence, naïveté, and sexual curiosity.

Recalling her decision to sign on to play Poppy in *Prime Cut*, a crime drama that reads as an exploitation film in its perpetual comparing of women's bodies to cattle and raw cuts of meat, Spacek recognizes, yet partially disavows, how her onscreen bodily integrity was compromised:

> I was officially offered the part in *Prime Cut*—my first real film! But there was one thing that made me hesitate: the role called for at least one nude scene. It wasn't an unusual requirement in those days; everyone seemed to be running around naked in the movies—and even on Broadway. So I figured if I wanted to be an actor, I'd better get over it. I called my parents and told them the good news. I'd gotten my first part in a movie, and it starred Lee Marvin and Gene Hackman. Then I told them the bad news: I wouldn't always be wearing clothes. After much deliberation, we decided that this was a wonderful opportunity, and the good far outweighed the bad. I packed my bags and never looked back.[24]

Fascinatingly, Spacek's description of her decision-making process in agreeing to play the role of Poppy in *Prime Cut* mimics her character's naïveté and childlike obedience. Remembering this moment in her early career, Spacek withholds from specifically discussing the gendered imbalance of nudity in New Hollywood cinema, and instead recasts the negative aspects of the era's limited and exploitative roles for women in a positive light by focusing on male stardom and her own "wonderful opportunity" to be featured and made visible in a mainstream movie, despite the sexist nature of her part. Yet this decision to star in *Prime Cut* and pack her bags for Hollywood, as signified by her use of the first-person plural pronoun "we," in her mind was not entirely her own, but rather one made only with her parents' approval and encouragement.

Spacek's rationalization for accepting a role requiring so much nudity is slightly disingenuous as well, since in *Prime Cut* the only actors "running around" naked are the women; in fact, nearly every woman in the film appears in the nude; to be precise, however, they are not exactly "running around," but lying down as they are depicted as lifeless bodies for sale—splayed out on beds of hay, caged in cattle pens, and housed in a barn. Even when wearing clothes, Spacek's Poppy remains, weirdly enough, even more exposed and "nude." In the film's oddest and most disturbing scene, immediately after Nick rescues Poppy from sexual slavery, he then decides to keep her as his lover/adopted daughter. During their first night together, he buys her clothes and directs her to wear them. He instructs her to put on an ultra-sheer, green evening gown and then takes her out to a fancy restaurant for dinner, where once again she is exposed and ogled by strange old men. In pornographic fashion, the camera fragments and frames her exposed breasts in close-up several times during this scene.

Nick gets off on controlling and parading her exposed body, while Poppy, with her orphan girl naïveté and ignorance regarding proper social and bodily

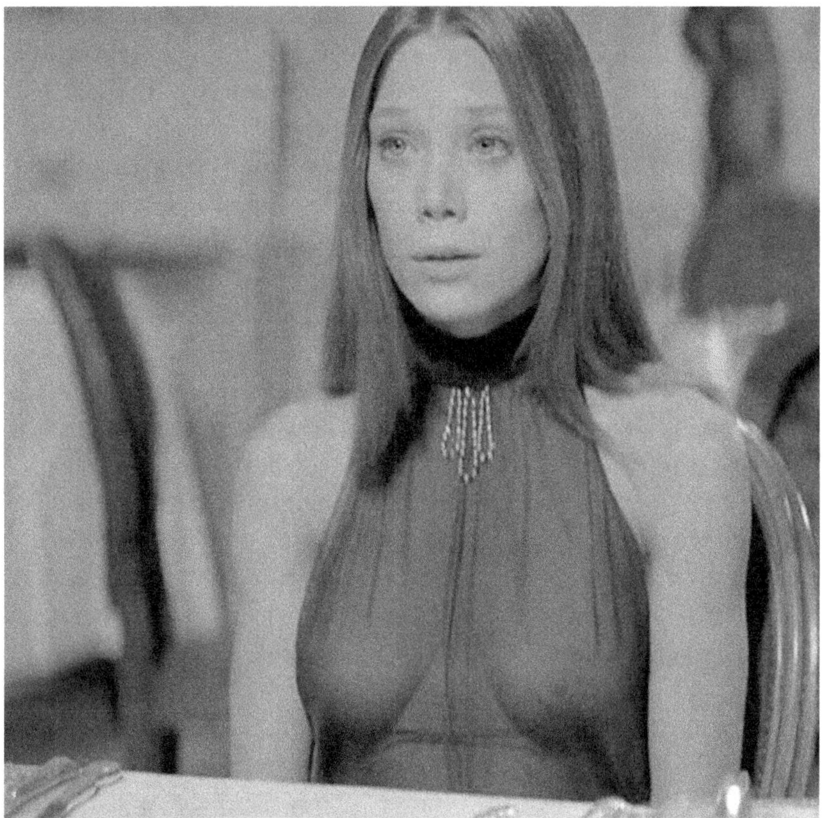

Spacek as Poppy in *Prime Cut* (1972), wearing the sheer dress gifted to her by Nick (Lee Marvin).

decorum, misrecognizes Nick's perverse gesture as a romantic and paternal kind of care. As the camera tilts up from her breasts to her face, she smiles warmly: she likes her new man, her new dress, and the fancy restaurant and food. Almost immediately, she falls in love with Nick, and becomes slavishly devoted to him despite their significant age difference. For the film's remainder, Nick repeatedly saves and protects Poppy; this is emphasized by one of the film's key visual refrains: Nick cradling Poppy's unconscious body in his arms and carrying her to safety. At the film's conclusion, Poppy and Nick's semi-incestuous relationship is secured, and the two vow to continue on together in his hometown of Chicago. She happily agrees to remain under his "care" and control.

In *Welcome to L.A.*, the fate of Spacek's character, Linda, appears less secure, though she maintains a higher degree of independence. After enduring a series of exploitative relationships with the various men in her life—her boss and rapist Jack, her dishonest and married lover (Harvey Keitel), and her drifter of a male roommate (Keith Carradine)—she winds up alone on Christmas, excitedly unwrapping gifts that she has purchased for herself. In the film's penultimate scene, costumed in a loose fitting top with her right breast hanging out, Spacek's Linda ends up almost exactly where she started—as an air-head but sweet hippie chick who fails to see herself and those around her clearly. She remains the eternal, ignorant, movie-struck girl in Los Angeles, one who will most likely continue to suffer at the hands of the city's unethical, selfish men.

In the gendered, narrative worlds of *Prime Cut* and *Welcome to L.A.*, Spacek's embodiment and placement might best be described as "slight" and "prone." Though she is a central character in both films, the meaningfulness of those characters is marginal: Poppy and Linda only "mean something" in relation to the key male characters around them, and how those key male characters find use for and inevitably abuse Spacek's characters' exposed, available body. Moreover, the bodily juxtaposition of her characters' almost constantly bared flesh and her freckle-faced innocence encourages a regressive vision of femininity, one that in the social context of the early to mid-1970s constitutes a dismissal of feminism. Here Kristeva's formula for abjection echoes Spacek's own rationalization for accepting such roles: "I abject *myself* within the same motion through which 'I' claim to establish *myself*" / "I'd better get over exposing my nude body if I want to establish myself as a Hollywood actress." For Spacek to bring her star text into being, similar to other "no name" actresses just beginning their careers in the seventies, she had no perceived options outside of "simultaneously beseech[ing] and pulveriz[ing]" herself as both a subject and performing body in order to achieve any kind of visibility, much less *voice*, on New Hollywood's screens.

THE DESTRUCTIVE BODY

While Spacek's early roles strangely work to diminish her subjectivity through the hyper-visibility that comes from her onscreen nudity, conversely, her most iconic roles of the seventies highlight her freckled, bared flesh, covered in blood and/or framed through the affective registers of resentment and rage. Unlike the "Exploited" category, in Spacek's "Destructive Body" films—*Carrie*, *Badlands*, and *Katherine*—her young characters' presence is made primary, constituting the visual, narrative, and affective center of each film. Far from "slight" and "prone," these characters embody contradictions and complexities that, while not explicitly feminist by any stretch, exhibit a partial alignment with and paranoia about the idea of female power. On the surface these characters appear passive and weak, as nubile bodies immediately on display at the beginning of each film—Carrie washing herself in the shower, Holly practicing her baton in hot pants, Katherine examining herself in a full-length mirror wearing only underwear. However, after these initial moments, these characters' girlish bodies prove massively powerful, harnessing violent and deadly powers, both physical and psychical. In *Carrie* and *Katherine* these bodies erupt in climactic moments of fierce, bloody spectacle—so disruptive in their abjection that their only fate, at the films' conclusion, is reluctant self-destruction. Carrie's own telekinetic powers ultimately lead to her death, and Katherine kills herself in a suicide bombing. Even though the bodies of Carrie and Katherine are "constructed as the source of horror," as Shelley Stamp argues, each film's rendering of those bodies "works to elicit profound sympathy, especially from female viewers."[25] *Badlands*, the most progressive film of the group, visualizes Holly's passive though nonetheless disruptive abjection as an internalized, violent rejection of dominant masculinity, a difference that affords her narrative survival at the cost of her father and boyfriend's deaths.[26]

The violence that each of these bodies eventually inflicts shares a similar purpose and target: to unmask and demolish patriarchal authority and ideological systems of domination. Bodily speaking, both the title character in *Carrie* and Holly in *Badlands* use the power of their eyes—their gaze—to retaliate against those who have perceivably harmed them. Carrie combines her telekinesis with the force of her steady look to unleash violence against everyone at her high school prom and her abusive mother at home, while Holly looks on complicitly as her father is murdered by her boyfriend, Kit (Martin Sheen), and then that same look sizes Kit up as a failure in his inability to master repeated attempts at performing a clichéd, "rebel" masculinity. Refusing to align herself with Kit's gaze by the film's conclusion, Holly lives on to narrate their story on her terms, while Kit dies offscreen.

As Katherine in the feature-length television movie *Katherine*, alternatively titled *The Radical*, Spacek undergoes multiple body transformations from feminine to masculine, bourgeois to homeless, pretty preppy to countercultural-feminist "revolutionary." The story of a privileged Wellesley girl turned political radical, loosely based on the life of Diana Oughton of the Weather Underground, *Katherine* provides Spacek with the opportunity to embody and emote anger and violent rage even more explicitly and realistically than does *Carrie*. Katherine unleashes power not just with her gaze, but with complete devotion to the cause of political and social revolution. She becomes increasingly masculine and empowered as her political attitudes shift from practicing non-violent passivity to armed, militant action.

The action that her character's body performs in each of these films emphasizes "movement" of some sort. Most obviously, Katherine joins up with multiple radical, political movements; Carrie's telekinesis allows her to violently move

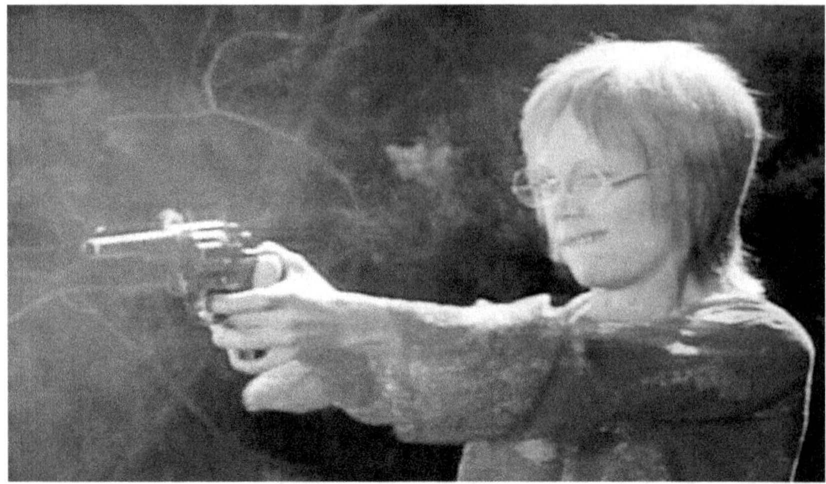

Spacek as a countercultural radical in *Katherine* (1975).

things with her mind; and Holly is "on the move" as she and Kit make their getaway from South Dakota to Montana. Always, in *Badlands*, Holly holds the map and drives the narrative forward through her narration and imagination.

By playing with the idea of female desire and independence vis-à-vis one woman's "movement" of people and things, *Carrie* and *Badlands* refract second wave feminist politics, albeit shallowly. However, *Katherine* engages it more explicitly by linking countercultural political movements to women's coalitions. During the film's most direct nod to its contemporaneous offscreen referents—radical feminist groups like the New York Redstockings and WITCH (the Women's International Terrorist Conspiracy from Hell)—Katherine heads up the Women's Militia of the Weathermen. Hair shorn, dressed in masculine countercultural militia wear, and donning a baseball bat, Katherine leads her fellow Weatherwomen in a "Day of Rage" action at a high school where she urges the students to reject the oppressive structures of their school and, by extension, the American government. The women break down doors and smash windows at the school, running through the halls united in an anarchistic sense of pleasure and purpose as they externalize their politics through physical action. Katherine charges the women forward with abandon, chanting to the students: "Strike because your classes are a bore; strike to show your opposition to the war and racism; strike to seize control of your lives. Take over!" Though "strike against sexism" is curiously absent in this scene's dialogue, by way of the film's framing of women's solidarity through political action, the iconography of radical feminist movement exercises a visual presence just the same.

The film's editing and its emphasis on Katherine's body also suggest such a connection. Briefly, in the scene immediately before the women's "Day of Rage" action, Katherine and her female comrades are united in a very different kind of bodily work: stripping. In order to devote their political lives to the "Weather Underground," the only anonymous and monetarily efficient mode of labor imagined to be available to these women is performing and selling the spectacle of their nude, feminine bodies. In this scene, Katherine—wearing only rainbow striped underwear and a mask of strategically overdone makeup—is watched closely by a series of middle-aged men in the strip club's audience, yet she herself never looks back at them. Cutting from a medium shot of the back of her dancing body to a close-up of her face, Katherine dances with her eyes closed, seemingly lost in the pleasure of her own performance, and charged by the idea that the joke is on these men: they pay to watch her body, but ultimately she is already strategizing the terms of what will be a decidedly violent payback.

While much of *Katherine* affords Spacek the opportunity to perform exaggerated embodiments of countercultural anger and resentment in nearly every scene, during these two moments in the film—just within a matter of three minutes of screen time—the transformation and juxtaposition of her body from a self-aware, strategic performance of passive *femininity* to militant, explosive "woman revolutionary" crystallizes the concept of *abject feminism*. These side-by-side scenes provide a perfect illustration of the era's abject feminist representational formula—its partial alignment to feminism—where "pulverizing" the female self constitutes *the only* means by which to assert female want and desire, in this case, one woman's desire to be recognized as a "revolutionary," political subject. *Katherine*, similar to other made-for-TV movies of the seventies and eighties, engages radical politics in a way that is surprisingly direct. However, as Elayne Rapping argues in her work on made-for-TV movies of this era, the film ultimately domesticates and dramatizes countercultural politics, and to a certain degree punishes Spacek's eponymous character.[27] On one hand, *Katherine* functions as a cautionary tale about the dangers of a liberal education for young women (i.e., "college-educated women are likely to become radicals"), yet on the other, her character remains empathetic, and is absolutely structured as a subject of identification throughout the film. Though she is depicted as an extremist, Katherine exercises care and compassion toward others, not only a feminine but a universal value.

As Katherine, Carrie, and *Badlands*' Holly, Spacek embodies characters with an unusually high degree of female authority for cinema of the New Hollywood era. Her performances of such authority work to *evoke* feminism—a violent, bloody, and/or threatening version of it, no doubt. Abject in their empowerment,

Spacek's characters in her "Destructive Body" films make some serious noise through their anger, terror, and rage.

THE TRANSFORMATIVE BODY

Gentler but equally resonant versions of Spacek's star body emerge in the "Transformative" category of her seventies-era work, which includes another made-for-TV movie, the cheesy but charming *Ginger in the Morning* (1974), along with Robert Altman's *3 Women* (1977) and, capping off the decade, *Coal Miner's Daughter* (1980). Passive aggression, control, and transformation—altering both the external and internal self, along with shifting gendered power imbalances in personal relationships—constitute the principal character and bodily contours in this grouping of Spacek's representational archive. Each of these films positively allegorizes a kind of liberal feminism through her characters' desire for self-integrity and validation from others, particularly women. At the conclusion of *3 Women* Pinky finds self through her maternal connections with Millie (Shelley Duvall) and Willie (Janice Rule); Loretta Lynn in *Coal Miner's Daughter* claims her talent and personal freedom not through her husband but through her friendship with Patsy Cline (Beverly D'Angelo); and hippie Ginger in *Ginger in the Morning* "frees" and feminizes her "square" and uptight boyfriend, even cloaking him in a bright yellow shawl in the film's final scene. Certainly, this category of Spacek's early work promotes a more progressive vision of female empowerment and feminine desire, yet these films are hardly overt celebrations of feminism. *3 Women*'s opacity makes its gesture toward feminism appear hollow, and *Ginger in the Morning*'s and *Coal Miner's Daughter*'s overemphasis on "the personal" as something detached from "the political" comes across as superficial readings of second wave demands.

Nonetheless, these films' engagement with feminist ideas makes them remarkable by New Hollywood's standards. For example, *3 Women* and *Coal Miner's Daughter* narrativize the process of female or "feminine" socialization under white patriarchal capitalism, yet Spacek's character comes to reject patriarchy and, at key points in the narrative, joins forces with other women, creating an alternative matriarchal family. At the conclusion of *Coal Miner's Daughter* and *Ginger in the Morning*, her characters ultimately transform the patriarchal order through their more ethical, feminine subjectivity and worldview. Resolution in these two films is imagined as mutual respect and shared domestic responsibility between men and women. Loretta's and Ginger's male partner, the key patriarchal figure, learns to "stand by" and actually "stand behind" his woman, cheering on her success in the public sphere and embracing his own traditionally "feminine" qualities. This is especially emphasized in *Coal Miner's Daughter*, where Spacek's Loretta Lynn finds her voice and authority as a successful country singer and takes ownership of her "public" persona and personal, desiring body, all despite her husband Doolittle's (Tommy Lee Jones) obsessive managing of her appearance, career, and bodily freedom. To claim control of her body and voice, and how they are represented to the public, Spacek's Loretta allies herself with a strong woman, her mentor Patsy Cline, and recognizes the special importance of her female fans as well.

However, her quest for personal ownership and integrity announces itself most strongly through the excessive nature of both her personal style and vocal performance. This radical shift in style and song—from clean-faced and simple hillbilly girl singing about romance to full-tilt Nashville diva vocally testifying onstage—occurs after Loretta and Patsy meet. Immediately, the two become near mirrors of one another, looking to each other for pleasure, validation, and support. In resisting her husband's demands that she maintain a "natural look" without makeup and flashy costumes, Loretta models herself after the hyper-feminine Patsy, finding independence and power by increasingly styling herself as a glamorous diva. First, she borrows Patsy's makeup and old costumes, and then, after Patsy's death, she creates her own "big," signature look. In classic musical biopic fashion, a montage sequence charts Loretta's rise in fame through the increasingly excessive "bigness" of her style. Successively, as her costumes become more puffed-up and colorful and her hair-dos progressively elaborate and large, she becomes a more powerful onscreen presence and, by implication, a woman in charge of her own destiny. The final scene in which Loretta stands at center stage with massive hair and sparkling gown, crooning her song "Coal Miner's Daughter" in a style more excessive and melodramatic than previously seen, may be superficial in terms of feminist content, yet it is deeply satisfying in terms of emotional payoff for female viewers.

CONCLUSION

Discussing American cinema's limited representations of women in the seventies, Robin Wood poses the key question to New Hollywood that relates especially to Spacek's star text of the decade: "What possibilities exist for a female (not necessarily feminist) discourse to be articulated within a patriarchal industry through narrative conventions and genres developed by and for a male-dominated culture?"[28] Spacek's "Destructive" and "Transformative Body" films begin to provide an answer: from *Badlands* to *Coal Miner's Daughter*, Spacek's characters' demolition and subsequent transformation of patriarchal authority set the stage for a productive, feminine, and perhaps even feminist power. New Hollywood's sublimation of second wave feminism vis-à-vis the abject bodily representations of young women, particularly Spacek's characters, proves historically substantial, since "film images have been and continue to be the repositories for many, if not most, of our notions of what bodies are supposed to do and look like" within a specific, sociocultural context.[29]

As her star text embodies not just her personification as an icon but also her various personae onscreen and her individuality as "just a person" with a personal body, Spacek will probably never escape the specter of *Carrie* or ever move far enough away from that place on the stage beneath that hovering bucket of blood. But why should she? Spacek's star text has thrived in large part precisely in that space of excess, anomalously drawing connections between the abject feminine and feminist angst and authority.

Spacek's female fans, in particular, seem to relish the peculiarity of her seventies-era star body and the abject, angsty contradictions it engenders—so much so that, according to Spacek, they are now marking their own bodies with her early star image. Concluding her 2012 memoir with this amusing story of embodied fandom, Spacek herself appears to relish the transference of her star body's abject femininity onto the body of one of her young fans:

> Not long ago I was walking through an old historic downtown mall in Virginia when a teenage girl came running up to me, all excited. "Sissy Spacek!" she squealed. "You're Carrie! You're Carrie!" She pulled back her sleeve to reveal a full color tattoo of me as Carrie in her prom dress, holding a bouquet of red roses. It was a beautiful tattoo, all pink and gold—it apparently captured the moment just before the bucket of pig's blood was dropped on my head—and I had to admire it, but I was still shocked that this lovely young girl would do such a thing. "Do your parents know about this?" I asked her. And more important: "Do they blame me?" Early in my career, I thought that making it in the business meant appearing on the Johnny Carson show. These days, a mark of success is having one of your characters tattooed on someone else's body part.[30]

Proof—in the flesh—of Spacek's iconic abject endurance.

NOTES

1. Mark Emerson and Eugene E. Pfaff Jr., *Country Girl: The Life of Sissy Spacek* (New York: St. Martin's Press, 1988), 29.
2. Noel King, "The Last Good Time We Ever Had: Remembering the New Hollywood Cinema," in *The Last Great American Picture Show*, ed. Thomas Elsaesser, Alexander Horwath, and Noel King (Amsterdam: Amsterdam University Press, 2004), 20.

3. Thomas Elsaesser, "American Auteur Cinema: The Last—or First—Picture Show?," in Elsaesser, Horwath, and King, *The Last Great American Picture Show*, 63.
4. Ibid.
5. Peter Krämer, *The New Hollywood: From Bonnie and Clyde to Star Wars* (London: Wallflower Press, 2005), 72.
6. Ibid., 87.
7. Molly Haskell, *From Reverence to Rape: The Treatment of Women in the Movies* (Chicago: University of Chicago Press, 1987), 325.
8. Celine Parreñas-Shimizu, *The Hypersexuality of Race* (Durham, N.C.: Duke University Press, 2007), 39–41.
9. Elsaesser, "American Auteur Cinema," 62.
10. See William Brown, "Jessica Lange and Sissy Spacek: Country Girls," in *Acting for America: Movie Stars of the 1980s*, ed. Robert Eberwein (New Brunswick, N.J.: Rutgers University Press, 2010).
11. Sissy Spacek, *My Extraordinary Ordinary Life* (New York: Hyperion, 2012), 180.
12. Charles Michener and Martin Kasindorf, "Year of the Actress," *Newsweek* (February 14, 1977): 56.
13. Ibid.
14. Ibid.
15. Ibid.
16. Peter Lev, *American Films of the 70s: Conflicting Visions* (Austin: University of Texas Press, 2000), 143.
17. Ibid.
18. Julia Kristeva, *Powers of Horror* (New York: Columbia University Press, 1982), 3.
19. Kate Cregan, *The Sociology of the Body* (London: Sage Publications, 2006), 96.
20. Ibid.
21. Vivian Sobchack, *Carnal Thoughts: Embodiment and Moving Image Culture* (Berkeley: University of California Press, 2004), 67.
22. Kristeva, *Powers of Horror*, 3.
23. Ibid., 5.
24. Spacek, *My Extraordinary Ordinary Life*, 129.
25. Shelley Stamp, "Horror, Femininity, and Carrie's Monstrous Puberty," *Journal of Film and Video* 43, no. 4 (1991): 41.
26. Barbara Jane Brickman, "Coming of Age in the 1970s: Revision, Fantasy, and Rage in the Teen-Girl Badlands," *Camera Obscura* 22, no. 3 (2007): 43.
27. Elayne Rapping, *Media-tions: Forays into the Culture and Gender Wars* (Boston: South End Press, 1994), 138.
28. Robin Wood, *Hollywood from Vietnam to Reagan . . . and Beyond* (New York: Columbia University Press, 2003), 187.
29. Adrienne McLean, "Feeling and the Filmed Body: Judy Garland and the Kinesics of Suffering," *Film Quarterly* 56, no. 3 (2002): 13.
30. Spacek, *My Extraordinary Ordinary Life*, 260.

11

LOVE HURTS, BUT NOT TOO MUCH: JULIA ROBERTS'S SCENES OF SUFFERING

R. Barton Palmer

STAR TURNS

NO CONTEMPORARY STAR HAS BEEN MORE PROMINENT IN REPRESENTING the complex appeals of romance, and the different narrative forms that romance can assume, than Julia Roberts. First achieving prominence in the industry with the surprising mega-hit *Pretty Woman* (Garry Marshall) in 1990, Roberts had become Hollywood's most bankable performer by the end of the decade; her agreement to participate in a project guaranteed pre-production financing. Even after making a number of career miscalculations, some rather serious, during the middle of that decade, Roberts emerged as one of the few actors at the close of the twentieth century whose name above the marquee could "open" a film. The first weekend's box office can generate sufficient attendance momentum in the weeks immediately following to ensure a film's solid financial success.

As a result, her up-front fee rose steadily during the decade until it reached a rumored $25 million (as widely reported for *Mona Lisa Smile* [2003]), a stratospheric compensation level that few, if any, of her fellow actresses at that time could even come close to matching. Only in the last decade have Reese Witherspoon and Cameron Diaz been reported to receive similar up-front compensation. Roberts's films through 2012 (not all offering her a starring role) have earned a staggering box office sum of $2.6 billion, an amazing total exceeded only by that of Cameron Diaz at $2.8 billion. Roberts is thus the second-highest producing female star in world cinema history.[1] Though exceptionally beautiful, Roberts has a disarming "everywoman" quality that endears her to fans, particularly females, who find her "relatable." Like Diaz and Witherspoon, with whom she shares much in common, Roberts is both a skilled comedienne and dramatic performer, with the versatility to take an occasional leading role in a "serious" film (as in *The Pelican Brief* [1993]) or in the comic action genre (as in *The Mexican* (2001), where her portrayal of a relationship-frustrated ditz compares favorably to Diaz's more celebrated performance in *Knight and Day* [2010]). And yet, like all stars, Roberts is certainly sui generis.

What is most unusual is that her growing appeal was in large part due to a turbulent personal life, hyped and reconstructed by the media, which generated enormous sustained interest around the world. She became not only a star but also a celebrity. Julia Roberts, as the industry publicity industry quickly emphasized, was the protagonist of an ongoing romance narrative in real life as well as in her various films roles. The star, as Richard Dyer has observed, possesses two bodies—the one that comes to signify, through complex gestures of impersonation and embodiment, a fabulized character, and the other—existentially coterminous with what has been confected—that signifies herself.[2] We might say that for Julia Roberts these two bodies have meant distinct, yet complexly interconnected narratives—the one, strictly fictional and constantly changing from text to text even while possessing its own general form; the other equally a confection, if based somewhat in the real, that played out on the other side of the screen and took shape in fanzine articles and newspaper accounts.

At the height of her career at the end of the 1990s, Roberts had become a figure whose professional and personal life constituted an irresistible subject for an extradiegetic text whose theme was romance writ large. Like many other female stars, Roberts has a dominant star narrative of courtship and love, despite her professional accomplishments. Following the paths of women like Marilyn Monroe, Grace Kelly, and Elizabeth Taylor, Roberts's struggles represent a perennial trope that reflects larger cultural concerns surrounding successful women devoted to their careers. This pattern in turn represents elements of an earlier Augustinian pattern of a restless search for the proper object of desire. Roberts's offscreen "life" came to constitute a narrative of episodic suffering, as one relationship after another proved to go nowhere. Anticipated conclusions (marriage to a Mr. Right and the establishment of some sort of satisfying domesticity) generated their own twists, turns, reversals, and suspense. James Spada's biography emphasizes the restlessness, inconclusiveness, and suffering of her various romantic connections: "the last-minute cancellation of her marriage to Kiefer Sutherland . . . brooding, intense relationship with Jason Patric . . . brief, shocking marriage to Lyle Lovett . . . and long liaison with Benjamin Bratt."[3] This version of her life constructed for fans emphasizes how Roberts's star persona was in large part defined by her offscreen misadventures in romance: she was portrayed as *amans amare*, in love with love, or so her tumultuous string of attachments suggested. Some have suggested that this press coverage, and its intrusive nosiness (which many, perhaps most, would find obnoxious), has turned Roberts into a near-tragic figure whose psychological health has survived only because of her inner resolve and self-confidence. "Roberts is certainly not the first Hollywood star to find the pressure of fame overwhelming. Comparisons were quickly made with the likes of Marilyn Monroe and Elizabeth Taylor—sometimes with sympathy, and sometimes not," writes one biographer.[4] Unlike the steely Taylor, however, Roberts comes across as Hollywood's ultimate survivor, appearing undamaged and undaunted by attention, favorable or not. Publicity of any kind has only boosted her visibility and professional viability, a calculation she is certainly shrewd enough to have made for herself. Both onscreen and off, she appears to have weathered well a series of emotional storms, but she has neither experienced nor portrayed passion in the traditional sense, nor its unavoidable pain, at least on the surface that appears to her public. The underlying reality is another question entirely.

LOVING TO LOVE

> *Nondum amabam, et amare amabam; quarebam quid amarem, amans amare.*
>
> I was not then experienced in love, and yet I was in love with love; I sought out what I might love, for loving is what I loved.
>
> Augustine of Hippo, *Confessions*

At this point in considering a star supposedly in love with love (at least in the superficial world of the box office), backtracking to older conceptions of love and romance may shed light on our subject. In Augustine's *Confessions*, the young narrator passes through an irresistible disposition toward eros to a self-indulgent carnality, a spiritual and existential drama that occupies much of his autobiography.[5] That self-indulgence leads, perhaps inevitably, to its renunciation, a state of refusal that constitutes the mirror image of the new life his desire to love had led him to seek. As he suggests, in the absence of the object proper to it, love is a painful lack that necessitates a restless searching, and yet possession of what love desires also dissatisfies. A way of life in which the erotic assumes a central, regular role finds its real meaning only in abjuration. The older man, reviewing his youthful follies and confessing them to God and his readers, offers this pattern of desire, satisfaction, and their discontents as an archetype. The *Confessions* is not just a bit of self-narration that, in the Dr. Phil sense, illuminates only the unique self, in the process revealing some hitherto undiscovered solution to unhappiness that is amenable to cognitive reordering. Instead, the narrative of Augustine points toward an inalterable existential condition that can only be endured, not to a maladjustment whose crookedness might be made straight.

We are to see ourselves in the all-defining intensity and pain of Augustine's experience—even if we do not share his commitment to a conversion that installs a becalming celibacy and a different object for our desire in the form of God. We want even before our wanting has found its object. It is the drama of erotic wanting and dissatisfaction—and the consequent discovery of some new form of living/loving—that provides the most pervasive, perhaps the most important theme of Western fiction, and Augustine is its first substantial chronicler. "Happy love has no history," states Denis de Rougemont, modernity's most penetrating analyst of our culture's "myths" of loving; "Romance," he says, "comes into existence when love is . . . doomed by life itself."[6] De Rougemont argues that our culture celebrates not "the happy contentment of the settled couple" or even "the delight of the senses." We seek passion in our representations of the erotic life (if not in the erotic life itself, where satisfaction is a more immediate and physiologically sanctioned goal). As its etymology suggests, passion means "suffering," and suffering, de Rougemont reminds us, is "the fundamental fact," the source of love's energy and the focus of our interest. Even though this is the realm of pain, "everything within and without us glorifies passion."[7] The proper end of love's suffering is death itself, as the "self-consciousness, intensity, variations, and delays of passion" point inexorably toward a "climax rising to disaster."[8] Such an ending, with its glorification of transfiguration within the order of passion, represents the "renunciation of terrestrial goods."[9] We celebrate with poignant pleasure the stories of Romeo and Juliet or Tristan and Iseult, the latter a chronicle of mutually unwilled passion, the "longing for what sears us and annihilates us in its triumph."[10]

In contrast, this "secret preference for the unhappy," this "transfiguring torment," is not what the traditions of popular culture create through their forging of a connection between love and matrimony.[11] Popular traditions have been decisively shaped toward the furnishing of a kind of collective release of potentially antisocial energies, in order that "the subversive desires of the individual mind shall be volatilized as sensual reverie." At the same time, this fictional tradition can be tolerated by society because it does not challenge the practical fact that marriage rests upon "financial foundations, prospects of inheritance . . . and so on."[12] The happy ending, with its required constitution of the couple, is thus nothing less than "the complete fusion of contradictory wishes: the wish that nothing shall be settled and the wish that everything shall be settled, the one romantic, the other middle class." And so the "tragic idealism" of pure erotic abandonment is turned into "a rather vulgar nostalgia, the idealization of tame desires" that leads toward a new life that is the fulfillment of the old, not its transfiguration.[13]

De Rougemont's characterization of the treatment of romance in modern popular culture is both revealing of the tension that romance displays between the volatilization of inner desire and the mild misery of its domestication that we call "contentment." However, it is far too simplistic to see this contentment, this finalizing of disruptive energies, as exclusively defined by the bourgeois notion of marriage as a social contract. This so-called contentment reduces to mere pathetic wistfulness the emotional and intellectual force of such representations, which are flexible enough to accommodate surprisingly different energies (such as the desire for authenticating selfhood beyond socially prescribed roles), even as they drive toward different ends (such as a satisfying balance between public and private demands on commitment and presence).

The essential thrust of romantic fiction designed to please a mass public, including the popular film, is more utopian than conformist or manipulative. It is therefore worthwhile to attempt symptomatic readings that identify the narrative's underlying social themes and thus transform the apparently simple romance into something strangely equivalent to a high cultural text. "Both modernism and mass culture," Fredric Jameson writes, "entertain relations of repression with the fundamental social anxieties and concerns, hopes and blind spots, ideological antinomies and fantasies of disaster, which are their raw material." The difference is that "mass culture represses them by the narrative construction of imaginary resolutions and by the optical illusion of social harmony," a process that in the case of romance promises and also delivers, if only fleetingly, a vision of the redemptive power of eros, the ability of love to make us over or make us new.[14] More generally, it is in the confection of impossibly perfect social visions that the Hollywood star can assume an especially prominent role.[15]

The utopian strain is strong in Roberts's breakthrough performance as a sympathetic young prostitute in *Pretty Woman*, a role that was straightforward wish fulfillment, a transgressing of class and moral barriers whose themes emerged from

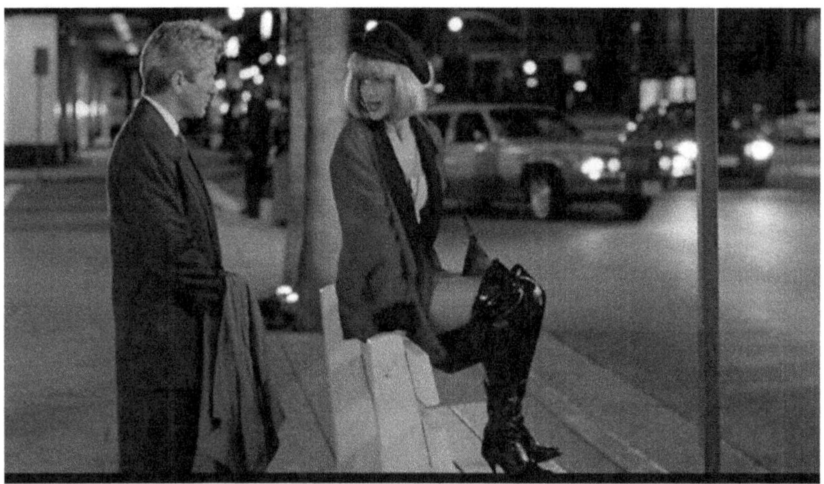

The pretty woman for rent: the body as commodity. Richard Gere and Julia Roberts in *Pretty Woman* (1990).

the Fabian Socialism of George Bernard Shaw's *Pygmalion*, its ideological basis the belief that all people are essentially the same, only superficially differentiated by the accidents of life. Though obviously lower class in manner, as incarnated by Roberts, Vivian Ward seems uncertain, almost shy rather than sleazy, vulnerable rather than mercenary. She possesses a modicum of self-worth and presence, and her appeal is not marred (beyond the not too offensive tattiness of her "work clothes") by any obvious bad habits. She appears not to use drugs, goes light on profanity, and avoids offensive aggression when talking business. Furthermore, no manager mister appears on the scene when Vivian is selected by the desire of an unusual "john," Edward Lewis (Richard Gere), who soon transforms himself (or, perhaps, is transformed by her) into a marital prospect driven to spend thousands at Rodeo Drive boutiques in order to provide her with a new image. Here is an enactment of transcendence (not more than one short step up from the ugly, debasing cheeriness of *The Price is Right*) that only a consumer culture, beguiled by the appealing shininess of the mass-produced, name-brand bling it inordinately values, could imagine as surpassing the thing-deprived penury in which Edward "discovered" her. Through this minimalization of the inevitable discontents of the sex trade, Roberts's pretty woman becomes the ideal wish fulfillment figure for female viewers less interested in building a respectable career and more taken with the romantic fantasy of being swept away by a rich (and, of course, also handsome) man, whose sole pleasure in life—beyond a bit of discreet and decidedly unkinky sex—seems to be providing the customary pleasures of upper-middle-class life.

The more interest Edward shows, the less professional their relationship becomes, until she finally signals a different kind of bargain by kissing him on the mouth, a demonstration that she no longer considers him a john. It is significant that the film's most important secondary character, the manager of the hotel where she is staying, takes on the role of instructing this Eliza Doolittle in what are for her the unfamiliar refinements of life at the top, teaching her about such matters as the proper use of silverware. Roberts's role demanded little more than being charming, beautiful, and appealingly vulnerable, as the only significant character arc in the film really belongs to Gere's Pygmalion figure, who becomes obsessed with effecting what viewers are expected to agree is a quite remarkable transformation, as an abasing past is wiped away by the possession of the latest status-conferring habiliments and accessories from Donna Karan and Oscar de la Renta.

Shorn of the patronizing class-leveling intentions of the protagonist in the original property (a man like Shaw, eager to show how much we are all the same), the narrative completely lacks plausibility, of course. The film's optical illusion of social harmony (Jameson's term seems especially appropriate in this instance) depends on a thoroughgoing suspension of disbelief. The social experimenting of Shaw's play is replaced by the chance eruption of an unfathomable desire on Edward's part (he is led to "her" part of Los Angeles by mistake and is seized with lust as he witnesses her plying her trade, surely a most strange instance of that once-resonant medieval cliché, love at first sight). Why, we might ask, would any good-looking rich man, despite an unfortunate marital past, have any interest in engaging a prostitute, and not a very high-class one at that, to satisfy desires that are absolutely conventional and might easily be catered to by companions not practicing the oldest profession, and who might also enjoy a Rodeo Drive shopping spree? In any case, Roberts functions admirably as the grateful yet feisty object of Edward's fascination and, later, recipient of his unexpected generosity, as she is lifted up and away from a life of poverty and degradation to a future of shopping in Beverly Hills' swankiest boutiques and dining in its toniest eateries (now that she has been taught by a helpful hotel manager what fork to use for the fish). An upscale home in the Valley surely looms as her ultimate reward. For what? For being "pretty," of course.

The suffering that Vivian endures is only mild and temporary—a series of adjustments made subject to a process over which she has surrendered control—as she exchanges one form of living and horizon of expectations for another. A man tells her what she must be, and she is spunky enough to resist that remaking, if only ineffectually. Is this a film about love? Of a sort, I suppose. What it is not is a film about passion. *Pretty Woman* offers a narrative, in fact, that fits

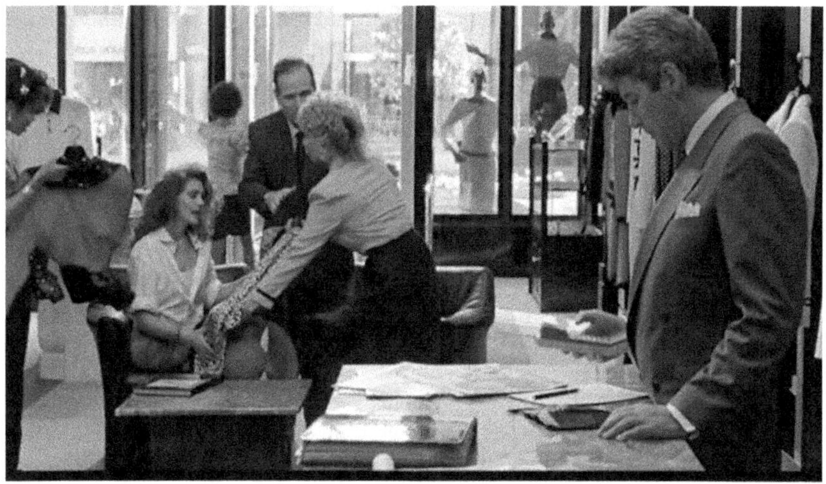

The pretty woman as consumer: the body as object to be adorned.

de Rougemont's notion of "vulgar nostalgia," providing, as it does, the deceptive appearance of social harmony—literally the disappearance of social class as an ineradicable marker of individual identity, which is achieved by its reduction to "manners" and "appearance" (a satiric point in Shaw, played for laughs, but here taken quite seriously indeed). As opposed to those social connections arising from birth, education, and residence, in *Pretty Woman* chance determines a romantic relationship. The sexual connection between Vivian and Edward seems more than a little awkward. More dangerously, perhaps, it is irrelevant, as desire is displaced onto a very conspicuous and deliberately spectacularized consumption. *Amans res*, Augustine might say, a cupidity for the material, not the potential disruptiveness of the love of desire itself, which is the desire, of course, to reach beyond the self.

Pretty Woman offers a transparent allegory for the star-becoming trajectory of Roberts's career in which the film played a central role. The young actress from Georgia becomes an internationally famous celebrity, an appropriate object of desire for an established star like Gere, who, interestingly enough, "discovers" her in Los Angeles in what can be read as the restaging of a time-honored Hollywood cliché. Some years later, a production designed to capitalize on the success of *Pretty Woman* in which Gere and Roberts were again paired as unlikely lovers offered a quite different way in which Roberts's two bodies might be represented. This film is more penetratingly evocative of Roberts's own star narrative, which by this time had become something of a worldwide cultural preoccupation. *Runaway Bride* (1999) imagines Roberts as Maggie Carpenter, a small-town girl led to the altar by a series of locals, yet each time refusing to go through with the marriage ceremony; only outsider Gere, as Ike Graham, a journalist interested in this woman's growing notoriety, can rescue her by demanding that she choose him as her love object. Disposing of the freedom that she now realizes she possesses, she consents to the subsuming of self in erotic passion for the other, and to the finality of the social form in which it must be expressed. The film's viewers could hardly forget that the real-life Roberts had abandoned fiancé Kiefer Sutherland just days before their planned wedding. Her subsequent marriage to Lyle Lovett lasted less than two years, and other prominently publicized relationships seemed to go nowhere. In *Runaway Bride*, the erotic is once again displaced from focus, as the film's narrative from the beginning configures Maggie as a "woman question," an oddball female who, with a furious, almost masculine energy, serially flees the commitment of marriage. Victimized by Maggie's inability to go through with their wedding ceremony, Graham eventually diagnoses her problem—that she has never taken possession of herself, never properly assessed what it is that she wants.

In a strangely conservative and somewhat misogynistic transformation, the desiring self of romance seeking its proper object, the *amans amare* of Augustine's formulation, is displaced in favor of an immature young woman whose life lacks proper direction (working as a store clerk and living in a small town, her prospects, as least as far as screen fantasy is concerned, seem slim). For her, going through with a marriage becomes the acid test of becoming her own person, as she follows unquestioningly the advice of Graham, who becomes something of a Pygmalion figure after initially taking only a journalist's interest in the oddness of Maggie as a serial refusenik. She must choose whom to love, he sternly advises her, meaning himself, of course, establishing himself as an all-disposing patriarchal figure. This fish, so he convinces her, does need a bicycle, rejecting the feminist injunction toward self-definition and the irrelevance of attachment to some man that her serial escapes seem so clearly to express. The notion that every young woman should be married, of course, is central as well to the extratextual narrative in which Roberts was at that time starring. The film's finale is a wedding, exactly the kind of "ending" to the restless romantic life of Julia Roberts the actress for which her fans at the time, and Roberts herself, were hoping, if her frequent statements to that effect are to be believed.

Not long after finishing *Runaway Bride*, Roberts agreed to participate in what was essentially a comparatively low-budget British project, at what was to be only a fraction of her usual asking price. The career-boosting appeal of the film was that it would offer an attractive version of the "Julia Roberts" story;

in this case the actor would not play some small-town girl unable to choose a mate, but a movie star and model whose serially unhappy experience with love has become the master narrative of her life. *Notting Hill* would be produced by Duncan Kenworthy (who had achieved considerable success with the ensemble dramedy *Four Weddings and a Funeral* [1994]) and directed by Roger Michell, whose sleek BBC television production of Jane Austen's *Persuasion* (1995) had met with similar critical and popular approval. Her interest in the proposed film, and her willingness to take a substantial pay cut, was surprising for other reasons. Though Roberts would be the film's star, she would by no means be the main character, a role that would fall to British actor Hugh Grant, who would reprise his role as a charmingly bumbling romantic lead, a characterization he had played to perfection in *Four Weddings* and a number of other mildly successful releases such as *Nine Months* (1995). Roberts would play the same role played by Andie McDowell in *Four Weddings* as a somewhat distant and infrequently glimpsed object of erotic longing. The film, in other words, would offer Roberts very little in the way of big scenes, and the script by Richard Curtis (who had also written *Four Weddings*), which she read with great approval, placed a good deal of emphasis on intriguingly grotesque or comic secondary characters, a significant feature also obviously recycled from *Four Weddings*. *Notting Hill* would by no means provide her with the screen prominence she had enjoyed in her recent box office successes such as *The Pelican Brief*, but it would focus on her character as a romantic problem in the same way that *Runaway Bride* had. If *Four Weddings* was essentially Grant's film, *Notting Hill* would be as well, but with a difference. *Notting Hill*, unlike its obvious model, offers an appealing and attractive version, replete with wish-fulfillment conclusion, of the offscreen/onscreen life of its glittering star presence, including the suffering, romantic and otherwise, that such a life had brought her.

Roberts had been reluctant at first to sign up for a project in which she was to play a famous, eminently bankable American actress named Anna Scott, who was exactly like Julia Roberts but, at least according to Roberts herself, entirely different. In fact, she seems to have hated the way in which the film, while ostensibly biographical, distorted the star persona she had carefully created ("Anna is still unsure of her own worth, whether as an actress or as a person. What is written about her concerns her a lot more than it would concern me," she observed to a reporter from *Vanity Fair*).[16] Roberts had perhaps forgotten her own desperate exasperation at the intense press coverage of her romantic life, especially the last-minute cancellation of her much-ballyhooed engagement to Kiefer Sutherland and then her startling marriage to singer Lyle Lovett, and subsequent unsurprising divorce less than two years later. In any event, reading carefully through Curtis's script, Roberts quickly realized that the project showed great potential, and she was correct ("Fuck, I'm going to do this movie!" she enthused when signing on).[17]

It is tempting to believe that Roberts eventually saw that the film's engagement with her filmmaking career and personal life would appeal to her fans and serve her career well, providing something of a capstone image of her mercurial success and well-publicized romantic difficulties. Though her fans certainly saw (and were meant to see) *Notting Hill* as intriguingly biographical, Roberts is of course correct that the film at first presents Anna Scott as lacking in self-confidence and vaguely dissatisfied with a life of stardom and the poisoned relationships it seems to engender. Because Anna is shown to be somewhat unwillingly entangled with a (tellingly) nameless lover played by an uncredited Alec Baldwin, whose turbulent romantic life offscreen was also well known at the time to one and all, viewers were strongly encouraged to endorse Anna's view that stardom, at least in terms of the romantic possibilities it offered with glamorous, narcissistic, and unreliable men, is not all that it is cracked up to be.

But if Anna starts out as a somewhat neurotic, even reticent version of a Julia Roberts famed for her brassy self-assertiveness, by film's end she has become an ideal version of the star, one who can be transported by eros back to an ordinariness and domesticity that would provide stability and privacy. She is now loved by and loves in return a relentlessly ordinary guy, William Thacker (Grant), and can fully possess herself at the same time. The fact that this ordinary guy looks like an internationally famous star such as Hugh Grant and can dispose of unlimited, self-deprecating charm is of course an essential element of the fantasy. As displaced star biography, *Notting Hill* is not only a romantic comedy but also a woman's picture, on both its fictional and metafictional levels. The film traces a pattern of maturing self-awareness that is connected not only to romantic fulfillment, but also, and perhaps more importantly, to the full acceptance of the responsibilities and discontents of cinematic stardom; the transforming power of love provides not a self-destructive rejection of "what we are," but rather a deliverance to another and double form of being, as Anna becomes "just a girl" but also remains Anna Scott. Her life with Thacker provides a sense of privacy and authenticity she has previously lacked.

Like Julia Roberts, Anna is not forced to choose between a husband (a metonymy for happy domesticity) and a satisfying career. Quite the contrary. *Notting Hill* makes it clear that the relationship with a man who comes without the baggage of his own career completes rather than replaces Anna's professional life,

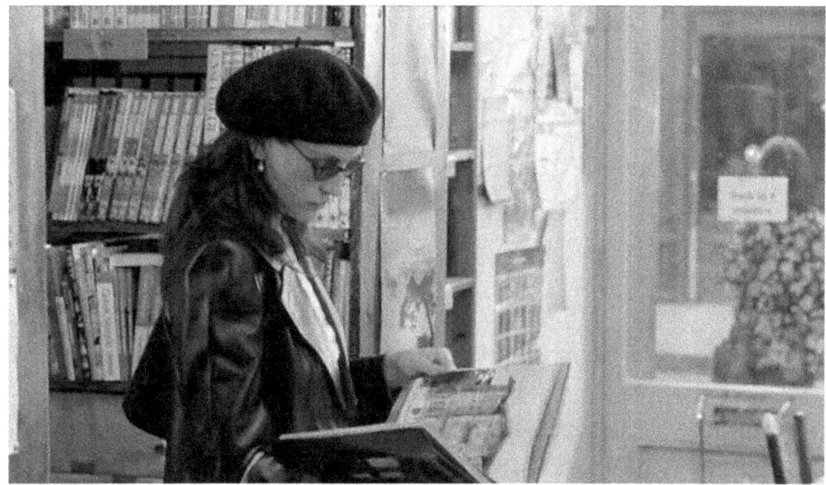

The star in disguise and despectacularized: "just a girl." Roberts in *Notting Hill* (1999).

promoting the notion of a woman liberated and empowered rather than entrapped by romance. Her drive for success is at least as important as what personal happiness her glamour and charm might win for her. It is no accident that the film repeats the narrative pattern of the nineteenth-century Bildungsroman, as Scott follows what, culturally speaking, had been an exclusively masculine trajectory toward maturity, with Thacker imagined as her peace-of-mind-conferring secondary attachment. As in *Runaway Bride*, the erotic nature of romance is reconfigured, as passion is directed more toward companionship, with William's ordinary way of life the greatest appeal he has to offer Anna, beset as she is by celebrity and suffering from the lack of privacy she craves. The narrative has a distinctive Jane Austen feel, as compatibility of character and sensibility emerges early as more important than erotic passion for a desirable other. From their first meeting, it seems clear that Anna is more interested in what William is (that is, a non-celebrity), as well as, more selfishly, what he might do for her, than William himself.

The intriguing doubleness of a woman fully in control of her acting career yet unable to sustain a satisfying romantic relationship had been an important element of the particular star fantasy that Roberts came to embody in the course of the 1990s. Mr. Right always seemed to be lurking just around the next corner in her life; there was never a lack of contenders, as one relationship ended only just before (or, sometimes, after) another began. Julia Roberts seemed destined to have her cake and eat it, too—the only question was when this would happen. Like Anna Scott, she confessed even early in her career to a desire for a fulfilling family life in addition to success as a performer. Speaking to an interviewer from *Rolling Stone* in 1990, Roberts said, "Movies will come and go, but family is a real kind of rich consistency . . . when you have family, friends, and there's love in your life, and you give in to that, you can see instant gratification."[18] Feature pieces on Roberts published throughout the decade routinely praise Roberts's onscreen successes while pointing out that she has yet to settle into a relationship that would provide her with a long-wished-for domestic happiness.

If Anna, according to the actress who came to embody her, initially lacks the self-confidence and immunity from criticism that Julia possessed aplenty, the film's narrative seemed carefully calculated to reproduce the substantially hyped version of Roberts's life that the media had been promoting since the release of *Pretty Woman*. As James Spada has observed with just a bit of hyperbole, "It is her personal life and the press and public's almost inordinate fascination with it that has elevated Julia Roberts from movie star to one of the cultural phenomena of the last twenty-five years. . . . Her love life . . . provides enough juice for a Jackie Collins miniseries."[19] In fictionalizing that life, *Notting Hill* skips over much of the "juice" Collins would have taken delight in (for example, her version of the abusive, egocentric, but devastatingly attractive lover played by Alec Baldwin, a compelling bad boy, would never have been reduced to a walk-on). The film instead concentrates its wish-fulfilling rhetoric on the kind of sentimental final act (straight out of the Austenian fantasies of mutual accommodation that screenwriter Curtis so admires) for which Roberts's millions of fans had been hoping against hope, as one romantic connection after another soured or fizzled.

The most important structural element of the film's versioning of the Roberts narrative may be that the star is not personalized even as she becomes the focus of the plot. In the transpersonal psychological drama that provides the solution to her unhappiness, Anna, like Julia herself, is seen from the outside, that is, from precisely the perspective from which fans and filmgoers view her performances and her life. The viewer is implicitly asked to believe that Anna's real life (that is, the life that matters, especially to us) is not inner, a matter of consciousness. This form of being belongs only to William, the film's ordinary protagonist, who can be imagined as a voice narrating his own story, unlike Anna, who must remain an objectified image, a self that is glimpsed rather than known. Anna does not lead the narrative but, rather, provides it with forward motion, with both its motive and goal. And yet she is the star around whom the film is built; Grant's character, attractive and appealing as he might be, is the stand-in for the viewer and fan, not really a protagonist in the classic sense. Anna is literally the stranger known to one and all who wanders accidentally into his life and in so doing transforms it, lifting this male Cinderella out of the dull sameness of his everyday life. Unlike the traditional romance, here the woman rather than the man constitutes the problem that must be solved in order for their mutual attraction to find social acceptability in marriage.

In this way, the film models the interest of viewers in the persona of a star like Julia Roberts, who is the passive agent of both seduction and wooing, the one who confers value on William simply by appearing in his shop and noticing him. At the same time, it is his interest in her as star and not just as an attractive woman that motors their relationship, establishing that her appeal is ontologically different from and superior to his own evident charm as a not-too successful, not-too-male admirer. Anna suddenly embraces William at first meeting. Is this an erotic whim, a sudden urge for connection with a seemingly sympathetic and unthreatening man, or an unplanned signaling of availability? It is impossible to say. But what is crystal clear is that this approach is a gesture that cannot be refused. Part of the star's essence is, in fact, her unrefusability. Her charisma and sex appeal, collectively established as beyond the unpredictability or whimsy of individual taste, have bestowed upon her the right to desire as she wills. As Curtis recognized, the film did not have to explain why he agrees to become her love object; consent in *Pretty Woman* clearly reflects the different places in the economic order occupied by Vivian Ward and her surprisingly generous john, but in *Notting Hill* consent seems a given, a shared recognition of Anna Scott's peculiar social standing and the power it confers upon her desire to have her erotic way. The stupefied William Thacker, who never presumes to query her motives for pursuing him, and does not seem to have much of a life in any case, is shown to understand perfectly that he is a commoner at the disposal of this so-familiar yet erstwhile stranger, eager to kiss him in his own hallway.

What matters is that through the connection she makes with him and his reciprocation, Anna escapes in the end from the uncertainty and ennui that plague her. This dissatisfaction, as it emerges, has been deep enough to provoke her to seek out real life (or at least the commercial cinema's version of it), which she does by visiting in easily seen-through disguise a small and persistently unprofitable niche bookstore in the charmingly funky London neighborhood evoked in the film's title, there encountering William. The shocked young owner, just recovering from being rejected by the woman he loves, is immediately smitten by the charms of a visitor from the seemingly unreachable world of global celebrity, and he is then led to think that she finds him attractive, when without a word and seemingly out of the blue she kisses him passionately. He is too surprised or too reticent, in the presence of secular royalty, to return the embrace, as his hands refuse seemingly of their own volition to grasp her body.

Persuaded to take her out on a date, William later introduces her to the lovable grotesques and relentlessly everyday folk who constitute his circle of friends and family. Anna, who has become accustomed to being the object of non-stop, probing attention, seems satisfied to be treated like just another guest at an informal dinner party, though she is of course widely known to the average person on the street to be a celebrity. Her being treated as "just one of the gang" emerges as a deception, of course. Ordinariness is not a realm of being that the star, once having transcended it, can ever reenter. After William escorts her out the door, the pair hear the other guests break out into howls of surprise and joy, hitherto repressed, at the exalted presence that happy accident has brought into their midst. That she can be just like everyone else is shown to be merely an effect of English reticence and politeness. The true meaning of her appearance among ordinary folks is signaled earlier in the sequence when William's wacky sister arrives at the party, spots Anna by her side, and explodes with a very loud "Holy fuck!" before lapsing into wordless awe. Anna Scott can only be Anna Scott. Likewise, Julia Roberts can never be a nobody. Having worked hard to become a star, why in any case would she then embrace some ordinary form of ordinariness that denies her much-admired particularity? She can only pretend to be just anybody since everybody knows she *is* somebody.

Anna's real life (that is, the life she has that matters) is contained in the objectified glamor of her image; it is not inner, not a matter of consciousness. Many shots in the film capture others capturing that image, especially in montage sequences meant to be read as characteristic of the life she leads, which seems centered on posing for photographers. These glamor shots explain the interest that inhabitants of the story world have in Anna Scott, but, metafictionally, they also remind viewers of *Notting Hill* why they bought tickets to see the film. This is an aspect of *Notting Hill* that has no equivalent in *Four Weddings*, a contrast explained in part by the substantial difference between Andie McDowell, a well-known supermodel, and Julia Roberts, whose position in the culture as a superstar was quite different. An interior view of the character would dispel the mystique that is the star's stock in trade. An inner being, the revelation of which confers familiarity, even intimacy, can belong only to William, even though he is mostly reduced to reacting to Anna's unexpected appearance and expressions of interest in him.

In order for William to be transformed into a simulacrum of the traditional male romantic protagonist, whose defining quality is an irresistible impulse to act on passion, *Notting Hill* must in fact generate a double ending. The relationship between screen queen and commoner is actually finalized when Anna, who had seemed distant and uninterested (precisely how the unexceptional William thinks she should feel, since he is a nobody), tells him that she wants them to spend more time together. William, suffering from hurt feelings and fear of further emotional injury, is allowed an initial refusal—a gesture of resistance that is the conventional response of a wooed woman, who, fearing being condemned as "fast," is unwilling to surrender too quickly to availability. Later, William, counseled by his friends about the absurdity of refusing an Anna Scott, recants that refusal, rushing to convince Anna of his sincerity in the midst of a press conference that positions him not as himself but as yet another petitioner, however faux, from the insatiable media. But William has hardly "won" her. Anna's acceptance of his recantation simply repeats in a more conventional form her earlier request that they continue their relationship. She is transformed in this scene from a petitioner (she had previously visited him in his store to reconnect with him) to a dominating injured party, quite visibly displaying the power she wields as a celebrity, as the center of a press conference. Their most private moment, so the irony here runs, is thoroughly public, generating as it does the news flash that Anna Scott refuses to return at this time to the United States, not that she has in effect agreed to marry the apparent nobody who has persuaded her to do so.

The entertainment press had been emphasizing for years in its continuing narrative of her love life that Julia Roberts had a problem; she could never manage to sustain a relationship with any of the high-powered and glamorous men (all of them in the entertainment business) to whom she became connected. If that problem had not yet been solved in real life, *Notting Hill* could do the trick onscreen, offering a wish fulfillment that was absolutely conventional. Girl and boy get each other in the end, triumphing over the obstacles of personality and character they themselves have in their insecurity erected to block their coupling, making the film in some sense simply an updating of *Pride and Prejudice.* Made miserable rather than happy by a succession of Alec Baldwins (his role in the film is an intriguing metonymy), Julia—I mean Anna—finds contentment this time with a man whose reticence and uncertainty mirror her own, but who is pointedly not being carried along by the ever-moving machine of a high-powered career.

Through her relationship to William, which properly begins with the kiss she bestows upon him (transforming him metaphorically from a frog to a prince?), Anna discovers an answer to the paradox of celebrity, which is the cause of the not insignificant suffering endured by Anna and, of course, by the actress who incarnates her. Celebrity, like such similar states as aristocratic birth, seems to offer freedom in conferring unanticipated power to shape relationships, a power that is only partially charged by the wealth that celebrity customarily brings. But this liberation from the restraints of ordinary living threatens a different form of entrapment. As Leo Braudy points out, "Fame promises a freedom from worry about the opinions of others, only to trap the aspirer inside an even larger audience. . . . Lurking behind every chance to be made whole by fame is the axman of further dismemberment."[20]

The film, lighthearted fantasy that it is, offers a penetrating example of such dismemberment, for which—we might add—a relationship with Thacker does not seem to promise a permanent cure. Scott flees to the seeming protection that Thacker's absolute anonymity provides (he is literally unfamous) when she discovers that some nude photographs she had consented to pose for when poor and unknown have been unearthed and may be circulated. The photos did not matter when Scott was literally a nobody—her body would then be read as any body, as an anonymous source of arousal or interest simply because it was female and attractive. They would be known but not known as hers; they would possess no powers of revelation (of body or of character) and thus could circulate without doing harm to the woman they represent. But now that same body, embodied in images whose form is only slightly different and more morally compromised from that in which her glamour is currently promoted, belongs to a somebody, a somebody in whom there is the most intense interest, both the cause and result of her success. The photos now mean everything because they testify to a hitherto unknown history, promising a further revelation of the star whose knownness is never satisfyingly complete; their release is but an extreme and harmful form of what celebrity essentially promises, the renown that, as Leo Braudy suggests, arouses frenzy. As such, the photos portend an embarrassment of global proportions that will never dissipate, at least as long as the public has an interest in Anna Scott.

Seeking anonymity in William's flat as she tries to recover from the shock of the sudden surfacing of the photos, Anna ironically makes her situation only worse by provoking yet another media sensation as reporters, fed the information that she is hiding in Notting Hill, cluster around Thacker's door, which he opens in a state hardly suitable for company. A crisis in their relationship follows as Scott, who had happily shared the young man's bed the night before, accuses him of selling her out to the press in order to acquire his own little bit of fame, a stolen portion of reflected celebrity, which would make him also "known" to the world. If in modernity, as Braudy points out, "fame promises a liberation from powerless anonymity," *Notting Hill* underlines the substantial discontents of that state of eminent, unbounded recognizability.[21] *Notting Hill* tellingly dramatizes how the star, to quote Braudy once again, must suffer from the fact that "we applaud our heroes, and we condemn them,"[22] but this is a harsh truth from which this otherwise conventional story quickly retreats, interestingly illustrating yet another function of a star like Julia Roberts: providing viewers with a wish fulfillment whose very implausibility is the most powerful element of its affective rhetoric, its most interesting evocation of the suffering celebrity body as a source of pleasure.

Through her connection with William, Anna emerges at film's end to become a less fictionalized version of Julia Roberts. The key to professional happiness, so the film suggests, is a satisfying personal life, which essentially means a life lived in appropriate privacy and in the familiar and valued form of the family. In such a space that she can occupy as an anybody, Anna learns how to be, and enjoy, "herself," and, although her relationship with William goes through the required twists and turns, also how to be loved and love in return. She becomes, in her own phrase, "just a girl, standing in front of a boy, asking him to love her." But, of course, Anna Scott, however much in one sense she wishes to be understood as "just a girl," remains a star whose most important quality is shown to be a glamorous charisma (Anna is constantly flashing the noted multi-million dollar Julia Roberts smile). The film does not disavow the attractions of a life of stardom; it only suggests that there is more to life than this kind of rare accomplishment and the resulting knownness. William does not demand that she give up her career but, on the contrary, seems eager and willing to participate in it. His sacrifice (if it is one) is to surrender an unfulfilling life of small-business ownership and, as the Cinderella, be transported suddenly, through a succession of happy accidents, from daily drudgery and genteel squalor to glamour and riches. The only man with whom Anna can be happy must not be pursuing a career that competes with hers; in fact, he must be available to escort her so that she can better promote herself. At the same time, what he has to offer is not only his compliance, but also a connection back to the ordinariness she has worked so hard to abandon but then suffered so much to reacquire.

The film's final scene, in fact, emphasizes how romantic fulfillment of the conventional kind (marriage, children, a life centered in some sense around loved ones) can be reconciled with endless, inevitably narcissistic performance and self-promotion. With poise and aplomb, Anna publicly accepts William's charmingly bumbling apology for rejecting her earlier offer to explore the possibility of a permanent connection. She agrees to cancel plans to return from the London where he lives to the Hollywood where another project awaits, proclaiming instead for all to hear that she will stay in the UK so that their courting can proceed. This bargain is sealed in the unlikely venue of a press conference as the two lovers become the targets of the assembled paparazzi. Their subsequent life together is revealed in the "characteristic" scenes of a post-finale sequence. Here director Roger Michell emphasizes both how Thacker makes an appropriately presentable partner for Scott at a gala premiere and also how the couple, now a part of his circle of friendship and love, make a place for themselves apart from the world of show business, whose intense pressures can tear a relationship apart, at least as conventional wisdom has it.

The cliché claims that life often imitates art, or, more precisely, imitates the way in which art imitates life. This was true for Roberts shortly after the 1990s ended, with a long-expected change in her personal life recalling the fairytale narrative of *Notting Hill.* A result of Roger Michell's influence, perhaps, the film's dramatization of a successful romance emphasizes the force of the inevitable discontents of the human condition, as these are magnified by Anna's stardom, which exposes the couple to the harsh glare of publicity and the promise that missteps, once part of the record, can never be truly expunged. Love triumphs, however, because mistrust, misunderstanding, and an unhealthy sense of vulnerability can be overcome by empathy, reason, humility, and the good offices of friends, a message about the path to human happiness that Jane Austen would likely endorse. And—how could it be otherwise?—a surprise soon emerged in the real world. Soon after the film's wildly successful release, and certainly against the odds, the celluloid match with Thacker found its biographical reflex in the romance that turned into a marriage between Roberts and cameraman Daniel Moder, a very good-looking and slightly younger man whom she had met on the set. According to Moder's outraged wife at the time, who at first refused to grant him a divorce, Roberts seduced her husband with sex and promises of future employment, aggressively pursuing him until he agreed to turn their affair into a long-term commitment. James Spada some years ago observed that "by numerous accounts, both Julia and Danny are insecure in their relationship's staying power—Danny because of Julia's history with men, and Julia because of Danny's proven appeal to the opposite sex."[23]

Love hurts, but apparently not too much when it has found its proper object, much as *Notting Hill* predicts. This film summarizes, even as it resolves, the discontents of her career, easily remedied by a partial return to ordinariness, the comforting lie that Anna can be "just a girl." But *Notting Hill* is not about passionate attachment; William is valued for what he means, what he can do, and not for who he is. Not one of Roberts's films is about passion in the Augustinian sense, with its drive toward transcendence, its characters dominated by the love of loving. Passion usually figures as a problem, not the essential state of desiring. In *Sleeping with the Enemy* (1991), for example, Roberts figures as the object of an obsessive love that is more pathology than passion, but she does not seem to have experienced such destructive attachment herself; the narrative's conclusion is satisfied with delivering her to safety, not fulfillment. If Method actors mine suffering, Roberts manages it, both onscreen and in real life. As she ages, the toughness she displayed as the eponymous lead in *Erin Brockovich* (2002) emerges as caricature and camp in her role as the evil queen who torments Snow White in Tarsem Singh's *Mirror Mirror* (2012). She seethes, storms, and shrieks as a bitter wife abandoned by her husband for a younger woman, and ridiculed by her heartless mother (played by Meryl Streep), in John Wells's film adaptation of Tracy Letts's melodramatic *August: Osage County* (2013). In *Closer* (2004), Roberts finds herself trapped in a Bergmanesque love quadrangle in which the polymorphousness of desire, as well as the demonstrated stupidity of firm commitment, fuels a depressing drama of misunderstanding, betrayal, and self-destruction. In this and other recent films, love appears as pathology or, more precisely, as the pathology *du jour* of restless young adults, adrift in a world where everything goes and nothing seems to work, including the romantic connections they seek and flee. In a world where passion cannot locate its object, is it any wonder that what de Rougement would term the "vulgar" accommodations of *Pretty Woman* and *Notting Hill* exert such an appeal, and that an actress such as Julia Roberts became so successful in dramatizing them?

NOTES

My thanks to Rebecca Bell-Metereau and Colleen Glenn for their comments and suggestions on this essay.

1. See boxofficemojo.com for the constantly updated figures on star earnings.
2. See Richard Dyer, *Heavenly Bodies: Film Stars and Society,* 2nd ed. (New York: Routledge, 2004).
3. From the back cover of James Spada, *Julia Roberts: Her Life* (New York: St. Martin's Press, 2004).
4. "Julia Roberts," in *International Dictionary of Films and Filmmakers,* 4th ed., galenet.galesgroup.com/servlet/BioRC, accessed June 2, 2010.
5. The passage quoted in the epigraph is *Confessiones* 3/1/1, from the edition of James J. O'Connell, *Augustine: Confessions* (Oxford: Oxford University Press, 1992).
6. Denis de Rougemont, *Love in the Western World* [L'Amour et L'Occident], trans. Montgomery Belgion (1940; New York: Harper, 1956), 15.
7. Ibid., 16.
8. Ibid., 52.
9. Ibid., 235.

10. Ibid., 30.
11. Ibid., 31.
12. Ibid., 234.
13. Ibid., 235.
14. Fredric Jameson, "Reification and Utopia in Mass Culture," in *Signatures of the Visible* (New York: Routledge, 1992), 25–26.
15. Some of this material appeared initially in a quite different form in my essay "Julia Roberts: Cultural Phenomenon," in *Pretty People: Movie Stars of the 1990s*, ed. Anna Everett (New Brunswick, N.J.: Rutgers University Press, 2012), 85–102.
16. Quoted in Frank Sanello, *Julia Roberts* (Edinburgh: Mainstream Publishing, 2000), 197.
17. Quoted in ibid., 195.
18. Quoted in *Newsmakers: 1991* (Detroit: Gale, 1991)
19. Spada, *Julia Roberts*, 8.
20. Leo Braudy, *The Frenzy of Renown: Fame and Its History* (Oxford: Oxford University Press, 1986), 8.
21. Ibid., 7.
22. Ibid., 8.
23. Spada, *Julia Roberts*, 419.

13

RE/INVENTING HALLE BERRY: MIXED-RACE STARDOM AND THE MELODRAMA OF FEMALE VICTIMHOOD

Charles Burnetts

> First of all I want to thank Warner Bros., for putting me in a piece of shit, godawful movie. You know, it was just what my career needed, you know? I was at the top and then *Catwoman* just plummeted me to the bottom. Love it. It's hard being at the top, much easier being at the bottom.
>
> Halle Berry, "Halle Berry Accepts Razzie Award for Worst Actress!"

THE RAZZIES (OR GOLDEN RASPBERRY AWARDS) ARE HELD EVERY YEAR IN Los Angeles on the evening preceding the official Academy Awards ceremony. In a highly unusual turn in 2005, a movie star actually showed up to accept the award (for her performance in the title role in *Catwoman* [2004]), something made all the more unusual by the fact that Halle Berry was the first Oscar-winning actress to do so. She began with a parody of her own Oscar acceptance speech three years previously, mimicking her own entrance, with dumbfounded tears and hand on heart, confessing with knowing irony that she "never in her life thought that she would be up here." She then, in comic fashion, turned to spread the derision leveled at her onto the wider nexus of Hollywood and the industry that had apparently put her there, including the manager who arranged her casting, her co-stars and writers, as well as the all agents, accountants, and lawyers who were involved in the casting and production arrangements of the notorious flop.

Such appearances by stars who have ostensibly gone off-script of course entertain us as movie fans, for they seem to reveal actors in a less mediated light, allowing us to feel closer to a more authentic version of the star's "self," without either the artifices of narrative and characterization or the shiny gloss of official trailers, interviews, promotional materials, and official awards speeches. Aided by magazines, reality TV, YouTube, and its equivalents, stars have never appeared so close to us in their unvarnished reality as they are now, with their humiliations, embarrassments, and parapraxes ever available to us at the click of a mouse. Such appearances as Berry's also reveal the deep ambiguities of getting close to stars, and the complex meanings associated with authenticity in our media culture. At a certain naive level, Berry's appearance seems to adhere to a moment of revelatory disclosure and melodramatic rebellion against the "system," where the oppressed individual gets her revenge on everyone who contributed to her being singled out for punishment and public humiliation.

Critics and scholars might consider alternative readings of such an event, however, by factoring in issues relating to the management and strategic promotion of stardom, and proposing Berry's appearance as a potential media opportunity over which she ultimately has some control. By this reading, the award becomes a publicity opportunity that allows Berry to address audiences at different registers, invoking a carefully calibrated balance of public humiliation, good-sportsmanship, and a dose of irreverence. Her performance facilitates fan identification by humorously invoking the melodrama of female victimhood and suffering at a public shaming, leading viewers to question what lies beneath Berry's "brave" countenancing of those who humiliate her. Moments in which stars suffer humiliation can thus be treated as symptoms of something larger within the systems of signification in which they operate, and as much as these ruptures entertain us, they also invite us to think critically and historically about what's really happening in such ritual display of pained humiliation. The following discussion proposes to do just that in relation to Berry and her surprisingly long career, situating her moment at the Razzies as an intervention on the part of both herself and her management within broader strategies of negotiation and struggle to control an excessively fragmented and mutable star image.

Berry's star persona is made particularly complex and problematic by her mixed-race origin and by a Hollywood culture that is notoriously rigid and hegemonic in its management and representation of difference. Analysis of Berry's career in Hollywood in fact reveals a star dogged by the problems and indeterminacies encountered by African American women in the entertainment industry in general, where skin color has traditionally limited employability and constrained minority talent to a restrictive typology. What becomes clear from such analysis is the extent to which Berry has negotiated her persona from an early stage with issues of artificiality and hybridity, aspects of which can be traced not only to her beginnings as a beauty-pageant queen and model but also to her skin color and its blurring of racial binaries. This essay seeks to account for both Berry's undoubted (and, for some, unexpected) success as an Oscar-winning actress and for the problems she has encountered in maintaining her place at "the top," as she refers to it, focusing in particular on the cultural work represented by Berry in relation to the suffering and invisibility of African American woman in U.S. culture more broadly.

INVENTING HALLE BERRY

Although hardly without precedent, Berry's career did not begin with the kind of acting or stage training common for Hollywood actors and stars. Beginning rather as a beauty-pageant winner from Ohio and following with work as a model, Berry moved into screen acting in a way that ostensibly invokes the "starlet" narrative. This paradigm, as Shelley Stamp argues, is driven by an ideology of being "discovered" through "passive acts of waiting and being looked at over the skill and effort required to succeed in the industry."[1] However, as with such comparable figures as Marilyn Monroe and Grace Kelly, Berry's career has also from early beginnings been about hard work, particularly in the star's efforts to gain legitimacy as an "acting" talent.

Berry's early role as Vivian, the crack-addicted partner of Gator (Samuel L. Jackson) in Spike Lee's *Jungle Fever* (1991), fulfilled a key function in developing Berry's status as a star. Although hers is a small role with few lines, the prestigious alignment with Lee as a contemporary auteur provided a race-oriented authenticity analogous to that of other African American stars such as Jackson and Wesley Snipes. Through Lee's deployment of ensemble casting, including himself and John Turturro, Berry benefits from associations with the geographical continuity of New York's ethnic neighborhoods, the film's artistic and political integrity, and a communitarian ethos not usually associated with the Hollywood culture of bottom-line, market-driven production priorities. Berry's performance

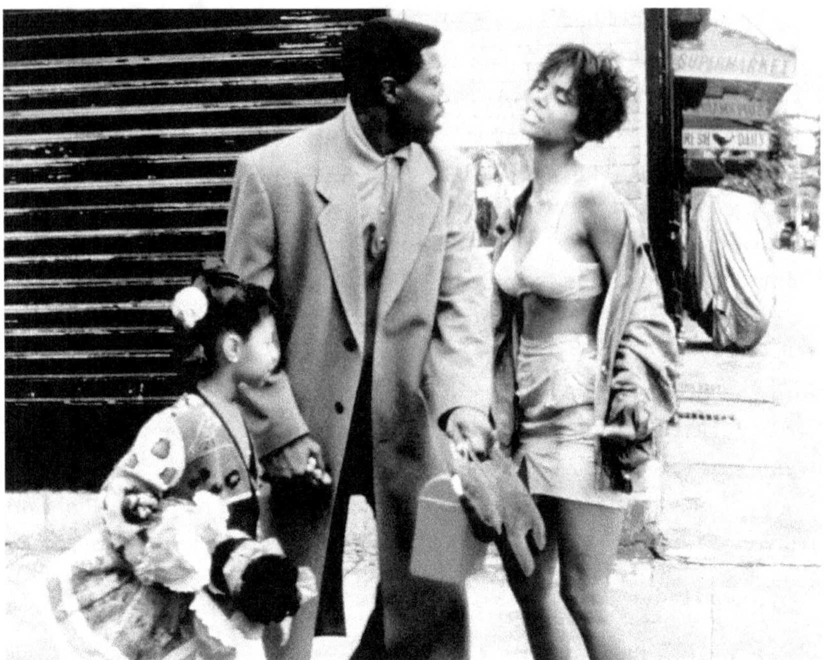

Berry as a crack addict turned prostitute in Spike Lee's *Jungle Fever* (1991).

thus shares in the film's connotations of artistic integrity, serving as a brave depiction of urban drug addiction, with its honest naturalism and concomitant de-prettification of the former beauty queen, aided by Berry's trademark short-hair, male style of dress, aggressively fast-paced speech, and overt drug use.

The character of Vivian was in many ways a signature role that helped Berry counter associations with pageants and beauty, and thus challenged a specific kind of classical femininity aligned with aspects of grace and deference to men. Moreover, and as attested by *Jungle Fever*'s explicit discussion of the problems of skin darkness for African American women, such conventions contrast with ideals of a particular white passivity and sensibility, as widely identified by literary theorists, where female beauty is firmly indexed to the sheltered, innocent, and deferential heroines of sentimental literature.[2] Applying such models to questions of black femininity, theorists of race can understand how these conditions set the terms for further discrimination and exclusion of black women, wherein "whiteness" becomes the baseline condition for visibility, before determinations of beauty become possible. As Jane Gaines argues in relation to the "placement of Black femaleness" in Western culture historically, the "Black female is either all woman and tinted black, or mostly Black and scarcely woman."[3] Put differently, black female bodies are subjected to discrimination at the level of both dominant race and gender constructions, where excesses of "blackness" in categories ranging from skin color to (masculine) displays of agency are understood as grounds for non-visibility and cultural dismissal.

Issues of "tinted" blackness are of particular import to considerations of Berry's status in Hollywood, owing to her mixed-race heritage and the instabilities such a racial profile engenders in the manufacture of stardom. While casting decisions, performance, makeup, hair preparation, guest appearances, interviews, and merchandizing opportunities are subject to market-driven calculation and scrutiny for all stars, these factors are particularly crucial to minority actors.[4] Berry's mixed lineage allows her to straddle the boundaries of racial differentiation and thereby maximize her casting potential and economic feasibility as a star. At the same time, she makes visible the conditions surrounding the negotiation of race and individuality in both Hollywood and the society it reflects. One of Berry's greatest assets, her mixed race also becomes her greatest problem, blurring the terms of her reality as an individual or icon—a finished product for consumption—even as her ambiguous identity maximizes her career opportunities. Richard Dyer argues that stars appeal to our fantasies of the "individual," of "certain peculiar, unique qualities that remain constant,"[5] as evidenced in the nexus of star, roles, movies, and promotional apparatus. It is thus often incumbent on the stars themselves, along with their managers, directors, and marketers, to define the parameters and limits of the particular field of meaning stars occupy.

"Tinted" blackness can thus be understood in Berry's case alongside a rubric of social and career mobility, at the same time as its ambiguities serve to threaten or undermine her individuality and unique commodity form, which ensure her financial reliability as a star. Such tensions become apparent very early in Berry's career, for just as her claims to racial authenticity and artistic integrity are marked by a preponderance of gritty, naturalistic roles throughout her career (*Jungle Fever*, *Losing Isaiah* [1995], *Bulworth* [1998], *Monster's Ball* [2001]), her success has been predicated equally, and indeed necessarily, on her flexibility as a "jobbing actor" in Hollywood for the first ten years of her career. This situation is perhaps most clearly evidenced by the various genres through which she gradually rose up the credit list, including television (*Knott's Landing* [CBS, in 1991]), action/adventure (*The Last Boy Scout* [1991], *Executive Decision* [1996]), comedy (*The Flintstones* [1994], *Race the Sun* [1996]), melodrama (*Losing Isaiah* [1996]), thriller (*The Rich Man's Wife* [1996]), and biopic (*Introducing Dorothy Dandridge* [1999]). Such flexibility, while ensuring that Berry stayed working within the profession, also reveals instabilities and indeterminacies with regard to who

Halle Berry "really" is, a query that so often proves inimical to the establishing of a "true" star and its invocation of continuity and presence. Indeed, while female stars are so often defined in the memory of fans and audience imaginations by their breakout hit (such as Vivien Leigh in *Gone with the Wind* [1939], Marilyn Monroe in *Gentlemen Prefer Blondes* [1953], Jane Fonda in *Barbarella* [1968], or Julia Roberts in *Pretty Woman* [1990]), Berry's diversity of roles signals a failure to be so defined. None of the films from this period in such respects can really qualify as breakout hits for Berry, despite her gradual rise to celebrity.

The instabilities surrounding Berry's persona are of course also attributable to issues of race and stereotyping in Hollywood more broadly, along with the way black female stardom has been historically constituted in the face of collective racism and gender bias. Key to such tensions are the limits to singularity and uniqueness that have characterized the representation of African American femininity in Hollywood, which was for so long associated, as bell hooks reminds us, with the "comfortable mammy image" in such films as *Gone with the Wind* and *Imitation of Life* (1959).[6] For hooks, such images long confined African American female identity to a position of invisibility and subordination to the white female star. Moreover, as the Berry vehicle *Introducing Dorothy Dandridge* demonstrates, while black male stars such as Harry Belafonte and Sidney Poitier rose to prominence and enjoyed sustained acting careers, black women had careers fraught with problems of both sexual and racial exploitation. For instance, Dandridge, who landed the title role in Otto Preminger's film musical *Carmen Jones* (1954), found her success mired not only in drug addiction and spousal abuse but also in the difficulties of consistently landing big roles as an African American woman in Hollywood. She faced the dilemma of either not working or damaging her name as a leading lady by accepting minor supporting roles.

Indeed, while the careers of contemporary black male stars in Hollywood, such as Denzel Washington, Jamie Foxx, Wesley Snipes, Don Cheadle, or Samuel L. Jackson, are in many ways prefigured by the successful career trajectories of earlier stars, a less stable precedent emerges for today's black women in Hollywood, a fact that Berry strategically deploys and exploits in her co-produced biopic of Dandridge (an HBO television movie). As a quintessential narrative of female suffering in Hollywood, Dandridge's story serves as a clear call for racial and gender inclusivity that self-consciously (and some may consider cynically) asks to be considered alongside Berry's own career at the time. If Berry is today's Dandridge, the film seems to say, Hollywood should strive hard to avoid repeating the abuses of its past by not passing up on, or exploiting, its young African American talent. By casting Berry in a "heritage" film of this kind, HBO indeed provides its own cautious solution to such a problem through the film's liberal unpacking of Hollywood prejudice and exploitation, while nevertheless leaving the question open as to how the movie industry (including HBO) can accommodate black female subjectivity in more specific terms. Despite the film's worthy contribution to the history of African American female stardom, the film remains constrained by the biopic's more pervasive conservatism with respect to the individual and his/her struggle. If the biopic is limited, as John Lupo and Carolyn Anderson note, by a "psychological approach to storytelling, with personal struggle as the nodal dramatic action," wider issues of race are all too often subordinated to mythologizing a great figure.[7]

A more interesting film in such respects is the earlier Eddie Murphy comedy *Boomerang* (1992), which stars Berry as a character who serves as a compromise formation between a variety of illegitimate subject-positions for black women in the early 1990s. Based in the culturally significant locale of a modern marketing department of a multinational cosmetics company called Lady Eloise, the film concerns itself with the problems of a successful, promiscuous executive, Marcus (Murphy), who must resign himself to the rise of successful black women in the company at both professional and personal levels. The film features not only Berry as a successful, talented art designer, but also Robin Givens as Murphy's new boss and Eartha Kitt as Lady Eloise, the company's original cover girl. Following the company's new campaign to rebrand itself by hiring a wild diva from Europe called Strangé (Grace Jones) as the new face of the company, the film foregrounds issues of self-conscious reinvention and manufacture in relation to key subject-positions of popular black female identity.

At the same time, the film remains highly problematic in terms of its misogyny. It is thus in full sympathy with the sexism of Murphy's character (and his two male friends) that the problem of all three central female characters is articulated around issues of excessive sexuality. Both Jones as Strangé and Kitt as Lady Eloise serve indeed as figures of black hypersexuality, both making advances on Marcus that he tries in vain to rebuff. While Lady Eloise succeeds in her seduction by implicitly offering Marcus a promotion opportunity at the company, Strangé's very public attempt in a restaurant results in his hasty retreat. Both women, however, conform clearly to the "wild animalistic sexuality"[8] attached to black women, which hooks describes in relation to pop star Tina Turner: "This tough black woman has no time for woman bonding, she is out to 'catch.' Turner's fictive model of black female sexual agency remains rooted in misogynist notions. Rather than being a pleasure-based eroticism, it is ruthless, violent; it is about women using sexual power to do violence to the male Other."[9] Hooks goes on to align displays of black female sexual aggression with the black prostitute's cynical reduction of sex and her body to commodity, whereby "sexual service" is "for money and power" while "pleasure is secondary."[10]

Age is also foregrounded in the way Marcus disgustedly rejects older women Lady Eloise and Strangé, compounding the extent to which the black woman's body is designated for the purpose of male gratification. Such hypersexuality finds continuities in the much younger character of Marcus's fellow marketing executive, Jacqueline Boyer (Givens), whose light skin, straightened hair, and corporate success and professionalism serve to merely obscure another eventual display of the black woman's intrinsically aggressive competence in bed. In one of various bedroom scenes with Marcus, for instance, Jacqueline assumes a dominant position on top, precipitating unusual shots of the man's face in the throes of sexual pleasure rather than the woman's, while in another scene she provocatively licks his face while he attempts to have a business phone call with a colleague. Such displays of aggressive sexuality prove Jacqueline more than equal to the task of pleasuring a man, foregrounding continuities not only with Lady Eloise and Strangé but the "hunter" typology more broadly conceived.

In the film's problematically antifeminist subtext, the problem of contemporary black femininity therefore emerges as one of excessive agency and hypermasculinization. Women like Jacqueline are more interested in the evening's basketball game, the latest sales figures, and "uncomplicated" sex than in romance, relationships, or even the traditional associations attached to appreciation of culture and art. Angela (Berry's character) serves as the longed-for antidote to such excesses in her adherence to more conventional feminine values of romance, compassion, meaningful sex, and understanding her man, while she is also shown to fully embrace her African American heritage. Despite her "whiteness," in terms of skin color and professionalism in the office environment, Angela decorates her house with traditional African art and volunteers at a school teaching children how to embrace their cultural heritage. By retaining these inoffensive aspects of African American culture that are acceptable within a liberal, market-based economy and its commodity-dictated tastes for "authentic" identity, Angela avoids offense in a way that her three contemporaries fail to finesse. Strangé's exhibitionism and politically inflected avant-gardism (as evidenced by a particularly "abject" ad demo that fails to impress the Lady Eloise committee) are supplanted by Angela's prioritization of marketable art design in commercials, and her implied acceptance of patriarchal domesticity with Marcus. Angela's compliant withdrawals from the spotlight are insufficient within the film's misogynist scheme, such that Marcus cannot resist a final fling with Jacqueline after falling for Angela. She stands first as a neglected figure in her relinquishing of agency, followed by her subordinated compromise and convenient forgiveness of Marcus before the final credits roll. As if two stars are contesting for dominance within an inequitable culture of patriarchal privilege in Hollywood, Berry/Angela must ultimately relinquish her integrity, as a function of its coherence, to Murphy/Marcus.

Such characterization and plotting indeed invite speculation on alignments between these characters and the stars who play them, with Berry firmly distinguished from the kinds of blackness represented by her precursors, Jones and Kitt. These older stars stand as icons of confrontation and agency, both in terms of their performances and star personae. Jones's performances in particular, as Steven Shaviro notes, have "appropriated, mocked, and inverted traditional (racist and sexist) signifiers of blackness and whiteness, and of femininity and masculinity,"[11] aspects of which are manifest in *Boomerang*. Here, though, Jones's character is subject to far more ridicule and internalized prejudice, and Jones thus plays true to the name of her character, Strangé, clearly placed within a frame of comic estrangement and disgust. By contrast, Berry's image of compliance and dignified deference, as borne out by her role in the film, conforms to what Richard Dyer describes as the "committed" star, an actor who exhibits an overall ethos of hard work and professionalism without the big ego, characteristics that Dyer identifies in the "technical mastery" of Fred Astaire or of Joan Crawford's "slogging away at all aspects of her image."[12]

If Jones's stardom adheres more to the kinds of "antagonism" that Dyer writes of in figures like Marilyn Monroe or Judy Garland—aspects of which crucially accord with issues of Jones's blackness and the traumatic histories of black performance—Berry's stardom is more self-effacing and genteel. The compromise that the character Angela represents, and that Berry's persona takes on, lies between aspects of an exhibitionistic, performative blackness and an innocuous whiteness, which both efface race and the visibility of what Gaines calls the "mostly black" woman. If such an image is not borne out by each and every role Berry took on in her first ten years in Hollywood, such a compromise becomes salient in terms of the overall aggregated impressions that she conveys as a star.

GONGS AND RASPBERRIES

By dint of an extended status as a working actor in Hollywood, appearing in a variety of genre films as characters ranging from the "girl-next-door" (*Boomerang*, *Bulworth*) to more vampish incarnations (*The Flintstones*), Berry had by the time of *Monster's Ball* cultivated an image of "committed" hard worker, who hung on in Hollywood thanks precisely to roles that had eluded her assumed forebear, Dandridge. Considering her trajectory to her Academy Award for Best Actress in 2001 for her performance as a near-destitute wife and mother in *Monster's Ball*, Berry benefited from a particularly self-conscious and media-savvy professionalism in the management of her racial profile in contemporary Hollywood. She had charted a course between the confrontational, ego-driven iconicity and ineffability of Grace Jones and the self-referential positions of passive, studio-era exploitation and limited demand for black female parts encountered by Dandridge.

Berry's appearance in the forgettable *Monster's Ball* served less as a particularly remarkable breakthrough hit for Berry (despite her worthy, naturalistic performance) than as a showcasing of Berry's professional resilience. Hollywood is always keen to reward those who embody a hard work ethic as much as an intrinsic talent. This "committed" persona is of equal importance, I would suggest, to considerations of Berry's race as such, notwithstanding the Academy's desire at the time of the award to redress its failure to award African American female actors. The numerous factors surrounding Berry's winning of the award are listed in John Patterson's *Guardian* profile:

> If you'd come to me a few years ago with a list of all the African American candidates potentially capable of winning the Oscar for Best Actress, just about the last name I'd have picked would have been Halle Berry's. In fact, I probably wouldn't have kicked up much a fuss if her name hadn't appeared on the list full stop, given all the Angela Bassetts and Alfre Woodards who, no disrespect intended, could act her to a standstill using only their little fingers. As it turned out, her performance in the deeply overrated *Monster's Ball* was expertly calibrated to become a favourite with Academy voters. Serious racial issues. A woman in great pain. Tits out (what courage!). All the necessary requirements to be taken seriously in airhead Tinseltown.[13]

Such emphasis on Berry's willingness to address the "necessary requirements" laid down by Hollywood allows for an understanding of her stardom that incorporates both textual and extra-textual components.

As is common with the "Best Actor" Oscar, performances are understood to be more often awarded for the star's adherence to certain criteria of courage, professionalism, and compliance with production requirements than for more traditional notions of talent or display of a star's essential iconicity in the film. Thus, stars (and perhaps Berry herself) can be created, reaffirmed, or promoted by recognition of the status of bankable stars within the industry, but these awards are rarely determined or based on stardom in its more romanticized senses. Indeed, comments from Berry's contemporary, Angela Bassett, in the wake of Berry's award, resound with snarky dismissiveness from an actress who had turned down the part, claiming that she "wasn't going to be a prostitute on film."[14] Such a remark, alongside her hope that she be awarded "for something I can sleep with at night," seems at first to simply misrepresent Berry's role as a woman who merely falls for Billy Bob Thornton's racist ex–prison guard, having lost both her husband and son. Yet Bassett's comments gain legibility in view of the film's critical reception, wherein Berry's character is framed as a vehicle through which Hollywood persists in its problematic treatment of "serious racial issues." Indeed, despite the naturalism of Berry and Thornton's performances, commentators were critical of the film's blandly liberal approach to issues of capital punishment, racism, and interracial marriage, both in terms of its invocations of a morally flawed man's redemption by the love of a good woman, and the deterioration of the film's love scenes into what film critic Peter Bradshaw describes as "very tacky softcore."[15]

Such considerations contribute to a picture of Berry that is dominated above all by a sense that her achievements are attributable to a well-calibrated machine of image manufacture, casting, promotion, and marketing over the more traditional virtues of individuality or uniqueness. These aspects of Berry's professionalism, along with connotations of impersonality and manufacture, may help explain not only her posturing alongside Dandridge, but also her notoriously tearful and "melodramatic" acceptance of the Best Actress statuette on Oscar night in 2002. In both cases, what Berry seemed to lack up to that point was a touching "story" of her own, a means by which the public could identify with Berry's brand as a vulnerable person, as opposed to a mere professional, as borne out by the variance of her roles before she was cast as a victim of oppression and racism in *Monster's Ball.* Whether those tears on Oscar's night were performed or not matters less, therefore, than the alignments she claimed between herself and stars like Dorothy Dandridge, Lena Horne, and Diahann Carroll, effacing her performance (and herself) in favor of situating her award alongside rubrics of social justice and civil rights. Adhering also to a traditional model of female suffering (and its legitimized place with regards to female subjectivity in Hollywood writ large), Berry here redresses any alignments she may have retained from her more social-realist outings (*Jungle Fever*, *Bulworth*) while negating any sense in which her star image adhered to the repudiated "hunter" sexuality described by feminist theorist bell hooks and invoked in films like *The Flintstones* (where she plays a woman who tries to seduce Fred away from Wilma).

Since the Oscars, however, Berry has struggled to stay on top, both in terms of the bankable star's ability to ensure the critical and/or commercial success of her films and in terms of maintaining her continuity as an iconic figure. Despite a preponderance of high-profile roles (like the ongoing role as Storm in the X-Men franchise and the ill-fated title role in *Catwoman*), issues of race and individualization are never far away from Berry in many of the projects she accepts. This pattern is especially evident in her assumption of roles traditionally coded "white," perhaps most saliently when she appears as a Bond girl in *Die Another Day* (2002), released immediately after *Monster's Ball*. As if to underline the use of a woman of color, Berry serves here as an unprecedentedly big-name actor to play Bond's primary love interest, CIA agent Jinx Johnson. The film is quite emphatic, too, about her character's standing as a primary "prize" for Bond, a term deployed by Ian Fleming in relation to Bond's final sexual conquest in *Live and Let Die*. In dialogue with the superstitious, voodoo-practicing Rosie Carver, played with animalistic gusto by Gloria Hendry in the 1973 film version of *Live and Let Die*, Jinx serves as a CIA agent who remains loyal to both the CIA and Bond, driven by shared strategic goals. Promotional materials surrounding the film, moreover, highlight Jinx's introductory scene, where she emerges from the sea in a bikini as seen from Bond's point of view, a detail paying direct homage to the now mythical scene in *Dr. No* (1962) introducing the first Bond girl, Honey Ryder (Ursula Andress). As if acknowledging its own anachronisms with regard to race and the Bond girl, the franchise deploys self-conscious imagery of unveiling, or even of birth, as a curvaceous Berry emerges, Venus-like, from the water. In this metaphorical washing away of prejudice, the franchise seems to signal a fresh start to Bond's treatment of race, in a visual rhetoric that is then imitated almost exactly in *Casino Royale* (2006), where Bond's own body emerges from the sea as an unveiling not only of its new star (Daniel Craig), but also of the franchise's foregrounding of Bond's eroticized body for visual pleasure.

Berry's appearance thus allows for the exotic otherness of African American women in the Bond franchise to be reworked in dialogue with its earlier problematics. While black actresses seemed in prior Bond films to be marginalized to a disposable and/or primitive status, Berry's character here invokes the familiar and the conventionally American. In counterpoint to the hostility and sexual aggressiveness of Grace Jones's May Day in *A View to a Kill* (1985), Berry's performance is arch and participates fully in the self-parodying style of the Pierce Brosnan years. Once out of the water, she and Bond meet and trade innuendos about Bond's pretense as an ornithologist, she commenting on the "mouthful" the word presents as she looks down and offscreen (toward his crotch). The film is thus particularly self-reflexive in its renegotiation of race, aligning Jinx with her stereotyped predecessors, May Day and Rosie Carver, only to finally dispel such associations by situating her as the loyal Bond girl after all. Contrasts between Jinx and the über-white British spy Miranda Frost, who turns out to be a traitor to Bond and MI6, meanwhile serve to compound the franchise's revisionism in relation to its earlier alignments between femininity, whiteness, and virtue. Berry's mixed race status thus signals a compromise with this older model, both in literal and figurative terms. Never able to fully occupy the place of the Bond girl as the ultimate figure of commodified white femininity, her star persona nevertheless benefits from such associations while foregrounding the tensions surrounding the renegotiation of race and gender in Hollywood.

DECLINE AND REINVENTION

Berry's apparently professionalized control of her star image remains bound up with larger questions relating to a star's position as a film artist, status as a genre actor, and manipulator of film franchise branding, subject to the persistently intransigent politics of representation. Such factors account as well for the key dominant narrative that has dogged Berry (in many ways justifiably) throughout her post-Oscar career, with regards to her poor film choices and general demise as a top-tier film star. Criticized for a number of badly received films, including *Gothika* (2003), *Perfect Stranger* (2007), and *Frankie and Alice* (2001), Berry experienced a career slump epitomized for many by the Razzie punishment for her title role in *Catwoman*, which once again saw her take on the role of a character strongly associated with white female actors, notably Michelle Pfieffer in Tim Burton's *Batman Returns* (1992). However, a recurring characteristic, with which Berry has countenanced such dismissal, has been her willingness to play along with such reviews with a good humor that is more than mildly infused with criticism of the Hollywood system itself. While such an appearance may sound ostensibly like an archetypal low point for any actor, Berry's speech in fact served as a reclamation of dignity through the honesty and humor with which she accepted the award. Aided by the irreverent ideology of the Razzies themselves, and their camp takedown of the Oscars' pomp and authority, Berry can even be considered here to have taken over, at a certain level, authorship of her star image through a rhetoric of ironic repetition and mimicry. Berry reverses her Oscar winner's invocations of female suffering and humble (raced) deference to the Academy, an intervention that importantly incorporates her—at least for an evening—into an event dictated by the carnivalesque and its "aesthetic of mistakes,"[16] alongside its implied reversals of power, scatology, and candor.

While a certain reading could therefore contextualize Berry's appearance within a rubric of "damage-limitation" or savvy star marketing, valid reasons remain for situating her appearance at the Razzies within a critical understanding of stardom and its instabilities, not least owing to the "antagonistic" aspects of Berry's appearance in this instance. It reveals in particular the extent to which stardom proves here to be a uniquely flexible, and thus a potentially critical, means by which individuality is negotiated within the complex conditions of film promotion, reception, and evaluation, such that no one ultimately has final say on what films and their stars can mean or signify. If, for one event, Berry reveals a more "antagonistic" persona, such an act remains significant and noteworthy in terms of its resistance to power and the status quo. Such defiance, although possibly or even probably scripted in its own right, is fueled by the will to make known the mechanisms image industries use to regulate and control their employees, along with the potentially restrictive conditions within which stars negotiate their images. As borne out furthermore by Berry's mention of her beauty-pageant roots toward the end of her speech, with overtones of confession or "coming out," such performance is suffused with the desire to tell one's own nuanced story as opposed to "playing the race card" (to use Linda Williams's terminology).[17]

Berry's star image is thus cautiously reintegrated here with the more personal individuality and history that are so often sacrificed or forfeited in the process of commodity production. The painful history and connotations surrounding race of course remain key to comprehending the full dimensions of Berry's resistance, yet I suggest it is manifest more at the level of form than content. Such reclamation is significant especially in terms of the cultural work Berry represents in the face of a repressed or excessive blackness, and the tensions inherent in those contradictions. *Catwoman* serves in many ways as recto to the verso of Berry's girl-next-door image, neither ultimately shifting questions of black femininity beyond the typologies of black "hunter" and white "prize." Her irreverence thus represents a fissure in the polished edifice of a system predicated on racial effacement or fetish, an almost Brechtian moment of revelation when the star takes off the mask and addresses the audience outside of character, script, and the ideology that surrounds them.

Indeed, Berry's Razzies speech represents one of only a few times that Berry has taken on the kinds of agency and performativity more associated with a figure like Grace Jones, notable too, perhaps, in terms of its greater proximity to fans and audiences than to the "official" movie business and its accepted forms of promotion and marketing. By contrast indeed, this period of Berry's career has been rather more populated by various embarrassments and gaffes in the public eye, from a hit-and-run car accident in 1997, for which Berry was sentenced to community service, to a joke on Jay Leno's *Tonight Show* that was construed as antisemitic, when she likened a digitally manipulated photo of herself to "her Jewish cousin," owing to the photo's enlargement of her nose.[18] This latter incident in particular serves as a revealing instance of an antagonism that lies outside the scope of Berry's racial profile, prefigured by a long-standing tradition of enmity between African American and Jewish American communities. It provides context, too, for Berry's more recent high-profile efforts to bring about a system of "color blind" casting in Hollywood, amidst long-standing reports that she is to star in a film that tells the true-life story of a white teacher.[19] Although the role has failed (as of this publication) to enter into any formal production context, Berry's various roles in *Cloud Atlas* (2012) speak also to her increased participation in Hollywood's racial politics, whereby she and a number of other high-profile Hollywood stars played characters varying in race, gender, age, sexuality, and historical setting. While the film in fact was criticized by a number of commentators owing to the deployment of "yellowface" for one of its white stars playing an Asian character (Jim Sturgess),[20] Berry's appearances were notable in the range of characters she played. Her role in particular as Jocasta Ayrs, a white German Jewish refugee from Nazi Germany, for which she received extensive makeup (including a prosthetic nose), serves as a meta-textual response to her earlier gaffe.

Berry's career has served to underscore the problems encountered by stars emerging from underrepresented groups in Hollywood, wherein race serves as both a catalyst and a constraint to stardom. Berry's role(s) in *Cloud Atlas* can be considered a promising intervention, for while her stardom has been propelled and facilitated by her racial profile, the film's radical casting allows racial difference to be situated alongside other forms of social difference such as age, sexuality, and gender. Like other films, such as Todd Solondz's *Palindromes* (2004), where the main character of Aviva is played by seven different actors who vary in race, age, and gender, *Cloud Atlas* foregrounds the casting as a convention that is all too often dogged by Hollywood's strict requirements for realism and verisimilitude at the expense of innovation, experimentation, and focus on formal procedures. Berry's usual complicity with such requirements has been a key condition of her successful rise to prominence as a screen star. She has also been brutally criticized by peers and critics owing precisely to the ways she has been deemed to toe the line of Hollywood's liberal yet problematic approach to race and gender politics. Her marginality in terms of race has served a complex function in such regards, endowing her with an "authenticity" that has allowed for effacements of her beauty-pageant roots, while equally allowing her to become

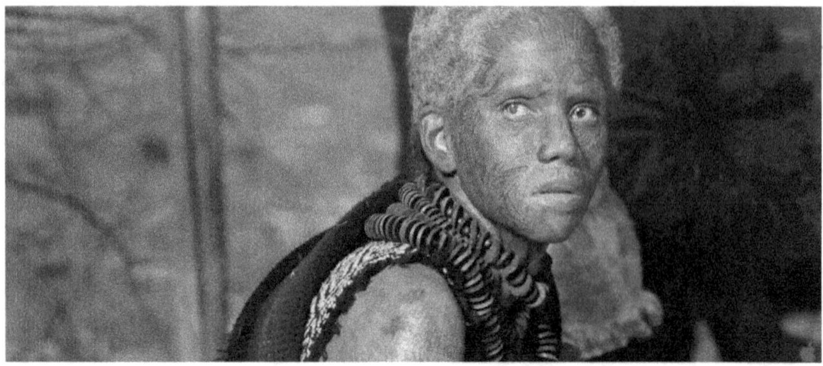

The various characters played by Berry in *Cloud Atlas* (2012) range widely in terms of race, gender, and age.

a figure of negotiation with respect to Hollywood's representation of African American femininity in an era of allegedly color-blind casting and racial diversification.

The fact that Berry (as the first black female winner of an Oscar for Best Actress) stands as a poster child for Hollywood's inclusivity and diversity has been a mixed blessing within the wider reception contexts of Hollywood culture. If anything, she has revealed the extent to which Hollywood has been reluctant to shift the parameters around which aspects of gender and race are represented. As the "committed" star who has invariably done what she is told, Berry has drawn critiques revolving around the way she is excessively sanitized and streamlined as a star—by virtue of the various roles and genres in which she has performed, the ease with which her persona has adhered to traditional models of female subordination, her domesticity in relation to male characters, or her melodramatic female sacrifice and suffering. Her moments of "blackness" in such films as *Die Another Day* and *Catwoman* meanwhile give the lie to any claim that Hollywood has been able to overlook race entirely. Instead, they reveal ongoing fetishization of the black woman as an exotic temptress and "hunter," in relation to whom white characters (and the white male gaze) are reinscribed within normative parameters.

A film like *Cloud Atlas*, which has been called the most costly "independent" film to date, serves as a profoundly ambiguous gesture toward racial inclusivity in the case of Berry's signification as a star. It both motions toward racial diversification and inclusivity and undermines the individuality that traditionally goes hand in hand with the star as a visual constant within a film narrative's trajectory. Owing to considerations not only of race but also of age (a well-documented problem for women over forty in Hollywood), Berry here reformulates her contract with a Hollywood that is increasingly reluctant to finance risky projects as she attempts once more to allow herself an even greater scope of parts to play. If such maneuvers ensure her continued employment as a successful star, they also go some way in dampening the extent to which stardom can be mythically equated with a certain kind of immutable screen immortality. What becomes visible, rather, are the conditions within which stars must negotiate and renegotiate their screen personae, wherein only a top tier of actors–usually white and male—have tenure. Other stars who are like Berry—black, mixed race, and female—must remain carefully, silently, and painfully aware of the social and racial boundaries within which their images circulate.

NOTES

1. Shelley Stamp, "'It's a Long Way to Filmland': Starlets, Screen Hopefuls and Extras in Early Hollywood," in *American Cinema's Transitional Era: Audiences, Institutions, Practices*, ed. Charlie Keil and Shelley Stamp (Berkley: University of California Press, 2004), 342.
2. See Claudia Johnson, "A 'Sweet Face as White as Death': Jane Austen and the Politics of Female Sensibility," *Novel: A Forum on Fiction* 22, no. 2 (1989): 159–74; Janet Todd, *Gender, Art and Death* (Hoboken, N.J.: John Wiley, 2013), 173–75.
3. Jane Gaines, "White Privilege and Looking Relations," *Cultural Critique* 4 (1985), reprinted in *Film Theory: An Anthology*, ed. Robert Stam and Toby Miller (London: Blackwell, 2000), 723.
4. See Richard Dyer, *Stars* (London: BFI Publishing, 1998), 5–32.

5. Richard Dyer, introduction to *Heavenly Bodies: Film Stars and Society* (New York: St. Martin's Press, 1986), reprinted in Stam and Miller, *Film Theory: An Anthology*, 609.
6. bell hooks, *Black Looks: Race and Representation* (New York: South End Press, 1992), 121.
7. Carolyn Anderson and John Lupo, "Hollywood Lives: The State of the Biopic at the Turn of the Century," in *Genre and Contemporary Hollywood*, ed. Steve Neale (London: Routledge, 2000), 92.
8. hooks, *Black Looks*, 69.
9. Ibid., 68–69.
10. Ibid., 69.
11. Steven Shaviro, *Post-Cinematic Affect* (London: Zero Books, 2010), 19.
12. Dyer, *Heavenly Bodies*, introduction, reprinted in Stam and Miller, *Film Theory: An Anthology*, 608.
13. John Patterson, "Profile: Halle Berry," *Guardian,* August 6, 2004.
14. See "Actor Says *Monster's Ball* Stereotypes Black Women," *Guardian,* June 24, 2002.
15. Peter Bradshaw, review of *Monster's Ball, Guardian,* June 6, 2002.
16. Stam and Miller, *Film Theory*, 262.
17. Linda Williams, *Playing the Race Card: Melodramas of Black and White from Uncle Tom to O. J. Simpson* (Princeton, N.J.: Princeton University Press, 2002).
18. Matthew Moore, "Halle Berry Apologises for 'Jewish Nose' Gaffe," *Telegraph*, October 25, 2007.
19. Benjamin Lee, "Can Playing a Racist Restore Halle Berry's Mojo," *Guardian*, October 2, 2009.
20. Nick Allen, "Cloud Atlas Criticised For 'Badly Done Yellowface,'" *Telegraph*, October 26, 2012.

BIBLIOGRAPHY

"Actor says *Monster's Ball* Stereotypes Black Women." *Guardian*, June 24, 2002.

Addison, Heather. "'Must the Players Keep Young?': Early Hollywood's Cult of Youth." *Cinema Journal* 45, no. 4 (2006): 4.

"The AFI Life Achievement Awards." American Film Institute. www.afi.com/laa/default.aspx.

"AFI's 100 Years. 100 Heroes & Villains." American Film Institute. www.afi.com/100years/handv.aspx.

Alba, Jessica. Interview by Howie Kahn. *Elle*, December 2010. Quoted in Thomas Fisher, "Acting Disaster." *Celebrity Studies* 3, no. 3 (November 2012): 344.

Allen, Michael J. 2003. *Contemporary US Cinema*. Harlow: Longman/Pearson Education, 2003.

Allen, Nick. "Cloud Atlas Criticised For 'Badly Done Yellowface.'" *Telegraph*, October 26, 2012.

"Amanda Bynes." Internet Movie Database. www.imdb.com/name/nm0004789/?ref_=sr_1.

Anderson, Carolyn, and John Lupo. "Hollywood Lives: The State of the Biopic at the Turn of the Century." In *Genre and Contemporary Hollywood*, ed. Steve Neale, 91–104. London: Routledge, 2000.

Andersen, Christopher. *Michael Jackson Unauthorized*. New York: Simon and Schuster, 1994.

Anderson, Paul Thomas, and Daniel Day-Lewis. Interview by Charlie Rose. *Charlie Rose*, PBS, December 21, 2007.

Anderton, Ethan. "Martin Scorsese Is Trying to Make 'Silence' His Next Project Yet Again." *FirstShowing*, January 21, 2013. www.firstshowing.net/2013/martin-scorsese-is-trying-to-make-silence-hist-next-project-yet-again.

Åström, Berit. "Referred Pain: Privileging Male Emotions in Narrative Instances of Female Physical Suffering." *Journal of Gender Studies* 20, no. 2 (June 2011): 125–37.

Atkinson, Michael. "Fire Bomb." *Village Voice*, January 31, 2006. www.villagevoice.com/2006-01-31/film/fire-bomb.

Avery, Jack. "The Construction of Daniel Day-Lewis's Star Persona." *Strange Enlightenments*, February 25, 2013. strangeenlightenments.wordpress.com/2013/02/25/the-construction-of-daniel-day-lewis-star-persona.

Ayers, Drew. "Bodies, Bullets, and Bad Guys: Elements of the Hardbody." *Film Criticism* 32, no. 3 (2008): 41–67.

Balsom, Erika. "'One Single Mystery of Persons and Objects': The Erotics of Fragmentation in Au Hasard Balthazar." *Canadian Journal of Film Studies* (*Revue Canadienne D'études Cinématographiques*) 19, no. 1 (Spring): 20–40.

Banita, Georgiana. "Fossil Frontiers: American Petroleum History on Film." In *A Companion to the Historical Film*, ed. Robert A. Rosenstone and Constantin Parvulescu. Malden, Mass.: Wiley-Blackwell, 2013.

Barkhorn, Eleanor, and Spencer Kornhaber. "Is It Wrong to Be Charmed by Reese Witherspoon's Drunk-Driving Tirade?" *Atlantic*, May 3, 2013. www.theatlantic.com/entertainment/archive/2013/05/is-it-wrong-to-be-charmed-by-reese-witherspoons-drunk-driving-tirade/275536/.

Barris, George. *Marilyn: Her Life in Her Own Words*. New York: Citadel Press, 2003.

Barton, Sabrina. "Face Value." In *All the Available Light: A Marilyn Monroe Reader*, ed. Yona Zeldis, 120–41. New York: Touchstone, 2002.

Basinger, Jeanine. Review of *Being Rita Hayworth: Labor, Identity, and Hollywood Stardom* by Adrienne McLean. *Film Quarterly* 60, no. 1 (Fall 2006): 61.

———. *The Star Machine*. New York: Vintage Books, 2007.

———. *A Woman's View*. Middletown, Conn.: Wesleyan University Press, 1993.

Bearak, Barry. "The Living Nightmare." *New York Times*, February 12, 2012.

Belázs, Béla. "The Face of Man." In *Film Theory and Criticism: Introductory Readings*, 2nd ed., ed. Gerald Mast and Marshall Cohen. Oxford: Oxford University Press, 1979.

Bell, Emma. "The Insanity Plea: Female Celebrities, Reality Media and the Psychopathology of British Pop Feminism." In *In the Limelight and under the Microscope: Form and Functions of Female Celebrity*, ed. Su Holmes and Diane Negra, 199–223. New York: Continuum, 2011.

Bell-Metereau, Rebecca. "Movies and Our Secret Lives." In *American Cinema of the 1950s: Themes and Variations*, ed. Murray Pomerance, 89–110. New Brunswick, N.J.: Rutgers University Press, 2005.

———. "Stealth, Sexuality, and Cult Status in *The Manchurian Candidate* and *Seconds*." In *A Little Solitaire: John Frankenheimer and American Film*, ed. Murray Pomerance and R. Barton Palmer, 48–61. New Brunswick, N.J.: Rutgers University Press, 2011.

Berger, Joseph. "Rock Hudson, Screen Idol, Dies at 59." *New York Times*, October 3, 1985.

Bigsby, Christopher. *Arthur Miller: 1915–1962*. Cambridge, Mass.: Harvard University Press, 2009.

Bingham, Dennis. *Acting Male: Masculinities in the Films of James Stewart, Jack Nicholson, and Clint Eastwood*. New Brunswick, N.J.: Rutgers University Press, 1994.

———. "'I Do Want to Live!': Female Voices, Male Discourse and Hollywood Biopics." *Cinema Journal* 38 no. 3 (Spring 1999): 3–26.

Blackwelder, Robert. "Respect from Theron Out." SPLICEDwire. splicedwire.com/03features/ctheron.html.

Blankstein, Andrew, and Richard Winton. "Natalie Wood: New Coroner's Report." *Los Angeles Times*, January 14, 2013. documents.latimes.com/coroners-report-death-natalie-wood.

Bordo, Susan. *The Male Body: A New Look at Men in Public and in Private*. New York: Farrar, Straus and Giroux, 1999.

———. *Unbearable Weight: Feminism, Western Culture, and the Body*. Berkeley: University of California Press, 1993.

Boucher, Geoff. "Harrison Ford Returns as Indiana Jones." *Los Angeles Times*, May 4, 2008.

"Bout Time: America's Fighting Women Set Their Sights on an Olympic Debut." *New York Times*, January 29, 2012.

"Box Office for *I'm Still Here*." Box Office Mojo. www.boxofficemojo.com/movies/?id=imstillhere.htm

Boys Don't Cry (press kit). Directed by Kimberly Peirce. Los Angeles: Twentieth Century–Fox, 1999.

Bradshaw, Peter. "Keeping It Real." *Guardian*, September 17, 2010.

———. Review of *Monster's Ball*. *Guardian*, June 6, 2002.

Braudy, Leo. *The Frenzy of Renown: Fame and Its History*. Oxford: Oxford University Press, 1986.

"A Breed Apart." Internet Movie Database. www.imdb.com/NewsFeatures/hford. Accessed April 3, 2014.

Breznican, Anthony. "Harrison Ford: A Portrait." *USA Today*, April 16, 2008.

Brickman, Barbara Jane. "Coming of Age in the 1970s: Revision, Fantasy, and Rage in the Teen-Girl Badlands." *Camera Obscura: Feminism, Culture, and Media Studies* 22, no. 3 (2007): 43.

Briefel, Aviva. "Monster Pains: Masochism, Menstruation, and Identification in the Horror Film." *Film Quarterly* 58, no. 3 (Spring 2005): 16–27.

Brown, William. "Jessica Lange and Sissy Spacek: Country Girls." In *Acting for America: Movie Stars of the 1980s*, ed. Robert Eberwein, 57–76. New Brunswick, N.J.: Rutgers University Press, 2010.

Brzecki, Patrick. "Martin Scorsese Scouts Locations for 'Silence' in Taiwan." *Hollywood Reporter*, February 7, 2014. www.hollywoodreporter.com/news/martin-scorsese-scouts-locations-silence-678187.

Burr, Ty. *Gods Like Us: On Movie Stardom and Modern Fame*. New York: Pantheon Books, 2012.

Cadwalladr, Carole. "I've Been to Hell. I'm Not Going Back There." *Guardian/Observer*, November 22, 2008. www.theguardian.com/film/2008/nov/23/mickey-rourke-interview.

Capote, Truman. "A Beautiful Child." In *Portraits and Observations: The Essays of Truman Capote*, 470–83. New York: Random House, 2007.

Caracalla, Laurence. *Harrison Ford*. San Francisco: Fitway Publishing, 2007.

Carlyle, Thomas. *The Best Known Works of Thomas Carlyle*. Rockville, Md.: Wildside Press, 2010).

"Casey Affleck Calls Sexual Harassment Lawsuit a Case of Sour Grapes." *PopEater*. www.popeater.com/2010/07/24/casey-affleck-lawsuit-blackmail-amanda-white.

Cassidy, Sarah. "Life Begins at Sixty, Says Harrison Ford." *Independent*, July 25, 2005. findarticles.com/p/articles/mi_qn4158/print.

"Charlize Theron profile." *Hello Magazine*. www.hellomagazine.com/profiles/charlizetheron.

Chavkin, Dan. "Action Figure." *Premiere* 15, no. 2 (2002): 62–88.

Churchwell, Sarah Bartlett. *The Many Lives of Marilyn Monroe*. New York: Picador, 2004.

Cohan, Steven. *Masked Men: Masculinity and the Movies in the 1950s*. Bloomington: Indiana University Press, 1997.

Comolli, Jean-Louis. "Historical Fiction: A Body Too Much." *Screen* 19, no. 2 (1978): 41–53.

Cregan, Kate. *The Sociology of the Body*. London: Sage Publications, 2006.

Crosbie, Lynn. "Complex? Yes. Odd? You Bet. Rapper? Uh . . ." *Globe and Mail*, January 20, 2009. www.theglobeandmail.com/arts/joaquin-phoenix-complex-yes-odd-you-bet-rapper-uh/article1146837.

Cullen, Jim. *Sensing the Past: Hollywood Stars and Historical Visions*. New York: Oxford University Press, 2013.

Custen, George. *Bio/Pics: How Hollywood Constructed Public History*. New Brunswick, N.J.: Rutgers University Press, 1992.

———. "The Mechanical Life in the Age of Human Reproduction: American Biopics, 1916–1980." *Biography* 23, no. 1 (Winter 2000): 137.

D'Addario, Daniel. "Cate Blanchett Thanks Woody Allen from the Oscar Podium." *Salon*, March 2, 2014. www.salon.com/2014/03/03/cate_blanchett_thanks_woody_allen_from_the_oscar_podium.

Daniel, Hugo. "Mickey Rourke Boxing Opponent Was Paid to Throw Fight." *Daily Mail Online* (UK), November 30, 2014. www.dailymail.co.uk/sport/boxing/article-2854855/Mickey-Rourke-s-opponent-paid-throw-fight-against-62-year-old-actor-sources-reveal-Elliot-Seymour-sleeping-rough-California-park.html.

"Daniel Day-Lewis on Playing Lincoln." *60 Minutes Overtime*, November 14, 2012. www.cbsnews.com/8301-504803_162-57536809-10391709/daniel-day-lewis-on-playing-lincoln.

Dannenbaum, Jed, Carroll Hodge, and Doe Mayer. *Creative Filmmaking from the Inside Out*. New York: Simon and Schuster, 2003.

Dargis, Manohla. "Running Away from the Circus." *New York Times*, September 10, 2010.

Davis, Wes. "Fighting Words." *New York Times*, February 26, 2005.

Day-Lewis, Daniel. Interview by Richard Brown. *Movies 101*. New York University, June 16, 2005.

———. Interview by Michael Parkinson. *Parkinson*. BBC, March 25, 2006.

———. Interview by Sophie Raworth. *The Andrew Marr Show*. BBC, January 27, 2013. www.bbc.co.uk/news/entertainment-arts-21227022.

DeAngelis, Michael. "Tom Cruise, The 'Couch Incident,' and the Limits of Public Elation." *Velvet Light Trap*, no. 65 (Spring 2010): 42–43.

DeCordova, Richard. *Picture Personalities and the Emergence of the Star System in America*. Urbana: University of Illinois Press, 1990.

Denby, David. "Fallen Idols." *New Yorker*, October 22, 2007.

De Rougemont, Denis. *Love in the Western World.* Trans. Montgomery Belgion. New York: Harper, 1956.

Dickinson, Kay. "Pop Stars Who Can't Act: The Limits of Celebrity 'Multi-Tasking.'" *Mediactive*, no. 2 (2004): 74–85.

Doane, Mary Ann. "Indexicality: Trace and Sign: Introduction." *differences* 18, no. 2 (2007): 1–6.

Doel, Marcus A., and David B. Clarke. "From Ramble City to the Screening of the Eye: *Blade Runner*, Death and Symbolic Exchange." In *The Cinematic City*, ed. David Clarke, 141–68. London: Routledge, 1997.

"Doris Day & Rock Hudson—Forever Friends." YouTube video, 2:47. Posted by "barayef." www.youtube.com/watch?v=z21shqPRTP8.

Doty, Alexander. *Making Things Perfectly Queer: Interpreting Mass Culture.* Minneapolis: University of Minnesota Press, 1993.

Du Bois, W.E.B. "The Talented Tenth." *The Negro Problem: A Series of Articles by Representative Negroes of To-day.* New York: James Pott and Company, 1903.

Duke, Brad. *Harrison Ford: The Films.* Jefferson, N.C.: McFarland, 2005.

Dyer, Richard. *The Culture of Queers.* London: Routledge, 2002.

———. *Heavenly Bodies: Film Stars and Society.* 2nd ed. London: Routledge, 2004.

———. "Rock—The Last Guy You'd Have Figured." In *You Tarzan: Masculinity, Movies and Men*, ed. Pat Kirkham and Janet Thumim, 27–34. New York: St. Martin's Press, 1993.

———. *Stars.* New ed. London: BFI Publishing, 2004.

Ebert, Roger. "Casey Affleck Levels about I'm Still Here." RogerEbert.com, September 22, 2010. blogs.suntimes.com/ebert/2010/09/casey_affleck_levels_about_im.html.

———. Review of *Aileen: Life and Death of a Serial Killer*, directed by Nick Broomfield. RogerEbert.com, September 7, 2010. www.rogerebert.com/reviews/aileen-life-and-death-of-a-serial-killer-2004.

———. Review of *I'm Still Here.* RogerEbert.com, September 7, 2010. rogerebert.suntimes.com/apps/pbcs.dll/article?AID=/20100907/REVIEWS/100909992.

———. Review of *Indiana Jones and the Kingdom of the Crystal Skull. Chicago Sun-Times,* May 18, 2008. rogerebert.suntimes.com/apps/pbcs.dll/article?AID=/20080518/REVIEWS/969461084/1023.

———. "Rock Hudson's Secret." RogerEbert.com, October 22, 2010. www.rogerebert.com/balder-and-dash/rock-hudsons-secret.

Eberwein, Robert, ed. *Acting for America: Movie Stars of the 1980s.* New Brunswick, N.J.: Rutgers University Press, 2010.

Edwards, Phil, and Alan McKenzie. "Interview with Ridley Scott." *Starburst*, no. 50 (1982): 24–31.

Ellis, John. "Stars as a Cinematic Phenomenon." In *Film Theory and Criticism*, ed. Leo Braudy and Marshall Cohen, 598–605. New York: Oxford University Press, 2004.

Ellmann, Richard. *Yeats: The Man and the Masks.* New York: Dutton, 1948.

Elsaesser, Thomas. "American Auteur Cinema: The Last—or First—Picture Show?" In *The Last Great American Picture Show,* ed. Thomas Elsaesser, Alexander Horwarth, and Noel King, 37–69. Amsterdam: Amsterdam University Press, 2004.

———. "Tales of Sound and Fury: Observations on the Family Melodrama." In *Home Is Where the Heart Is: Studies in Melodrama and the Woman's Film*, ed. Christine Gledhill, 61–62. London: BFI Publishing, 1987.

Emerson, Mark, and Eugene E. Pfaff Jr. *Country Girl: The Life of Sissy Spacek*. New York: St. Martin's Press, 1988.

Enty Lawyer. "The Amanda Bynes—Joaquin Phoenix Theory." *Crazy Days and Nights*. www.crazydaysandnights.net/2012/10/the-amanda-bynes-joaquin-phoenix-theory.html.

Fairclough, Kirsty. "Fame Is a Losing Game: Celebrity Gossip Blogging, Bitch Culture and Postfeminism." *Genders*, no. 48 (2008). www.genders.org/g48/g48_fairclough.html.

Fanon, Frantz. *Wretched of the Earth*. New York: Grove Press, 1963.

Feinberg, Scott. "Q and A with the *Lincoln* Team." *Hollywood Reporter*, December 14, 2012, www.hollywoodreporter.com/video/q-a-lincoln-team-403077.

Felperin, Leslie. Review of *I'm Still Here*. *Variety*. September 19, 2010. www.variety.com/review/VE1117943443?refcatid=31.

———. Review of *K-19: The Widowmaker*. *Sight and Sound* 12, no. 11 (2002): 48–49.

Filipovic, Jill. "Amanda Bynes' Public Meltdown Says More about Us Than about Her." *Guardian*, May 29, 2013. www.guardian.co.uk/commentisfree/2013/may/29/amanda-bynes-meltdown-why-we-watch.

"Final Bravery of Rock Hudson Moves Actors." *Sydney Morning Herald*, October 4, 1985, 10.

Finstad, Suzanne. *Natasha: The Biography of Natalie Wood*. New York: Three Rivers Press, 2001.

Fisher, Thomas. "Acting Disaster." *Celebrity Studies* 3, no. 3 (November 2012): 343–45.

Fleming, Michael. "Harrison Ford: The Playboy Interview." *Playboy Magazine*, July 2002.

Foucault, Michel. *Discipline and Punishment*. New York: Vintage Books, 1995.

Foundas, Scott. "Andrew Garfield to Star in Martin Scorsese's *Silence*." *Variety*, May 7, 2013. variety.com/2013/film/news/andrew-garfield-to-star-in-martin-scorseses-silence-exclusive-1200470625.

"Fox Settles Lawsuit with Woman Depicted in Film." *McCook Daily Gazette*, March 22, 2000.

Freer, Ian. "The Top Ten Harrison Ford Performances." *Empire*, April 2006, 137.

Gaines, Jane. "White Privilege and Looking Relations." *Cultural Critique* 4 (1985). Reprinted in *Film Theory: An Anthology*, ed. Robert Stam and Toby Miller, 715–32. London: Blackwell, 2000.

Gallagher, Mark. *Action Figures: Men Action Films and Contemporary Adventure Narratives*. New York: Palgrave Macmillan, 2006.

Gamson, Joshua. *Claims to Fame: Celebrity in Contemporary America*. Berkeley: University of California Press, 1994.

———. "The Unwatched Life Is Not Worth Living: The Elevation of the Ordinary in Celebrity Culture." *PMLA* 126, no. 4 (2011): 1063.

Gardner, Eriq. "Martin Scorsese Defends Taking 22 Years (and Counting) to Make 'Silence.'" *Hollywood Reporter*, November 27, 2012. www.hollywoodreporter.com/thr-esq/martin-scorsese-defends-taking-22-394439.

Gates, Philippa. "Acting His Age? The Resurrection of the '80s Action Heroes and Their Aging Stars." *Quarterly Review of Film and Video* 27 (2010): 276.
Gates, Phyllis. Interview by Larry King. *Larry King Live*. CNN, March 20, 2004.
Geraghty, Christine. "Re-examining Stardom: Questions of Texts, Bodies, and Performance." In *Rethinking Film Studies*, ed. Christine Gledhill and Linda Williams, 183–201. London: Arnold, 2000.
Girgus, Sam B. *Levinas and the Cinema of Redemption: Time, Ethics, and the Feminine*. New York: Columbia University Press, 2010.
Gledhill, Christine, ed. *Home Is Where the Heart Is: Studies in Melodrama and the Woman's Film*. London: BFI Books, 1987.
———. *Stardom: Industry of Desire*. New York: Routledge, 1991.
Gleiberman, Owen. Review of *I'm Still Here*, directed by Casey Affleck. *Entertainment Weekly*, September 17, 2010. www.ew.com/ew/article/0,,20419430,00.html.
———. Review of *Morning Glory*. *Entertainment Weekly*, November 12, 2010. www.ew.com/ew/article/0,,20440727,00.html.
Glock, Allison. "Blade Runner." *Telegraph Magazine*, May 10, 2008, 47–50.
Goode, James. *The Story of the Misfits*. New York: Bobbs-Merrill, 1963.
Goode, Mike. "Knowing Seizures: Julian Barnes, Jean-Paul Sartre, and the Erotics of the Postmodern Condition." *Textual Practice* 19, no. 1 (2005): 149–71.
Goodwin, Christopher. "Is Joaquin Cracking?" *Sunday Times*, November 4, 2012. www.thesundaytimes.co.uk/sto/culture/film_and_tv/film/article1157610.ece.
———. "What Makes Daniel Day Lewis Tick?" *Week*, January 21, 2008. www.theweek.co.uk/27833/what-makes-daniel-day-lewis-tick.
Govil, Nitin. "Conversion Narratives." *Media Fields Journal*, no. 2 (2011): 1.
Griffin, Nancy. "Harrison Ford: Hollywood Hero." *AARP: The Magazine*, July/August 2011. www.aarp.org/entertainment/movies-forgrownups/info-05-2011/harrison-ford-interview-full-throttle.html.
Grossberger, Lawrence. *Rolling Stone*, July 8, 1982.
Guiles, Fred Lawrence. *Legend: The Life and Death of Marilyn Monroe*. Lanham, Md.: Scarborough House Press, 1992.
Gwynedd, Myrddin. "Joquin Phoenix Makes a Shocking Debut . . . as a Rapper." *New Zealand Herald*, January 19, 2009. www.nzherald.co.nz/entertainment/news/article.cfm?c_id=1501119&objectid=10552547.
Hadleigh, Boze. *Conversations with My Elders*. New York: St. Martin's Press, 1988.
Hale, Mike. "Before an Actor Became an 'Actor.'" *New York Times*, March 17, 2013. www.nytimes.com/2013/03/17/arts/television/daniel-day-lewiss-1980s-bbc-dramas.html.
"Halle Berry Accepts Razzie Award for Worst Actress! [Krowns.com][Boardgame Cafe]." YouTube video, 5:25. Posted by "BizkitProductions," December 1, 2007. www.youtube.com/watch?v=NxLa73N6Rls.
Hansen, Kelly Dean. "Opus 77." *Listening Guides to the Works of Johannes Brahms*. www.kellydeanhansen.com/opus77.html.
Hansen, Miriam. *Babel and Babylon: Spectatorship in American Silent Film*. Cambridge, Mass.: Harvard University Press, 1994.

———. "Pleasure, Ambivalence, Identification." In *Star Texts: Image and Performance in Film and Television*, ed. Jeremy G. Butler, 266–98. Detroit: Wayne State University Press, 1991.

Hart, Hugh. "Ford Lightens Up (a Little)." *Boston Globe Online*, June 8, 2003.

Haskell, Molly. *From Reverence to Rape: The Treatment of Women in the Movies*. Chicago: University of Chicago Press, 1987.

Haun, Harry. "Rourke Mania: Darren Aronofsky Directs Portrait of Aging Wrestler." *Film Journal*, November 25, 2008. www.filmjournal.com/filmjournal/content_display/news-and-features/filmmakers/e3ifcb7b0c6e00764408fab87945d105104.

"Her (2013)." Internet Movie Database. www.imdb.com/title/tt1798709.

"Hilary Swank Interview." Contactmusic.com. www.contactmusic.com/interview/hswank.

Hill, James. *Rita Hayworth: A Memoir*. New York: Simon and Schuster, 1983.

Hirschberg, Lynn. "The New Frontier's Man." *New York Times Magazine*, November 11, 2007. www.nytimes.com/2007/11/11/magazine/11daylewis-t2.html?pagewanted=all&_r=0.

Hochman, David. "Harrison Ford Interview: Ford in Focus." *Readers' Digest*, May 2008.

Hodgens, R. M. Review of *Love with the Proper Stranger*. *Film Quarterly* 17, no. 3 (1964): 62.

Hofler, Robert. *The Man Who Invented Rock Hudson: The Pretty Boys and Dirty Deals of Henry Willson*. New York: Carroll and Graf, 2005.

Holmes, Su, and Diane Negra, eds. *In the Limelight and under the Microscope: Form and Functions of Female Celebrity*. New York: Continuum, 2011.

Holmes, Su, and Sean Redmond. *Framing Celebrity: New Directions in Celebrity Culture*. New York: Routledge, 2006.

Holmlund, Christine. "Celebrity, Ageing and Jackie Chan: Middle-aged Asian in Transnational Action." *Celebrity Studies* 1, no. 1 (2010): 97.

———. *Impossible Bodies: Femininity and Masculinity at the Movies*. New York: Routledge, 2002.

hooks, bell. *Black Looks: Race and Representation*. New York: South End Press, 1992.

Horeck, Tanya. "From Documentary to Drama: Capturing Aileen Wuornos." *Screen* 48, no. 2 (Summer 2007): 141–59.

———. *Public Rape: Representing Violation in Fiction and Film*. London: Routledge, 2004.

Horkins, Tony. "In Conversation with Harrison Ford." *Empire*, April 2006, 133–40.

Horowitz, Josh. "Mickey Rourke Explains His Preparation for 'The Wrestler': 'I Had Some Demons.'" MTV, September 11, 2008. www.mtv.com/news/articles/1594599/mickey-rourke-talks-about-training-wrestler.jhtml.

Howell, Peter. "Pity If Phoenix Packs It In." *Toronto Star*, April 10, 2009. www.thestar.com/news/2009/04/10/two_lovers_pity_if_phoenix_packs_it_in.html.

Howes, Keith G. "Hudson, Rock (1925–1985)." *GLBTQ Encyclopedia*. www.glbtq.com/arts/hudson_r.html.

"The Immigrant (2013)." Internet Movie Database. www.imdb.com/title/tt1951181. Accessed May 19, 2014.

"I'm Still Here (2010)." Box Office Mojo. boxofficemojo.com/movies/?id=imstillhere.htm.

"Indiana Jones and the Kingdom of the Crystal Skull (2008)." Internet Movie Database. www.imdb.com/title/tt0367882/business?ref_=tt_ql_dt_4.

Jackson, Laura. *Daniel Day-Lewis: The Biography*. New ed. London: John Blake, 2013.

Jameson, Fredric. "Reification and Utopia in Mass Culture." In *Signatures of the Visible*, 25–26. New York: Routledge, 1992.

Jarvinen, Lisa. Review of *Latina/o Stars in U.S. Eyes: The Makings and Meanings of Film and TV Stardom* by Mary C. Beltrán. *Journal of American Ethnic History* 31, no. 3 (2012): 72–76.

Jeffers, Tamara. "'Very Little Wrist Movement': Rock Hudson Acts Out Sexual Heterodoxy." *Canadian Journal of Communication* 31 (2006): 843–58.

Jefferson, Margo. *On Michael Jackson*. New York: Pantheon Books, 2006.

Jeffords, Susan. "The Big Switch: Hollywood Masculinity in the Nineties." In *Film Theory Goes to the Movies*, ed. Jim Collins, Hilary Radner, and Ava Preacher Collins, 196–208. New York: Routledge, 1993.

———. *Hard Bodies: Hollywood Masculinity in the Reagan Era*. New Brunswick, N.J.: Rutgers University Press, 1994.

———. *The Remasculinization of America: Gender and the Vietnam War*. Bloomington: Indiana University Press, 1989.

Jenkins, Garry. *Daniel Day-Lewis: The Fire Within*. London: Pan Books, 1995.

———. *Harrison Ford: Imperfect Hero*. New York: Pocket Books, 1998.

Jenkins, Patty. "Interview with Patty Jenkins and BT." *Monster*, directed by Patty Jenkins. Los Angeles: DEJ Productions, 2003. DVD.

———. "The Making of *Monster* Featurette." *Monster*, directed by Patty Jenkins. Los Angeles: DEJ Productions, 2003. DVD.

Jermyn, Deborah, and Sean Redmond, eds. *The Cinema of Kathryn Bigelow: Hollywood Transgressor*. New York: Wallflower Press, 2003.

"Joaquin Phoenix." Internet Movie Database. www.imdb.com/name/nm0001618.

"Joaquin Phoenix on Drugs, on Letterman (Full, HD)." YouTube video. February 12, 2009. www.youtube.com/watch?v=zVg-c9P2CKc&feature=related.

"Joaquin Phoenix on Letterman 9/22, Full Interview." YouTube video. Posted by "Jamie767," September 23, 2010. www.youtube.com/watch?v=xl3c_L2sy90&feature=related.

Johnson, Claudia. "A 'Sweet Face as White as Death': Jane Austen and the Politics of Female Sensibility." *Novel: A Forum on Fiction* 22, no. 2 (1989): 159–74.

Johnson, Michael L. *New Westers: The West in Contemporary American Culture*. Lawrence: University Press of Kansas, 1996.

Johnson, Sharon D. "Shaded Lives: African-American Women and Television." *Black Issues Book Review*, no. 44 (2002): 52–53.

Juhasz, Alexandra, and Jesse Lerner, eds. *F is for Phony: Fake Documentary and Truth's Undoing*. Minneapolis: University of Minnesota Press, 2006.

"Julia Roberts." In *International Dictionary of Films and Filmmakers*, 4th ed. galenet.galesgroup.com/servlet/BioRC.

Kael, Pauline. "Saint Cop." In *Deeper into Movies*. Boston: Little, Brown, 1972.

Kauffmann, Stanley. Review of *Sunday in New York*. *New Republic*, February 8, 1964, 24–25.

Keegan, Rebecca. "Harrison Ford." *Time*, February 13, 2006, 99.

Kemp, Philip. "Close-Up: Genre Bender." *Sight and Sound* 13, no. 7 (2003): 66.

Kermode, Mark. "The Year Hollywood Made a Mockery of the Documentary." *Observer*, January 9, 2011.

Kessler, Elizabeth Rodriguez. "Language, Nature, Gender, and Sexuality: Theoretical Approaches to Chicana and Chicano Literature." Ph.D. diss., University of Houston, 1998.

Khan, Yasmin Aga. "Remembering Rita." *People*, June 1, 1987, 72.

Kim, Ellen A. "Getting Ugly for Oscar." *Today.com*, February 26, 2004. today.msnbc.msn.com/id/4113650/ns/today-entertainment/t/getting-ugly-oscar.

King, Barry. "Stardom, Celebrity, and the Money Form." *Velvet Light Trap* 65 (Spring 2010): 7–19.

King, Neal. "Old Cops: Occupational Aging in a Film Genre." In *Staging Age: The Performance of Age in Theatre, Dance, and Film*, ed. Valerie Barnes Lipscomb and Leni Marshall, 57–81. New York: Palgrave Macmillan, 2010.

King, Noel. "The Last Good Time We Ever Had: Remembering the New Hollywood Cinema." In *The Last Great American Picture Show*, ed. Thomas Elsaesser, Alexander Horwarth, and Noel King, 19–36. Amsterdam: Amsterdam University Press, 2004.

Klinger, Barbara. *Melodrama and Meaning: History, Culture, and the Films of Douglas Sirk.* Bloomington: Indiana University Press, 1994.

Knee, Adam. "Celebrity Skins: The Illicit Textuality of the Celebrity Nude Magazine." In *Framing Celebrity: New Directions in Celebrity Culture*, ed. Su Holmes and Sean Redmond, 161–76. London: Routledge, 2006.

———. "The Dialectic of Female Power and Male Hysteria in *Play Misty for Me*." In *Screening the Male: Exploring Masculinities in the Hollywood Cinema,* ed. Steven Cohan and Ina Rae Hark, 87–102. London: Routledge, 1993.

Kobal, John. *Rita Hayworth: The Time, the Place and the Woman*. New York: W. W. Norton, 1977.

Krämer, Peter. *The New Hollywood: From Bonnie and Clyde to Star Wars*. London: Wallflower Press, 2005.

Krebs, Albin. "Rita Hayworth, Movie Legend Dies." *New York Times*, May 6, 1987. www.nytimes.com/learning/general/onthisday/bday/1017.html.

Kristeva, Julia. *Powers of Horror*. New York: Columbia University Press, 1982.

Kushner, Tony. *"Lincoln": The Screenplay*. New York: Theatre Communications Group, 2012.

Lacey, Nick. *Blade Runner*. London: York Press, 2000.

Lai, Adrienne. "Glitter and Grain: Aura and Authenticity in the Celebrity Photographs of Juergen Teller." In *Framing Celebrity: New Directions in Celebrity Culture*, ed. Su Holmes and Sean Redmond, 215–29. London: Routledge, 2006.

Lambert, Gavin. *Natalie Wood: A Life*. New York: Back Stage Books, 2005.

Lankester, Mark. "The Craziest Ways Daniel Day-Lewis Prepared for Roles." *Yahoo! UK Movies Features*, January 28, 2013. uk.movies.yahoo.com/the-craziest-ways-daniel-day-lewis-prepared-for-roles-171013867.html.

LaSalle, Mick. Review of *Crossing Over*. *San Francisco Chronicle*, March 13, 2009. www.sfgate.com/cgibin/article.cgi?f=/c/a/2009/03/13/DDoC16DE15.DTL.

Lauren [pseud.]. "Joaquin Phoenix Rejoins Hollywood Just to Complain about Hollywood." *Crasstalk*, October 18, 2012. crasstalk.com/2012/10/joaquin-phoenix-rejoins-hollywood-just-to-complain-about-hollywood.

Lazar, Rochelle L. "The Achievement of Harrison Ford." American Film Institute, 2000. www.afi.com/tvevents/laa/laa00.aspx.

Leaming, Barbara. *If This Was Happiness*. New York: Viking, 1989.

———. *Marilyn Monroe*. New York: Three Rivers Press, 1998.

Lee, Benjamin. "Can Playing a Racist Restore Halle Berry's Mojo." *Guardian*, October 2, 2009.

Lev, Peter. *American Films of the 70s: Conflicting Visions*. Austin: University of Texas Press, 2000.

Levitt, Linda. "Death on Display: Reifying Stardom through Hollywood's Dark Tourism." *Velvet Light Trap* 65 (2010): 62–70.

"Liberace to Be Tested for AIDS." *Sun Sentinel*, February 7, 1987. articles.sun-sentinel.com/1987-02-07/news/8701080508_1_sabas-rosas-coroner-raymond-carrillo-death-certificate.

"Liberace, Behind the Candelabra: Life Story of Liberace Generates Huge Buzz at Cannes." *New Zealand Herald*, May 23, 2013.

"Lincoln 2012." Box Office Mojo. www.boxofficemojo.com/movies/?id=lincoln.htm.

Lincoln, Anne E., and Michael Patrick Allen. "Double Jeopardy in Hollywood: Age and Gender in the Careers of Film Actors, 1926–1999." *Sociological Forum* 19, no. 4 (December 2004): 611–31.

Lipkin, Steven N., Derek Paget, and Jane Roscoe. "Docudrama and Mock-Documentary: Defining Terms, Proposing Canons." In *Docufictions: Essays on the Intersection of Documentary and Fiction Filmmaking*, ed. Gary D. Rhodes and John Parris Springer, 11–26. Jefferson, N.C.: McFarland, 2006.

Littler, Jo, and Steve Cross. "Celebrity and Schadenfreude: The Cultural Economy of Fame in Freefall." *Cultural Studies* 24, no. 3 (May 2010): 395–417.

Loewestein, Lael. "The Buddy Factor." *New York Daily News*, June 8, 2003.

Lopes, Valerie. "Joaquin Phoenix—Screw You Too . . . A Letter from a Lingering Fan." *Open Salon*, February 13, 2009. open.salon.com/blog/valerie_lopes/2009/02/13/joaquin_phoenix_screw_you_too_a_letter_from_a_lingering_fan.

Loselle, Andrea. "Freud/Derrida As Fort/Da and the Repetitive Eponym." *MLN* 97, no. 5 (December 1982): 1180–85.

Low, Shari. "Overgrrown Chaps Give Me a Hairy Fit." *Daily Record*, February 5, 2009. www.dailyrecord.co.uk/news/politics/overgrown-chaps-give-me-a-hairy-fit-1008336.

Lucia, Cynthia. "Natalie Wood." *Oxford Bibliographies*. www.oxfordbibliographies.com/obo/page/cinema-and-media-studies. January 7, 2013.

———. "Natalie Wood: Studio Stardom and Hollywood in Transition." In *The Wiley-Blackwell History of American Film, Volume III: 1946 to 1965*, ed. Cynthia Lucia, Roy Grundmann, and Art Simon, 26–61. Malden, Mass.: Wiley-Blackwell, 2012.

Luciano, Dana. "Coming Around Again: The Queer Momentum of *Far from Heaven*." *GLQ: A Journal of Lesbian and Gay Studies* 13, no. 2–3 (2007): 249–72.

Luckett, Moya. "Toxic: The Implosion of Britney Spears's Star Image." *Velvet Light Trap*, no. 65 (Spring 2010): 39–41.

Luitjers, Guus. *Marilyn: The Never Ending Dream*. London: Plexus Publishing, 1986.

Lyman, Rick. "Marlon Brando, Oscar-Winning Actor, Is Dead at 80." *New York Times*, July 2, 2004. www.nytimes.com/2004/07/02/movies/02CND-BRANDO.html.

MacKinnon, Kenneth. *Love, Tears, and the Male Spectator*. London: Associated University Presses, 2002.

"Mae West–Rock Hudson 1957 Award Show." YouTube video, 2:06. Uploaded by Mann George, August 4, 2007. www.youtube.com/watch?v=mZUVP_nsRjw.

Mailer, Norman. *Marilyn*. New York: Grosset and Dunlap, 1974.

Maltby, Richard. *Hollywood*. 2nd ed. Oxford: Blackwell, 2003.

Marshall, P. David. *Celebrity and Power: Fame in Contemporary Culture*. Minneapolis: University of Minnesota Press, 1997.

Mauceri, Joe. "What Lies Beneath. A Shivers Interview." *Shivers* 82 (2000): 30–32.

May, Elaine Tyler. *Homeward Bound: American Families in the Cold War Era*. New York: Basic Books, 1988.

Mayne, Judith. "Walking the *Tightrope* of Feminism and Male Desire." In *Men in Feminism*, ed. Alice A. Jardine and Paul Smith, 62–70. New York: Methuen, 1987.

McCann, Graham. *Rebel Males: Clift, Brando, and Dean*. New Brunswick, N.J.: Rutgers University Press, 1991.

McDonald, Paul. *Hollywood Stardom*. Malden, Mass.: Wiley-Blackwell, 2013.

McGrath, Charles. "Abe Lincoln as You've Never Heard Him: Daniel Day-Lewis on Playing Abraham Lincoln." *New York Times*, November 4, 2012. www.nytimes.com/2012/11/04/movies/daniel-day-lewis-on-playing-abraham-lincoln.html?pagewanted=all.

McLean, Adrienne. *Being Rita Hayworth: Labor, Identity, and Hollywood Stardom*. New Brunswick, N.J.: Rutgers University Press, 2004.

———. "Feeling and the Filmed Body: Judy Garland and the Kinesics of Suffering." *Film Quarterly* 56, no. 3 (2002): 2–15.

———. "I'm a Cansino: Transformation, Ethnicity, and Authenticity in the Construction of Rita Hayworth, American Love Goddess." *Journal of Film and Video* 44, no. 3–4 (1992–93): 8–25.

McLellan, Dennis. "Obituaries: Phyllis Gates, 80; Former Talent Agency Secretary Was Briefly Married to Rock Hudson in '50s." *Los Angeles Times*, January 12, 2006. articles.latimes.com/2006/jan/12/local/me-gates.

McNary, Dave. "Liam Neeson Joins Martin Scorsese's 'Silence.'" *Variety*, January 31, 2014. variety.com/2014/film/news/liam-neeson-joins-martin-scorseses-silence-1201080196/.

Menard, Valerie. "Luscious Latinas." *Hispanic* 10, no. 5 (1997): 20–25.

Mercer, Kobena. "Monster Metaphors: Notes on Michael Jackson's Thriller." In *Stardom: Industry of Desire*, ed. Christine Gledhill, 305–21. London: Routledge, 1991.

Metz, Christian. *The Imaginary Signifier: Psychoanalysis and the Cinema*. Trans. Celia Britton et al. Bloomington: Indiana University Press, 1982.

Meyer, Richard. "Rock Hudson's Body." *Inside/Out: Lesbian Theories, Gay Theories*, ed. Diana Fuss, 259–90. London: Routledge, 2013.

Meyers, Jeffrey. *The Genius and the Goddess: Arthur Miller and Marilyn Monroe*. Urbana: University of Illinois Press, 2009.

Michener, Charles, and Martin Kasindorf. "Year of the Actress." *Newsweek*, February 1977, 56–66.
"Mickey Rourke." *Boxrec.* www.boxrec.com/media/index.php/Mickey_Rourke.
"Mickey Rourke's Spirit Award Speech: Hilarious & Curse-Laden (VIDEO)." *Huffington Post*, February 22, 2009. www.huffingtonpost.com/2009/02/22/mickey-rourkes-spirit-awa_n_168965.html.
"Mickey Rourke—Trivia." Internet Movie Database. http://m.imdb.com/name/nm0000620/trivia.
Migliore, John. Review of *Firewall. Premiere Magazine*, February 2006. www.premiere.com/moviereviews/2478/firewall.html.
Miller, Arthur. *After the Fall.* New York: Penguin Books, 1964.
———. *I Don't Need You Any More.* New York: Bantam Books, 1968.
———. "Making *The Misfits.*" Directed by Gail Levin. *The Misfits,* directed by John Huston. Image Entertainment, 2001. DVD.
———. *The Misfits.* London: Methuen, 2002.
———. "My Wife Marilyn: An Affectionate Tribute to Her Feat." *Life*, December 22, 1958, 146–47.
———. *Timebends: A Life.* New York: Grove Press, 1987.
Miller, Arthur, and Serge Toubiana. *The Misfits: Story of a Shoot.* London: Phaidon Inc Ltd., 2000.
Mitchell, Elvis. "Joaquin Phoenix." *Interview Magazine*, October 18, 2012. www.interviewmagazine.com/film/joaquin-phoenix.
Modleski, Tania. *Feminism without Women: Culture and Criticism in a Postfeminist Age.* London: Routledge, 1991.
———. "Time and Desire in the Woman's Film." *Cinema Journal* 23, no. 3 (1984): 19–30.
Monaco, Paul. *History of the American Cinema, Volume 8: The Sixties: 1960–1969.* Berkeley: University of California Press, 2001.
Monroe, Marilyn, with Ben Hecht. *My Story.* Lanham, Md.: Taylor Trade Publishing, 2007.
Moore, Dick. *Twinkle, Twinkle, Little Star (But Don't Have Sex or Take the Car).* New York: Harper and Row, 1984.
Moore, Matthew. "Halle Berry Apologises for 'Jewish Nose' Gaffe." *Telegraph*, October 25, 2007.
Morella, Joe, and Edward Z. Epstein. *Rita: The Life of Rita Hayworth.* New York: Delacorte Press, 1983.
Morgan, Piers. "When Piers Met Mickey Rourke." *GQ.com* (UK), July 22, 2010. www.gqmagazine.co.uk/entertainment/articles/2010-07/22/gq-film-piers-morgan-interviews-mickey-rourke.
Morrison, Toni. *The Bluest Eye.* New York: Plume, 1994.
Morrissey, Tracie Egan. "Amanda Bynes: Breakdown of a Meltdown." *Jezebel*, September 18, 2012. jezebel.com/5944292/amanda-bynes-a-breakdown-of-a-meltdown.
"The Movie Show." Special Broadcasting Service. www.sbs.com.au/films/video/11682371946/interview-with-kimberly-peirce-and-hilary-swank.
"Movie Star into Actress." *Newsweek*, February 26, 1962, 54–57.

Mulvaney, Kieran. "The Manny/Freddie/Mickey Story." ESPN, March 8, 2010. sports.espn.go.com/sports/boxing/news/story?id=4974064.

Mulvey, Laura. *Visual and Other Pleasures*. 2nd ed. Hampshire: Palgrave MacMillan, 2004.

———. "Visual Pleasures and Narrative Cinema." *Screen* 16, no. 3 (Autumn 1975): 6–18.

Naremore, James. *Acting in the Cinema*. Berkeley: University of California Press, 1988.

"Natalie Wood: Child of Change." *Look* 27, no. 16 (1963): 91–94.

"Natalie Wood Investigation Prompted by Boat Captain's Comments." *Los Angeles Times*, November 17, 2011. latimesblogs.latimes.com/lanow/2011/11/natalie-wood-investigation prompted-by-boat-captain-comments.html.

Nathan, Ian. "The New Ford Solo." *Empire*, November 2002, 115–19.

Neale, Steve. "Questions of Genre." *Screen* 31, no. 1 (1990).

———. "Reflections on Men and Mainstream Cinema." Prologue to *Screening the Male: Exploring Masculinities in the Hollywood Cinema*, ed. Steven Cohan and Ina Rae Hark, 9–22. New York: Routledge, 1993.

"*Newsweek*'s 2008 Oscar Roundtable." Youtube video, 4:49. Posted by "NewsweekVideo," January 18, 2008. www.youtube.com/watch?v=Hbm9KgdLk9s&list=PLA1F8BE3AADAFA035.

Nunn, Heather, and Anita Biressi. "'A Trust Betrayed': Celebrity and the Work of Emotion." *Celebrity Studies* 1, no. 1 (2010): 49–64.

O'Connell, James J. "Confessiones 3/1/1." *Augustine: Confessions*. Oxford: Oxford University Press, 1992.

Oliver, Myna. "James Hill; Producer-Writer Married Rita Hayworth, Teamed with Burt Lancaster." *Los Angeles Times*, January 16, 2001, B12.

Olivier, Sir Laurence. "The Prince and the Showgirl." In *All the Available Light: A Marilyn Monroe Reader*, ed. Yona Zeldis McDonogh, 150–64. New York: Touchstone Books, 2002.

Oppenheimer, Jerry, and Jack Vitek. *Idol Rock Hudson: The True Story of an American Film Hero*. New York: Villard Books, 1986.

O'Sullivan, Michael. "Is He Putting Us On? Maybe." Review of *I'm Still Here*, directed by Casey Affleck. *Washington Post*, September 10, 2010. www.washingtonpost.com/gog/movies/im-still-here-2010-i,1168087/critic-review.html#reviewNum1.

Palmer, Martyn. "'I Know What It's Like to Be the Outsider': Hilary Swank on Her Journey from Trailer Park to Tinseltown." *Daily Mail*, January 7, 2011. www.dailymail.co.uk/home/you/article-1341187/Hilary-Swank-journey-trailer-park-Tinseltown-I-know-like-outsider.html.

———. "In Private, I Live a Quiet Life. My Extreme Sport Is Acting." *Mail Online*, October 20, 2012. www.dailymail.co.uk/home/moslive/article-2219521/Joaquin-Phoenix-In-private-I-live-quiet-life-My-extreme-sport-acting.html.

Palmer, R. Barton. "Julia Roberts: Cultural Phenomenon." In *Pretty People: Movie Stars of the 1990s*, ed. Anna Everett, 85–102. New Brunswick, N.J.: Rutgers University Press, 2012.

———, ed. *Larger Than Life: Movie Stars of the Fifties*. New Brunswick, N.J.: Rutgers University Press, 2010.

Parreñas-Shimizu, Celine. *The Hypersexuality of Race*. Durham, N.C.: Duke University Press, 2007.

Patterson, John. "Profile: Halle Berry." *Guardian*, August 6, 2004.

———. "What's Up, Joaquin?" *Guardian*, March 17, 2009. www.guardian.co.uk/film/2009/mar/17/joaquin-phoenix-letterman-show.

Pearlman, Cindy. "Ford Stays Focused Despite Hollywood 'Hardships.'" *Chicago Sun-Times*, June 8, 2003.

Peirce, Kimberly. "Featurette." *Boys Don't Cry*. Directed by Kimberly Peirce. Los Angeles: Twentieth Century–Fox, 1999. DVD.

———. Interview by Scott Tobias. *A. V. Club*, October 27, 1999. www.avclub.com/articles/kimberly-peirce,13626.

Peña Ovalle, Priscilla. *Dance and the Hollywood Latina*. New Brunswick, N.J.: Rutgers University Press, 2011.

Pepitone, Lena, and William Stadiem. *Marilyn Monroe Confidential*. New York: Pocket Books, 1979.

Perren, Alisa. *Indie, Inc.: Miramax and the Transformation of Hollywood in the 1990s*. Austin: University of Texas Press, 2012.

Persall, Steve. "Phoenix Isn't Rising." *St. Petersburg Times*, September 16, 2010.

Petersen, Anne Helen. "Rules of the Game: A Century of Hollywood Publicity." *Virginia Quarterly Review* 89 (2013). www.vqronline.org/articles/rules-game.

Pidduck, Julianne. "Risk and Queer Spectatorship." *Screen* 41, no. 1 (2001): 98.

Porton, Richard. "Acting in the Grand Manner: An Interview with Christopher Plummer." *Cineaste* 34, no. 4 (2009): 12–17.

Priore, Domenic, and Becky Ebenkamp. *Look! Listen! Vibrate! Smile!* New York: Last Gasp, 1995.

Rader, Dotson. "Dark Star. Harrison Ford: Hollywood's Melancholic Hero." *Sunday Times Magazine*, August 11, 2002.

Rappaport, Mark. "Notes on *Rock Hudson's Home Movies*." *Film Quarterly* 49, no. 4 (Summer 1996): 16–22.

———. "The Sirk-Hudson Connection." *Criterion Collection*, January 21, 2009. www.criterion.com/current/posts/935-the-sirk-hudson-connection.

Rapping, Elayne. *Media-tions: Forays into the Culture and Gender Wars*. Boston: South End Press, 1994.

Rea, Steven. "Funny, Filthy, Careful, Compassionate." *Philadelphia Inquirer*, December 23, 2012. articles.philly.com/2012-12-23/news/35983981_1_skyfall-james-bond-magic-mike.

Redmond, Sean. "Intimate Fame Everywhere." In *Framing Celebrity: New Directions in Celebrity Culture*, ed. Su Holmes and Sean Redmond, 27–43. London: Routledge, 2006.

Redmond, Sean, and Su Holmes, eds. *Stardom and Celebrity: A Reader*. London: Sage Publications, 2007.

Reed, Christopher. "Phyllis Gates: Token Wife to a Star." *Guardian*, March 15, 2006. www.guardian.co.uk/news/2006/mar/16/guardianobituaries.obituaries.

"Rock Hudson—On 'Douglas Sirk'—1980." YouTube video, 3:00, posted by "KayRHvids cellar," December 23, 2012, www.youtube.com/watch?v=enk3x23a030.

Rogin, Michael Paul. *Ronald Reagan, the Movie: And Other Episodes in Political Demonology*. Berkeley: University of California Press, 1987.

Rojek, Chris. *Celebrity*. London: Reaktion Books, 2004.

Rosen, Philip. *Change Mummified: Cinema, Historicity, Theory*. Minneapolis: University of Minnesota Press, 2001.

Rottenberg, Josh. "Joaquin Phoenix's Rap Career: An Elaborate Hoax?" *Entertainment Weekly*, January 27, 2009. insidemovies.ew.com/2009/01/27/joaquin-phoenix-2.

Rourke, Mickey. Interview by James Lipton. *Inside the Actor's Studio*. Bravo, August 31, 2009.

———. Interview by Piers Morgan. *Piers Morgan Tonight*. CNN, November 19, 2011. transcripts.cnn.com/TRANSCRIPTS/1111/19/pmt.01.html.

"Rourke Rebounds with Wrestler." *Sydney Morning Herald*, January 8, 2009. www.smh.com.au/entertainment/movies/rourke-rebounds-with-wrestler-20100218-ofcc.html.

Rulli, Marti, with Dennis Davern. *Goodbye Natalie, Goodbye Splendour*. Beverly Hills, Calif.: Medallion Publishing, 2009.

Sanello, Frank. *Julia Roberts*. Edinburgh: Mainstream Publishing, 2000.

Schickel, Richard. *Conversations with Scorsese*. New York: Alfred A. Knopf, 2011.

Schnabel, Julian. "Ring Free." *German Vanity Fair*, January 2009. Reprinted on *The Fashion Spot* forums, forums.thefashionspot.com/f50/mickeyrourke-77485-10.html.

Schwarzbaum, Lisa. Review of *Firewall. Entertainment Weekly Online*, July 2006. www.ew.com/ew/article/0,,1157675,00.html.

Scorsese, Martin. "Director Commentary." *Gangs of New York*. Directed by Martin Scorsese. Burbank, Calif.: Miramax Lionsgate, 2011. DVD.

Scott, A. O. "To Feel a City Seethe." *New York Times*, December 20, 2002. www.nytimes.com/2002/12/20/movies/film-review-to-feel-a-city-seethe.html?pagewanted=all&src=pm.

Seitz, Matt Zoller. "I'm Still Here: Joaquin Phoenix's Fascinating Performance Art." *Salon*, September 10, 2010. www.salon.com/2010/09/10/im_still_here_joaquin_phoenix.

Sellers, Robert. *Harrison Ford: A Biography*. London: Warner Books, 1993.

Sessums, Kevin. "Fighting Irish." *Vanity Fair*, July 1991. www.vanityfair.com/hollywood/features/1991/07/mickey-rourke-199107.

Sharkey, Betsey. "Joaquin Phoenix Can Leave Hollywood—As Long as He Comes Back." *Los Angeles Times*, October 24, 2012. articles.latimes.com/2012/oct/24/entertainment/la-et-mn-joaquin-phoenix-essay-20121025.

Shaviro, Steven. *Post-Cinematic Affect*. London: Zero Books, 2010.

"The Show Goes On in AIDS Battle." BBC News. November 24, 2003. news.bbc.co.uk/2/hi/entertainment/3281609.stm.

Sirk, Douglas. "Commentary." *Magnificent Obsession*. Directed by Douglas Sirk. Hollywood: Paramount, 2009. DVD.

———. *Sirk on Sirk: Interviews with Jon Halliday*. London: Faber and Faber, 1997.

Skerpan-Wheeler, Elizabeth. "The First 'Royal': Charles I as Celebrity." *PMLA* 126, no. 4 (October 2011): 912–34.

Sklar, Robert. *City Boys: Cagney, Bogart, Garfield*. Princeton, N.J.: Princeton University Press, 1992.

———. "*Million Dollar Baby:* A Split Decision." *Cineaste* 30, no. 3 (June 2005): 8.

Slade, Brian. "Rock Hudson's Hollywood." *Harvard Gay and Lesbian Review* (Spring 1996): 18–20.

Sloane, Judy. "What Lies Beneath." *Starburst* 268 (December 2000): 22–25.

Smith, David. "People: Is Joaquin Phoenix Just Another Actor in Meltdown, or Is This a Hoax?" *Observer*, February 15, 2009. www.guardian.co.uk/film/2009/feb/15/joaquin-phoenix-letterman-behaviour.

Smith, Neal. Review of *Firewall*. BBC, March 2006. www.bbc.co.uk/films/2006/03/17/firewall_2006_review.shtml. 27/04/2007.

Smolowe, Jill. "Harrison Ford." *People*, March 8, 1999, 155.

Soares, Andre. "AIDS/Lifecycle 2012: A Letter from Doris Day." *Alt Film Guide*. www.altfg.com/blog/movie/doris-day-rock-hudson-aids/.

Sobchack, Vivian. *Carnal Thoughts: Embodiment and Moving Image Culture*. Berkeley: University of California Press, 2004.

Solomons, Jason. "Observer Review: Venice Film Festival." *Observer*, September 12, 2010. www.guardian.co.uk/film/2010/sep/12/venice-film-festival-vincent-gallo-joaquin-phoenix.

Sontag, Susan. *Against Interpretation*. New York: Farrar, Straus and Giroux, 1961.

Spacek, Sissy. *My Extraordinary Ordinary Life*. New York: Hyperion, 2012.

Spada, James. *Julia Roberts: Her Life*. New York: St. Martin's Press, 2004.

Spoto, Donald. *Marilyn Monroe: The Biography*. New York: Harper Paperbacks, 1993.

Stacey, Jackie. "Feminine Fascinations: Forms of Identification in Star-Audience Relations." In *Stardom: Industry of Desire*, ed. Christine Gledhill, 145–68. London: Routledge, 1991.

———. *Hollywood Cinema and Female Spectatorship*. London: Routledge, 1994.

Stam, Robert. *Film Theory: An Introduction*. Oxford: Blackwell Publishers, 2000.

Stam, Robert, and Toby Miller, eds. *Film Theory: An Anthology*. London: Blackwell, 2000.

Stamp, Shelley. "Horror, Femininity, and Carrie's Monstrous Puberty." *Journal of Film and Video* 43, no. 4 (1991): 33–44.

———. "'It's a Long Way to Filmland': Starlets, Screen Hopefuls and Extras in Early Hollywood." In *American Cinema's Transitional Era: Audiences, Institutions, Practices*, ed. Charlie Keil and Shelley Stamp. Berkley: University of California Press, 2004.

"Steven Spielberg's 'Obama.'" YouTube video, 1:56. Posted by "The White House," April 27, 2013. www.youtube.com/watch?v=ZyU213nhrho.

Stone, Jay. "The Fine Line between Reality and Hoax." *Gazette*, September 24, 2010, final edition.

"Strange Doings of Actress at Practice." *Life*, January 28, 1957, 96–100.

Studlar, Gaylyn. *This Mad Masquerade: Stardom and Masculinity in the Jazz Age*. New York: Columbia University Press, 1996.

Sullivan, Chris. "I've Hacked Off So Many People in Hollywood: Who the Hell Would Give Me an Oscar?" *Daily Mail*, February 20, 2009. www.dailymail.co.uk/tvshowbiz/article-1150506/Mickey-Rourke-Ive-hacked-people-Hollywood-hell-Oscar.html.

Taraborelli, J. Randy. *The Secret Life of Marilyn Monroe*. New York: Grand Central Publishing, 2009.

Tartaglione-Vialatte, Nancy. "Can Scorsese 'Silence' Daniel Day-Lewis?" *Hollywood.com*, February 3, 2009. www.hollywood.com/news/movies/5389081/can-scorsese-silence-daniel-day-lewis?page=all.

Tasker, Yvonne. *Spectacular Bodies: Gender, Genre and the Action Cinema*. New York: Routledge, 1993.

Tate, Ryan. "Did Robert Downey Jr. Really Just Accuse Kirk Douglass of a Brutal Rape?" *Gawker*, March 15, 2012. gawker.com/5893793/did-robert-downey-jr-really-just-accuse-kirk-douglas-of-a-brutal-rape.

Taylor, Aaron. "Playing to the Balcony: Screen Acting, Distance, and Cavellian Theatricality." In *Stages of Reality: Theatricality in Cinema*, ed. André Loiselle and Jeremy Maron, 185–203. Toronto: University of Toronto Press, 2012.

Thomas, William. "Hall of Fame." *Empire*, June 2002.

Thomson, David. "Biographical Dictionary of Film, No. 29: Johnny Depp." *Guardian*, January 10, 2008. www.guardian.co.uk/film/filmblog/2008/jan/11/biographicaldictionaryoffil9.

Todd, Janet. *Gender, Art and Death*. Cambridge: Polity Press, 2013.

"Tom Cruise." Internet Movie Database. www.imdb.com/name/nm0000129/?ref_=sr_1.

"Tom Cruise Goes Crazy on Oprah (Danger)." YouTube video. Posted by "Approvedby-Chuck," September 8, 2008. www.youtube.com/watch?v=frI_BUkH5OY.

"Tom Cruise Kills Oprah Extended Version." YouTube video. Posted by "maxishine," September 21, 2006. www.youtube.com/watch?v=CRbhE3GRiUE.

Toole, F. X. "Million $$$ Baby." *Rope Burns: Stories from the Corner*. New York: Harper-Collins, 2000.

"Top Ten Money Making Stars." Quigley Publishing Company. www.quigleypublishing.com/MPalmanac/Top10/Top10_lists.html.

Turner, Graeme. *Understanding Celebrity*. London: Sage Publications, 2004.

"2008 Yearly Box Office Results." Box Office Mojo. boxofficemojo.com/yearly/chart/?view2=worldwide&yr=2008.

Vincent, William. "Rita Hayworth at Columbia: The Fabrication of a Star." In *Columbia Pictures: Portrait of a Studio*, ed. Bernard F. Dick, 118–30. Lexington: University Press of Kentucky, 1992.

Wagner, Robert J., with Scott Eyman. *Pieces of My Heart: A Life*. New York: Harper Entertainment, 2008.

Wallace, Debra L. "Harrison Ford: el último gran héroe." *Cinemanía* 138 (March 2007): 84–87.

Walsh, Keri. "Why Does Mickey Rourke Give Pleasure?" *Critical Inquiry* 37, no. 1 (2010): 131–62.

Waxman, Sharon. *Rebels on the Backlot: Six Maverick Directors and How They Conquered the Hollywood Studio System*. New York: HarperCollins, 2005.

Weatherby, W. J. *Conversations with Marilyn*. New York: Paragon House, 1992.

Wilcox, Earl J. "Abraham Lincoln on Daniel Day-Lewis." *New Verse News*, November 29, 2012. newversenews.blogspot.com/2012/11/abraham-lincoln-on-daniel-day-lewis.html.

Williams, Linda. *Playing the Race Card: Melodramas of Black and White from Uncle Tom to O. J. Simpson*. Princeton, N.J.: Princeton University Press, 2002.

Williams, Rebecca. "From Beyond Control to In Control: Investigation Drew Barrymore's Feminist/Agency/Authorship." In *Stardom and Celebrity: A Reader*, ed. Sean Redmond and Su Holmes, 111–25. London: Sage Publications, 2007.

Windolf, Jim. "Keys to the Kingdom." *Vanity Fair*, February 2008.

Winter, Jessica. "Hail to the Chief." *Time*, November 5, 2012. entertainment.time.com/2012/10/25/daniel-day-lewis-in-lincoln-hail-to-thechief/.

Wolfe, Donald H. *The Assassination of Marilyn Monroe*. New York: Warner Books, 1999.

Wood, Lana. *Natalie: A Memoir by Her Sister Lana Wood*. New York: G. P. Putnam's Sons, 1984.

Wood, Robin. *Hollywood from Vietnam to Reagan . . . and Beyond*. New York: Columbia University Press, 2003.

"Writer: David Letterman Faked Interview with Joaquin Phoenix." *PopEater*. www.popeater.com/2010/09/20/david-letterman-faked-interview-joaquin-phoenix.

Yarbrough, Jeff. "Rock Hudson: On Camera and Off, The Tragic News That He Is the Most Famous Victim of an Infamous Disease, AIDS, Unveils the Hidden Life of a Longtime Hollywood Hero." *People*, August 12, 1985.

Zacharek, Stephanie. Review of *Extraordinary Measures*. *Salon*, June 2010. www.salon.com/topic/extraordinary_measures/.

Zakarin, Jordan. "Steven Spielberg Reveals Daniel Day-Lewis' Original *Lincoln* Rejection Letter." *Hollywood Reporter*, January 8, 2013. www.hollywoodreporter.com/news/steven-spielberg-reveals-daniel-day-409709.

CONTRIBUTORS

PETER J. BAILEY is the author of *Reading Stanley Elkin*, *The Reluctant Film Art of Woody Allen*, and *Rabbit (Un)Redeemed: The Drama of Belief in John Updike's Fiction*. With Sam B. Girgus, he co-edited Wiley-Blackwell's *Companion to Woody Allen*. He is Piskor Professor of English Emeritus at St. Lawrence University in Canton, New York, where he teaches creative writing and film.

REBECCA BELL-METEREAU, professor of English and director of the Media Studies Minor at Texas State University, is the author of *Hollywood Androgyny*, *Simone Weil on Politics, Religion and Society*, and chapters in *A Little Solitaire: John Frankenheimer and American Film*; *Acting for America: Movie Stars of the 1980s*; *Authorship in Film Adaptation*; *Cinema and Modernity*; *American Cinema of the 1950s: Themes and Variations*; *Film and Television after 9/11*; *Ladies and Gentlemen, Boys and Girls: Gender in Film at the End of the Twentieth Century*; *Bad: Infamy, Darkness, Evil, and Slime on Screen*; and *Cultural Conflicts in Twentieth Century Literature*, as well as articles in *College English*, *Journal of Popular Film and Television*, and *Quarterly Review of Film and Video*.

DENNIS BINGHAM is professor of English and director of the Film Studies Program at Indiana University-Purdue University Indianapolis. He is the author of *Acting Male: Masculinities in the Films of James Stewart, Jack Nicholson, and Clint Eastwood*; *Whose Lives Are They Anyway? The Biopic as Contemporary Film Genre*; articles in *Cinema Journal* and *a/b: Auto/Biography Studies*; essays in numerous anthologies; and entries in *Oxford Bibliographies Online* and *The Schirmer Encyclopedia of Film*.

CHARLES BURNETTS teaches film in the Department of Philosophy and Religious Studies at Kings University College, The University of Western Ontario. He is the author of *Improving Passions: Sentimental Aesthetics and American Film*. He has published articles in the *Journal of Film and Video, New Review of Film and Television Studies*, and *Scope*, and has contributed chapters to *The Women of James Bond* and *Time-Travel in the Media*.

MEGAN CARRIGY is the assistant director for Academic Programs at NYU Sydney. Before joining New York University, she was the Education Projects Manager at the Australian Film Television and Radio School (AFTRS). She has taught film and media studies at the University of New South Wales (UNSW) and at the University of Technology, Sydney, in Australia. For four years, she programmed Sydney's annual queerDOC and Mardi Gras Film Festivals, building partnerships with local and international distributors, filmmakers, festivals, and community organizations. She was awarded the Best Doctoral Thesis Prize in the Faculty of Arts and Social Sciences at UNSW in 2011 for her Ph.D. thesis entitled "Performing History, Troubling Reference: Tracking the Screen Reenactment." She has also been awarded the Mari Kuttna Memorial Prize for Film Studies at the University of Sydney. Her research interests include contemporary film theory, reenactment, film stars, early American cinema, and the cinema of Ritwik Ghatak.

COLLEEN GLENN is an assistant professor at the College of Charleston (South Carolina), where she teaches courses in film studies and writing. Glenn received her Ph.D. from the University of Kentucky, completing a dissertation on Jimmy Stewart's post–World War II films and their relationship to war trauma. Her research focuses on star studies, masculinity studies, and film exhibition. Glenn's essay "The Traumatized Veteran: A New Look at Jimmy Stewart's Post-WWII Vertigo" has been published in the *Quarterly Review of Film and Video*, and "Which Woody Allen?" appears in *A Companion to Woody Allen*.

TODD GRAY photographed Michael Jackson over a period of ten years, often as Jackson's chosen photographer. He has shot numerous album covers and directed music videos, and his photo-based artwork is in the permanent collections of museums in the United States and abroad. The author of *Michael Jackson: Before He Was King*, Gray is a professor of art and photography at California State University, Long Beach.

ALISON HOFFMAN-HAN is assistant professor and director of Film Studies at Moorpark College (California), where she teaches cinema history, documentary studies, and courses on gender, racial, and sexual difference in American and global film cultures. Her writings on women's and experimental film, contemporary world cinema, and classical and New Hollywood have been published in the *Journal of Japanese & Korean Cinema*, *Film Quarterly*, as well as in anthologies such as *There She Goes: Feminist Filmmaking and Beyond* and *Billy Wilder, Movie-Maker*.

CYNTHIA LUCIA is professor of English and director of the Film and Media Studies Program at Rider University. The author of *Framing Female Lawyers: Women on Trial in Film* and co-editor of *The Wiley-Blackwell History of American Film*, she has written for *Film Journal International*, *The Guardian*, *Oxford Bibliographies in Film and Media Studies*, and *Cineaste*, where she has served on the editorial board for over two decades. Her essays have appeared in *A Companion to Woody Allen*; *Law, Culture and Visual Studies*; *Modern British Drama on Screen*; and *Authorship in Film Adaptation*, among other anthologies.

VIRGINIA LUZÓN-AGUADO is a permanent lecturer at the University of Zaragoza in Spain, where she completed her doctoral dissertation on masculinity and stardom in the films of Harrison Ford. She is a member of the research team that pioneered Film Studies in English in Spain. She has published work on Harrison Ford, star studies, and film genres.

NINA K. MARTIN is an associate professor and director of the Film Studies Program at Connecticut College, where she teaches feminist film theory and criticism, animation, and cult and exploitation film and television. She has published articles in *Atlantis: A Women's Studies Journal*, *Journal of Film and Video*, *Jump Cut*, and the *Quarterly Review of Film and Video*. She is the author of *Sexy Thrills: Undressing the Erotic Thriller*, and is currently working on a book on postfeminism and the Hollywood remake.

LINDA RADER OVERMAN is an adjunct professor of English at California State University, Northridge. She holds a Ph.D. in Creative Writing from Lancaster University (United Kingdom) and a Master of Fine Arts in Creative Writing from California State University, Chico. Her debut novel *Letters Between Us* was selected as a finalist in the 2008 National Best Books Awards, in the category of Fiction & Lit: Chick Lit/Women's Lit. Her work has appeared in many anthologies.

R. BARTON PALMER is Calhoun Lemon Professor of Literature at Clemson University, where he also directs the Film Studies Program. Along with Linda Badley, he is the founding/general editor of the *Traditions in World Cinema* and *Traditions in American Cinema* series at Edinburgh University Press and, with Tison Pugh, founding/general editor of the *South on Screen* series at the University of Georgia Press. Palmer is the author, editor, or general editor of more than sixty books devoted to various literary and cinematic subjects. His most recent monograph is *Shot on Location: The Use of Real Space in Postwar American Cinema* (forthcoming). Also forthcoming are *Thinking in the Dark* (with Murray Pomerance), *Multiplicities* (with Amanda Klein), and *Hitchcock and the Moral of the Story* (with Homer Pettey and Steven Sanders).

INDEX

Note: Italicized page numbers indicate illustrations.

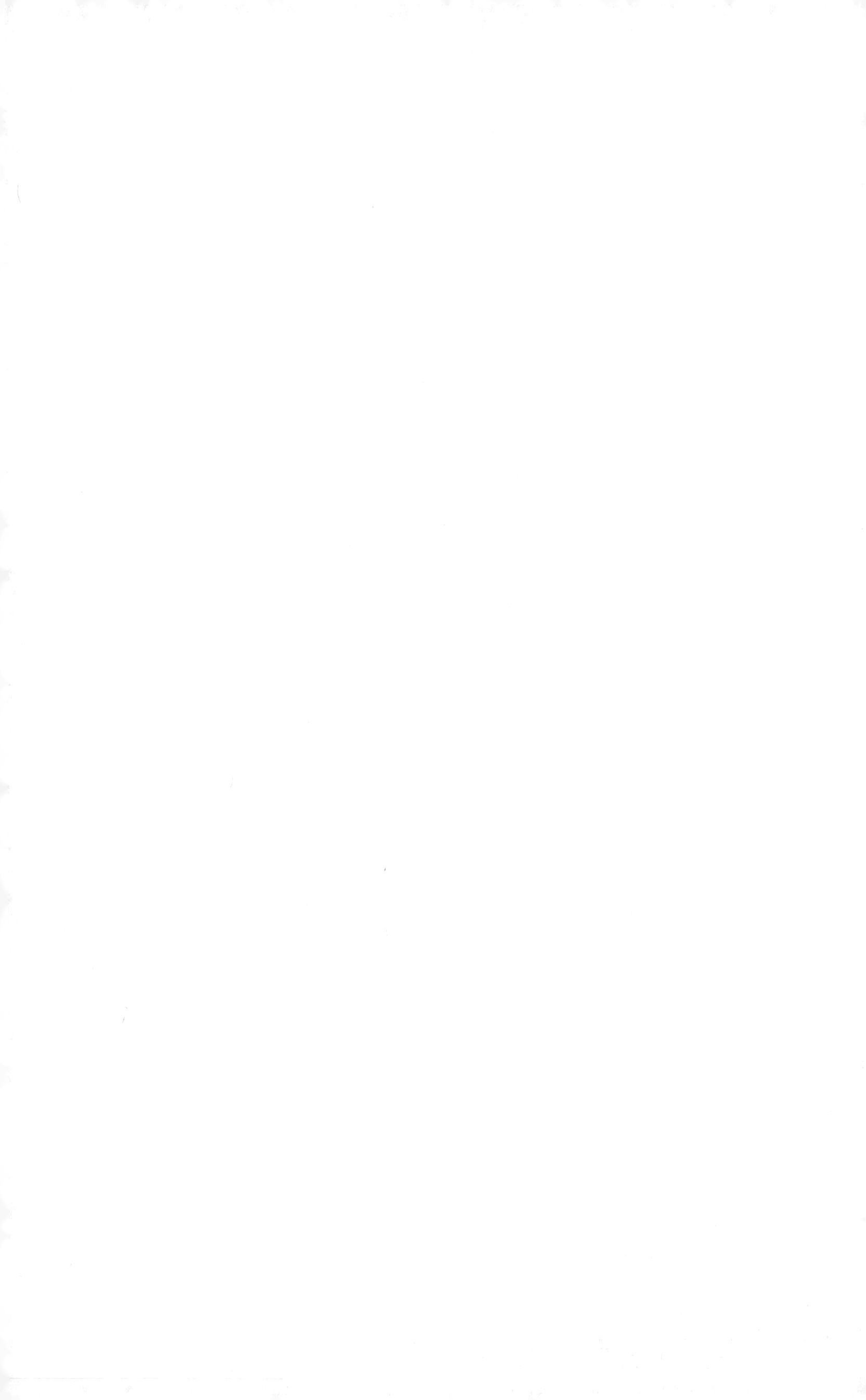

www.ingramcontent.com/pod-product-compliance
Lightning Source LLC
LaVergne TN
LVHW020436080826
844660LV00033B/1299
* 9 7 8 0 8 1 4 3 3 9 3 9 8 *